OXFORD ADVANCED HISTORY

BRITAIN

1846-1964 | The Challenge of Change

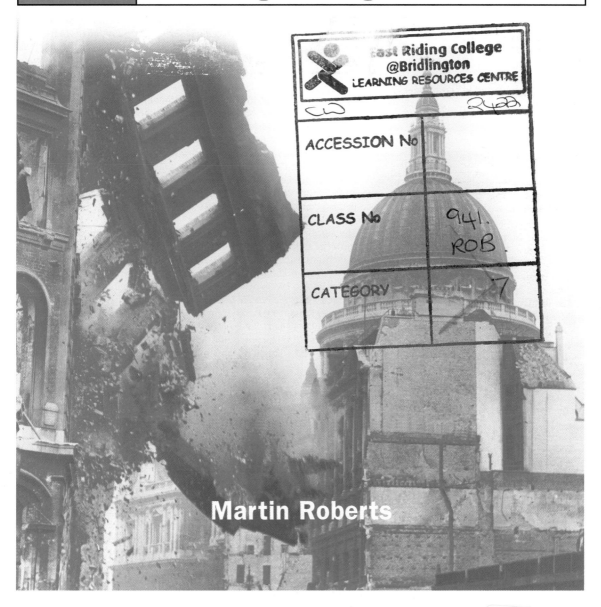

Martin Roberts

OXFORD
UNIVERSITY PRESS

OXFORD
UNIVERSITY PRESS

Great Clarendon Street, Oxford OX2 6DP

Oxford University Press is a department of the University of Oxford.
It furthers the University's objective of excellence in research, scholarship, and education by publishing worldwide in Oxford New York
Athens Auckland Bangkok Bogotá Buenos Aires Cape Town Chennai Dar es Salaam Delhi
Florence Hong Kong Istanbul Karachi Kolkata Kuala Lumpur Madrid Melbourne Mexico City Mumbai Nairobi Paris São Paulo Shanghai Singapore Taipei Tokyo Toronto Warsaw with associated companies in Berlin Ibadan

British Library Cataloguing in Publication Data
Data available

ISBN 0 19 9133735
Designed by Peter Tucker, Holbrook Design (info@holbrook-design.co.uk)
Maps by Jeff Edwards
Printed in Italy by Canale

With special thanks to Katharine Burn, Series Consultant, who provided invaluable support and advice throughout the development of this project.

Acknowledgements

The author and publisher would like to thank the following for their permission to reproduce the following photographs:
Advertising Archives: 220cr; Art Archive: 69ca, 178tr; © Associated Newspapers: 265tc; © The Bodleian Library, University of Oxford/ C.P.A.1923/1: 184tc, /C.P.A. 1945/12: 259cl, /C.P.A. 1959/2: 268cl, /C.P.A. 1964/27: 274br; Bridgeman Art Library /Forbes Magazine Collection, New York: 27tr, /Imperial War Museum: 160c, /Private Collection: 19tl; Camera Press: 263clb; Centre for the Study of Cartoons & Caricature, University of Kent, Canterbury: 79b, 229clb, 238tl | © Associated Newspapers:261crb, 271bc; © Corbis: 164tc; Mary Evans Picture Library: 8tl, 25clb, 72crb, 78tc, 80cla, 92c, 113tl, 115cl, 123tc, 128tr, 138tr, 141bl, 148bl, 158br, 167clb, 181br, 198cr, 217clb, 226c, 235tl; © Express Newspapers: 224bl; Hulton Archive: 9tl, 9clb, 10c, 18bl, 23cla, 24cl, 24br, 46br, 51cra, 51clb, 55tr, 64cla, 77cla, 82bl, 86tr, 129tl, 131c, 144cl, 147clb, 157tr, 162br, 163tl, 165bl, 170c, 185cl, 204tc, 207tr, 212bl, 218br, 219tr, 220bl, 234crb, 256cr, 266tr; Illustrated London News: 11tl, 38clb, 49cra, 80r, 84crb, 89tl, 130bl, 158tr, 255tl, 255cla; Marx Memorial Library, London: 118cl, 214bl: © Lewis Morley/Akehurst Bureau: 273bc; National Museum of Ireland: 62bl; National Museum of Labour History: 116bl, 258cl, 274cra; National Museum of Photography, Film & Television/SSPL: 208cla, /Daily Herald Archive/SSPL: 208bc; PA Photos: 196cr; Popperfoto: 64bl, 64bc, 64cr, 66cra,250cl, 253cr; Public Record Office: 78tl, 188ca; Punch Ltd: 22cl, 29tc, 70clb, 88cr, 97tl, 105bl, 120c, 134tl, 140cl, 145tl, 177tr, 193tc,199tl, 232bc, 242crb; Topham Picturepoint: 8bl, 54tl, 59tl, 64br, 108c, 146cr, 154tl, 197clb, 201cl, 203bc, 243tl, 264tl, 276c, 279tc, 283bl; Collection Ulster Museum, Belfast, courtesy MAGNI: 58t; V & A Picture Library: 44cl.

The author and publisher gratefully acknowledge permission to reprint from the following copyright works –Robert Blake: extracts from *The Conservative Party from Peel to Major* (Wm Heinemann, 1997), by permission of The Random House Group Ltd; extracts from *Disraeli* (Prion Books, 1966), by permission of the publishers. Peter Clarke: extracts from *The Penguin History of Britain: Hope and Glory* (Allen Lane. The Penguin Press, 1996), copyright © Peter Clarke 1996, by permission of Penguin Books Ltd. R F Foster: extracts from *Modern Ireland 1600–1972* (Allen Lane, 1988), copyright © R F Foster 1988, by permission of Penguin Books Ltd. K T Hoppen: extracts from *The Mid-Victorian Generation: 1846–1886* (OUP, 1998), copyright © K Theodore Hoppen 1998, by permission of Oxford University Press. T O Lloyd: extracts from *Empire to Welfare State: English History 1906–1967* (OUP, 2nd edition 1979), copyright © Oxford University Press 1970, 1979, by permission of Oxford University Press. A Marwick: extracts from *Britain in Our Century* (Thames & Hudson, 1984), by permission of the publisher. Kenneth Morgan: extracts from *Keir Hardie* (Weidenfeld & Nicolson), by permission of the publishers; extracts from Labour People (OUP, 1987), by permission of David Higham Associates. Martin Pugh: extracts from *The Making of Modern British Politics* (Blackwell, 1982), by permission of the publishers; extracts from *Lloyd George* (Longman, 1988), by permission of Pearson Education. Andrew Roberts: extracts from *Lord Salisbury: Victorian Titan* (Weidenfeld & Nicolson), by permission of the publishers. Siegfried Sassoon: lines from 'Base Details' from *Collected Poems* (Faber & Faber, 1961), by permission of Barbara Levy Literary Agency. Harold L Smith: extracts from *The British Women's Suffrage Campaign* (Longmans, 1998), by permission of Pearson Education. A J P Taylor: extracts from *English History 1914–1945*, first published as volume 15 of *The Oxford History of England*, (OUP, 1965), copyright © Oxford University Press 1965, by permission of Oxford University Press Trevor Wilson: extracts from *The Downfall of the Liberal Party* (Collins, 1966), by permission of HarperCollins Publishers Ltd.

Contents

Meeting examination criteria: A map of this book

Chapter		AQA	EDEXCEL	OCR
1	Parties in change 1846–1865 (and Lord Palmerston)	–	AS The Age of Gladstone and Disraeli	AS Britain 1846–1906, A2 Gladstone and Disraeli 1846–1880
2	Gladstone versus Disraeli	–	AS The Age of Gladstone and Disraeli	AS Britain 1846–1906, A2 Gladstone and Disraeli 1846–1880
3	Britain and Ireland 1868–1921	AS Britain 1895–1918 AS Unionism and Nationalism in Ireland c1895–1921	A2 Policies and Parties in Britain 1886–1906	AS The Irish Question in the Age of Parnell 1877–1894, AS Britain 1846–1906, AS Britain 1906–1964
4	The Conservative Ascendancy 1885–1905	AS Britain 1895–1918	A2 Policies in Britain 1886–1906, A2 The Decline of the Liberal Party	AS Britain 1846–1906, AS England in a New Century 1900–18
5	The British Empire 1870–1914	AS Britain 1895–1918	AS The Age of Gladstone and Disraeli, A2 Britain and De-colonisation c.1870–1980	AS Britain 1846–1906, AS Britain 1906–1964
6	Foreign Policy 1890–1914	AS Britain 1895–1918	A2 The Road to War 1890–1914	AS England in a New Century 1900–18, AS Britain 1846–1906, AS 1906–1964
7	The Labour Movement 1868–1906	AS Britain 1895–1918, AS The New Liberalism	AS The Liberal Government 1905–15, A2 Policies and Parties, 1886–1906, A2 The Decline of the Liberal Party	AS England in a New Century
8	Votes for Women 1867–1928	AS Britain 1895–1918, AS The New Liberalism	AS Votes for Women c.1880–1918, AS the Liberal Government 1905–15, A2 the Decline of the Liberal Party	AS Britain 1846–1906, AS Britain 1906–1964, AS England in a New Century 1900–1918
9	The last Liberal government 1905–15	AS Britain 1895–1918, AS The New Liberalism	AS The Liberal Government 1905–15, A2 The Road to War 1890–1914	AS England in a New Century, AS Britain 1906–1964
10	The First World War and its effects	AS Britain 1895–1918	A2 British Foreign Policy between the Wars	AS Britain 1906–1964
11	The decline of the Liberal Party 1906–1935	AS Britain 1895–1918, A2 Britain 1918–1951	A2 the Decline of the Liberal Party	AS England in a New Century, AS Britain 1906–1964
12	The inter-war years: Conservative, Labour, National	A2 Britain 1918–1951	AS British Society between the Wars, A2 the Decline of the Liberal Party	AS Britain 1906–1964
13	Economic and social issues 1918–1939	A2 Britain 1918–1951	AS British Society between the Wars	AS Britain 1906–1964
14	British foreign policy 1919–1939	A2 Britain 1918–1951	A2 British Foreign Policy between the Wars	AS Britain 1906–1964, A2 Chamberlain and Anglo–German Relations 1918–38
15	The Second World War	A2 Britain 1918–1951	A2 Britain and De-colonisation	AS Britain 1906–1964
16	Labour in power 1945–51	A2 Britain 1918–51	–	AS Britain 1906–1964
17	Britain 1951–1964	–	–	Britain 1906–1964
18	British imperial and foreign policy 1945–1964	–	A2 Britain and De-colonisation 1870–c1980	AS Britain 1906–1964

Documents/Interpretations exercises*	Key skills activities**	
pp. 20–1 Palmerston as Prime Minister	–	1
pp. 36–7 The Eastern Question crisis 1876–1878; pp. 40–1 What kind of reformer was Gladstone after 1868?; pp. 41–2 Does Disraeli deserve to be taken seriously as a political thinker?	p. 43 Communication 3.2 and 3.3	2
pp. 52–3 The 1886 Home Rule crisis; pp. 62–3 The Easter Rising	–	3
–	p. 75 Communication 3.1b	4
–	–	5
p. 97 The significance of the Anglo-Japanese Treaty of 1902	p. 103 Information Technology 3.1	6
–	–	7
pp. 133–4 The contribution of the WSPU and NUWSS to female emancipation; pp. 138–9 The role of the war	p. 133 Information Technology 3.2	8
p. 153 Social reform, Lloyd George and New Liberalism; pp. 154–5 The significance of the Liberal social reforms	p. 159 Communication 3.2	9
pp. 168–9 Lloyd George as war leader	p. 169 Communication 3.1b	10
pp. 185–6 The death of liberalism	p. 181 Communication 3.2	11
pp. 198–9 Baldwin's leadership; pp. 200–1 MacDonald in 1931 – traitor to the people's cause or courageous patriot?	–	12
pp. 214–5 Revolutionary in intent?; pp. 224–5 The hungry thirties	p. 223 Communication 3.3	13
pp. 237–8 Italy and Abyssinia; pp. 248–9 The argument about appeasement	p. 241 Communication 3.3	14
–	p. 257 Information Technology 3.1	15
pp. 266–7 Real progress or illusion?	–	16
	p. 275 Communication 3.2	17
pp. 281–2 The Suez crisis 1956	–	18

* These provide examination-style questions

** See page 6

5

Using this book

The way in which you use this book will obviously depend on the examination specification you are following, and the particular options within it that you have chosen to study. The contents map on pages 4–5 makes clear how different chapters relate to the main AS and A level specifications, while within each chapter a clear introduction and list of key questions outline how the main issues are dealt with. Concise conclusions are offered in the end of chapter summaries.

Where there are important differences of interpretation between historians, the main text will introduce you to these controversies and suggest further reading. However, there are also specific sections that focus on major historical debates. These explore the different reasons why historians have such conflicting views, and set out criteria that you will find helpful in comparing interpretations and assessing their value.

Key Skills

Since the study of history involves information gathering (i.e. research) and processing (assessing the value and implications of different kinds of evidence) in order to reach conclusions which you then have to communicate, it can obviously contribute significantly to the practice of two of the designated *Key Skills:* Communication and Information Technology. The spread of activities within this book has, therefore, been carefully planned to provide opportunities for you to develop and demonstrate these Key Skills.

The specifications for these Key Skills at level 3 are as follows:

Communication

C3.1a   Contribute to a group discussion about a complex subject.
C3.1b   Make a presentation about a complex subject, using at least one image to illustrate complex points.
C3.2   Read and synthesize information from two extended documents about a complex subject. One of these documents should include at least one image.
C3.3   Write two different types of documents about complex subjects. One piece of writing should be an extended document and include at least one image.

Information Technology

IT3.1   Plan and use different sources to search for, and select, information required for different purposes.
IT3.2   Explore, develop and exchange information and derive new information to meet two different purposes.
IT3.3   Present information for two different purposes and audiences. Candidates' work must include at least one example of text images and one example of numbers.

The contents map on pages 4–5 provides a clear indication of the pages where Key Skills activities can be found and which elements of the specifications they cover. A Key Skills logo on the page itself also indicates which activity is being referred to. These Key Skills activities arise naturally out of the work that you are doing and can be used as part of your teacher-assessed portfolio of evidence, demonstrating the application of these skills.

Spotlight
These sections provide opportunities for a detailed focus, either exploring significant issues within a chapter, or examining the impact of particular policies through specific case studies. They generally include a range of different kinds of source material, with structured questions and activities to help you to engage with the issues and reach your own conclusions.

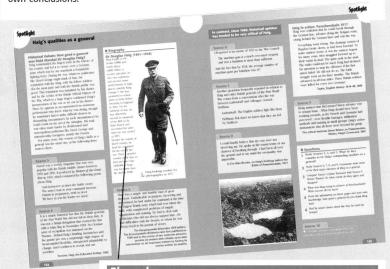

Biography
These boxes provide short biographies of key individuals, helping you to assess their significance, and to place specific actions or decisions in the context of their wider careers.

Note

These boxes provide additional information or reminders. They alert you to issues that may influence the judgements you may make about certain events, individuals or historical interpretations.

Timeline

These provide useful summaries of the main developments explained in the text. They help you to develop an overview of the particular issue or sequence of events and to locate particular incidents within a wider chronology.

Activity

The activities include a range of exercises that will help you to make sense of all that you have read. Structured tasks encourage you to manipulate information – organising it in different ways – to complete summary charts; to analyse and compare different explanations, and to assess the consequences of particular developments. The activities take a variety of forms, including research work, decision-making exercises, role-play, discussion and debate, as well as exam-style sequences of structured questions and essays.

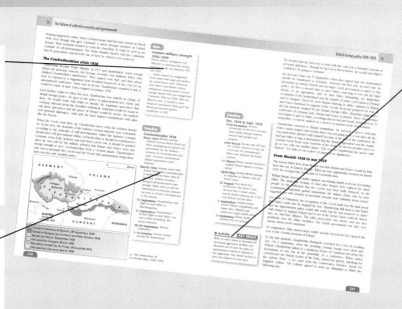

Examination-style exercises

Each chapter includes specific assessment exercises modelled on the details provided in AS and A level specifications and specimen papers. A large number of structured *document exercises* provide plenty of opportunity for exam practice, while those chapters that deal specifically with major issues of historical controversy include similar structured exercises focused solely on issues of historical *interpretations*.

Source

A large number of sources are presented within each chapter. Primary sources give you access to the kinds of evidence on which our understanding of the period has been built, while extracts from historians' accounts give you an insight into their particular interpretation of events.

Further reading

Suggestions here include texts written specifically for AS and A level students as well as accessible works by prominent historians. Some include guidance as to how the books might be read and which sections may prove particularly relevant or enjoyable. Where appropriate, the place of these books in key historical controversies is also made clear.

Cross reference

These boxes alert you to relevant sections elsewhere in the book that may extend or enhance your understanding of the text you are reading.

Think about

Most sources are linked to a 'think about' encouraging you to reflect on the evidence or historical interpretation offered. The questions posed help you to relate the source to your developing knowledge of the topic and to assess its value and implications.

'Think about' boxes relating to the main text also help you to think critically about what you are reading: making links, drawing comparisons and predicting likely outcomes.

Facts and figures

These boxes present statistical information or specific details to exemplify and substantiate more general claims made in the main text.

Introduction

Britain in 1846

▲ Where the destinies of the nation were, usually, decided. The new Houses of Parliament, designed by Barry and Pugin, near completion in 1855. The old buildings had been destroyed in a catastrophic fire in 1834.

◀ Railways and factories, dynamic elements in the Victorian economy. The Glasgow-Garnkirk line in the 1840s.

A young German in 1844

Sixty, eighty years ago, England was a country like every other, with small towns, few and simple industries, and a thin but proportionately large agricultural population. Today it is a country like no other, with a capital of two and a half million inhabitants; with a vast manufacturing industry that supplies the world; with an industrious, intelligent, dense population, of which two-thirds are employed in trade and commerce...forming, in fact, with other customs and other needs, a different nation from the England of those days.

Frederick Engels, *The Condition of the Working Class in England in 1844,* London 1943 (first published in Germany in 1845)

■ Think about

Engels' father was a cotton manufacturer who set up a successful business in Manchester. Well-off and well-travelled, Frederick became the lifelong friend of Karl Marx, the founder of communism.

▶ Why did Engels consider England to be 'a country like no other'?

▶ How reliable would you consider his description of England in 1844?

Changed circumstances 1846–1964

▲ Lord John Russell, Prime Minister in 1846. This portrait of this reforming Whig/Liberal dates from c.1850.

- Britain in 1846 was by far the richest nation in the world. This wealth came from her advanced industry and her trading skills. Between 1846 and 1876, Britain exported between 30 per cent and 40 per cent of the world's manufactured goods.

  In 1964, Britain was, comparatively, much less rich than the USA and, though amongst the world's richest nations, was losing ground to Japan and to Western Europe. Manufacturing played a smaller part in the British economy and the service sector (e.g. the media, finance, the health service) was expanding.

- Because of her wealth and her navy, Britain in 1846 was the most powerful nation in the world. That future international superpower, the USA, was still in the process of nation-building and industrialization. In Europe, Germany and Italy did not yet exist as independent nations and the Russian Empire, though vast, was economically and socially primitive.

  Britain in 1964 was dwarfed by the superpowers of the USA and the USSR. She was also isolated from an increasingly dynamic Western Europe, co-operating and prospering as the European Economic Community (EEC). Britain had applied to join the EEC in 1962 but had had her application turned down.

- The British Empire of the 1840s reflected Britain's power. It was the largest the world had ever seen and centred on the Indian sub-continent. In the next 50 years it would get much larger, especially in Africa.

  By 1964 the Empire was collapsing. Most colonies had either won their independence or would soon do so.

- Only one in five men (and no women) could vote in the Britain of the 1840s. However, in contrast to most other nations, her elected parliament was far more powerful than her hereditary monarch (in 1846, Queen Victoria).

  By 1964, Britain was fully democratic, with all adults entitled to vote. By then, however, most of the Western industrialized world had adopted democratic forms of government.

In a period of a little over a century, these were some of the changes to which Britain had to adapt. It was a period that marked a substantial fall in Britain's comparative power and prosperity in the world, and one to which the word 'decline' is frequently attached. However, in that same period, most British people became incomparably richer. They lived longer and enjoyed better health and education. Their lives were improved by innumerable technological advances, e.g. gas, electricity, radio, television and motor vehicles. Not only did all adults have the vote, but society became more tolerant and fairer with much less discrimination on the basis of gender or of class.

▲ Harold Wilson, the Labour leader in 1964, with his familiar pipe. This photograph was taken just before his victory in the 1964 general election, which ended 13 years of Conservative rule.

An aim of this book is to explain how Britain's circumstances changed in these years. Often, as in the case of the two world wars, the changes were substantial. How well did the nation cope with the difficult process of adaptation? How effectively did her politicians lead the country through them?

Chapter 1

Parties in change 1846–1865 (and Lord Palmerston)

Source 1

▶ A man of great privilege and power. John Wodehouse, Earl of Kimberley, was a Whig/Liberal landowner who with others of his class dominated British politics for a generation between 1846 and 1874. Kimberley lived until 1902 and was one of Gladstone's most loyal supporters (see Chapter 2).

Introduction

1846 is a significant date in British history. It was then that Sir Robert Peel, Conservative Prime Minister since 1841, decided that he must repeal the Corn Laws. A Conservative government had introduced these laws in 1815 to protect British farmers from foreign competition. Their abolition had two important consequences. Firstly, it made clear that the age of 'protection' was over. For the next 60 years British politicians believed in 'free trade' with an almost religious conviction. Secondly, Peel's action caused a bitter split in the Conservative Party.

This chapter deals with the years from 1846 to 1865, during which politicians came to terms with the split of 1846. The Whigs usually had the support of those Conservatives who stayed loyal to Peel (known as the Peelites), and formed most of the governments of the next 20 years. By 1867, they had transformed themselves into the Liberal Party. For the Tories (Conservatives) these were years in the wilderness. Not until 1874 were they strong enough to form a lasting government. The most influential politician was Lord Palmerston who began his long career as a liberal Tory and ended it as conservative Liberal.

Key questions

- What were the effects of the repeal of the Corn Laws on (a) the Conservatives and (b) the Whigs?
- How did the Whigs stay in power for most of the period 1846 to 1865 and, in the same period, turn themselves into Liberals?
- What were the main issues of foreign policy facing British governments in these years? How successfully did they handle them?
- Why was Palmerston the most dominant politician of these years? How successful was he both at home and abroad?

Peel and the repeal of the Corn Laws

Sir Robert Peel was an exceptionally able man. In 1810, when he was only 22, he became a government minister. He held office in Conservative governments for most of the next twenty years. He gained a reputation for being a hard-working, efficient and far-sighted minister but also for having a readiness to change his mind on important policies.

Though Peel opposed the famous Reform Act of 1832, he realized that the Conservative Party needed to accept that the country was changing and to change with it. In his so-called Tamworth Manifesto of 1835, he committed himself and his party to accept the spirit of the 1832 Reform Act and 'judicious (well-considered) reforms'.

For many years, Peel himself had been moving towards a 'free trade' position and against the Corn Laws. The question was how and when to persuade his party that they must go. The intense national campaign of the Anti-Corn Law League, which started in 1838, may have influenced his thinking and the dreadful Irish famine which began in 1845 persuaded him that he must delay no longer.

Peel, however, for all his great abilities, was an arrogant man and a poor party manager. Convinced that he knew what was in the best interests of the nation, he expected his party to follow him. The great majority did not. Led by Lord George Bentinck and by Benjamin Disraeli, they turned on their leader, crying 'treachery'. After some of the most bitter debates of the century in the House of

▲ Hero or villain? Sir Robert Peel in the 1840s.

The 1832 Reform Act

This Act, which the Tories fiercely opposed, increased the number of middle-class voters and abolished many small constituencies that had been in the 'pocket' of the local landlord. It was the first step in the nineteenth century towards the creation of a democratic society.

Quotation

I keep horses in 3 counties, and they tell me that I shall save £1,500 a year by free trade. I don't care for that. What I cannot bear is being sold.

Lord George Bentinck

[Peel] is a burglar of other people's intellects...there is no statesman who has committed political petty larceny [theft] on so great a scale...I know, Sir, that all confidence in public men is lost.

Benjamin Disraeli, speaking in the House of Commons

Commons, Peel was only able to get the repeal of the Corn Laws through Parliament with the support of the Whigs. Then he had no choice but to resign.

The nature of mid-Victorian politics

Whigs and Tories

These party names go back to the late seventeenth century and the so-called 'Glorious Revolution' of 1688. Then Parliament encouraged the Dutch Protestant, William of Orange, to drive the Catholic James II into exile and to rule Britain as William III, with a strong Parliament. The Whigs supported Parliament and William III, the Tories supported James II.

By 1830, Tories (or Conservatives as they then became known) were the party of the Crown and the Anglican Church (the Church of England). They disliked the ideas of the French Revolution and saw themselves as the protectors of the established order, especially of the farming interest.

The Whigs, in contrast, saw themselves as the party of individual freedom and representative government. They were less afraid of change and more tolerant of religious groups outside the Anglican Church, like the Nonconformists. Though most of the Whig leaders, like the Tories, were great landowners, they were committed to free trade.

The Peelites

In the 1841 election, the Conservatives had had a majority of 76 over the Whigs. After the 1847 election the Whigs had 81 seats more than the Conservatives. If the 89 Peelites were ready to vote with the Whigs, then the Whigs could count on a large majority. Without exception, Peel's ministers followed their leader and left the Conservative Party. Among them were some of the ablest politicians of that generation – Gladstone, Graham, and Cardwell for example. For some years they hovered between the parties. Not until 1859 did Gladstone, for example, finally decide to commit himself to the Whigs/Liberals.

The Conservative Party of Derby and Disraeli

The Conservatives needed a generation to recover from the split. Although they had seen that protection was a vote loser, they would not immediately abandon it. Almost all their best men had gone over to the Liberals, but Lord Stanley, the future Earl of Derby, led them shrewdly from the Lords. In the Commons, their most talented MP was Disraeli. He was in effect their leader, but, for many years, he did not inspire the trust of his backbenchers (see page 25).

Mid-Victorian attitudes to religion

Religion dominated Victorian thinking. Governments could flourish or fail on religious issues like whether or not in 1851 Roman Catholics should be allowed to have their own bishops. Though the religious census of 1851 showed that barely half the population regularly attended church, the vast majority of the respectable and educated classes did and were shocked by the failure of the less respectable to do so.

The 1851 census also showed that Anglicans were slightly outnumbered by the Nonconformists, i.e. those Christians who did not conform (agree) with important aspects of the Church of England and formed their own separate Church or denomination; for example the Methodists, Presbyterians, and

Facts and figures

Number of parliamentary seats:

	1841	1847
Whigs	291	324
Conservatives	367	243
Peelites		89

Quotation

They could not be got to attend business when the hunting season was on…They never read… they learnt nothing useful and did not understand the ideas of their own time.

Disraeli on Conservative MPs

■ Biography

Jeremy Bentham (1748–1832)

Bentham was the son of a lawyer, educated at Westminster School and Oxford. He failed to make a career both in law or politics but achieved an international reputation in 1789 with the publication of his *Introduction to the Principles of Morals and Legislation*. In this book he explains that the chief function of government is to create the 'greatest happiness of the greatest number'. His philosophic radicalism, along with that of his followers, the Mills, was the most influential political philosophy in nineteenth-century Britain.

Quotation

[Laissez-faire] should be the general practice; every departure from it, except required by some great good, is a certain evil.

John Stuart Mill, *Principles of Political Economy Vol II*, 1857

■ Think about

▶ Why do you think the utilitarians thought that 'laissez-faire' was the best way of achieving 'the greatest happiness of the greatest number'?

■ Think about

▶ What effects did the repeal of the Corn Laws in 1846 have on the Conservative and the Whig/Liberal Parties?

▶ Why did the Whigs/Liberals have a greater electoral appeal than the Conservatives for the next 30 years?

Quakers. The Methodists were particularly strong in Wales, the Presbyterians in Scotland. A major aim of the Nonconformists was to ensure that the privileged position of the Church of England was, wherever possible, reduced, especially in education, so they tended to vote Whig/Liberal rather than Conservative.

Mid-Victorian attitudes to the duties of the State

Ideas about the role of government at this time were strongly influenced by the ideas of a group of philosophers known as the utilitarians. The most important among them were Jeremy Bentham, James Mill and his son John Stuart Mill. Bentham believed that on the whole, the State should 'be quiet' or, using the French phrase 'laissez-faire', leave things alone. The more people were left to take responsibility for their actions the better they and society would be. The freer trade was, the more the economy would flourish and people's living conditions improve.

In practice, 'laissez-faire' meant that mid-Victorian politicians saw their main duty as making sure Britain's defences were secure, her international position maintained and the laws of the land obeyed. Taxes should be kept as low as possible. They had a reluctance to pass laws or to spend money on social improvements. That said, between 1830 and 1870, there were many examples of socially improving laws, e.g. the Factory Acts and the setting up of a General Board of Health in 1848. However, the intention was more to eliminate obvious 'abuses' than to achieve large-scale social improvement. In addition, the Westminster government tended to delegate responsibility for deciding to take action to the localities, rather than insisting on nationwide reforms.

How the Whigs became Liberals

These characteristics of mid-Victorian Britain helped the Whigs more than the Conservatives. They also helped to turn the Whigs into Liberals. In the 1840s and 1850s, there were three distinct groups in Parliament which, more often than not, voted together to keep the Conservatives in opposition:

● The Whigs proper – wealthy aristocratic landowners linked by marriage and friendship. They were particularly strong in the House of Lords and frequently held ministerial posts.
● The Radicals – who were committed to further parliamentary reform and to the reduction of privileges. They were enthusiastic about free trade and had strong Nonconformist support.
● The Peelites – whose commitment to free trade and balanced budgets pushed them away from the Conservatives, who only slowly abandoned protection, and towards the Whigs/Radicals.

However, up to 1858, these groups, without an agreed leader, did not vote together in a disciplined way and twice allowed the Conservatives to form a government, the first in 1852, the second in 1858–1859.

Consequently on the 6 June 1859, 274 Whig, Peelite and Radical MPs met at Willis' Rooms, a London dining club. Lords Russell and Palmerston, whose rivalries had harmed their cause in recent years, helped each other on to the platform and, amidst resounding applause, declared that they would each be happy to serve under the other. This meeting marks the beginning of the Liberal Party. Five days later, it voted out the Conservatives. Palmerston became Prime Minister, Russell Foreign Secretary, and the Peelite Gladstone Chancellor of the Exchequer.

The appeal of liberalism to the middle and working classes

Voting behaviour tends even today to be mysterious. In the Victorian period, evidence was more limited than nowadays, so generalizations about how particular classes then voted need to be very cautious. On the whole, though, since the middle classes stood to gain from further parliamentary reform, from the reduction of privileges and from free trade, and since many of them were Nonconformists, they seem to have favoured the Liberals. However, as early as 1852, the middle class reforming impulse showed signs of weakening. For example, Gladstone received a letter in 1852 from a Manchester businessman who was a committed Liberal on free trade and other grounds but declared himself 'decidedly conservative in all that relates to the further infusion of democratic elements into our constitution'.

The Liberals also seemed to attract the support of skilled working people, most of whom did not yet enjoy the right to vote and saw the Liberals as their best hope for further parliamentary reform. They saw themselves as the people who were building the nation's future and for them the Tories were too rooted in the past. Many of them would also have been Nonconformists and proud of their respectability. They worked hard and stood on their own two feet. Gladstone became their hero because of his careful budgets, which made savings, kept taxes low and displayed an open and honest approach to government expenditure.

The support of the Press

Another advantage to the Liberals was the backing they had from newspapers. Between 1855 and 1861, the newspaper industry boomed. One reason for this was technological change – like the steam press, the electric telegraph and the railways. Newspapers were cheaper to produce, more fully and speedily informed and distributed across the country overnight. Another was Gladstone's abolition of the tax on newsprint. The owners of papers like the *Daily Telegraph*, the *Leeds Mercury* and the *Sheffield Independent* gave warm support to the Liberal Party.

Political events 1846–1865

The politics of these years are complicated (see timeline). Party organizations were weak. Different groups combined to bring down governments and then split up again. The early setbacks of the Crimean War led to groups of Whigs, Radicals and Conservatives combining to force the resignation of Lord Aberdeen in 1855. His successor, Lord Palmerston, was brought down in 1858 by a combination of Conservatives and Radicals.

The Crimean War 1853–1856: causes, events and consequences

The Crimean War was a particularly futile war, which the great powers involved – Russia, France and Britain – simply muddled into.

The Turkish Empire was weak and getting weaker. The Russian Tsar, Nicholas I, wanted to strengthen Russia at the Turks' expense. Napoleon III of France was looking for an international success to improve his relations with the Roman Catholic Church. Britain regarded Russia as the greatest threat to the British Empire, so supported Turkey.

Timeline

1846 Peel defeated, Whig government formed.
1852 Derby forms a minority Conservative government. General election returns the Whigs/Peelites. Aberdeen PM.
1854-6 Crimean War.
1855 Palmerston replaces Aberdeen as PM.
1857 Indian Revolt.
1858-9 Derby forms another minority Conservative government.
1859 General election Liberal victory, Palmerston PM.
1865 Death of Palmerston. Russell becomes PM.
1866-7 Derby/Disraeli form another minority Conservative government and pass the Second Reform Act (1867).

▶ The Crimean War 1853–1856

Timeline

Crimean War

1852 Holy Places dispute between France and Russia.

1853 Russia threatens the Turkish provinces of Moldavia and Wallachia. British fleet sent to Besika Bay. Russia occupies Moldavia and Wallachia. Turks declare war on Russia. Russian fleet defeats Turkish fleet at Sinope.

1854 Britain and France declare war on Russia. Win minor victories at the River Alma, Balaclava and Inkerman.

1855 Britain and France capture Sebastapol, threaten naval assault on St Petersburg.

1856 Treaty of Paris ends the war

France and Russia quarrelled over which monks should look after the Holy Places in Turkish-held Palestine. Napoleon backed the Roman Catholic monks, the Russians the Orthodox ones. Nicholas threatened the Turks and moved his troops towards the Turkish-held provinces of Moldavia and Wallachia. In response, the British and French moved their fleets close to Constantinople.

When Russian troops occupied Moldavia and Wallachia, the Turks declared war on Russia in October 1853. They soon lost much of their fleet at the Battle of Sinope. The British Cabinet dithered. The Prime Minister, Aberdeen, did his best to keep the peace, while Russell and Palmerston pressed for war. Eventually, Britain and France declared war on Russia in March 1854.

Ultimately, at the cost of 22,000 lives, Britain achieved most of her aims:
- The Turkish Empire did not collapse.
- By the Treaty of Paris, Russia's claims over the Turkish Empire were much reduced.
- Russian warships could not enter the Black Sea.
- Moldavia and Wallachia became more independent, both of Russia and Turkey.

However, the war revealed a number of serious problems, reported in detail by W.H. Russell, the first war correspondent of *The Times*. At Balaclava, the Light Brigade charged the wrong guns with heavy loss of life. Living conditions during the first harsh winter and the work of Florence Nightingale at Scutari hospital showed that the British army was in great need of modernization. Its officers were poor, its weapons out of date and its care of the wounded appalling. British public opinion came to realize that all was not well with the British army and that reforms would be required.

Palmerston's foreign policy 1846–1865

To what extent was it (a) successful, (b) honourable?

Some principles of Palmerston's foreign policy:

His main principle:

- On each occasion as it arises, to act in Britain's best interest.

Following from this:

- to maintain the balance of power in Europe, achieved in 1815, since that suited Britain well
- to restrain Russia even if this meant supporting illiberal Austria against popular risings
- on other occasions to support Liberal governments against illiberal ones
- with smaller and weaker nations to defend aggressively Britain's interests
- to win the support of public opinion for an apparently aggressive policy which in practice was usually aimed at keeping the peace.

Issues faced as Foreign Secretary from 1846 to 1851

1846 The Spanish Marriage. Palmerston aimed to prevent Luisa, the sister of the heiress to the Spanish throne, from marrying a French prince. He failed and damaged Anglo-French relations.

1848–1849 Liberal revolutions in Europe. While most British Liberals sympathized with the Italians and Hungarians trying to overthrow Austrian rule, Palmerston did nothing to weaken the Austrians. In fact he only declared his sympathy for the revolutionary causes when he was sure that they would not be successful. His main aim was for Austria to survive.

1850 The Don Pacifico Incident. Don Pacifico was a Portuguese Jew living in Greece who held a British passport because he was born in Gibraltar. His house in Athens was burnt down by an anti-Jewish mob. When the Greek government turned down his claim for £27,000 of compensation, he wrote to Palmerston asking for help. Palmerston had the British fleet blockade the port of Piraeus until some compensation was paid. While this action gained him much popularity with the British public, and he easily survived a vote of censure in Parliament, it annoyed France, Austria and Russia and gave him a reputation as a bully of small nations.

Issues faced as Prime Minister from 1855 to 1865

1856–60 China.

In 1856, Chinese officials in Canton had arrested the crew of a small ship, the *Arrow*, which had been robbing local shipping. The *Arrow*, however, had been flying the British flag. The British consul in Canton demanded that the crew be released and that the Chinese apologize for insulting the British flag. When the Chinese refused to apologize, the Governor of the British colony of Hong Kong sent warships to bombard Canton. Palmerston not only backed this action but launched, with French support, a full-scale attack on the Chinese coast to open up the Chinese trade to European business. Both Canton and Peking were captured. This aggression forced the Chinese government to agree in 1860 to allow Europeans to trade through a number of their ports. As a result of this war against China, Palmerston became extremely popular in Britain.

1859–60 Italian Unification.

The Italians rose against their foreign rulers. Palmerston skilfully timed his declarations of British support for the Italians against Austria to help the risings in the north, while British warships guarded the force of the Italian hero Garibaldi when he invaded the tyrannical Kingdom of Naples. The Italians triumphed so the new united Kingdom of Italy was friendly towards Britain.

1861–65 The American Civil War.

Britain officially stayed neutral. However, Palmerston's government fell out badly with the Union (Northern states) government which eventually won the war. The Confederates (Southern states) had placed orders for warships with British shipyards. The Union government protested that by allowing these ships to be built, Britain was hardly behaving as a neutral. One of these warships, the *Alabama*, slipped away from Liverpool disguised as a merchant ship in 1862 and did considerable damage to Union shipping. There would not have been an issue if Russell, the Foreign Secretary, had acted more swiftly to prevent the *Alabama* from leaving Liverpool but neither he nor Palmerston were prepared to accept any responsibility for the incident. Relations between the USA and Britain were strained and Palmerston and Russell's successors had to find a solution to this problem.

European Issues 1863–64.

Poland: In 1863, the Poles rose in revolt against Russia. Supported by Prussia, the Russians crushed the rising with great cruelty. Palmerston, having appeared ready to take action in support of the Poles, in the event did nothing and Britain appeared weak.

Denmark: Much the same happened a few months later when Denmark and Prussia came into conflict over Schleswig-Holstein. Palmerston offered strong verbal support to Denmark, but when it came to the crunch and Prussia quickly defeated the Danish forces, Britain did nothing. The foreign policy of the government in 1863 and 1864 was no more than 'meddle and muddle', declared Lord Derby, with justification.

Source 2

I believe that the principles on which we have acted are those which are held by the great mass of the people in this country. I am convinced that these principles are calculated, so far as the influence of England may be properly exercised with respect to the destinies of other countries, to conduce to the maintenance of peace, to the advancement of civilization, to the welfare and happiness of mankind …[just as] the Roman, in days of old, held himself free from indignity, when he could say '*Civis Romanus sum*' [I am a Roman citizen]; so also a British subject, in whatever land he may be, shall feel confident that the watchful eye and strong arm of England will protect him against injustice and wrong.

Palmerston defends his actions during the Don Pacifico incident in the House of Commons

Source 3

The Queen has [this] complaint to bring against Lord Palmerston…his policy has generally had the effect that England is universally detested, mistrusted and treated with insult by even the smallest powers. There is not a sovereign or a government who is not convinced that their internal disagreements and sufferings are stirred up by England, in order to keep them weak and unable to compete with English manufacturers. Since 1846, Britain has not had a single success [in foreign affairs].

Prince Albert, the husband of Queen Victoria

Source 4

Towards the end of his career, Palmerston had come more and more to resemble a poker player who regularly and predictably outbids the value of his cards.

Hoppen, The Mid-Victorian Generation 1846–1886, 1998

■ Activity

1 Read Source 2 What actions had Palmerston taken to help Don Pacifico? On what principles does he say he was acting? Do you agree with him?

2 In what ways were the Don Pacifico and the Arrow incidents similar?

3 Why was Palmerston unpopular with the Queen (Source 3) but popular with the British people?

4 To what extent do you agree with Hoppen's comment (Source 4)?

5 Using the information on pages 14–15 and 18, and this spotlight, answer the question: 'To what extent was Palmerston's foreign policy between 1846 and 1865 (a) successful and (b) honourable?'

The Indian Revolt (Mutiny) 1857–1858

One of the unhappier episodes in British imperial history occurred while Palmerston was Prime Minister.

By 1857, Britain controlled most of India. Much of the sub-continent had been won by conquest. Alliances with numerous princes secured the rest. A Governor-General exercised control through a small civil service and an army which was made up mostly of Indian troops (sepoys) and British officers. The British view was that their rule brought obvious benefits to their Indian subjects. They had colossal confidence in their superiority and in their ability to rule India indefinitely.

Consequently, when sepoys at Meerut rose against their English officers and killed a number of them in May 1857, the immediate British reaction was astonishment. This astonishment increased when the rebels captured Delhi and proclaimed a descendant of the Mogul emperors as king. It turned to horror when a large area of northern India joined the revolt and massacres of Europeans, including women and children, took place.

In fact, there were many reasons for the revolt. The British had confiscated land in a high-handed way. They had interfered with Indian religious customs, which they neither understood nor respected. British manufactured goods harmed Indian producers. The actual spark of the revolt was the thoughtless requirement of the army officers at Meerut that the cartridges of the new Enfield rifle had to be torn open with the teeth before loading. The cartridges were greased. Hindu sepoys feared that the grease contained fat from cows which were sacred to them, while Muslims feared equally that it contained the fat of pigs, which to them were unclean.

Though most of India remained at peace and the revolt was a scattered affair with no effective leadership, a year was needed restore order. In crushing the rebels, the British committed atrocities as bad as those of the Indian rebels. The main consequence of the revolt was the Government of India Act. It abolished the East India Company, created the new post of Viceroy with extensive powers, reformed the army by strengthening the British element within it, and reduced the amount of interference in Indian religious and social customs.

In Britain the revolt, or 'mutiny' as Britons preferred to call it, had virtually no impact on national politics. Palmerston treated it as a national emergency and the Conservatives supported him.

■ Think about

▶ Why do you think the British in India were so surprised by the revolt?

▶ Indian civilization was different from European civilization but it was as old and as advanced. Why, then, did most Britons of the 1850s think of themselves as superior to Indians? When do you think ideas of racial superiority began to wither away?

◀ The Indian Revolt. The British win back control. Here a Highland regiment regains the guns at Cawnpore in 1857.

Palmerston and home affairs

We have considered Palmerston's foreign policy (see pages 14-18). His popular historical reputation is very much the swashbuckling patriotic British politician who sent gunboats at a drop of a hat to secure British interests around the world. In reality, he was much more considerable and many-sided.

Early career

▲ Lord Palmerston, now Prime Minister, addresses the House of Commons. (As an Irish lord, he could stay a member of the Commons.)

Born in 1784, Palmerston attended Harrow School and first Edinburgh, then Oxford Universities. In 1802 he succeeded to his father's peerage, which, since it was an Irish one, meant that he sat in the House of Commons when he began his political career in 1807.

He started as a Tory and for nearly twenty years (1809–1828) held the post of Secretary of War. Though he was a hard-working and effective junior minister, he was best known as a pleasure-loving man of fashion.

On the reforming side of the Tory Party and no friend either of the Duke of Wellington or of Sir Robert Peel, he joined the Whigs in 1830 and became Foreign Secretary in the Whig government which held power for most of the 1830–1841 period. In these years he made his reputation as an aggressive, popular and successful Foreign Secretary. His main achievements were securing the independence of Belgium in 1831, safeguarding Britain's interests in the Eastern Mediterranean by the Straits Convention of 1841 and seizing Hong Kong from China at the end of the Opium War of 1839–1842, which he had provoked.

At the Home Office 1852–1855

In 1852, he took the post of Home Secretary in Aberdeen's government. Here he achieved much. Underneath his jaunty, cynical man-of-the-world exterior lay a genuinely compassionate person. Throughout his political career he fought the slave trade with vigour, and, while at the Home Office, his prime concern was to improve factory conditions for women and children.

In his three years as Home Secretary, he:
- reduced the maximum time women and children could work to 10.5 hours, by the Factory Act of 1853
- supported measures for improved public health
- improved prison conditions, by the Penal Servitude Act (1853) and the Reformatory Schools Act (1854)

As Prime Minister

Palmerston was Prime Minister twice, from 1855 to 1858 and from 1858 to 1865. He has the unfair reputation for getting little done. He is partly to blame for this himself. When asked in 1864 what his government's plans were, he is said to have rubbed his hands in apparent glee and said that there was nothing to be done and that laws could not be added continuously to the statute book.

In fact, he was a good chairman of talented Cabinets who were by no means short of ideas.

Between 1855 and 1865, reforming laws were passed with regard to divorce, company law, the Poor Law, police, criminal law and public health. In addition, he had from 1859, in Gladstone, a great reforming Chancellor of the Exchequer.

When he became Prime Minister again in 1859, Palmerston was 75. In his old age he enabled the Liberal Party to take shape so that it could flourish under Gladstone. His great personal popularity and ability to hold together within his government very different personalities, gave time for Whigs, Peelites and Radicals to work out how to co-operate with each other.

His own qualities were great. He always worked hard and had exceptional staying power. As he grew older, he became more patient and tactful. He took trouble and used his considerable sense of humour to resolve differences between his colleagues. He travelled throughout the country, addressing large crowds and enjoying their affection. Perhaps his most striking quality was his vigour. He spent most of his 80th birthday on horseback, inspecting fortifications on the south coast.

Quotation

Lord Shaftesbury, perhaps the leading social reformer of the time, commented that he had:

'never known any Home Secretary equal to Palmerston for readiness to undertake every good work of kindness, humanity and social good, especially to the child and working class.'

Document Exercise: Palmerston as Prime Minister

Source A
Palmerston 'more Tory than the Tories'

On 18 October, Palmerston died quite suddenly two days before his eighty-first birthday. It was the end of an era. 'Our quiet days are over; no more peace for us', Sir Charles Wood (an old colleague) was heard to say as he walked sadly away from the funeral. Palmerston's incongruous (strange) position as a Whig who was in many ways more Tory than the Tories had blurred and confused the real dividing lines in politics. His death created a new situation.

Blake, *Disraeli*, 1966

Source B
Disraeli's view of Palmerston in 1855

He is really an imposter, utterly exhausted, at best only ginger-beer, and not champagne, and now an old painted pantaloon (clown) very deaf, very blind, and with false teeth, which would fall out of his mouth when speaking if he did not hesitate...so in his talk.

Source C
Palmerston on the franchise

My belief is that...the Country at large, including the Great Bulk of the Liberal Party, do not want or wish for any considerable changes in our Electoral System.

Source D
A historian on Palmerston in 1855

...Palmerston had made himself the embodiment (expression) of a very wide spectrum of opinion both within and outside the restricted government circles of the time. He had done so by being in many respects the most modern politician of his day: by cultivating the Press, appealing to public opinion on grounds of national pride, taking his policies – however indirectly – to 'the people'. He had done this too by sheer professional skill...As an orator he could reach considerable, though unpredictable heights. His progressive rhetoric (praise for liberal and national movements) abroad and support for enough reform to distance himself from complete reaction at home allowed him to achieve a unique place in political life.

Hoppen, *The Mid-Victorian Generation*, 1998

■ Examination-style questions

1 Comprehension in context

Explain what Hoppen means (in Source D) by Palmerston's 'support for enough reform to distance himself from complete reaction at home'?

2 Comparing the sources

To what extent does Source C support Blake's comments in Source A that Palmerston was 'more Tory than the Tories'?

3 Assessing the sources

Using your own knowledge assess the value to a historian of Disraeli's assessment of Palmerston in 1855 (Source B).

4 Making judgements

Using the sources and your own knowledge, explain how far you agree with the view of Palmerston as 'the most modern politican of his day' (Source D).

Summary

- The Repeal of the Corn Laws in 1846 transformed British party politics. The consequences for the Conservatives were very serious. They split and, in the split, virtually all their leaders left the Party. Though there were short-lived, minority Conservative governments in 1852, 1858–1859 and 1866–1867, the Party did not fully revive until 1874. In contrast, the Whigs, strengthened by the addition of the Peelites, became, for the next 30 years, the natural party of government.

- The Whigs held on to power for most of the years from 1846 to 1865 by following policies of free trade and reform which were attractive to the Peelites, to Radicals and to the electorate among whom the middle and some of the skilled working classes were important elements. They were helped considerably by the weakness of the Conservatives.

- The main issues of foreign policy which Britain faced during these years arose from the balance of power in Europe and from the need to strengthen the British Empire and British trade. The weakness of the Turkish Empire and liberal and nationalist movements in regions like Italy and Poland affected the European balance of power. China had particular potential for the development of British trade. British governments had their fair share of successes and failures in these years. The successes were more at the expense of weak nations rather than of strong ones.

- The great personal popularity which Palmerston's apparently aggressive foreign policy gained for him was one reason for his dominance. Other reasons included his ability to appeal to a wide cross-section of the Liberal Party and his apparently inexhaustible vigour. He had mixed success, if great fame, as Foreign Secretary. At home he achieved more than he is usually given credit for.

■ Further reading

Paul Adelman, *Peel and the Conservative Party**

M.E. Chamberlain, *British Foreign Policy in the Age of Palmerston**

Jasper Ridley, *Palmerston,* 1970

H.C.G. Matthew, *Gladstone,* 1982

P. Smith, *Disraeli, a Brief Life,* 1996

T.A. Jenkins, *The Liberal Ascendancy,* 1994

Robert Blake, *The Conservative Party from Peel to Thatcher,* 1985

* Books particularly suitable for students

Chapter 2

Gladstone versus Disraeli
The greatest political rivalry of the century

Gladstone as an author

Gladstone's *Iuventus Mori* is a study of Homer, a great, many people would say the greatest, poet of ancient Greek civilization. It was a serious subject, treated seriously and it sold far fewer copies than *Lothair*.

Disraeli as an author

Disraeli wrote the novel *Lothair* in 1869. With wit and a lightness of touch, it tells of the adventures of a young English aristocrat in Italy and was a great success with the reading public.

Source 1

◄ This *Punch* cartoon by Tenniel in 1870 shows Gladstone, on the left, reading Disraeli's *Lothair* and Disraeli reading Gladstone's *Iuventus Mori*. Both books were published in 1870 when Gladstone was Prime Minister of a Liberal government and Disraeli leader of the Conservative opposition.

Source 2

Posterity will do justice to that unprincipled maniac Gladstone – extraordinary mixture of envy, vindictiveness [given to revenge], hypocrisy and superstition; and with one common characteristic – whether preaching, praying, speechifying or scribbling – never a gentleman!

Disraeli on Gladstone, in writing to Lady Derby in 1876

Source 3

As he lived, so he died – all display without reality or genuineness.

Gladstone on Disraeli, in conversation with his personal secretary, Edward Hamilton, about Disraeli's funeral

Introduction

Gladstone and Disraeli were political opponents from 1846 and rival party leaders from 1868 to 1881, the year of Disraeli's death. They were very able, very different and as Sources 2 and 3 illustrate, they disliked each other greatly. Seldom has there been a rivalry so intense in the history of British politics.

Key questions

- What were the main characteristics of liberalism and conservatism in the 1860s?
- How did party politics change between 1865 and 1885?
- What were the relationships of the two men to their respective parties?
- What did each achieve?
- How have their reputations stood up to the investigations of historians?

Gladstone's career to 1867

Born in 1809, the fifth of six children, William Ewart Gladstone had a start in life which gave him an easy entry into national politics. Both his parents were Scots but his father, Sir John Gladstone, had moved to Liverpool, where he had made a considerable fortune as a merchant. He also became a Tory MP. He sent William to Eton and then on to Christ Church, the Oxford college for future political leaders. The young Gladstone did not make a particular mark at Eton but at Oxford he excelled, gaining a double first in Greats (classics) and in Mathematics.

By the time he left university, Gladstone had acquired the deep religious faith which he kept for the rest of his life and which was the foundation of his political activities. He thought of becoming a priest but his father persuaded him to enter politics. One of his Oxford friends was the son of the Duke of Newcastle and, in 1832, through the Duke's influence, he became Tory MP for Newark.

He soon made his mark as a committed Tory. In his maiden speech he defended his father's conduct as a West Indian slave owner and his first published book was a strong defence of the Church of England as the conscience of the nation.

His abilities soon caught the attention of Peel, who was the Tory/Conservative Prime Minister from 1841 to 1846. Working at the Board of Trade first as Vice-President and then from 1843 as President (which brought him into the Cabinet at the age of 34), Gladstone simplified considerably the many tariffs (customs duties) which were hampering the country's trade.

In the great Corn Law crisis of 1846 which caused a bitter split within the Tory Party, he supported Peel and free trade against the majority of the Party which favoured protection (see pages 11–12).

During the 1850s, Gladstone moved towards the Liberals. He was an outstanding Chancellor of the Exchequer in the 1850s and 1860s. Following Palmerston's death in 1865 and Lord Russell's retirement in 1867, he emerged unchallenged as Liberal leader.

Gladstone was a man of high intelligence, extraordinary energy and intense Christian commitment. His first political boss, Sir James Graham, said of him that he could do in four hours what would take other men 16 and he worked 16 hours a day. His career in Parliament lasted more than 60 years, as a Cabinet minister off and on for 50. He was Prime Minister four times. He also found the

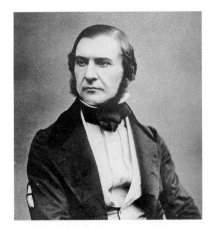
▲ Gladstone in his forties.

Note

Gladstone's diaries

Gladstone started his journal at Eton and kept a daily record of his activities, almost without a break, for most of the rest of his life. Collected together in 14 volumes and brilliantly edited by H.C.G. Matthew, it is an exceptionally fascinating and valuable source for understanding his long and complex life.

time to read an enormous range of books, write extensively, travel widely both in Britain and abroad, care actively for an extensive family and, as his main relaxation, cut down trees.

Catherine Glynne, whom he married in 1839, proved an ideal partner. She was a charming and witty woman who devoted herself to their eight children and his political career.

She also appears to have been remarkably tolerant of her husband's unusual practice with prostitutes. Often late at night after parliamentary debates, he used to seek them out, talk to them and try to persuade them to change their ways. Sometimes he brought them home for tea with Mrs Gladstone. He always stressed the charitable nature of this activity and cared nothing about the gossip that it caused. However, though he never seems to have been unfaithful to his wife, he knew he gained a sexual thrill from these meetings. A symbol in his diaries suggests he whipped himself as a punishment.

> **Quotation**
>
> William, if you were not such a great man, you would be an awful bore.
>
> **Mrs Gladstone to her husband**

◀ Gladstone in his seventies relaxing from his favourite hobby, tree felling. With him are Mrs Gladstone and his family, with the family home, Hawarden Castle in Flintshire, in the background.

▼ The young Disraeli irritating the Irish members with his maiden speech in the House of Commons in 1837.

Disraeli to 1867

In contrast, Disraeli was an outsider. Both his paternal grandparents were Jews. His grandfather had emigrated from Italy. His grandmother was Portuguese. Isaac, his father, was a successful writer and lived comfortably in London. Since Jews could not take part in national politics until 1858, perhaps the best thing Isaac did for Benjamin's political career was to quarrel with his local synagogue and have his son baptized a Christian.

Benjamin Disraeli was born in 1804. He attended a local day school and, at his father's request, started training as a lawyer in 1821. He was, however, an ambitious romantic who was determined to make his mark in the world. The next ten years went badly. Having left legal work, he tried and failed to start a national newspaper and amassed huge debts (which were to haunt him for much of his life) by gambling in South American mining shares. He quarrelled with his friends and found his first novels harshly criticized. He had a nervous breakdown from which he only seemed fully recovered after an extensive tour in the Mediterranean and Near East.

Henrietta Sykes

Henrietta Sykes was beautiful, passionate and unhappily married. Disraeli met Lord Lyndhurst through her. The two men became friends and Lyndhurst was able to help Disraeli with his career. Disraeli had an intense affair with Henrietta before she deserted him for the handsome painter of this picture. His affair with Mrs Sykes and the gossip, probably true, that he shared her with Lyndhurst caused him to be regarded for many years as a thoroughly disreputable character.

■ Think about

▶ Consider the characteristics which made the young Disraeli so disliked and the qualities which eventually helped him to the top of British politics.

▲ Mrs Mary Lewis, the rich widow whom Disraeli married in 1839. She was to provide him with vital emotional (and financial) support through his turbulent political career.

By 1831 he had decided that his future lay in politics and he became well-known in London society for his striking looks and dandified dress. His reputation as a novelist was growing, especially after the publication of the semi-autobiographical *Contarini Fleming* in 1832. He had a famous quarrel with the Irish leader, Daniel O'Connell, and a different kind of fame through his affair with Henrietta Sykes. Though married, she became his mistress.

After three failures, he was finally elected Tory MP for Maidstone in 1837. His maiden speech was a disaster. The Irish members took against him for his extravagant dress and dramatic manner and shouted him down. He ended his speech with the declaration: 'I will sit down now but the time will come when you will hear me'. He made that prophecy come true. Disraeli's determination and political courage were remarkable.

He had many disappointments still to face. He had hoped for a post in Peel's government in 1841 but was offered nothing. He then built up his position within the Tory Party with a group of friends who gained the nickname, Young England. They strongly criticized what they considered the too-commercial, too-middle-class approach of Peel and looked back to a golden age when nobles and people were united by a single Church and caring monarch. Disraeli was the most intelligent and imaginative of the group and two of his novels – *Coningsby* (1844) and *Sybil; or the Two Nations* (1845) – contained many of its ideas.

In alliance with Lord George Bentinck, Disraeli led the assault on Peel during the Corn Law crisis of 1846. His anti-Peel speeches were brilliant, savage and personal. After Peel had been driven from office and Bentinck had died in 1848, Disraeli became the Tory leader in the House of Commons. Lord Stanley, the future Earl of Derby, led the Party from the House of Lords.

Disraeli became leader in the Commons because he was indispensable, not because he was liked or even respected. On the contrary, he was distrusted because he was an outsider, un-English in appearance, and with a bad reputation in matters of money and women. However, since most of the able Tories like Gladstone had left the Party with Peel, he was so much the Tories' best parliamentary performer that they had to tolerate him.

Being intensely ambitious, he found the next 20 years of almost continuous opposition most frustrating. Divisions amongst the Liberals allowed Derby to form short-lived governments in 1852 and 1858–1859. In both, Disraeli was Chancellor of the Exchequer. In 1852, he found his budget proposals demolished by Gladstone in a long and devastatingly successful speech which did much for the latter's reputation and nothing for Disraeli's. Then, in 1865, came the death of Lord Palmerston and new opportunities for Disraeli which he seized with both hands.

In 1839 he married Mary Lewis, 12 years his senior and the widow of a political colleague. She was pretty, talkative, a trifle eccentric and had money. After a fiery courtship, he persuaded her to marry him and won her devotion for the rest of her life. He probably married her for her money but soon became equally devoted to her. When she died in 1872, he was devastated. They had no children.

How the parties were organized

By modern standards, and by the standards of the 1880s, party organizations were amateur and weak. They reflected the widespread belief of the time that politics should be the part-time occupation of men of property. What little central organization existed was the responsibility of the parliamentary Whips. They had to make sure that there were enough candidates at election time and enough money for election expenses. In the counties and boroughs, local worthies ran the show. The big London political clubs – the Reform (Liberal) and the Carlton (Conservative) – co-ordinated national and local efforts.

> **Note**
>
> In Parliament, Whips were, and are still, the party officials who make sure that MPs are well-organized and vote as the leadership requires.

Disraeli and the Conservative Party

The name Conservative began to replace Tory from the 1840s, with 'Tory' surviving as a nickname. The original eighteenth-century Tories defended the monarchy and the Church of England. They disliked the French Revolution and opposed electoral reform. They were mainly a party of the landed and farming interest and broke with Peel when he tried to make the Party more attractive to the flourishing middle classes. After 1846, the Conservatives continued for some years as the party of protection, which lost them votes. Disraeli realized that protection was a dead issue and persuaded the Party to take up a free-trade position. He also encouraged it to become more sympathetic to electoral reform. None the less, in the 1860s, the Conservative Party remained out of touch with the most dynamic elements of British society.

Disraeli took his political beliefs less seriously than Gladstone and changed them less significantly. His novels are the best guide to them, especially *Coningsby* and *Sybil*. He was a Tory because he believed that the Whigs had done enormous damage to Britain. In his opinion, they were a small group of selfish wealthy families who with the industrialists had divided Britain into two nations, the rich and the poor. The Conservatives would make sure that the monarchy, aristocracy and Church would govern well and reduce the gap between rich and poor by social reforms.

In 1867, however, Disraeli's simple aim was to get the Conservatives back into power by whatever means possible (see spotlight on pages 28–29).

Gladstone and the Liberal Party

By 1867 Gladstone's views had changed greatly from the extreme Toryism of his youth. He was now a Liberal because:
● His travels in Italy and support for Italian unification made him a champion of freedom and an enemy of tyrants.
● His experience first as a Peelite and then as a long-serving and successful Chancellor of the Exchequer had convinced him of the importance of free trade, low taxes, and 'laissez-faire'.
● While he remained a loyal member of the Church of England, he had developed a more tolerant attitude to other denominations.
● He developed a warm opinion of working people, and though never a democrat, favoured the extension of the franchise.

However, Gladstone always kept a distance between himself and his Party. In a sense he was bigger than it. His powerful personality, his well-publicized speaking tours and the backing he received from the Press made him a national figure. Nicknamed 'the People's William', he was an important vote-winner in his own right. As the years passed and the divisions amongst Liberals grew, his personality held them together, even if his ideas were becoming out of date.

Gladstone's first ministry 1868–1874

As described in Chapter 3, (page 47) Gladstone's first reaction when he heard the 1868 election result was to think of Ireland and the opportunity this gave him to try to bring peace. During this ministry, Ireland remained his central concern. His government also proved to be one of the most energetic reforming governments of the century. Little, however, of this reforming drive came from Gladstone himself, since he was broadly satisfied with the free trade, low tax, and sparingly regulated society which he with his Peelite-Liberal colleagues had helped to create. The main reason why he allowed ministers like Forster and Cardwell to push forward a reform programme, was to keep the support of the Nonconformist radicals.

The major and mainly successful reforms

Forster's Education Act (1870)

The aim of this Act was to fill the gaps left by the voluntary system of education, in which most schools were Church schools subsidized by a national grant. Though the size of this grant had risen considerably, many children (as many as nine out of ten in some industrial cities) still went without education. A mainly Nonconformist National Education League, founded in 1869 and based in Birmingham, campaigned for compulsory, free education and for a reduction of the influence of the Church of England in educational matters. The Education Act set up school boards which could create new schools, known as Board Schools, where they were needed, which were paid for out of local rates.

This was a major step forward for education in Britain. Between 1870 and 1880 the number of children receiving elementary education doubled to 3 million. The most controversial parts of the Act were its religious aspects. To please the Nonconformists, the government allowed the Act to include the so-called Cowper-Temple Clause, which stated that, if religious education was taught in Board schools, it must be non-denominational. However, it angered Nonconformists by its Clause 25 which laid down that the fees of poor children attending Church, mainly Anglican, schools, should be paid out of the rates.

The Reform Act of 1867

In 1866–1867, the rivalry between Gladstone and Disraeli began in earnest. Though Lord Russell led the Liberals and the Earl of Derby the Conservatives, Gladstone and Disraeli dominated the House of Commons and both saw themselves as future Prime Ministers.

The issue over which they fought was a major one – giving the right to vote to a larger proportion of the population.

The 1832 Reform Act had given the vote to only one in five adult males. Hardly any working men had gained the vote and the industrial cities remained under-represented when compared to the more rural counties. As the country grew richer and industrialization advanced, skilled working men became more prosperous and confident. They formed trade unions to campaign for better pay and working conditions. They also began to demand the right to vote in general elections. Their champion was the Radical Liberal MP John Bright. In 1865 he helped to set up the Reform League, the aim of which was to persuade the government to increase substantially the number of men with the right to vote.

Both Gladstone and Disraeli favoured a new Reform Act. However, both faced strong opposition within their own parties, Gladstone from a group led by Robert Lowe, Disraeli from one led by Lord Cranborne (later Lord Salisbury) who did not believe that the new voters would cast their vote responsibly.

In 1866, Russell and Gladstone introduced a Reform Bill to Parliament. The right to vote was based on property qualifications, so they proposed including householders paying a rent of £7 per year or more and to leaseholders paying £14 per year. This bill would have added about 400,000 voters to the electorate.

Though the Liberals outnumbered the Conservatives in the Commons by 360 to 290, Russell and Gladstone could not get their bill through. Lowe and his supporters, who became known as the Adullamites, combined with the Conservatives to defeat it.

Derby with Disraeli formed a Conservative government with the intention of postponing further discussion of the franchise until 1868. However, there was anger now in the country. The Reform League campaigned harder. A crowd banned from meeting in Hyde Park simply broke down the railings and met anyway. The Queen was anxious. In February 1867, Disraeli introduced a new Reform Bill to the Commons.

It started off as much the same as Gladstone's but changed greatly during the debates in the Commons. Disraeli had by now just one real aim, to get a major bill through Parliament to prove to the country that the Conservatives, after 20 years in opposition, could be seen as a party of government.

How, though, could he get this bill through? The Conservatives were a minority. Lord Cranborne would oppose him within his own Party as would Gladstone who did not wish him to gain the glory of passing a new Reform Act. What he did was this. He found a group of Radical Liberals who would co-operate with him if he would produce a more far-reaching bill than his original. Then, by a clever and rapid use of tactics within Parliament, he accepted amendment after amendment of his bill by the Radicals. He lost Cranborne and a few others, but held the rest of the Party together by offering them the exciting prospect of 'dishing the Whigs'. One of the amendments he accepted from the Liberals, that of Hodgkinson, added 500,000 to the voting lists by abolishing the practice of 'compounding' by which rate-payers could pay their rates through their landlord rather than personally. By the time the bill had passed through the Commons and the Lords it created 830,000 new voters in the boroughs and 290,000 in the counties. In the towns, one in two adult males now had the franchise.

The 1867 Reform Act had alongside it a Redistribution Act, which slightly increased the number of seats in the big cities. However, the countryside and the south where the Conservatives were strong remained over-represented at the expense of the cities and the north.

Derby described the Reform Act as a 'leap in the dark' since no one knew what would be the electoral consequences of the Reform Act. In the long run it probably made little difference. In the short run it brought no benefit to Disraeli who lost the 1868 election to Gladstone by the wide margin of 112 seats. (A short sharp economic depression seems to have been the main reason for this defeat.)

Key term

The Adullamites
The nickname comes from the Old Testament in the Bible. A group of discontented Israelite warriors hid in the cave of Adullam.

Historical debate

For years historians argued about why the 1867 Reform Act ended up more far-reaching than Disraeli's original proposal. There was a Liberal myth that he was simply forced to go further because of well-organized Liberal pressure. There was also a Conservative myth that Disraeli was, as he put it, educating his Party. He wanted all along a wider franchise but knew that his Party would not go so far. So he used the Radical Liberals to get him to his goal. However, in the 1960s, M. Cowling and F.B. Smith made a thorough analysis of the events of 1867 and there is little doubt now that Disraeli's main concern was to get any bill anyhow through Parliament. The final shape of the 1867 Reform Act, therefore, was the result of complicated party manoeuvrings with no-one having a clear idea where precisely they would lead.

THE DERBY, 1867. DIZZY WINS WITH "REFORM BILL."

Mr. Punch. "DON'T BE TOO SURE; WAIT TILL HE'S *WEIGHED.*"

Source 6

[Any man] who is not presumably incapacitated by some consideration of personal unfitness or of political danger, is morally entitled to come within the pale of the constitution.

Gladstone in the Commons in 1864

Source 7

The future principle of English politics will not be a levelling principle; not a principle adverse to privilege, but favourable to their extension. It will seek to ensure equality, not by levelling the Few, but elevating the Many.

Disraeli speaking through Egremont, one of the characters in his novel *Sybil* (1845)

Source 8

Disraeli's performance was an outstanding exhibition not only of parliamentary skill but of mental and physical endurance for a man in his sixty-third year. He thought at first the task was impossible.

The historian Paul Smith. Smith, *Disraeli: a Brief Life,* 1996

Source 4

The carpenter commented to Disraeli's secretary that 'Mr Disraeli had laid Mr Gladstone on his back'.

A carpenter in Shropshire

Source 5

A smash, perhaps, without example.

Gladstone

■ Questions

1 Explain in your own words the views expressed by Gladstone in Source 6 and Disraeli in Source 7.

2 Why, in Source 8, did Disraeli first think his task impossible? How did he succeed?

3 What are the carpenter and Gladstone getting at in Sources 4 and 5? Gladstone thought of resigning from the leadership of the Liberals in the Commons. Why?

4 What does the Reform Act crisis tell you about Disraeli's political skills?

5 What does the cartoon show? Explain the caption including Mr Punch's comment 'Wait till he's weighed'.

Entry to the civil service (1870)

Merit as measured by competitive examinations replaced patronage (getting jobs through family or friends) for entering the civil service. Robert Lowe (forgiven for his Adullamite action) was responsible for this overdue reform. However, it upset some aristocrats who lost their influence. Lord Granville, Foreign Secretary, refused to introduce the reforms to the Foreign Office.

The University Test Act (1871)

This ended the monopoly of the Anglican Church to provide teachers and students at Oxford and Cambridge universities. Students from all religious backgrounds were allowed entry and could become teachers. It was part of the drive against privilege, particularly religious privilege, to which Radical Liberals gave high priority.

Cardwell's army reforms

There were a number of these. The government saw them as a necessary attack on inefficiency and aristocratic privilege. The army had distinguished itself neither during the Crimean War (1854–1856) nor during the rising in India (the so-called Indian Mutiny) of 1857. Wealthy young men could become officers simply by buying 'a commission'. The Duke of Cambridge, who was both stupid and reactionary as well as a cousin of the Queen, was Commander-in-Chief and obstinately opposed all change.

Cardwell combined the various military departments under one roof at the War Office, reorganized the regiments and abolished the purchase of commissions. Instead, promotion should be through merit. He made the Commander-in-Chief answerable to the Secretary for War. The conditions of ordinary soldiers were improved by the end of flogging in peacetime and the reduction in the length of overseas service from twelve years to six. He also secured more modern weapons, notably the Martini-Henry breech-loading rifle.

These were successful and timely reforms which gave Britain an efficient, if small, army, well-designed for colonial wars. However, they also angered the aristocracy and only the influence of the Queen got them through the House of Lords.

Other effective reforms included the Ballot Act (1872) which introduced the secret ballot (voting in secret rather than in public) and greatly reduced the incidence of bribery and intimidation at election time, and the Judicature Act (1873) which modernized the legal system.

Two less successful reforms

Trade unions

Various unions had founded the Trades Union Congress (TUC) in 1868, and, following some incidents of industrial violence, were anxious to put trade unions on a secure legal basis and to legalize strikes. This the Trade Union Act of 1871 did, but the Criminal Law Amendment Act of the same year forbade peaceful picketing (the right of strikers to try to persuade other workers from entering strike-bound factories). The law courts interpreted the Act in a manner hostile to the unions. Consequently, the government lost much support among skilled working people.

■ Biography

Edward Cardwell (1813-1886)

Cardwell was a close ally of Gladstone for many years. Educated at Winchester and Oxford, he too was a Peelite and held a number of ministries in the 1850s and 1860s, where he proved himself hard-working and efficient. As Secretary for War from 1868 he had to push his reforms through stiff opposition and had a lengthy dispute with Gladstone in 1874 over army funding. He was exhausted when the government fell in 1874 and took no further part in politics.

■ Activity

Gladstone later looked back to this ministry as 'an era of liberation'. He was thinking particularly of those measures which ended privilege and opened up opportunities for men of merit. At the same time, it was a ministry which controlled people more through regulation. This tension between liberation and regulation was one which the Liberal Party found very difficult to resolve.

Draw up a chart of 3 columns.
1 In the first column list the reforms of the Liberal government of 1868–1874.
2 In the second, note whether they were 'liberating' or 'regulating'.
3 In the third, explain the reasons for your judgement.

■ Think about

Many people at the time, and later, thought that Gladstone's confidence in a new law of nations (Source 9) was completely unrealistic and that it was not possible for nations to have ethical or moral foreign policies.
▶ What is your opinion?

Quotation

The 'exhausted volcanoes' quotation is worth noting more fully since it is Disraeli at his best, He was reminded 'of one of those marine landscapes not very uncommon on the coasts of South America. You behold a range of exhausted volcanoes. Not a flame flickers from a single pallid crest. But the situation is still dangerous. There are occasional earthquakes, and ever and anon the dark rumbling of the sea.'

The Licensing Act (1872)

Excessive alcohol consumption was a serious problem in Victorian Britain and a 'temperance' movement aimed at reducing drinking had considerable support, especially among Nonconformist Liberals. Consequently in 1872, the government passed a Licensing Act which gave magistrates the power to issue licences to pubs so their number could be controlled and forced pubs to close at midnight in towns and 11 p.m. in the country. This Act proved highly unpopular both with working men who disliked the closing hours and with brewers.

There was a general unease about the way the government was intervening in social customs. As a bishop put it during the debate in the House of Lords, he would 'prefer an England free to an England sober'.

Foreign policy 1868–1874

Gladstone's unusually moral approach to politics guided his foreign policy. As he wrote in an article for the *Edinburgh Review* in 1868, he was confident that:

Source 9

...a new law of nations is gradually taking hold of the mind...of the world; a law which recognises independence, which frowns on aggression, which favours the pacific [peaceful], not the bloody settlement of disputes...which recognises, above all, as a tribunal [court], of paramount authority, the general judgement of civilised mankind.

The first major foreign crisis he faced was the Franco-Prussian War of 1870–1871. The crushing Prussian victory led to the unification of Germany around Prussia and the German seizure of the provinces of Alsace and Lorraine. Gladstone made clear to Prussia that Britain would come to the aid of Belgium if that small country were attacked in the course of the war.

A problem left over from previous government was the *Alabama* affair (see page 17). The *Alabama* was a Confederate warship built in Britain which did great damage to the Union side during the American Civil War. Since Britain was officially neutral, it should never have been allowed to leave British waters but the government was careless and it did. Consequently, the victorious Union government sued for damages. Throughout a complicated and often bitter dispute, Gladstone accepted that the American government had a case and insisted, patiently, that a settlement be found. After complicated negotiations, an international arbitration panel in 1872 fixed Britain's liability as £3.25 million, which, though a considerable sum for those days, Gladstone immediately agreed to pay. His action showed that he took seriously the 'general judgement of civilized mankind' and greatly improved Anglo-American relations.

Defeat 1874

Disraeli made one of his most memorable criticisms of his opponents in a speech in Manchester in 1872. He explained to his audience how Gladstone and his ministers reminded him of a range of 'exhausted volcanoes' It was a powerful and appropriate image. Gladstone and his ministers had been very energetic but between 1872 and 1874 they ran out of steam. They also quarrelled amongst themselves.

Source 10

There is now no cause, no great public object on which the Liberal Party are agreed and combined.

Gladstone writing in his diary in March 1873

The Nonconformists were angry about the Education Act; working-men about the trade union laws and the Licensing Act; the Whigs about the army reforms and the Irish land policies (see page 48). Gladstone planned to win the 1874 general election by abolishing income tax but he did not carry his Cabinet colleagues with him. His announcement of the election date took everyone by surprise, not least his Party officials.

The election result of February 1874 was a disaster for the Liberals. In 1868 they had had 387 MPs against the Conservatives 271. In 1874 they had only 251, the Conservatives had 342 and the Irish Nationalists, appearing for the first time, returned 59.

Gladstone had a simple explanation. As he wrote to a colleague:

Source 11

We have been swept away in a torrent of gin and beer

He was fooling himself. The situation was more complicated and serious. The country as a whole was tired of change. The middle classes were turning to the Conservatives. The Irish vote was lost, permanently. Many Nonconformists had abstained from voting.

At the age of 65, Gladstone decided that the time had come for him to retire from politics and to prepare to meet his Maker.

Disraeli 1868–1880

Opposition 1868–1874

His defeat in 1868 had depressed Disraeli greatly. He was 64 and had already experienced the frustrations of opposition for too many years. From 1868 to 1871 he did so little as the leader of the opposition that Lord Salisbury and Lord Derby discussed whether Derby should replace him as leader.

In 1872, however, he found renewed vigour and the plots behind his back ceased. In two major speeches, the one in Manchester and the other at the Crystal Palace, he set out what he considered to be the main strands of Conservatism:
● Maintaining the historic institutions of the nation, notably the Crown, the House of Lords and the Church of England
● Upholding the Empire of England
● Improving the condition of the people through social reform

Otherwise, he stayed clear of major policy statements and concentrated on attacking Gladstone's government, since he realized, correctly, that the 1874 election would be won by the electorate feeling negative about the Liberals rather than positive about the Conservatives.

■ **Activity**

Draw or plan the main elements of a political cartoon that you think more accurately than Source 8 reflects the range of reasons why the Liberals did so badly in the election of 1874.

Quotation

Power! It has come to me too late. There were days when, on waking, I felt I could move dynasties and governments; but that has passed away.

Disraeli in 1878

■ Biography

Richard Cross (1823–1914)

Cross was born in Lancashire and educated at Rugby School (where he became a friend of Lord Derby) and Cambridge University. A successful lawyer and businessman, he became an MP in the 1860s. Though he had been active in local government, he was by far the least experienced of Disraeli's ministers. However he proved himself both shrewd and efficient, though he was a boring public speaker. After Disraeli's death, his political career failed to flourish, though he became a viscount in 1892. His social reforms of 1874 made him particularly popular in Lancashire; hence this rhyme:

'For he's a jolly good fellow, whatever the radicals may think. He's shortened the hours of work and lengthened the hours of drink.'

Prime Minister at last 1874–1880

Disraeli was 69 when he became Prime Minister. He was often ill and his wife was soon to die. As the quotation suggests, he was very conscious of the effects of age. His poor health and lack of energy often worried his colleagues.

None the less, his was a strong government which achieved much. However physically fragile he may have been, he was a powerful Prime Minister. He continued to dominate the House of Commons in debates. His Cabinet ministers, who included a duke, three earls, a marquis, two lords, a baronet and four commoners, were talented and he let them get on with their jobs. His most surprising appointment was Richard Cross as Home Secretary, who proved very successful. Disraeli only interfered on really important matters like foreign policy and when his ministers were in trouble. He had a particularly warm relationship with Queen Victoria.

That said, he had no clear programme for his government. In his *Memoirs* (1903) Cross described his first Cabinet meeting:

Source 12

From all his speeches I quite expected that his mind was full of legislative schemes, but such did not prove to be the case; on the contrary, he had to rely on the suggestions of his colleagues…

He also exasperated his colleagues by his refusal to discuss with them important details of their work. Lord Carnarvon, his Colonial Secretary once exploded: 'He detests details…He does no work!'

Social reform

Other people, however, did work. In 1874, Cross effectively repealed the Liberals' Licensing Act of 1872. In the same year he produced a Factory Act which reduced the maximum hours women and children could work per week to 56.5 hours. Children under 14 were only to be employed half-time, while children under 10 were not to be employed at all.

Probably the most important achievement of Cross, with the active backing of Disraeli, was his trade union legislation of 1875. He repealed the Liberals' Criminal Law Amendment Act of 1871 and produced an Employers' and Workmen's Act and a Conspiracy and Protection of Property Act. Strikers no longer needed to worry about being prosecuted for conspiracy and they could also picket peacefully. Disraeli was probably exaggerating when he claimed that these measures would 'retain for the Tories the lasting affection of the working classes' but they certainly helped to reduce the traditional suspicions which factory workers had of the Conservatives.

Cross produced another major act in 1875, the Artisans' Dwelling Act. The cholera epidemic of 1866–1867 had raised considerable concern nationally about extensive slums in the large cities. The Act permitted local authorities to purchase land compulsorily and build and rehouse people where appropriate. It also made cheap loans available for this purpose.

Another active reformer was George Sclater-Booth, who was in charge of the Local Government Board. He piloted through Parliament:

- A Public Health Act (1875) which built on previous Acts of 1866 and 1872, improving standards of sewage disposal and of controlling contagious diseases
- A Sale of Food and Drugs Act (1875) which encouraged authorities to appoint inspectors to check on the adulteration of food (e.g. chalk in flour)
- A River Pollutions Act (1876) which allowed the cleansing of Britain's contaminated rivers.

Other reforms included a very limited measure in 1875 to regulate the Friendly Societies which were an important source of insurance for working people, and an Agricultural Holdings Act (1875) which gave tenants greater safeguards against eviction from their homes. Sandon's Education Act of 1876, which aimed to boost school attendance, was also intended to strengthen Anglican schools in rural areas.

The Merchant Shipping Act of 1876 was very much the achievement of the Liberal MP, Samuel Plimsoll, who was concerned about how the lack of regulations about seaworthiness and overloading was risking sailors' lives. After many delays, this Act was passed which required the 'Plimsoll Line' to be painted on ships' hulls to indicate the level of safe loading (but see margin note).

Towards the end of 1876, in poor health, Disraeli talked much about retiring. Both the Queen and his Party, however, considered him indispensable and persuaded him instead to move to the House of Lords as Lord Beaconsfield. He remained leader of the Party and Stafford Northcote, Chancellor of the Exchequer, led the Conservatives in the House of Commons. Disraeli missed the cut and thrust of the Commons but his health improved, though this may have been a result less of the move than his doctor insisting that he drank claret instead of port.

For the rest of his term of office, his chief concerns were imperial (see Chapter 5) and foreign.

Foreign Policy

The Eastern Question

From 1876 to 1878, events in the Balkans gripped the attention of most of Europe's leaders, including Disraeli. They also brought Gladstone out of retirement. These events were another act in the drama which became known as the 'Eastern Question'.

The Eastern Question was this: what would happen to Eastern Europe and the Eastern Mediterranean when the Turkish (Ottoman) Empire collapsed?

Between 1400 and 1700, the Ottoman Turks had created a huge Empire, ruled from Constantinople, which stretched from Hungary in the north to Egypt in the south and Persia in the east. Its rulers were Muslim, its European subjects were, for the most part, Christian. During the nineteenth century Turkish power declined, its government was often cruel and corrupt and in the area known as the Balkans (see map on page 35), a number of mainly Christian peoples with different (mainly Slav) languages and history began to demand their independence.

> **Note**
>
> Samuel Plimsoll and the Merchant Shipping Act (1876). Plimsoll was so infuriated by the delays which occurred in the passing of this Bill that he lost his temper in the Commons, shouting 'villains' and shaking his fist at the Conservative ministers.
>
> Even when the Act became law, shipowners undermined its effect by painting the Plimsoll Line where they wished. Not until 1890 did it really become effective.

> **Note**
>
> Permissive legislation means passing laws which allow communities to take action but do not force them. In Disraeli's opinion, permissive legislation was right for a free country. The problem was that often it meant little change when change was needed, e.g. six years after the Artisans' Dwelling Act had been passed, only 10 out of 85 towns in England and Wales had made use of it, despite their slums and health hazards.

> ■ **Activity**
>
> Make a chart of three columns for the reforms of Disraeli's ministry. In the first, list the reforms. In the second, note whether they were 'permissive' or 'compulsory'. In the third, give the reasons for your judgement.

There were three European powers particularly interested in the Eastern Question:

● Russia, which bordered on the Ottoman Empire and, because of its own mainly Slav population, had warm feelings towards the Balkan Slavs. Since its European ports were ice-bound in winter, it liked the idea of having Constantinople as a warm-water port. Russian governments usually did their best to speed the Ottoman decline and increase their influence.

● Austria-Hungary, which also had a common border with the Ottoman Empire and did not want Russia to become too strong. Austrian governments usually worked to weaken Turkey as long as Russia did not gain too great an advantage.

● Britain, which had important trading interests in the Eastern Mediterranean and also regarded Russia as a serious threat to the British Empire in Asia and the sea-route to India, which went through Egypt via the Suez Canal. British governments usually propped up the Turkish government against Russian pressure.

Timeline

1853-6 Crimean War
Britain, France and Turkey against Russia.

1856 Treaty of Paris ends the war. (see page 15).

1870s Unrest in the Balkans. Cruel repression by the Turks.

1876 Russia, Austria and Germany demand that the Turkish government reforms. Disraeli disagrees with them. He is sure that Britain should support Turkey.

1876 News emerges that the Turks have massacred thousands of innocent Bulgarians.
Gladstone writes the best-selling pamphlet on 'The Bulgarian Horrors'.

1877 Russia invades Turkey and advances on Constantinople. Disraeli orders the British fleet to Constantinople.

1878 (March) Russians force the Turks to sign the Treaty of San Stefano.
Britain and Austria think this much too favourable to Russia.

1878 (June–July) Congress of Berlin ends with the Treaty of Berlin, which is a much better settlement from the British point of view.

▷ The Eastern Question crisis 1876–8. South-east Europe after the Treaty of Berlin, 1878. The lands indicated in the lighter blue were part of the Ottoman Empire before 1878.

Note

The crisis of 1876–1878, when Britain and Russia nearly went to war, brought the word 'jingoism' into the language. It means excessive nationalism and was inspired by this music hall rhyme:

'We don't want to fight but, by jingo, if we do,
We've got the men, we've got the ships and we've got the money too.'

Disraeli showed a clear head and strong nerves during this crisis. He led the British delegation at the Congress of Berlin and there put on an impressive performance. As the document exercise on pages 36–37 shows he got what he wanted – a revision to the Treaty of San Stefano which made Bulgaria (and Russia's influence) smaller and Turkey stronger. He returned to Britain a hero. He had achieved, he said, 'peace with honour'. He had prevented the Russians from entering Constantinople, kept the sea-route to India secure and added the island of Cyprus to the British Empire.

The difference of opinion which Gladstone and Disraeli had over the Eastern Question crisis of 1876-8 was very bitter and the final stage of their long rivalry. There was much at stake; exceptional cruelty by an ally of Britain on the one hand and the danger of a major European war on the other. Who was right?

Document exercise: The Eastern Question crisis of 1876–1878

Source A

Gladstone condemns the Bulgarian atrocities

Let the Turks now carry away their abuses in the only possible manner, namely by carrying off themselves. Their Zaptiehs and their Mudits, their Bimbashis and their Yuzbashis, their Kaimakans and their Pashas, one and all, bag and baggage, shall I hope clear out from the province they have desolated and profaned.

Extract from 'The Bulgarian Horrors and the Question of the East'

Source B

A historian's assessment of Disraeli's aims and achievement

Disraeli did not want war. He wished to preserve as much of Turkey as he could, stop the Russians entering Constantinople...if possible without war, but he did not flinch at war if there was no alternative. He succeeded in his object, despite the division of the Cabinet, despite the opposition of Derby [see margin note], who was not only Foreign Secretary but one of the most powerful figures in the Conservative Party, despite deep divisions in the country, despite Gladstone and despite his own bad health...the Berlin Settlement....was followed by almost as long a period of peace between the European great powers as the interval separating the Crimean war (1854-6) and the Congress of Vienna (1815).

Blake, *Disraeli*, 1966

Source C

Disraeli's appeal to 'deeper sentiments'

I say absolutely the policy of Europe and not merely the policy of England...has been this – that by the maintenance of the territorial integrity and independence of the Ottoman Empire, great calamities may be averted in Europe, wars may be averted, and wars of no ordinary duration...It has been said that the people of this country are deeply interested in humanitarian considerations [i.e. the Bulgarian atrocities]...involved in the Eastern Question. All must appreciate these feelings. But I am mistaken if there be not yet a deeper sentiment on the part of the people of this country...and that is the determination to maintain the Empire of England.

Disraeli addressing the House of Lords, 1877 Hansard

Note

When Gladstone heard the news of the massacres in Bulgaria, his religious and liberal beliefs convinced him that he must lead a crusade against Turkish rule in the Balkans. It was evil both because it was savagely cruel and because it was denying freedom to the Balkan people.

Gladstone's Bulgarian atrocities pamphlet, which he wrote in three days while in bed with lumbago, proved a best-seller in Britain and also in translation in many other countries. Disraeli's remark that 'it was the worst of the Bulgarian atrocities' struck many at the time as intolerably flippant in the circumstances.

Note

The Derby referred to in Source B was the 15th Earl, the son of the 14th Earl who had been Prime Minister in the 1860s (see page 25). He and Disraeli had been close friends for many years but they fell out in 1878. Though he was Foreign Secretary, Derby thought Disraeli was supporting the Turks too much. Disraeli passed much of the detailed negotiations to Salisbury and led the British delegation to Berlin. Derby resigned and joined the Liberal Party.

Note

Disraeli had to put up with some public hostility from those who thought he was not standing up enough to the Russians. 'What are you waiting for', a fervently pro-Turk lady called out to him at a banquet in 1877. 'At this moment, ma'am, for the potatoes', was Disraeli's reply.

Note

When Britain and Russia seemed close to war early in 1878, Gladstone and his wife had, in London, to take refuge from an angry crowd. They also had the windows of their London house broken.

Source D

An alternative view of the outcome

Because the Congress of Berlin failed to address the issues of Balkan nationalism, 'the direct and logical outcome of the Berlin Settlement was the Serbian-Bulgarian War of 1885, the Bosnian Crisis of 1908, the two Balkan Wars of 1912-13, and the murder of Archduke Ferdinand in 1914.'

Stavrianos, *The Balkans since 1453*, 1958

■ Biography

John Gorst (1835–1916)

Gorst studied Maths at Cambridge before having an adventurous time in New Zealand. On returning to England he became a lawyer and joined Parliament in 1865 as a Conservative. After losing his seat in the 1868 election, Disraeli asked him to improve the Party's organization. This was the most substantial achievement of his life. He became an MP again but despite his intelligence and energy he never held high office, partly because of his quarrelsome nature. In the 1880s he was part of Randolph Churchill's Fourth Party which harassed the ageing Gladstone in debate. He left the Conservatives over tariff reform in 1906 and joined the Liberals.

■ Examination-style questions

1 Comprehension in context

Using Source B and your own knowledge, explain why Disraeli was so anxious to preserve the Ottoman Empire.

2 Comparing the sources

Study Sources B and D. How and why do they differ in their interpretations of the outcome of the Congress of Berlin.

3 Assessing the sources

How useful is Source A to historians seeking to understand public opinion in Britain in relation to the Bulgarian atrocities?

4 Making judgements

Using the sources and your own knowledge, explain how far you agree with the view that Disraeli's policy in relation to the Eastern Question crisis was a successful one.

Organization of the parties after 1868

The 1867 Reform Act significantly increased the electorate and both parties got better organized to fight elections in this new situation.

Disraeli reacted to the defeat of 1869 by setting up a Conservative Central Office and appointing John Gorst as party agent. Gorst was an efficient administrator and far-sighted too. His priority was to get good candidates into the large boroughs and to capture the new working class vote. Disraeli and Gorst also strengthened the National Union which had been founded in 1867 to co-ordinate Party activities throughout the country, and moved it into Gorst's offices. It circulated Conservative propaganda.

Gorst became an MP in 1875 and the organization lost its edge. After the bad 1880 election result, Lord Randolph Churchill (see page 72) tried to take over the National Union and turn it into the policy-making group of the Party, thus weakening the power of the leadership. However, he was outmanoeuvred by Lord Salisbury and the Union returned to the control of the Party leadership. At the end of the century, the Conservative Party was very well organized under the direction of Lord Salisbury the Party leader, Akers-Douglas the Chief Whip, and Captain Middleton the Party agent.

The Liberals improved their organization but, in contrast to the Conservatives, from the bottom up rather than the top down. The Radical Liberals of the Birmingham area who had created the National Education League turned it into the National Liberal Federation in 1877. Joseph Chamberlain (see page 70) was its President and Jesse Collings its Secretary. It was tightly organized with a Central Committee of 600, a Central Executive and a Council of Ten at the top. It became known as the 'Caucus' and the Liberal leaders in London regarded it with suspicion. They believed that Chamberlain would use it to try to force his own particular programme on the Party as a whole. However, it proved an effective election-winning organization first in local elections and then in the general election of 1880.

Gladstone's Midlothian Campaigns 1879–1880

Gladstone transformed British politics by two intensive speech-making tours in the Edinburgh region (Midlothian) in November 1879 and March 1880. On the surface he was fighting to win the Midlothian constituency which had nominated him as its parliamentary candidate. In reality he was leading a national campaign against Disraeli and all his works – Beaconsfieldism he sometimes called it. An additional reason for crusading on big broad issues was to encourage the separate and often squabbling sections of the Liberal Party to unite under his leadership.

What was new about the Midlothian campaign was that it was organized to capture the national imagination through coverage by the Press. Thanks to stenographers and the electric telegraph, the electorate could read Gladstone's Midlothian speeches at their breakfast tables the next day. This was politics for the new voters, who thanks to the secret ballot, could not be easily influenced by local pressures. They were interested in national causes and their hearts and minds had to be won by national campaigning using the most modern means of communication. Such was his personality and his skill as a public speaker, Gladstone did this better than anyone else.

Gladstone savaged Beaconsfieldism on moral grounds. It supported the beastly Turks against the Christian Balkan peoples. Its imperial adventures in Africa and Asia (see Chapter 5) were ending in disaster and harming the native peoples. It was corrupt and spendthrift.

The 1880 general election

For Gladstone, the 1880 general election was a triumph, the Liberals winning a majority of 114 seats. His campaigning was one important cause of success but there were others. Disraeli, misled by two favourable by-election results, called the election during an industrial and agricultural depression when confidence in the government was low. In comparison with Gladstone, the Conservative leaders campaigned feebly and, at a local level, the Liberals were far better organized. Joseph Chamberlain joined the Cabinet in 1880 and Schnadhorst, who had succeeded Collings as Secretary of the NLF, moved to London where he also became Secretary to the Liberal Central Office. When in 1886, Gladstone and Chamberlain split over Home Rule (see page 53) the NLF stayed with Gladstone.

Gladstone's second ministry 1880–1885

In 1880, Gladstone was 71 and supposedly retired but, after his Midlothian successes, he was convinced that he had to make good the harm done by Beaconsfieldism. Lord Hartington, Party leader since 1875, gave way to him.

However, once in office, he found himself forced to wrestle with difficult problems in Ireland (see Chapter 3) and the Empire (see Chapter 5) which left him little time for other matters. Compared to 1868, he had a less clear programme and the tensions with radicals like Chamberlain and Dilke who wanted substantial social reform were greater.

One important achievement was the Corrupt Practices Act of 1883, which limited spending at general elections.

The major achievement of this ministry, however, was the Reform Act of 1884. It had Gladstone's full support since for him it was less a move towards full democracy (of which he was suspicious) than a measure to distribute the vote more fairly. Its main effect was to simplify the franchise by giving male householders in the counties the same voting rights as those in the boroughs. It was essentially a cautious step – Gladstone would not allow votes for women nor proportional representation, though some Liberal MPs favoured these ideas. None the less it increased the number of voters by 60 per cent, more than the other two Reform Acts of 1832 and 1867.

The Lords, which now had a large Conservative majority, were uneasy about it and voted it down. They played for time by arguing that since the constituencies varied too greatly in size and should be redistributed, a Redistribution Bill was needed alongside the Franchise Bill. The Liberals campaigned on the slogan 'peers against the people' and Gladstone on his tours once again met huge cheering crowds. Behind the scenes, Lord Salisbury for the Conservatives worked hard with his friend Dilke for the Liberals and a settlement was reached. The Reform Act became law in 1884, followed by a Redistribution Act in 1885. Under this Act, 159 old parliamentary seats disappeared to be replaced by 175 new ones. For the first time Britain had a reasonably fair distribution of seats.

Once the Reform Act crisis was passed, Liberal unity collapsed. Defeated on a budget vote, Gladstone resigned, and, now aged 76, once again expected to retire and prepare for death.

Gladstone's third and fourth ministries

However, he had another crusade to lead, this time for Irish Home Rule (see Chapter 3). His third ministry (1886) lasted five months and ended with the defeat of his Home Rule Bill and a bitter Party split (see also Chapter 4, pp. 70–71). None the less he remained Party leader. Only he and the Home Rule crusade seemed able to hold what was left of the Party together.

In opposition from 1886 to 1892, the Liberals managed to recover and, with the support of the Irish Nationalists, Gladstone was able to form his fourth ministry in 1892. Somehow the 84 year old Prime Minister found the strength and skill to get a Home Rule Bill through the Commons only for the Lords to kill it

■ Biography

Lord Hartington, (1833–1908)

Lord Hartington (who became the 8th Duke of Devonshire) was the leading Whig aristocrat in Gladstone's 1868 government in which he held the post of Secretary of State for Ireland. It was he who became leader of the Party on Gladstone's first retirement in 1875 and gave way to him in 1880. He was increasingly uneasy about his chief's Irish policy and split away from him over Home Rule. Leader of the Liberal Unionists he held office under the Conservatives. A capable and conscientious rather than gifted politician, he was particularly interested in horse-racing.

■ Biography

Sir Charles Dilke (1843–1911)

Dilke was one of the most promising Liberal politicians of his generation. Elected to Parliament in 1869, he became notorious for his criticisms of the monarchy. A close friend of Chamberlain he was one of the most effective members of Gladstone's second ministry and was tipped as a future Prime Minister. However he was cited as the correspondent in a divorce case by a 22-year-old wife of a Liberal lawyer. While she was probably lying, it emerged that he had been the lover of her mother. Public opinion, especially Nonconformist public opinion was unforgiving and he never held office again.

quickly with a massive majority. Gladstone considered beginning another crusade – this time against the House of Lords – but he was at last too old and his colleagues had no stomach for such a fight. After quarrelling in the Cabinet about funding for the navy, he finally retired in 1894.

Historical debate

Historians have been divided in the assessments they have made of the political careers of Gladstone and Disraeli. They have questioned the extent to which Gladstone was committed to reform and the nature of his achievements given the divisions within his Party. In analysing Disraeli's motivation, they have questioned the extent to which he can be regarded as a serious political thinker.

Interpretation exercise 1: What kind of reformer was Gladstone after 1868?

Source A

A contemporary view of Gladstone as a reformer

Another great principle has been established – that public office shall not henceforth be bought by the rich to the exclusion of those who are less rich. Or are poor.

There is another principle that has been established and that is that a secret ballot is the right of electors…

The State has admitted its responsibility for the education of the people by… public rates and the partial application of the power of compulsion.

These five years have been memorable years and its measures will bear comparison with those of any government which has ever preceded it.

> John Bright, a leading Radical Liberal, speaking in Birmingham in 1873 when he was a member of Gladstone's government. He presents Gladstone as the committed leader of an enthusiastically reforming government.

■ Think about

Bright was a Quaker and a radical campaigner of long-standing, first against the Corn Laws and then in favour of parliamentary reform. Gladstone gave him his first governmental post, President of the Board of Trade, and took much trouble to seek his advice as he saw him as very influential among the Nonconformists.

▶ How reliable do you think Bright is likely to be in assessing the success of Gladstone's first ministry?

Source B

A historian's view of Gladstone as a 'radical conservative'

It was Gladstone's problem that [in 1868] his career had hitherto been associated with great legislative successes and many of his supporters expected legislation of a dramatic sort…to follow the great electoral victory…Buoyed up by the great Nonconformist revival of the 1860s, Dissenters saw the victory of 1868 as the occasion for the assertion of the political priorities of Nonconformity: general disestablishment, abolition of university tests, a Burials Bill. The disestablishment of the Anglican Church would lead to social and political equality in the same way that Peelite finance had led to fiscal and economic equality. Allied to these proposals were those of the intellectuals, especially demanding educational reform, the abolition of university tests, the ballot, and equality of opportunity in entrance to the Civil Service. Most of these Gladstone regarded with caution, and some with hostility. He particularly disliked the complete repeal of the university tests, which he succeeded in avoiding in its extreme form. He also regretted the introduction of the ballot which he came to see as unavoidable but with a 'lingering reluctance', and whose various delays he contemplated with some satisfaction, partly because the issue helped to hold the Party together in 1871 and 1872. Certainly the days were over when, as in the later years of Palmerston, Gladstone had been regarded by many…as almost a Radical.'

> Matthew (the editor of Gladstone's diaries), *Gladstone*, 1999

■ Questions

Study Sources A, B, and C

1 How do they differ in their judgements on Gladstone's reforming ministry of 1868–1874?

2 To what extent do they explain the reasons for their varied interpretations of Gladstone as a reformer?

3 'An enthusiastic reformer', 'a conservative radical' or 'a cautious party manager'. Which of these phrases do you consider to be the most accurate description of Gladstone between 1868 and 1874? Give reasons for your judgement.

Source C

An alternative view of Gladstone as a cautious manager

Given the problems which it faced, what is remarkable about …the ministry of 1868-74 is not that it ultimately fell into disarray, but that it functioned successfully for so long. The nature of the demands of the various sections within the Party meant that none of them were likely to be completely satisfied with the compromises which government ministers felt necessary to construct to retain broad-based support. Assessments of Gladstone's role during these difficult years must not lose sight of this continuing susceptibility to sectionalism and the undeniable fact that the problems which the Party experienced with him as leader were nothing to those which it would have faced without him. His leadership strategy revolved around two central requirements: the delivery of just enough in the way of legislative action and political rewards to stave off outright revolt by any section, and the support of causes under whose banner all could enthusiastically unite to bully into submission a hostile, Tory-dominated House of Lords and to appeal confidently to the electorate for continued support.

Winstanley, *Gladstone and the Liberal Party*, 1990

Interpretation exercise 2: Does Disraeli deserve to be taken seriously as a political thinker?

Source A

Disraeli's political ideas as expressed in his fiction

Disraeli's novels contain his most interesting political ideas. In this scene the aristocratic hero Egremont meets two strangers at sunset and falls into conversation with them. The reader later discovers that they are Chartist sympathizers.

'Well society may be in its infancy,' said Egremont slightly smiling, 'but, say what you will, our Queen reigns over the greatest nation that ever existed.'

'Which nation,' said the younger stranger, 'because she reigns over two…Two nations between whom there is no intercourse; who are as ignorant of each other's habits, thoughts and feelings, as if they were dwellers in different zones or inhabitants of different planets; who are formed by a different breeding, are fed by different food, are ordered by different manners, and are not governed by the same laws.'

'You speak of -' said Egremont, hesitatingly,

'THE RICH AND THE POOR.'

Disraeli, *Sybil*, 1845

Source B

A historian dismisses Disraeli as a political thinker

How seriously, then, should we take Disraeli's 'philosophy'? And how far does it affect the merits of his novels? The answer to the first question is probably 'not very'. Disraeli was writing partly to please his Young England friends, partly to assuage his own feelings as a disappointed place-seeker – the political satire is at times very bitter – but above all to puncture the balloon of early Victorian complacency....When he became a leading political figure he never attempted seriously to carry out the sort of programme which he and his friends seem to have envisaged.

Blake, *Disraeli,* 1966

Source C

Another historian's explanation of Disraeli's aims

The social, political, religious and racial ideas which he propounded so vigorously in the 1830s and 1840s...are an attempt to create and impose a definition of the identity, needs and destiny of the Tory Party and the English nation...[Later in his book Smith compares a comment Disraeli made to the House of Commons during the 1867 Reform Act debates with an observation made by Egremont in Sybil]. He [Disraeli] explained to the Commons:

'Popular privileges are consistent with the state of society in which there is great inequality of provision. Democratic rights, on the contrary, demand that there should be equality of condition as the fundamental basis of the society which they regulate...We do not, however, live – and I trust that it will never be the fate of this country to live – under a democracy.'

He was saying no more and no less than he had caused Egremont to say in *Sybil* more than twenty years earlier: 'The future principle of English politics will not be a levelling principle; not a principle adverse to privileges, but favourable to their extension. It will seek to ensure equality, not by levelling the Few, but by elevating the Many'.

Smith, *Disraeli, a Brief Life,* 1996

■ Questions

Study Sources A, B, and C.

1 How and why do the authors of Sources B and C differ about Disraeli as a political philosopher?

2 Once in power what did Disraeli do to reduce the gap between the two nations which he describes in *Sybil*? (Source A)

3 To what extent can Disraeli be described accurately as a 'Tory democrat'?

Summary

The Liberal Party which Gladstone led from 1868, was united in support of representative government, individual freedom, toleration and low taxes. However it was liable to disunity since its main constituents – Whig aristocrats, Nonconformist radicals and skilled working men – had their own distinct and sometimes conflicting agendas.

Disraeli's Conservative Party in 1868 was united in support of the Crown, the landowning classes and the Church of England. It had little, then, to offer the middle and skilled working classes. Since it had spent most years since 1846 in opposition, Disraeli's policy was to make it a serious alternative government.

Between 1868 and 1885, Gladstone held power for 11 years and Disraeli for 6. In this period, both parties were thoroughly reorganized and became more professional at fighting elections.

Gladstone held his divided Party together by the strength of his personality and by finding big crusading issues like the Bulgarian atrocities. Many of his Party disliked him but knew that they could not do without him. As the years passed he became a national as well as a Party figure.

Before 1867 Disraeli was barely tolerated by many Conservatives. His success in 1867 won their confidence. Both before and after that date, he was the leading Conservative policy maker. He returned from the Congress of Berlin a national hero.

Their achievements

Gladstone was one of Britain's best finance ministers before he became Prime Minister. He led a powerful reforming ministry between 1868 and 1874. Though his Irish policies failed and split his Party, he managed to hold most of the Liberal Party together. Britain changed greatly during his lifetime and he contributed greatly to ensuring that this change was achieved peacefully.

A statesman is a politician who is wise and far-sighted. Gladstone certainly had those qualities. If he had succeeded with Home Rule, the tragedy of Anglo-Irish relations in the twentieth century would probably have been avoided. If he could have persuaded more leaders to share his approach to quarrels between nations and imperial expansion, the world would have been far more peaceful. His religious faith required him to try to make the world a better place and his exceptional abilities enabled him to make a huge and mainly beneficial contribution to his country's development for more than 50 years.

Disraeli helped to make the Conservatives electable. His foreign policy was very successful too, in the short-term. He was the most effective parliamentary operator of his generation and, in Gladstone's opinion, was among the most determined and courageous politicians he had known.

He also had an imaginative feel for the manner in which the nation was evolving. His readiness to accept parliamentary reform, to commit his Party to improving social conditions and to expanding the Empire all helped the Conservatives to replace the Liberals as the natural party of government.

Their historical reputations are secure. Gladstone is regarded as one of Britain's greatest statesmen and Disraeli as one of her most skilful politicians.

■ Activity   KEY SKILLS

Use the cartoon on page 22, the information on pages 27–31 and all the sources on pages 40–42.

1 List 3 of the reforms of Gladstone and 3 of Disraeli.

2 Note 2 criticisms of Gladstone as a serious social reformer and 2 of Disraeli as a serious political thinker.

3 What impressions of the two politicians does the cartoon of page 22 aim to give?

4 Summarise Winstanley's comments on Gladstone and Smith's on Disraeli.

5 Write two contrasting plans of campaign for the 1874 general election, one for the Conservatives emphasising Gladstone's weaknesses and the other for the Liberals, which stresses Disraeli's failings.

■ Further reading

Paul Adelman, *Gladstone, Disraeli and Later Victorian Politics,* 1970

H.C.G. Matthew, *Gladstone,* 1996

Roy Jenkins, *Gladstone,* 1995

Robert Blake, *Disraeli,* 1998 edn

Paul Smith, *Disraeli, A Brief Life,* 1999 edn

Chapter 3

Britain and Ireland 1868–1921
A cursed relationship?

AN IRISH JIG.
JOHN BULL *to* UNCLE SAM:—"See what your American food has done! I've got to lick it out of him again."

■ Think about

▶ By what means did the *Puck* cartoonist (Source 1 opposite) communicate his ideas about the Irish situation in 1880?

Timeline

1170 Norman invasion. Henry II claims the 'lordship' of Ireland; English rule effective in the Pale, around Dublin.

1500s Reformation. While England becomes Protestant, Ireland stays Roman Catholic.

1599–1602 Army of Elizabeth I strengthens English rule.

Early 1600s Scots Protestants settle in Ulster.

1649 Cromwell's cruel campaign breaks Irish resistance.

1690–1 Protestant William III defeats Catholic James II at the Battle of the Boyne and secures 'the Protestant Ascendancy'.

1798 Nationalist revolt.

1800 Act of Union. End of Dublin Parliament.

1820s, 1830s and 1840s. Led by Daniel O'Connell, Irish nationalism grows stronger.

1845–49 Potato blight and the Great Famine.

1850s Emergence of the Irish Republican Brotherhood (IRB) or Fenians.

1867 Fenian attacks in England.

1868 Gladstone becomes Prime Minister.

The Pale c. 1550

Dublin

0   100 km

Introduction

Many histories of nineteenth-century Britain refer to 'the Irish Question'. From 1868 to 1921 it was one of the most difficult problems that British politicians had to face.

The question they had to answer was this: how do you keep within the United Kingdom and the British Empire the many Irish who have a real sense of nationhood, hate English governments for a number of good reasons and are prone to revolt, terrorism and rural violence?

What made the answer hard to find was the readiness of the English to stereotype the Irish as lazy, backward and violent and the Irish equally to stereotype the English as vicious, tyrannical and greedy (see Source 1).

This chapter describes how the politicians failed tragically to find a peaceful answer to the Irish Question and explains, with the help of three document exercises, how their failures had far-reaching effects on British as well as Irish politics.

Key questions

● Why was there so much hostility between the English and the Irish during the nineteenth century?
● Why did Liberal governments fail to grant Home Rule to Ireland between 1886 and 1914?
● What effect did these Home Rule crises have on British politics?
● In what ways did the events of the First World War lead to the partition of Ireland in 1921?

The origins of Anglo-Irish conflict

The relationship between England and Ireland had been unhappy through history. Almost the only characteristic which the Irish and English shared was their location as islands off the north-west coast of Europe. They differed in every other respect. The English were mainly Anglo-Saxon and spoke English and the Irish were mainly Gaelic-speaking Celts. The English were always more numerous, economically more advanced and militarily stronger. They were also more aggressive. The first English (Norman) invasion took place in the twelfth century and in 1172 Henry II of England proclaimed himself to be 'overlord' of Ireland. During the Middle Ages English rule in Ireland was concentrated in Dublin and the area around it known as the Pale.

Religious differences

The Reformation of the sixteenth century added a major element of tension to the relationship between the two islands, since England became Protestant while Ireland remained loyal to the Roman Catholic Church. Remember that at this time people did not understand the meaning of the word 'tolerance' and were ready to kill each other over differences in Christian belief. The tensions were not only religious. They were political and strategic too, since Protestant England became the enemy of two of the strongest Catholic powers of Europe, Spain and France. Ireland could be the strategic backdoor to England where Spanish and French troops might land and threaten England's security from the west.

Conquest and 'the Protestant Ascendancy'

Ireland suffered three English invasions between 1599 and 1691. Each was carried out to make sure that Ireland was ruled by Protestants and kept firmly under English control. The first was in the last years of the reign of Elizabeth I. The second in 1649, which was led by Oliver Cromwell in person, was both speedily effective and enormously cruel. The third and the most significant was that of the Dutch Protestant William of Orange, whom the British Parliament had made King William III to replace the Catholic James II. William defeated the Catholic armies of James II first at the River Boyne in 1690 and then at Aughrim in 1691. These victories cemented English rule over Ireland.

Simultaneously, land had passed out of Irish hands into English and Scottish ones. English and Scottish Protestants, aided by the English government, settled in 'plantations' on land confiscated from the many Irish who were disloyal to the English Crown. These plantations were especially extensive in the north-eastern province of Ulster. During the eighteenth century, in the period known as 'the Protestant Ascendancy', a small Protestant minority held much economic and all political power. A Protestant parliament met in Dublin but its powers were limited by the officials of Dublin Castle who acted for the British government.

Early Irish nationalism and the Act of Union 1800

Even these limited powers of government were ended in 1800 when the parliament was abolished. This followed a nationalist rising in 1798, when Wolfe Tone, inspired by the events of the French Revolution, led a revolt of the 'United Irishmen'. British forces easily suppressed the revolt and Tone committed suicide. One consequence of the 1798 rebellion was the Act of Union which abolished the Irish parliament in Dublin. The British government feared that a separate parliament might encourage Irish nationalism. For the whole of the nineteenth century a British Viceroy ruled Ireland from Dublin Castle and the British Parliament in London, which Irish MPs attended, made laws for whole of the United Kingdom, including Ireland.

In the 1820s, Daniel O'Connell successfully concentrated Irish nationalist feeling behind a campaign to gain for Catholics the right to become MPs and to hold high political office. This level of 'Catholic Emancipation' was achieved in 1829. O'Connell's 1840's campaign against the Act of Union and in favour of a separate Irish parliament in order that the Irish could have greater self-government, was less successful.

The Great Famine 1845–1849

Catastrophe came to Ireland between 1845 and 1849 when the potato crop failed and famine overwhelmed many regions. Of a population of more than 8 million, far too many were dependent on the potato for survival.

The crisis would have tested the best-organized and most generous government of modern times but the British government of the mid-nineteenth century had neither the resources nor the attitude of mind to take effective action. It did not believe in welfare payments nor in interfering with the freedom to trade. As a result, ships sailed from Ireland carrying food for export while people starved to death along the coast. Between 700,000 and 1,000,000 people died from starvation or disease, another 1,500,000 emigrated. Between 1845 and 1914 the Irish population fell from over 8 million to 4.4 million.

Main area of Scottish Protestant plantations in the 17th Century

Londonderry
ULSTER
Belfast
Dublin

0   100 km

■ **Think about**

▶ What could the British government have done to stop the Irish dying of starvation, 1845-49?

▶ Why do you think it did so little?

■ **Further reading**

An extremely readable and moving account of this terrible event of the Famine is *The Great Hunger* by Cecil Woodham-Smith (1972); more analytic is *The Famine in Ireland* by Mary Daly (Dublin Historical Association 1986).

Note

The Fenian violence which outraged Britain in 1867 was the result of failed attempts to rescue other Fenians; the attack in Manchester was on a police van; the other was an attack on Clerkenwell prison in London which caused some civilian deaths.

Note

The names of nationalist groups

The Fenians was another name for the IRB or Irish Republican Brotherhood. They were the most extreme Irish Nationalists during the nineteenth century.

Sinn Fein and the IRA belong to the twentieth century.

Sinn Fein began as a cultural and political movement in 1905. Many Fenians joined Sinn Fein as it grew rapidly between 1914 and 1918 (see pages 59–61).

The Irish Republican Army (IRA) emerged in 1919 as the secret terrorist group which fought the Black and Tans between 1919 and 1921 (see page 61). It kept this secret terrorist character throughout the twentieth century.

◀ The Great Famine, Ireland 1849. A mother and children search desperately for healthy potatoes.

Certainly some Irish believed that the British had done their best to ensure that the Famine killed as many Irish people as possible (see page 44).

The Fenians

The number of extreme nationalists grew. They believed that British rule could only be ended by force. Some formed the Young Ireland movement, others the Irish Republican Brotherhood (IRB) or Fenians, a secret revolutionary society which emerged in the 1850s and was ready to murder and maim to achieve Irish independence. Irish Nationalists could count on both moral and financial support from Irish emigrants in the USA. In 1867 they shocked British opinion by violence in Manchester and London as well as Ireland and in Canada.

Gladstone and Ireland 1868

When the news of his 1868 election victory came through, Gladstone was taking exercise, as was his custom, by felling trees on his Hawarden estate. 'Very significant,' he said to his companion, 'my mission is to pacify Ireland'.

He believed that three particular grievances needed to be resolved:
● Religion: 88 per cent of the Irish were Roman Catholics. However, the official 'established' Church in Ireland to which they had to pay tithes (a form of tax) was the Protestant Church of Ireland.
● Land: most Irish were tenants. Their landlords were often English, Protestant and absentee. Landlords had few restrictions on their powers over their tenants. They decided what rents to charge and could evict at will, without paying compensation.
● National identity: the Irish regarded themselves as different from the British, who ruled them badly. Increasingly they demanded either self-government or independence. A growing number of them would no longer tolerate this state of affairs, as the Fenian violence of 1867 showed.

Like all Liberal and Conservative leaders of the nineteenth century, Gladstone in 1868 believed that Ireland must remain part of the United Kingdom. The two islands were too closely bound by history and by economic and social links to part. More importantly, Ireland was vital to the security of the British Isles. A London government could not allow Ireland to pass into possibly hostile hands.

Gladstone and his many admirers maintain that his sustained commitment to Ireland was because his sense of justice convinced him that the British had done wrong in Ireland and he must put right this wrong. His critics argued that, typically and hypocritically, Gladstone disguised clever party political calculations behind his talk of justice for Ireland. The Liberals were in fact very divided in 1868 over the extension of the franchise. Gladstone was looking for an issue which would unite them. For this purpose Ireland served him very well.

Reform and coercion

The recipe which Gladstone and other British politicians used to keep Ireland part of the United Kingdom was on the one hand reform – to remove the most serious grievances and so reduce opposition; and, on the other 'coercion' – using force to hold down the Irish opposition. This 'reform/coercion' package eventually failed. British governments gave the Irish too little, too late and too often grudgingly.

Reform – the Irish Church Act (1869)

Gladstone first tried to lessen the anger of the Roman Catholic majority about the privileged position of the Protestant Church of Ireland.

His Irish Church Act (1869) disestablished the Protestant Church of Ireland. This meant that it was no longer the official State Church. The Act removed much of its wealth and used it to improve schools, hospitals and workhouses. Most important of all, Roman Catholics no longer had to pay tithes (taxes) to support it. This Act was a success, ending the most serious grievances of the Roman Catholic Church in Ireland.

However, Gladstone failed to gain either Protestant or Catholic support for his university reforms. He proposed the creation of a University of Dublin which would both admit Catholics and include the Protestant Trinity College. But both Catholics and Protestants wanted separate universities and, in 1873, his proposals were defeated in the Commons.

Reform – the Irish Land Act (1870)

Gladstone knew that he had to get a better deal for Irish tenants. His first attempt was the Irish Land Act of 1870. Its main aim was to protect tenants against unpredictable evictions, often by absentee landlords whose only interest was to increase their income from rents. Only in Ulster was there any system of protection from eviction and compensation in the event of eviction, and Gladstone aimed to spread this 'Ulster Custom' throughout Ireland. The Act had three main elements.

1 Magistrates were to prevent landlords from charging exorbitant rents.
2 Evicted tenants who had improved their holdings should be paid compensation, even if they had been evicted for non-payment of rent.
3 Damages would be payable for evictions (except for the non-payment of rent) in proportion to the size of the holding.

Most historians treat the 1870 Irish Land Act as a failure: it did not define 'the Ulster Custom' clearly enough and took no action to prevent landlords from increasing rents when they felt like it. The Act also failed to meet the tenants' main need, which was greater security of tenure. However R.F. Foster (1988) describes it as an 'astute if insubstantial' measure. By agreeing that tenants deserved compensation for eviction, Gladstone was challenging the landlords' property rights and accepting 'the Irish historical sense of a certain vested right in the land which had allegedly been expropriated [taken by force] from their ancestors'.

Disappointment with the Irish Land Act led to violence in the countryside. This prompted Gladstone's government to pass a Coercion Act (1871) which gave extra powers to the police to arrest those they suspected of violence and hold them in prison.

Home Rule, the Land League and Parnell

Meanwhile, the Irish were getting better organized inside and outside Parliament. Isaac Butt, a successful lawyer and MP, had become convinced that the London Parliament could not properly take care of Irish affairs. Consequently he created the Home Rule Association in 1870. Its aim was to re-establish an Irish parliament in Dublin responsible for Irish domestic matters. It secured the support of some Catholic bishops as well as Fenians. By 1874, 59 out of the 105 Irish MPs were Home Rulers, rather than Liberals or

■ Further reading

Strongly recommended is R.F. Foster's *Modern Ireland 1600-1972,* 1989. Foster was born in Waterford, Ireland and graduated from Trinity College, Dublin. His *Modern Ireland* skilfully links together social, economic and political history. He is often described as an outstanding revisionist historian, by which is meant that he challenges (revises) the views of other nationalist historians of Ireland who have presented Irish history as a hard-fought, though eventually successful, battle of nationalist heroes against the English enemy. Foster is not afraid to point out that some at least of Ireland's problems were not England's fault.

Conservatives, and they were ready to make their presence felt on the floor of the House of Commons.

Then, in 1879, came the worst agricultural crisis since the Great Famine struck in 1845. After many parts of Ireland had enjoyed a number of years of comparative prosperity, the potato crop failed again, following two poor harvests, and affected the large tenant farmers and shopkeepers as well as those tenants living near subsistence. The crisis caused much distress, which the Fenians were able to turn into anti-English agitation in Ireland.

Source 3

▶ This picture from the *Illustrated London News* in 1881 shows Land League leaders, in a rain-swept Kildare market-place, burning the hated leases which gave mainly English landowners economic control of much of Ireland.

■ Think about

▶ The affect of landownership on English/Irish relations. How had the English gained control of so much Irish land, and why were the land leases so hated by the Irish?

Michael Davitt, a leading Fenian, founded the Land League in 1879. Its immediate aims became known as the 3 Fs: Fixity of tenure (no evictions if the rent was paid), Free sale and Fair rents. It concentrated its efforts against the landlords, using intimidatory tactics. There were a few murders, for example Lord Mountmorres in 1880, but more frequent methods were threatening letters, the withholding of rent and the refusal of local communities to have any dealings with the local landlord and his agent. This refusal to allow normal links - which is now known as a boycott - gained its name from the unfortunate Captain Boycott, a land agent in Mayo. When he could not get anyone to harvest the crops, Boycott had to buy in 50 Protestants who then had to be protected by 1000 policemen at the cost of £10,000.

Davitt invited Charles Stewart Parnell, the rising star of the Irish Parliamentary Party, to become President of the Land League in 1879. The following year, Parnell was elected leader of the Irish Parliamentary Party. For the next 11 years, this remarkable politician (see pages 54–55) was to bring the Irish Question into the centre of British politics.

Gladstone's second ministry 1880–1885: Coercion–Reform–Coercion

Gladstone had won the 1880 election by his furious attack on the foreign and imperial policies of Disraeli. Ireland had not been an election issue. Indeed, the Prime Minister had no new plans for Ireland. However he could not ignore the troubles in Ireland which the campaign of the Land League was causing and, as in the past and as it would be in the future, his government's recipe was coercion and reform.

The Coercion Act (1881)

So effective was the intimidation used by the Land League that W.E. Forster, the Irish Secretary, persuaded the government to pass a Coercion Act in 1881, which allowed the police to hold in custody people suspected of intimidation without having to bring them to trial. Michael Davitt was imprisoned under the terms of this Act, as were other leaders of the Land League. So furious were Parnell and his Irish MP colleagues about these arrests, that 36 of them were temporarily expelled from the House of Commons for the violence of their language.

Reform – the Second Land Act (1881)

Reform followed swiftly in the shape of Gladstone's Second Land Act (1881). This was a bold political measure since it agreed to the 3Fs, (Fixity of tenure, Fair rent and Free Sale) demanded by the Land League. Over the years, rents fell and the position of tenants in relation to their landlords improved. The weakness of the Land Act was that it did not properly consider some of the most important reasons for Irish rural poverty – particularly the shortage of cultivable land and the primitive methods of farming.

The Second Land Act placed Parnell in a difficult situation. His more extreme followers in the Land League wanted to reject the Act and to continue the violence. However, his more moderate supporters in the Irish Parliamentary Party believed that the Act went most of the way to meeting their demands and should be supported. One of Parnell's strengths as a leader was staying silent at vital moments. In this situation, he criticized some details of the Act and otherwise played for time.

■ **Think about**

▶ Gladstone's Land Act of 1881 is described here as a bold political measure. Why?

▶ What arguments might his Conservative opponents have used against this Act?

The Kilmainham 'Treaty' 1882

Soon the government did him a favour. Because some members of the Land League continued with violence, the government locked Parnell in Kilmainham gaol, further boosting his popularity. He therefore appeared as a martyr. Since the violence increased during his imprisonment, he was also regarded as the 'uncrowned king of Ireland' without whose co-operation the government would not solve its Irish problems.

After holding him in prison for six months, Gladstone decided to do a deal with Parnell, the so-called Kilmainham 'Treaty'. To gain his freedom, Parnell agreed to do his best to end the violence and help make the Land Act a success. For his part, Gladstone promised that tenants who had fallen behind with their rent during the Land League campaign would not have to pay the arrears. W.E. Forster, the Irish Secretary responsible for security, resigned in disgust when he heard of this deal.

The Phoenix Park murders and more coercion

In place of Forster, Gladstone appointed Lord Frederick Cavendish who was married to one of his nieces. Hardly had Cavendish arrived in Dublin when he was hacked to death walking in Phoenix Park with his second-in-command, Thomas Burke. The knife-wielding assassins were a terrorist group called 'The Invincibles'. These Phoenix Park murders were a dreadful setback, in the short-term at least, to the peace process. For Gladstone it was a personal tragedy, since Lord Frederick Cavendish was like another son to him. For the government and for British public opinion more generally it seemed proof that Irish nationalism was irredeemably savage and that the only sensible policy was further coercion. Parnell for his part was genuinely shocked and condemned the violence. The 'Invincibles' were eventually arrested, tried and hanged and for the next few years Ireland settled into an exhausted calm.

Source 4

▶ The Phoenix Park murders in 1882. In this illustration from a French magazine, Lord Frederick Cavendish is being murdered with Burke already lying dead.

■ Think about

▶ What effect did this shocking crime have on English and Irish politics between 1881 and 1886?

▶ Is there any evidence that it reduced Parnell's popularity in Ireland or changed Gladstone's Irish policies?

The response to Parnell's success

As the following table shows, the 1885 election was a triumph for Parnell's Home Rulers who won 85 seats in Ireland and one in Liverpool. The Irish Liberals were wiped out and the Irish Conservatives limited to mainly Protestant Ulster. British party politics was never the same again.

Year	Liberal	Lib.Unionist	Con	Home Rule	Irish Nat.
1868	387		271		
1874	251		342	9	
1880	353		238	61	
1885	335		249	86	
1886	191	77	317		85
1892	273	46	269		80

Before the election, Gladstone's Liberal government had been struggling. It was increasingly divided between a Whig faction made up of rich land-owning families who had sustained the Liberal Party in the 1860s and 1870s, and a radical faction with strong roots in the cities and in Nonconformist Churches. This group had social reform as its priority. Only Gladstone's remarkable personality held the Party together. However, he was now 76, and few shared his obsession with Ireland.

Before 1885, Gladstone had consistently argued against Home Rule but, during the summer of 1885, he realized that greater self-government was the only way forward for Ireland. However he kept this vital change of mind secret except from his immediate family.

Gladstone had two main reasons for acting in this unusual way. Firstly, he knew that Home Rule would split the Liberal Party. He hoped that the Conservatives, encouraged by Parnell, would pass a Home Rule Act. This was not, in 1885, as far-fetched a hope as later Conservative behaviour might suggest. Parnell himself turned towards the Conservatives because some of their leading members were hinting to him that they might be sympathetic

Source 5

▲ In this cartoon of 1885, Parnell is shown as an Irish terrorist, threatening Gladstone.

towards greater self-government for Ireland. A Conservative government would be better placed to persuade the House of Lords, which had a huge in-built Conservative majority, to agree to Home Rule.

Gladstone's second reason was that he did not wish to be accused of changing his mind simply to win the Irish vote and so return to power.

Herbert Gladstone and the 'Hawarden kite'

Herbert Gladstone was a Liberal MP. In his opinion the greatest danger to the Liberal Party lay in the ambition of a radical faction led by Joseph Chamberlain to force his father's retirement and take the Party over. Because he believed his father's silence about his changed attitude to Home Rule was harming both the Party and his father, he leaked the secret to the national press (the so-called 'Hawarden kite'). This bombshell shocked the Liberal leaders, seriously damaging Gladstone's relations with many of them. Parnell immediately switched his support to Gladstone while Lord Salisbury committed the Conservatives to uncompromising opposition to Home Rule.

The 1886 Home Rule Bill

The Home Rule scheme which Gladstone presented to the House of Commons would have set up an Irish parliament in Dublin with an elected lower chamber and an upper chamber consisting of men of property and Irish lords. It would have been responsible for all Irish domestic affairs while the Imperial Parliament in London would keep control of defence, foreign policy, international trade and customs and excise. Alongside the Home Rule Bill was a land purchase proposal to buy out the Irish landlords at a cost to the British Treasury of £50 million. By this plan, Gladstone intended to end the tension between tenants and landlords which had so damaged Ireland in recent years.

The Liberals split

Unfortunately, he failed to convince 93 of his former supporters including a leading Whig, Lord Hartington, and a leading Radical, Joseph Chamberlain. They had three main concerns. Firstly, Home Rule for Ireland might lead to the break-up of the United Kingdom and the British Empire. Secondly, the Irish Nationalists could not be trusted to deal fairly with the many Protestants scattered across Ireland. Thirdly, the province of Ulster, which had a Protestant majority (and returned many Conservative MPs to Westminster), was passionately opposed to Home Rule. In combination the Conservatives and Liberal Unionists voted out the Bill and brought Gladstone's government to an end.

Document exercise: The 1886 Home Rule crisis

Source A

Parnell's nationalist appeal

I do not know when this great question will be settled. I do not know whether England will be wise in time, and concede to the constitutional arguments and methods of restitution of that which was stolen from us towards the end of the last century…But no man has the right to fix the boundary to the march of a nation. No man has the right to say to his country, 'thus far shalt thou go and no farther.'

Parnell speaking in Ireland in January 1885 about the Irish nation

Note

Gladstone and Chamberlain

These two leading Liberals never got on. They belonged to different generations and Gladstone never had as high opinion of Chamberlain, as he (Chamberlain) thought he should. Gladstone dealt with him particularly clumsily in 1886 when he formed his new government and turned down Chamberlain's request for the post of Secretary of State for the Colonies, apparently implying that he was not up to it.

Timeline

Home Rule 1885–1893

June 1885 Conservatives with Irish support form a government. Gladstone decides secretly that Home Rule must come.

November 1885 General Election. With his 86 MPs Parnell holds the balance of power in the Commons.

December 1886 Gladstone's son Herbert breaks the secret of his father's conversion to Home Rule to the national press.

January 1886 Gladstone becomes Prime Minister, with Irish support, and immediately introduces a Home Rule Bill. Liberal Party splits. Liberal Unionists oppose Home Rule

June 1886 Home Rule Bill defeated by 343 votes to 313.

1886 General Election produces massive Conservative victory.

1892 Liberal electoral victory

1893 Gladstone carries Home Rule Bill through the Commons only to have it defeated overwhelmingly in the Lords.

Source B

A historian's assessment of the 'Land War'

The 'Land War' of 1879–82 had political significance far beyond the successful struggle for tenant power...The objectives of the Land League included self-government, and by 1880 it was in effect the constituency organisation of parliamentary nationalism with its demand for devolution of Irish affairs to a 'Home Rule' parliament in Dublin. The effect of collaboration [with the Land League] was to transform the Home Rule body from a loose medley without local organisation except at elections into a tight-knit political party whose parliamentary weight was immeasurably increased by the menace of mass mobilisation.'

David Fitzpatrick writing in Foster (ed), *The Oxford Illustrated History of Ireland*, 1988

Source C

Gladstone asking the Commons to support Home Rule

I ask that we should apply to Ireland the happy experience we have gained in England and Scotland, where the course of generations has now taught us...that the best and surest foundation we can find to build upon is the foundation afforded by the affections, convictions and the will of the nation; and it is there, by decree of the Almighty, that we may be enabled to secure at once the social peace, the fame, the power and the permanence of the Empire.

Gladstone addressing the House of Commons, 1886

Source D

Chamberlain's opposition to Home Rule

The furthest he would go in appeasing Irish claims was devolved local government. His objection lay in a deep veneration for Britain's imperial mission...Moreover he believed that Home Rule was irrelevant, if not positively harmful to both Britain and Ireland. What Ireland urgently needed was development of its resources, not political meddling. Britain desperately required a programme of welfare reforms, not ...constitutional wrangles.

Jeremy Smith in Kelly and Cantrell (ed), *Modern British Statesmen*, 1997

Source E

George Curzon, Conservative, opposes Home Rule

Home Rule is a policy which shatters the authority of Parliament and Crown, intensifies friction, where it affects [pretends] to create harmony between England and Ireland; and if carried would be a source of danger to the one, and of disaster, social and economic, to the other.

■ Examination-style questions

1 **Comprehension in context**
   Using Source B and your own knowledge explain how the activities of the Land League changed the Home Rule party in Ireland.

2 **Comparing the sources**
   Study Sources C and D. How far do Gladstone and Chamberlain differ in their assessment of how to solve the 'Irish Question'.

3 **Assessing the sources**
   How useful is Source E to historians seeking to understand why the Conservatives opposed Home Rule in 1886?

4 **Making judgements**
   Using the sources and your own knowledge, assess the importance of Parnell in the Home Rule Crisis of 1886.

The rise and fall of Charles Stewart Parnell

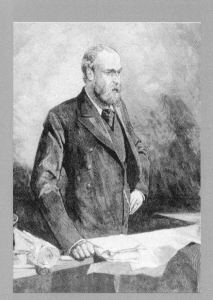

▲ Parnell in his prime, c.1885, looking not the least like a terrorist.

■ Questions

The rise of Parnell

1 What were the personal characteristics which helped Parnell to become leader of the Irish Parliamentary Party?

2 What did he do to make this party a more effective political force?

3 Study Sources 6 and 7. What impressed Healy about Parnell and what does he mean by the 'canvas of a national hero'? How reliable is Healy as a source on Parnell's rise?

4 What does Foster, Source 7, mean by Parnell's 'unerring instinct'?

5 Using the sources and your own knowledge, explain why, by 1885, British politicians had to take Parnell very seriously indeed.

Parnell was the outstanding Irish Nationalist leader of the second half of the nineteenth century

He was a most unusual person by any standards. Born into one of the leading families of the Protestant Ascendancy and educated at English public schools and Cambridge University, he kept through his turbulent life some of the characteristics of an aloof, arrogant English aristocrat. His mother, however, was an American with strong anti-British views and, by the time he became an MP in 1875, when he was 29 – as much out of boredom as anything else - he was a convinced Home Ruler.

Once elected he made his presence felt. He joined those Home Rulers like J.G. Biggar and O'Connor Power who were disrupting Commons business by filibustering (making speeches of immense length on each and every subject). In addition, Parnell had no hesitation in criticizing Isaac Butt for his weak leadership. 'At no time have you shown that you had any policy at all,' he told Butt in 1877, 'much less that you were carrying it out boldly or actively.'

Davitt invited Parnell to become President of the Land League. Parnell accepted the invitation because he was confident that it would force the British government and the landlords to take Home Rule more seriously. He was careful, though, to avoid giving any public support to its intimidation and violence. After a hugely successful money-raising tour of the USA, he returned to fight the 1880 general election. He was re-elected in April as were another 60 Home Rulers. The following month he was also elected as leader of the Irish Parliamentary Party, though he was still only 34.

Perhaps Parnell's greatest achievement was to transform the Irish Parliamentary Party into an efficient election–winning machine in Ireland and within Parliament into a disciplined group sharply focused on the Home Rule issue. His leadership was undisputed. His followers referred to him as 'the Chief' and he inspired fear as well as respect.
In Ireland, the National League, which had succeeded the Land League, provided the Party's organization. With more than a thousand branches, it was dominated by Parnell's followers, mainly young men from middle-class backgrounds like business, journalism and the law. Well-funded from the USA, it made sure that in every Irish constituency there was a good Home Rule candidate. In the run-up to the 1885 election, the Franchise and Redistribution Acts of 1884–1885 helped Home Rulers greatly, since they added to the electoral registers some 500,000 voters who were mainly small farmers and agricultural labourers sympathetic to Home Rule. Furthermore, most Irish boroughs were absorbed into the new and more winnable county constituencies.

Source 6

We (the Irish Nationalist Party) created Parnell and Parnell created us. We seized very early in the movement the idea of this man with his superb silences, his historic name, his determination, his self-control, his aloofness – we seized that as the canvas of a great national hero.

Tim Healy Irish Nationalist MP from 1880–1910 and one-time secretary of Parnell

Source 7

If land was the priority for the farmers, for the fenians and the Irish Parliamentary Party, it patently was not…What mattered was that the Land War created the Irish Parliamentary Party as accredited national leaders; and Parnell, with his unerring instinct, swung political energy back to the parliamentary field in 1882. The Parliamentary Party could now deliver.

R.F. Foster On the land war 1879–1882 in Foster, *Modern Ireland 1600-1972*, 1988

▲ The cause of Parnell's downfall – Kitty O'Shea.

Note

It was difficult to maintain his image as a national hero when the divorce court heard how he had had to shin down the fire escape of a Brighton hotel so as not to be caught with Kitty O'Shea by her husband.

The Fall of Parnell 1890–1891

In these years, Irish nationalism was gravely weakened by the scandalous end of Parnell's career and its effect on the party which he had largely created.

In 1890, Parnell was more popular than he had ever been. In 1887 The Times newspaper had published letters which seemed to prove that he had supported the violence of the Land League. However in 1889 a Parliamentary Commission proved that the letters were forgeries and he received an ovation in the House of Commons.

A year later his career was in ruins after he had been publicly named as an adulterer in a divorce case by one of his colleagues, Captain O'Shea. The truth was that he had maintained an affair with O'Shea's wife Kitty for many years and spent as much of his time with her as he could. She gave birth to his child while he was in Kilmainham gaol and they married in 1891 as soon as her divorce had come through.

Parnell had hoped to carry on as normal but he could not withstand the moral outrage of the Churches. First the Nonconformist Church leaders, who were amongst Gladstone's most important supporters, made it clear to the Liberal leader that his alliance with Parnell must cease. Then the Irish Catholic leaders turned against him and his followers. 'You cannot remain a Parnellite and remain Catholic' was the line of most parish priests. Parnell fought his corner bitterly but his party split with most deserting him. He died suddenly in 1891, aged 45. Not until 1900 was John Redmond able to reunite the Irish Nationalist Party.

■ Questions

Parnell's fall

1 Who was Kitty O'Shea?

2 Why was the O'Shea divorce case so damaging to Parnell?

3 Parnell at first intended to continue as leader of the Irish Parliamentary Party. Why did so many of the Party refuse to support him any more?

The second Home Rule Bill 1893

The Liberals won the 1892 election, mainly on issues of social reform. Gladstone's main interest, however, remained Home Rule and he managed to get a Home Rule Bill through the House of Commons. The House of Lords, however, threw it out by a colossal majority – 419 against, and only 41 in favour. Gladstone resigned and Home Rule became a dead issue until 1912.

New influences on Irish nationalism

Killing Home Rule with kindness

The Irish policy of Lord Salisbury's government was to maintain law and order by coercion but also to 'kill Home Rule with kindness'. Between 1887 and 1905, three Irish Secretaries - Arthur Balfour, his brother Gerald and George Wyndham introduced a number of land and land purchase acts which, building on those of Gladstone, effectively replaced 'landlordism' in Ireland with peasant ownership. Agriculture was modernized and local government reformed.

The new cultural nationalism and the Boer War

The Gaelic Athletic Association was founded in 1884 to encourage physical fitness and native Irish sports. It was followed in 1893 by the Gaelic League. The main aim of the League was to revive the use of the Gaelic language. Its leaders like Douglas Hyde saw themselves as part of an Irish-Ireland movement which would steadily de-Anglicize (remove English influences from) their country. How influential these cultural movements were on nationalist thinking is hard to judge. The number of members of these associations remained small but they wrote fluently and often had their writings published.

Irish nationalism found a new lease of life from 1900, and the Boer War (1899-1902) was undoubtedly influential. Irish Nationalists easily identified themselves with the Boers, a small country fighting bravely for its freedom against the aggressive British Empire. The Boer War boosted membership of the Gaelic League (107 branches in 1900, nearly 400 by 1902) and in Belfast Catholic gangs took the names of Boer generals.

The war also focused the energies of the political organization which would become known as Sinn Fein. In 1900, Arthur Griffith, editor of the newspaper the *United Irishman*, started an anti-war organization which in 1905 he turned into a more broadly nationalist political movement known as Sinn Fein or 'We Ourselves.'

■ **Think about**

▶ Read about the Boer War on pages 88–90. Why should the Boer War have had this effect on Irish Nationalists?

The third Home Rule crisis 1912–1914

The position of Ulster

Ulster was the province which had been settled by Scottish Protestants in the seventeenth century, and 57 per cent of the population of the nine counties were Protestant. The highest concentration was in the four eastern counties of Londonderry, Antrim, Down, and Armagh. Here the Protestants were very conscious of being a strong minority outnumbered and surrounded by Catholics. They demonized the Pope as head of the Roman Catholic Church and were convinced that 'Home Rule' would mean 'Rome Rule'.

Ulster was also economically more advanced than the rest of Ireland, with a flourishing linen and ship-building industry. The province had done well since

Source 8

▶ The nine counties of historic Ulster, showing the proportions of Catholics and Protestants in each. Donegal, Monaghan and Cavan remained part of the South in 1921. Compare this map with that on page 46.

■ Think about

▶ Study Source 8. What does it tell you about the Protestant settlement of Ireland?

▶ Why were so many Ulster people so strongly against Home Rule?

▶ When politicians argued about whether Ulster ought to become separate from the rest of Ireland, some thought Ulster should be 4 counties, some 6 and some 9. Study the map and explain why this was so. Who would have preferred 4 and who 9?

Note

The Orange Order

This organization had been founded in 1795 to resist the nationalism of the United Irishmen. Its aim was to defend the Protestant Ascendancy. It had local lodges all over Ireland and was particularly strong in Ulster. With its marches and its banners it was regularly and publicly anti-Catholic and fostered a strong almost tribal loyalty to the British monarch and the Protestant Church.

the Act of Union. Since the Ulster economy was closely tied to the British one, the province might suffer particularly badly if a Home Rule government put protective tariffs on imports from Britain.

Many Ulster people believed that a Home Rule government would be run by Fenian extremists who would seek complete independence from the British Empire at the earliest opportunity.

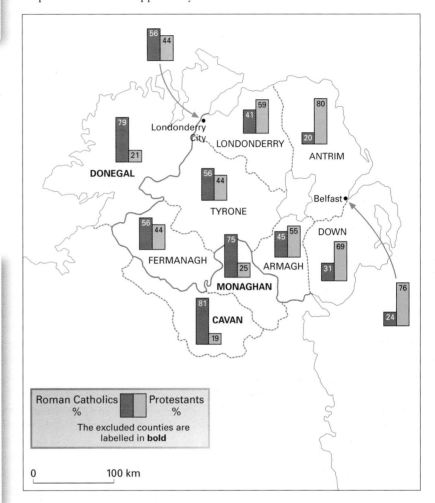

Roman Catholics % — Protestants %
The excluded counties are labelled in **bold**

0   100 km

Opposing Home Rule

From the first, Ulster Protestant opposition to Home Rule was clear and strong. All the Protestant Ulster MPs who were Liberals deserted Gladstone to become Liberal Unionists, if they were not already Conservative, and an Ulster Defence Association was formed. They also looked for active support from the Conservative Party and found it in Lord Randolph Churchill who liked slogans: 'Ulster will fight,' he declared, 'Ulster will be right.'

Worry in 1905 that the Conservative government under Arthur Balfour might be thinking of giving too much self-government to Ireland through local government reform led to the formation of the Ulster Unionist Council. This was a formidable body including members of both Houses of Parliament, the Churches and the Orange Order, which could act for the whole province in a time of crisis.

ULSTER'S PRAYER
Dont let go!

The Ulster Unionists' view of the proposals for Home Rule before the First World War.

Source 9

We must be prepared, in the event of Home Rule passing, with such measures as will carry on for ourselves the government of those districts of which we have control. We must be prepared - and time is precious in these things - the morning Home Rule passes, ourselves to become responsible for the government of the Protestant Union of Ulster.

Edward Carson in 1911

■ Think about

▶ What was Carson threatening? Do you think he was bluffing?

Timeline

1910 General election: Liberals stay in power with Irish Nationalist support.

1911 Parliament Act ends the power of the House of Lords to block bills from the Commons. A Home Rule Act now possible.

1912 Asquith introduces Home Rule Bill to the Commons.
250,000 Ulstermen sign the Solemn League and Covenant, pledging themselves to go to all lengths to stop Home Rule. Bonar Law, the Conservative leader, declares his support for Ulster resistance.

1913 Ulster Volunteer Force (UVF – Unionist) set up.
Irish Volunteer Force (IVF – Nationalist) set up.

1914 UVF import arms (Larne). IVF import arms (Howth).
Some army officers at the Curragh camp indicate that they would not be prepared to fight against Ulstermen (the Curragh Mutiny). Discussions begin to exclude Ulster from the Home Rule Act. The First World War begins. Home Rule for Ireland postponed.

The Home Rule Bill of 1912

The third Home Rule Bill, which Asquith introduced to the House of Commons in 1912, was very similar to Gladstone's of 1893, though the Imperial Parliament in London was to keep rather more powers including administration of the new old age pensions and national insurance. As well as having its own two-chamber assembly, Ireland would send 42 MPs to Westminster. Asquith did not consider excluding Ulster from the Bill since he knew that Redmond and the Irish Nationalists believed Ireland to be a single nation.

While the Home Rule Bill was approved in the Commons by a majority of 100, the House of Lords threw it out. As a result of the Parliament Act (see page 150), its supporters could now be confident that it would eventually become law, but only after a delay of about two years.

The Home Rule Crisis 1912-14

Ulster opposition now stiffened. Led by Sir Edward Carson and James Craig, the Ulster Unionist Council organized massive protest meetings. At one in Belfast, on Easter Tuesday 1912, where the main speakers were Carson and the Conservative leader, Bonar Law, 100,000 Ulstermen attended, as did 70 Conservative MPs. Later that year, on the 28 September, which the Ulster Unionist Council proclaimed to be Covenant Day, a quarter of a million men signed 'the Solemn League and Covenant' through which they promised to use all means to protect their union with Britain. A similar number of women signed a supporting document. Like Randolph Churchill in 1886, so Bonar Law in 1912 supported Ulster in its determination to defy the Liberal government.

This Unionist postcard was published in 1914 in Belfast.

■ Think about

Consider the message of Source 10. Explain the Union Jack and the caption.

▶ Who had deserted whom?

▶ How well does Source 10 reflect Carson's attitude in Source 11?

■ Questions

1 Who signed the Solemn League and Covenant? Why?

2 What did they mean in Source 11 by: (a) 'disastrous to our civil and religious freedom'? (b) 'destructive of our citizenship'? (c) 'perilous to the unity of the Empire'? (d) 'using all means which may be found necessary'?

3 The Liberals were profoundly shocked by Bonar Law's response in Source 12. Why?

4 How close did Ulster come to civil war between 1912 and 1914?

5 What else might Asquith have done at the beginning of 1914, rather than 'wait and see'?

Source 11

Being convinced in our consciences that Home Rule would be disastrous to our civil and religious freedom, destructive of our citizenship, and perilous to the unity of the Empire, we do hereby pledge ourselves…to stand by one another in defending for ourselves and our children our cherished position of equal citizenship in the United Kingdom and in using all the means which may be found necessary to defeat the present conspiracy to set up a Home Rule Parliament.

Ulster Solemn League and Covenant September 1912

Source 12

I can imagine no length of resistance to which Ulster can go in which I should not be prepared to support them.

Bonar Law, the Conservative leader, offering his support in 1912

1914 – Gun-running and the 'Curragh Mutiny'

Asquith believed that 'to wait and see' was often sensible and for many months let Ulster continue its defiance. This, however, was not wise since, far from calming down, the Ulster resistance prepared to fight. An unofficial army, the Ulster Volunteer Force, began training in secret and received considerable supplies of guns and ammunition from Germany through a gun-running operation at Larne, which the government made no real effort to stop. The reaction of the Irish Nationalists was to create their own army, the Irish Volunteer Force, and to buy in arms for it too. Their gun-running operation which came through Howth was much less secret than the UVF one at Larne. The government sent troops to intervene and in the resulting disturbance, three civilians died, to the fury of the Nationalists. Ulster seemed to be moving rapidly towards civil war.

Meanwhile, following a confused incident at the Curragh, the British army headquarters in Dublin, Asquith was informed that a number of officers were indicating that they would not obey orders to use force against Ulster resistance. This 'Curragh mutiny' and the gun-running convinced Asquith, somewhat late in the day, that he must consider excluding Ulster from his Home Rule Act. King George V summoned the party leaders to Buckingham Palace on 21 July to discuss how exclusion might work. Should four counties be excluded or six or nine (see page 57)? The Buckingham Palace Conference ended after three days without agreement. Before any other discussions could take place, the First World War began and the Home Rule Act was shelved for as long as the war lasted.

Another act in the Irish tragedy

The First World War transformed Irish politics. By its end, the Irish Parliamentary Party had collapsed. Sinn Fein, a tiny party in 1914 had taken its place. Home Rule was out of date; the Irish demand was for independence. Such a change could not have taken place in peacetime.

The saying was that 'England's adversity was Ireland's opportunity' and between 1914 and 1918 England's adversity had never been so great. While the Irish Parliamentary Party supported the British war effort and 150,000 Irishmen had enlisted by 1916, Redmond made a bad mistake in committing these men to wherever Britain needed them. Irish opinion preferred them to be used to defend Ireland and somewhere between 3000 and 10,000 left Redmond's National Volunteers to form themselves into the Irish Volunteers. Increasingly they co-operated with Sinn Fein and the IRB on anti-war and anti-English projects.

By 1916, there was much discussion of a revolution in IRB and Sinn Fein circles. Some, like Roger Casement, argued for a rebellion co-ordinated with a German landing; some were for using the Irish Volunteers in a guerrilla war; and some like Patrick Pearse preferred a dramatic rising in Dublin which might provoke a massive popular revolt or, if it failed, would provide inspiration to later generations as a 'blood sacrifice'.

The Easter Rising 1916

Eventually it was Pearse and his group who gained control of the Military Council of the IRB and planned a rising. What happened was an extraordinary muddle. Communications with German contacts broke down. The gun-running steamer ran aground. Casement was put ashore by a German submarine and promptly arrested. None the less, after hours of angry discussion, the Military Council ordered the rising to proceed, a day late on Easter Monday.

It was a 'blood sacrifice' with no chance of military success. The positions occupied by the rebels like the General Post Office had no military significance. They were chosen because they were very visible in the centre of Dublin. The Rising lasted six days and was very destructive. By the time Pearse decided to surrender, 64 of his force had died, as had 132 soldiers and policemen. Civilians suffered the most: 1318 died, 2217 were wounded and the centre of Dublin was wrecked.

The results of the Easter Rising

The immediate reactions of most Irish were first disbelief and then anger against the rebels. Had Asquith's government acted calmly and cautiously, making sure that the rebels had a fair trial, Pearse and his fellow rebels might have come to be seen as unbalanced adventurers of little significance in Irish history. Instead, angry and fearful because the war against Germany was going badly, Asquith's government allowed a massive and heavy-handed retaliation by the British army.

General Maxwell, the Military Governor, declared martial law, during which a number of appalling incidents took place, the most notorious being the murder by a British officer of the popular Francis Sheehy-Skeffington who was trying to prevent looting. Maxwell had 3500 people arrested and 15 of the rebel leaders swiftly executed without dignity. The reaction was a revulsion of opinion against the British. The leaders of the Rising became martyrs and support for the IRB and Sinn Fein soared. Redmond, who had denounced the Rising as pro-German treachery, found himself and his Irish Parliamentary Party deeply unpopular.

Conscription 1918

In 1917 Sinn Fein started to win by-elections and gained another great boost in

■ Biography

Patrick Pearse

Patrick Pearse was a journalist, playwright and a leading member of the Gaelic League. He led the Irish Volunteers, was the IRB Director of Military Operations and led the Easter Rising. He was 37 when he was executed.

Quotation

Life springs from death, and from the graves of patriotic men and women spring living nations

From Pearse's graveside eulogy to O'Donovan Rossa

■ Biography

Roger Casement (1864–1916)

Roger Casement was born in Dublin and had a distinguished career as a British consul with an international reputation for exposing some of the evils of colonialism. He then became a committed Irish Nationalist and went to Germany during the war to get German aid. Arrested in 1916 he was hanged for treachery. The government exposed his homosexuality to turn public opinion against his gaining a reprieve.

Eamonn de Valera (1882–1975)

Eamonn de Valera was born in New York. He joined the Gaelic League and then the Irish Volunteers. One of the leaders of the Easter Rising, his American citizenship saved him from execution. He became President of Sinn Fein and of the Dail Eireann. Opposed to the Anglo-Irish Treaty of 1921, he fought with the anti-Treaty forces during the Civil War. He later had a distinguished career as Prime Minister and President of the Irish Republic. He died in 1975 aged 93.

■ **Think about**

▶ Why should Ulster have been happy with the Government of Ireland Act?

Timeline

1916–1921
1916 Easter Rising.
1917 Sinn Fein wins two by-elections.
Failure of Irish Convention
De Valera becomes President of Sinn Fein.
1918 Conscription introduced to Ireland with mass disobedience.
General election: Sinn Fein 73 Unionists 26 Nationalists 6.
1919 Sinn Fein MPs refuse to go to Westminster; set up their Dail in Dublin.
Violence across the country between IRA and the Black and Tans.
1920 Government of Ireland Act
1921 General election Sinn Fein triumph.
Anglo-Irish Treaty partitions Ireland.

the spring when Lloyd George, responding to the pleas of his generals on the Western Front, who were being driven back by a massive German offensive, ordered conscription to be extended to Ireland. It was a disastrous decision in every way for British rule. Sinn Fein, with the backing of virtually every important group in Ireland including the Church, organized a successful anti-conscription campaign. In the general election of December 1918, Sinn Fein campaigned on resisting British power 'by all and every means', withdrawal from Westminster and presenting Ireland's case for independence at the Versailles Peace Conference. It won 73 seats against the Parliamentary Party's 6.

Anarchy and partition 1918–1922

The Sinn Fein MPs refused to go to London. Instead they set up their own assembly, the Dail Eireann in Dublin and elected Eamonn de Valera as their President. They also set up an alternative government all over the country. Not surprisingly, law and order broke down. The IRA (Irish Republican Army), an extremist group of the Irish Volunteers, began a campaign of assassinating policemen and soldiers. The response of the British government was to send in reinforcements – ex-soldiers, known as Auxiliaries or Black and Tans (because of their uniforms). The Black and Tans were as brutal as the IRA. They set fire to the centre of Cork, for example, and, in November 1920, fired into a football crowd causing 12 deaths, in revenge for an IRA killing of 11 unarmed British officers.

The Government of Ireland Act 1920 and the Anglo-Irish Treaty of 1921

Lloyd George now brought his formidable negotiating skills to find a way out of this shambles which was doing Britain's international reputation no good. In 1920, he got through Parliament the Government of Ireland Act which set up separate parliaments for Ulster in Belfast and for the rest of Ireland in Dublin, both of which would send some MPs to the Imperial Parliament in London. This Ulster happily accepted. Sinn Fein, through the Dail Eireann, did not. Violence continued.

Lloyd George did not give up. After two months of intense negotiation in London, an Anglo-Irish Treaty was agreed. Britain accepted that the 26 counties of Ireland, to be known as the Irish Free State and excluding the 6 counties of Ulster, should be essentially independent, though they would be part of the British Empire with Dominion status. Britain would retain some naval bases. As for the potentially difficult question of the size of Ulster, Lloyd George hid that away behind the promise of a Boundary Commission with the vaguest guidelines for its function. Ulster got six counties in 1921 and kept them for the rest of the century.

What bothered the Sinn Fein negotiators most was the nature of the Dominion status and having to take an Oath of Fidelity to the British monarch. The Dail Eireann only approved the terms of the Treaty by a tiny majority and the opponents, including de Valera, were prepared to fight a Civil War (1922–1923) before they would accept it.

The Problem of Northern Ireland

At last Britain and most of Ireland could live peaceably alongside each other, yet the curse on Anglo-Irish relations was still not fully exorcized. The Ulster problem remained unsolved. The troubles of the late twentieth century would cost thousands of lives, all too frequently of innocent civilians.

Source 13

[It] can be seen as both a remarkable historical settlement and a contemporary political failure. A British politician had had the vision, the skill and the luck to undertake successfully something which, since the Act of Union, had evaded all other politicians and statesmen who had approached it, a workable solution to the Anglo-Irish question...The political failure lay in the fact that the Treaty was necessarily a compromise. The Unionists were left feeling betrayed by Lloyd George's willingness to give in to what they regarded as Republican terrorism. The Nationalists could not forget his use of the 'Black and Tans'; nor could they regard it as anything other than a concession reluctantly and belatedly extracted from a British government who granted it only when all other means of maintaining the union had failed.

The historian Michael Lynch on Lloyd George and the 1921 Settlement.
Lynch, *Lloyd George and the Liberal Dilemma*, 1993

■ Activity

Study Source 13
Using the source and your own knowledge;
1 Explain why British governments found the Irish problem so difficult to solve between 1914 and 1921?
2 Explain how Lloyd George's Anglo-Irish Treaty of 1921 could be considered both 'a remarkable historical settlement and a contemporary political failure'?

Document exercise: The Easter Rising

Source A

The First World War should be seen as one of the most decisive events in modern Irish history. Politically speaking, it temporarily defused the Ulster situation; it put Home Rule on ice; it altered the conditions of military crisis in Ireland at a stroke; and it created the rationale for an IRB rebellion.

A historian assesses the importance of The First World War.
Foster, *Modern Ireland 1600-1972,* 1988

Source B

A report to Asquith from the Chief Secretary for Ireland

During the last few weeks I have read nothing but uncomfortable figures about the Irish Volunteers, who are steadily, month by month increasing...The newspapers are poor enough both in circulation and in ability but I think I notice an increasing exaltation of spirit and a growth in confidence...I feel the Irish Situation one of actual menace.

A. Birrell, writing to Asquith in late 1915

Source C

Another historian describes the effects of the Easter Rising

What transformed the situation was the government's crass response...Above all in the eyes of most ordinary Nationalists, the execution of the ringleaders turned them into martyrs, and Redmond's denunciation of it [the Rising] as a German plot turned him into a stooge. The scenario in which Asquith and Redmond would lead their nations to reconciliation through an Irish Home Rule Act was brought to a bloody end.

Peter Clarke, *Hope and Glory,* 1996

Source D

◀ Making martyrs. British troops execute one of the leaders of the Easter Rising in Kilmainham Gaol.

An anonymous reaction to the Black and Tans

What probably drove a peacefully inclined man like me into rebellion was the British attitude towards us, the assumption that the whole lot of us were a pack of murdering corner-boys [lads hanging around with nothing to do and looking for trouble].

■ **Further reading**

Paul Adelman, *Great Britain and the Irish Question 1800–1922*, 1996

Grenfell Morton, *Home Rule and the Irish Question*, 1992

Roy Foster, *Modern Ireland, 1688–1922*, 1989

Robert Kee, *Ireland, a History*, 1982

R.F. Foster (ed.), *The Oxford Illustrated History of Ireland*, 1989

■ **Examination-style questions**

1 Comprehension in context
Using Source A and your own knowledge explain what Foster means when he refers to an 'IRB rebellion'.

2 Comparing sources
To what extent do Sources B and C confirm the views of the author of Source A?

3 Assessing the sources
How reliable do you think the author of Source B is about the situation in Ireland in 1915?

4 Making judgements
Using the sources and your own knowledge, explain how far you agree with the view that Britain behaved very stupidly in Ireland between 1916 and 1921.

Summary

● There was so much hostility between the English and the Irish in the nineteenth century because an English minority which was socially different and had different religious beliefs had seized much of the land and ruled Ireland in the interests of Britain, not of the Irish majority. This hostility was increased by the contempt in which most English held the Irish and the fear and suspicions which the Irish had towards the English.

● The Liberals failed to grant Home Rule to Ireland between 1886 and 1914 because in 1886 Gladstone was unable to keep his Party united. A group of Liberal Unionists, of whom Joseph Chamberlain was the most important, were prepared to split the Party and put the Conservatives into power rather than grant more self-government to Ireland and weaken the British Empire. From 1893 to 1911 the House of Lords vetoed the Liberal Home Rule Bill. Though the Liberals finally passed a Home Rule Act, opposition from Ulster and the outbreak of The First World War meant it never took effect.

● The Home Rule crisis of 1886 ended 40 years of Whig/Liberal dominance of British politics. 1886 to 1906 were years of the Conservative ascendancy. The 1893 Home Rule crisis served to show how weak Gladstonian Liberalism had become. While the Grand Old Man wanted to challenge the power of the Lords, his colleagues had no stomach for that fight and were out of power within two years. From 1910 the Irish Home Rulers kept Asquith's Liberals in power. With Ireland close to civil war in 1914, Home Rule might again have had major consequences for British politics had not The First World War intervened.

● The events of The First World War, the manner in which the British suppressed the Easter Rising of 1916 and their later attempt to impose conscription on Ireland turned the majority of Irish in favour of independence rather than Home Rule. They voted for Sinn Fein rather than the Irish Nationalists and Sinn Fein showed that it was prepared to fight for Irish independence. Lloyd George solved the problem of Ulster for 50 years – though not permanently, by persuading Sinn Fein to accept that Ireland should be partitioned.

4

The Conservative Ascendancy 1885–1905
The 'Hotel Cecil'

◄ An apt symbol of the influence of the Cecil family, of which Lord Salisbury was the head, this impressive building is the Hotel Cecil, which was built on Cecil-owned land on the Strand in London.

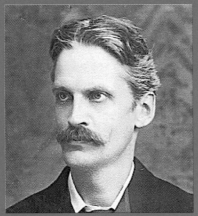

Note

The Cecil Family in 1900

Lord Salisbury was head of the Cecil family, which had become one of the leading aristocratic families of England in the sixteenth century, thanks to the services of William Cecil, and his son Robert, to Queen Elizabeth I.

In 1900 Lord Salisbury was Prime Minister and was taking good care of his large family. His nephew, Arthur Balfour, was Leader of the House of Commons and First Lord of the Treasury. Another nephew, Gerald Balfour, was President of the Board of Trade. Yet another nephew, Evelyn Cecil, was his parliamentary private secretary. A son-in-law, Lord Selborne, was First Lord of the Admiralty, a nephew-in-law, James Lowther, chaired the influential Commons Ways and Means Committee. His eldest son, Lord Cranborne, was Under-Secretary at the Foreign Office.

When Lord Salisbury made public the members of his government in 1900, he had to face an enormous amount of criticism because of his favouritism towards his family. The Liberal leader, Lord Rosebery, sarcastically complimented Salisbury 'on being the head of a family with the most remarkable genius for administration ever known'! His nephew Arthur Balfour was criticized similarly when he became Prime Minister in 1902. His Liberal opponents took to referring to Balfour's government as 'the Hotel Cecil'.

◀ Relatives who did well thanks to Salisbury's patronage:
(top) Arthur Balfour
(Bottom row left to right)
James Lowther, Gerald Balfour, Lord Selborne

Introduction

The Liberal split of 1886 over Home Rule, in which Joseph Chamberlain played a leading part, helped the Conservatives back into power. Twenty years later, a Conservative split over Tariff Reform, in which Joseph Chamberlain again played a leading part, helped to give power back to the Liberals. In the intervening years, Lord Salisbury, often assisted by his relations (see page 64), kept the Conservative Party in the ascendant. This chapter explores the reasons for these political developments, considering the impact of particular individuals and single issues in the context of wider social and economic trends.

Key questions

● What were the trends in the voting behaviour of the electorate between 1885 and 1906?
● What was the impact of Joseph Chamberlain on the fortunes of the Liberal and Conservative parties?
● Why were the Conservatives the dominant party between 1885 and 1906?
● How good a Prime Minister was Lord Salisbury?
● Why did the Liberals win such a massive victory in 1906?

Robert Gascoyne-Cecil, 3rd Marquess of Salisbury

Of the 20 years from 1885 to 1905, the Conservatives held power for 17 and Lord Salisbury was Prime Minister for 14.

Though Salisbury was one of the most able and successful Prime Ministers of the nineteenth century, his shy, complicated and unusual personality had prevented him from winning the fame and popularity which Gladstone and Disraeli came to enjoy. He gained respect; that was all. As we shall see, historians have reached very different judgements about him.

He had an unhappy childhood. He was afraid of his father and his mother died when he was only nine. Very bright but no games player, he was bullied so atrociously at Eton that he persuaded his father to remove him. Though plagued by ill-health at Oxford, he held office in the Union, the university debating society which was the place where many British politicians served their first apprenticeship. After Oxford he spent two years touring the British colonies to the benefit of both his health and his knowledge of the world. On returning to Britain in 1853, he became Tory MP for Stamford, a town where the Cecil family influence was strong.

In 1859 he made one of the best decisions of his life, which was to propose marriage to and be accepted by Georgina Alderson. He was highly strung and subject to serious depressions. She was intelligent, cheerful, energetic and ambitious for him. Not only did she bear him eight children but was a strong support and a lively companion throughout his political career. His father, however, opposed the marriage. Though she was a judge's daughter, he considered her much too middle class for a Cecil! None of the family attended the wedding.

Estranged from his family and his family's wealth for some years, Robert Cecil, as he then was, made a living as a journalist writing about politics and reviewing a vast range of books. He wrote fluently with a an often vitriolic wit. Disraeli, his future leader, he once described as 'the grain of dirt which clogs the whole machine [of the Conservative Party]'.

In his magazine articles in the 1850s and 1860s he set out his political philosophy which changed little during the rest of his life. He was an Anglican and as religious as Gladstone. Unlike Gladstone, he was deeply pessimistic about the future. Democracy would be the ruin of the country and it would destroy, as would social reform, the aristocracy and Church which provided the nation with the best possible political and moral leadership. The task of the Conservative Party and of himself when he became Prime Minister was to hold at bay the forces of destruction for as long as possible.

On the death of his elder brother in 1865, he became heir to the Salisbury title and estates so his financial worries ceased. He became Marquess of Salisbury when his father died in 1868.

In the Derby/Disraeli government of 1866/7 he (now Lord Cranborne) was Secretary of State for India. While he was in office, more than a million Indians died of famine in the state of Orissa. Though he was not really at fault, since his official in India passed on the relevant information far too slowly, he blamed himself for the rest of his life for not taking action earlier. In the 1867 Reform Act crisis, he considered Disraeli's tactics reckless and deceitful and resigned from the Cabinet, dramatically, taking General Peel, the Secretary for War and Lord Carnarvon, the Colonial Secretary with him.

Disraeli, however, realized his abilities and, when he won the 1874 election, persuaded him (now Lord Salisbury) to join his Cabinet, once again as Secretary of State for India. After a sticky start, their relations steadily improved, to such an extent that in 1878, at the height of the Eastern Question crisis, Disraeli made him Foreign Secretary. Salisbury's acute intelligence and mastery of detail contributed considerably to Britain's success at the Congress of Berlin.

Clearly he was now well-placed to succeed Disraeli, though being in the House of Lords was regarded increasingly as a disadvantage. During Gladstone's second Ministry from 1880 to 1885, he led the opposition in the Lords while Sir Stafford Northcote, Disraeli's Chancellor of the Exchequer from 1874 to 1880, led in the Commons. In these five years, Salisbury's performance was much more commanding, not least in the negotiations about the 1884 Reform Act and the Redistribution Bill (see page 39). Consequently, when in 1885 Gladstone's government resigned, Queen Victoria had no hesitation in asking Salisbury to form the next government.

Electoral trends 1880–1906

General election results 1880–1906

Date	Cons	Liberal	Irish Nat.	Liberal Unionist	Labour	Prime Minister
1880	238	353	61			Gladstone
1885	250	334	86			Gladstone
		Liberals split over Home Rule				
1886	316	191	78	78		Salisbury
1892	268	273	81	47		Gladstone Rosebery
1895	341	177	82	70		Salisbury
1900	334	184	82	68	2	Salisbury/ Balfour
		Conservatives split over Tariff Reform				
1906	132	400	83	25	30	Campbell-Bannerman

▲ Lord Salisbury in the 1890s.

It is tempting to explain Salisbury's success from 1886 to 1902 and then the failure of his successor, Balfour, in 1906 simply in terms of party splits. The explanation runs like this: Salisbury had little difficulty holding power for nearly twenty years, because Gladstone split the Liberals over Home Rule; then in 1906, the Liberals came back with a huge majority because Joseph Chamberlain split the Conservatives over Tariff Reform.

This explanation, however, is too simple. While the splits were very important, there were some significant trends in voters' behaviour quite separate from these big issues. Most of these trends were linked to particular social classes.

The aristocracy

In these years the Liberals lost the old Whig aristocracy to the Conservatives. In 1880 the Whigs made up about 40 per cent of the parliamentary party and provided many of its leaders. By 1895 this proportion had fallen to 8 per cent. Gladstone's Irish policies were one reason for the defection of the Whigs. Another was their concern about the effects which the broadening of the franchise and social reform would have on their wealth and social standing. The Conservatives, under Lord Salisbury's leadership, seemed to offer much more security than the Liberals. An important consequence of this change was that the House of Lords became overwhelmingly Conservative and a serious obstacle to Liberal governments. In 1892, for example, though Gladstone gained a Commons majority for his Home Rule Bill, Salisbury had it thrown out of the Lords by 419 to 41 votes. Consequently, at the turn of the century, the Liberal leadership added the reform of the House of Lords to their agenda.

The middle classes

The more wealthy middle classes – industrialists and businessmen, professionals like lawyers and doctors – were moving into suburbs and becoming more sympathetic towards the Conservatives. Their smart new suburban villas gave rise to the phrase 'villa Toryism'. Gladstone's one-issue crusades worried them, as did the social reform programme of the Radical Liberals. They appreciated the calm and stability which the Conservatives offered.

However, this trend should not be exaggerated. The Liberal Party kept the loyalty of a substantial section of middle-class voters, especially of those from Nonconformist backgrounds.

The lower middle class

The increase both in shops and in clerical work created another group, which is best described as lower middle class. Its members had some education. They were moving into the suburbs and prided themselves on their respectability. They avoided getting their hands dirty. They cannot be easily classified as mainly Conservative or mainly Liberal. They probably included the greatest amount of 'floating' voters among their number.

The working classes

The 1867 and 1884 Reform Acts increased the proportion of the electorate that was working class. Of those who could vote, a majority appears generally to have voted Liberal because of Gladstone's reputation and the linking of social reform with radical liberalism. The Trades Union Congress (TUC), which was founded in 1868, showed little interest before 1900 in supporting a separate

Note

Gladstone's Irish policies and the Duke of Argyll

In 1868, the Duke of Argyll was a leading Whig aristocrat and a pillar of the Liberal Party. Like Gladstone he had held office under Palmerston and he was in Gladstone's Cabinet from 1868 to 74. In fact he was a personal friend of Gladstone with whom he would discuss deep religious issues. However, Argyll became increasingly unhappy with Gladstone's Irish policies. Because of these he resigned from the Cabinet in 1881 and voted against the Home Rule Bill in 1886. For the rest of his life he was a leading Liberal Unionist.

■ **Think about**

▶ Why do you think so many Whig aristocrats, like the Duke of Argyll, were unhappy about Gladstone's Irish policies?

Labour Party. (See Chapter 7 for the origins of the Labour Party.) When mainly working-class constituencies like Morpeth in Northumberland and the Rhondda in south Wales voted into Parliament uncompromisingly working-class MPs, these called themselves Lib-Labs and usually supported Gladstone.

However, the late nineteenth-century working classes consisted of a variety of groups. Skilled shipyard workers on Tyneside might earn three or four times the wage of a general labourer in London who, as often as not, would depend on casual rather than regular employment. Of approximately 10 million workers in 1895, about 1 in 7 were members of a union.

About 1 in 3 working-class voters appear to have voted Conservative. There seems to have been three main reasons why they did so. The first was 'deference' – the belief that the Conservative upper classes, because of their wealth, upbringing and position in society, were destined to rule. The second was the patriotic enthusiasm which many working men felt for the monarchy and for the expansion of the Empire. Thanks to Disraeli (and also to Gladstone's anti-imperialism), the Conservatives were able to market themselves successfully as the national and imperial party. Thirdly, alongside their enthusiastic imperialism and patriotism, they disliked foreigners. In Lancashire, where there were many Irish immigrants, Conservative candidates benefited from anti-Irish feelings, and in the East End of London, which in the late nineteenth century received Jewish immigrants from Eastern Europe, from anti-Semitism.

How the workers voted and would continue to vote as more and more of them gained the franchise was clearly one of the most crucial questions facing the party leaders.

Agricultural workers

Conservatives before 1870 had assumed that they could rely on the rural vote since most farmers and farm-workers who could vote would vote how their local landowner and parish priest (who were usually Tory) told them to. However in the 1880s, a long-lasting agricultural depression began which caused many agricultural workers to lose their jobs. In addition, the Reform Acts of 1867 and 1884 had increased their numbers, while the Ballot Act of 1872 had made it harder for local landowners to put pressure on them at election time. Agricultural trade unions and Nonconformist Churches helped rural radicalism. In the 1880s and 1890s, such was the readiness of rural voters to look to the Liberals rather than the Conservatives, that Conservative Party officials advised Salisbury to fix general election dates at harvest time. Then the turnout of rural voters would be lower than at other times of the year.

Party organization

In these years the Conservatives had two major advantages over the Liberals.

The first was the quality of the Party's organization headed by Akers-Douglas, the Chief Whip, and Captain Middleton, the Chief Agent. Akers-Douglas made sure that as far as possible Conservative MPs were disciplined and loyal. He kept the Prime Minister well informed about Party opinion and Lady Salisbury would ask his advice about how she could use invitations to her receptions to the Party's advantage. Middleton, whom Salisbury met regularly, was hugely well informed about opinion in the constituencies. He organized the Party's propaganda campaigns and registration drives, sought out possible candidates for elections and raised funds. As the historian Andrew Roberts has observed,

■ **Think about**

Regional voting trends

In those regions where Nonconformists and working people were numerous – the North, Wales and Scotland, Liberalism tended to be strong. Southern England was more Conservative. The more Nonconformist radicals dominated the Liberal Party, the more the suburban middle classes turned to conservatism.

▶ However, in working-class Lancashire and London they tended to vote Conservative. Why do think this was?

Note

The Agricultural Depression of the late nineteenth century

This began because of some poor harvests but continued because reliable steamships brought in cheap corn from North America and then refrigeration made it possible to import cheap beef and lamb from the Americas and Australasia. While most European countries protected their farmers by putting tariffs (custom duties) on foreign food, in Britain the tradition of free trade was too strong for this to happen. Many farmers were ruined but the population enjoyed cheaper food.

Source 1

Every department of political organisation, especially in mobilising the 'Villadom' of suburbia, proved invaluable to Salisbury in the latter half of the 1890s.

Roberts, *Salisbury, Victorian Titan*, 1999

Source 2

▶ Much appreciated, no doubt, at Primrose League socials, A.G. Tarbet's Primrose Waltz. Note the cover with the portrait of Disraeli, the primrose wreath and the Union Jack.

The second advantage was the Primrose League. Founded in 1883, it named itself after Disraeli's favourite flower and aimed to promote what it considered to be the principles of Disraeli's conservatism, namely, 'the maintenance of religion, of the estates of the realm and of the Imperial Ascendancy of Great Britain'. As important as what it did was how it did it. Membership offered lively social as well as political activities. In 1886 its membership had reached 237,000; by 1891 a million and by 1910 two million.

At election time it energetically circulated Party propaganda and the Warden of the local habitation (the head of the local organization) often had the responsibility of keeping voters' lists up to date and for organizing canvassing. It also involved women in the political process. Upper and middle-class Conservative supporters proved very capable at organizing social events with a political purpose and helping get the voters to the polling booths at election time. The Liberals had nothing quite like it.

■ Activity

Study Sources 1-3

1 What does Pugh (Source 3) mean by 'the stability of the Conservative vote between the 1880s and 1914 compared with the more volatile Liberal performance?

2 What do you think Roberts (Source 1) means by the 'Villadom of suburbia'?

3 Explain the success of the Primrose League.

4 What did it do for the Conservatives electorally?

5 What other advantages did the Conservatives have in terms of Party organization?

Source 3

...the Primrose League generated the voluntary labour so necessary under the reformed electoral system of the 1880s ...By extending the Conservative influence beyond small groups of partisans the League succeeded where politicians invariably failed in keeping the cause healthy between elections, which goes some way to explaining the stability of the Conservative vote between the 1880s and 1914 by comparison with the more volatile Liberal performance.

Pugh, *The Making of British Politics 1867-1939*, 1982

British party politics and the Home Rule crisis of 1885–1886

1885 June Gladstone resigns. Salisbury forms a minority government.
Secret meetings suggest to Parnell that Conservatives might favour Home Rule. Gladstone in contact with Parnell and by the autumn had privately decided that Home Rule must be granted.

1885 November General Election gives Liberals a majority.

December 'Hawarden kite' Herbert Gladstone tells Press that his father favours Home Rule.

1886 February Gladstone forms his third ministry.

June Home Rule Bill defeated by 341 votes to 311; 93 Liberals vote against. Gladstone resigns again.

Source 4

THE FINISH.

The key politicians

Gladstone

His starting point was that 'Parliament could not go on as it had done'. He came to believe that Home Rule was the only way forward for Ireland because of the failure of his other Irish policies. Irish crises (see Chapter 3) had prevented the Liberals from carrying out much of their programme for the rest of Britain.

Chamberlain

In 1885 Joseph Chamberlain was, after Gladstone, the most formidable Liberal politician in the land and a possible future Prime Minister. Born in 1836, he was Gladstone's junior by 27 years, a different generation. He came from a London Nonconformist business family. At the age of 18, his father sent him to Birmingham to join the screw-making firm of Nettlefolds. He quickly made a fortune and was able to devote his considerable energies and organizing abilities to politics. He was an outstandingly effective Mayor of Birmingham and the driving force first of the National Education Association and then of the National Liberal Federation.

Leader of the radicals with an ambitious programme of social reform, he was President of the Board of Trade in Gladstone's second ministry. He and his friend Dilke were the most vigorous ministers in a government otherwise distracted by Irish affairs.

Gladstone and he did not get on. Gladstone respected Chamberlain's abilities in a distant kind of way but he easily irritated the younger man. Chamberlain once described his leader as 'a magnificent lunatic' and found his Anglican religion and lack of interest in social reform particularly irksome. Since in 1885 Gladstone was 76, his remarkable capacity to stay leader of the Liberal Party was blocking Chamberlain's ambitions.

Salisbury

Through 1885 and 1886 Salisbury played his cards with cunning. He never had any intention of backing Home Rule, but in 1885 he let his colleagues give Parnell and Gladstone the impression that he might. Consequently Gladstone seems genuinely to have believed that he might have had support from the Conservatives for his radical scheme to end the Irish problem permanently. Salisbury did not come out in person against Home Rule until May 1886, by which time Hartington and Chamberlain had made public their differences with Gladstone. He also stated that those Liberals who voted against Home Rule would not have to face Conservatives standing against them in the election which would follow if Gladstone was defeated on the Home Rule issue. This obviously made it much easier for the future Liberal Unionists to vote down the Home Rule Bill since the risk to their political futures was much less.

Source 5

[The nature of this crisis is usually] misunderstood…Superficially it appears merely a divisive, weakening factor that deprived the Liberal Party of its radical strength. The reality was different. It clarified Liberal politics by introducing a simple test of orthodoxy (being in favour of Home Rule for Ireland)…The purging of the Whig elements had been proceeding apace during 1880–5…Of the 73 Liberal Unionist MPs who survived the 1886 election, only 20 were radical supporters of Chamberlain; by 1892 only 11 of the latter remained and several had rejoined the Gladstonians. In short, 1886 virtually completed the radicalization of liberalism. Although only 191 Gladstonians were returned in 1886, they comprised a much more cohesive party than ever before.

Martin Pugh assesses the effects of the Home Rule crisis. Pugh, *The Making of Modern British Politics*, 1982

Source 6

In his biography of Gladstone, Roy Jenkins, himself a senior politician when the Labour Party split in the early 1980s, suggested that the tactical plan for Gladstone in 1886 should have been as follows:

…to keep the gulf between Chamberlain and Hartington as wide as possible and Chamberlain so engrossed in and satisfied with his departmental work that he became reluctant to leave the government. On this basis, Gladstone might have been Emperor of the West, dealing with Ireland more or less as he wished, and Chamberlain, if not the Emperor, at least the Viceroy of the East, pursuing reform in England. Such a dual approach would also have had the effect of keeping Liberals – both MPs and active supporters – a good deal happier. Out of respect for Gladstone, provincial Nonconformists embraced the cause of Catholic Ireland with remarkable enthusiasm, but they did not want their eggs all in one basket.

The politician and historian Roy Jenkins. Jenkins, *Gladstone*, 1995

Instead, Gladstone handled Chamberlain with monumental tactlessness. Chamberlain asked for the Colonial Office. In turning down his request and offering him the Board of Trade again, Gladstone gave Chamberlain the impression that he wondered whether he was good enough for the Colonial Office. He then made matters worse by recommending a cut in pay, as a general economy measure, of one of Chamberlain's closest colleagues and removed staff from the Local Government Board to prepare the Home Rule Bill.

Chamberlain finally resigned from the government in March 1886. His main reason was his belief that to give the Irish a separate parliament in Dublin would seriously damage the unity of the British Empire. His powerful criticisms of the Home Rule bill were a major cause of its failure.

■ Questions

1 Study Source 4. Explain the cartoon and, in particular, why one runner is wearing the Union Jack.

2 Outline the parts played by Gladstone, Chamberlain, and Salisbury in the Home Rule crisis of 1885-6. What did they each gain or lose in terms of their political aims?

3 Read Source 5. To what extent did the Home Rule Crisis weaken the Liberal Party between 1886 and 1906? (See Chapter 3.)

4 Read Source 6. Roy Jenkins suggests that if Gladstone had handled the crisis differently, he might have persuaded Parliament to agree to Home Rule for Ireland in 1886? Do you agree with this view?

Salisbury and Lord Randolph Churchill

One of the first problems Salisbury had in 1886 was his Chancellor of the Exchequer, Lord Randolph Churchill.

Churchill (as well as being the father of Winston Churchill) was the third son of the Duke of Marlborough. When his father was Viceroy of Ireland from 1876 to 1880, he acted as his Secretary.

Randolph Churchill was clever, witty, impetuous, without scruple and very ambitious. He made himself out to be the natural successor to Disraeli, talking enthusiastically about Tory democracy and making conservatism more attractive to working men.

He became famous during the 1880–1885 Parliament when the Conservatives were in opposition. The leader of the Conservatives in the Commons was Sir Stafford Northcote, who had once been Gladstone's Private Secretary and found it next to impossible to stand up to the Grand Old Man in debate. Unhappy with this state of affairs, Lord Randolph with a group of friends attacked Gladstone with unusual force and ridicule (for example over the Bradlaugh affair – see marginal note). Alongside Churchill were Arthur Balfour, Sir James Drummond-Wolff and Sir John Gorst. Together they became known as 'the Fourth Party'. They also attacked Sir Stafford Northcote whom they referred to as the 'Grand Old Woman' because of his weakness when dealing with Gladstone. They would try to distract him when he was speaking by laughing at inappropriate moments.

Churchill and the National Union

Churchill became popular in the Conservative constituencies and the Primrose League because of his speaking skills and vitality. He tried to make the National Union (see page 37) more representative of local Party activists and more influential in the making of Party policy in London. He succeeded in getting himself elected to the leadership of the National Union in 1884 and challenged Salisbury and Northcote to give the National Union more influence in developing national policies.

Faced with this threat to his authority, Salisbury outmanoeuvred Churchill. He seems to have promised him a Cabinet post when the Conservatives were next in power, in return for which Churchill gave up the leadership of the National Union. Salisbury also appeared to agree to some of the minor changes in Party organization but he would not allow the National Union a greater say in the creation of Party policy. Control of the National Union returned to the national Party organizers, Akers-Douglas and Captain Middleton. (see page 68).

Churchill as Chancellor of the Exchequer

When Salisbury became Prime Minister in 1886, he made Churchill Chancellor of the Exchequer and leader of the House of Commons.

Immediately he proved an impossible colleague. He quarrelled with other ministers and, confident of his popularity with the Party, aimed to dominate the Cabinet. He used the threat of resignation to try to get his way. When in December 1886, after a disagreement about military spending, he wrote a letter of resignation to Salisbury, to his great surprise, the Prime Minister accepted. Even more to his surprise, he discovered that out of office whatever popularity he had gave him no real influence. The rest of his life was tragic. He had syphilis which caused partial paralysis and mental disorder. He spoke less and

The Bradlaugh affair

The Commons refused to allow an MP called Charles Bradlaugh to take his seat because he was an atheist. The Fourth Party used this event to launch their most vicious attacks on Gladstone. The Liberal Prime Minister argued in favour of Bradlaugh being allowed to take his seat but, because his own deep religious beliefs were well known, the Fourth Party accused him of inconsistencies and hypocrisy.

▲ Lord Randolph Churchill. A thorn in Salisbury's side.

■ Think about

▶ If Randolph Churchill was so dangerous a rival and so unprincipled a personality, why then did Salisbury make him Chancellor of the Exchequer in 1886?

less frequently in the Commons and when he did, he was often so confused that many members would leave in embarrassment. He was only 45 when he died.

Salisbury's second and third ministries

The second ministry 1886–1892

Salisbury needed the new Liberal Unionists as allies. They had two powerful politicians in their ranks, Hartington and Chamberlain. Salisbury cleverly gained Hartington's support by asking him to become Prime Minister with himself as Foreign Secretary. Hartington turned down the offer but he was flattered and, from then on, co-operated with Salisbury. However there was no offer to Chamberlain, whose enthusiasm for social reform Salisbury regarded with feelings little short of horror.

Once Churchill had resigned, Salisbury faced no rivals for the rest of his career. He led from the House of Lords as Prime Minister and Foreign Secretary. W.H. Smith (founder of the bookshop and stationery empire), led the Conservatives in the House of Commons. He was respected as a thoroughly decent and effective colleague. In place of Churchill at the Exchequer, Salisbury appointed George Goschen, a Liberal Unionist and 'safe pair of hands'. The Presidency of the Board of Trade went to another former businessman, C.T. Ritchie. To the tough post of Irish Secretary he appointed his nephew Arthur Balfour (see page 56).

Legislation

The major reform of this ministry was the Local Government Act of 1888 which created 62 elected county councils. The councils were given responsibility for roads, bridges and lunatic asylums. They also shared the supervision of the police with local magistrates.

With regard to education, the government set out to improve the technical skills of young people entering industry by the Technical Instruction Act (1889). There was national concern that Britain's manufacturing standards were falling behind those of international competitors like Germany and that young people entering industry needed better technical training. The government established the Board of Education and spent 2 million pounds to ensure free compulsory elementary education. It also gave grants to universities for the first time.

In addition, there was a steady stream of minor legislation. For example, the Housing for the Working Classes, Public Health and Factories Acts continued initiatives begun between 1868 and 1874.

Rural voters benefited from two reforms. The first was the Tithes Act of 1891. Tithes were land taxes of 10 per cent which were paid to local churches. They dated back to the Middle Ages and had become very unpopular because of the agricultural depression. During the winter of 1887–1888, the government had to send in the army to end anti-tithe riots in Wales. The Tithes Act abolished the payment of tithes by tenant farmers. The second was the Allotments Act which was intended to lessen the harm done by the agricultural depression to agricultural workers. The Cabinet forced an extremely reluctant Prime Minister to agree to the compulsory purchase of land to create allotments.

The 1892 election and Gladstone's last ministry

In this election Gladstone won with an overall majority of about 40 (see page 39). The Liberal 'Newcastle Programme' of social reform appears to have been the decisive factor. Salisbury was disappointed but not excessively so. He believed that the Liberals were so disunited that they would have difficulty surviving. He also knew that he could use the huge in-built Conservative majority in the Lords to block any Liberal measures that he particularly disliked.

Which is how things turned out. Gladstone was now 83 and clearly an old man. His only interest was Home Rule for Ireland. He did not really believe in the Newcastle Programme. Otherwise, his Party had no coherent policies, rather particular fads and fancies, and most of its initiatives were blocked by the Lords.

When Gladstone finally retired in 1894, Lord Rosebery succeeded as Prime Minister. He was clever and very rich but temperamentally unsuited to such a difficult inheritance. He openly quarrelled with Harcourt, his Chancellor of the Exchequer, and was happy to resign when his government was defeated on a snap vote of censure.

Salisbury won by a landslide in the 1895 election. So disunited were the Liberals that all he had to do during the election campaign was make a few vague commitments to further agricultural and social reforms.

Salisbury's third ministry 1895–1900

In 1895, Salisbury appeared to have a government of great promise. He had a large majority and an experienced Cabinet. The country was enjoying economic growth. Yet the government achieved little. This was partly because it became bogged down in foreign and imperial affairs, culminating in the Boer War of 1899 (see pages 88–90). It was also partly because Salisbury insisted on keeping government spending low.

The Conservatives and social reform

As the nineteenth century drew to its close, the enlarged electorate of the 1884 Reform Act looked to government for more social reform. On this major issue, Salisbury was extremely cautious, as the following judgements by historians suggest.

Source 7

Although Salisbury generally did not like change, and thought it usually for the worse, if established interests were not too badly damaged he was willing to countenance it for a specific, verifiable public benefit, and occasionally, of course, for electoral advantage.

Roberts, *Salisbury, Victorian Titan*, 1999

Note

The Newcastle Programme
This was a number of social reforms agreed at the Liberal Party Conference at Newcastle in 1891. These included more controls on drinking, the disestablishment of the Welsh and Scottish Churches, land reform and elected parish councils. However, Gladstone's only interest was Home Rule, and the divisions within the Party were too great to be healed by such a mixed bag of social reforms.

■ Think about

The Home Rule issue had badly split the Liberals. Many of his colleagues thought that Gladstone should retire.

▶ Why then did the Liberals win the 1892 general election?

Note

Salisbury and the Liberal Unionists in 1895
In 1895 Salisbury made a formal coalition with the Liberal Unionists. Hartington (now the Duke of Devonshire) became Lord President of the Council and Chamberlain, to Salisbury's surprise, chose the Colonial Office.

Source 8

A possible hypothesis about electoral behaviour [between 1880 and 1906] can be advanced…[It assumes] that the most persistent factor in the choice made by the enlarged electorate was the desire for … social reform in the interests of the newly enfranchised urban and rural householders, but this, at the moments of crisis, particularly when some national issue came to the fore, could be elbowed out. After … the Conservative failure to carry any further instalment of the reforms passed in 1875-6, it would be natural in spite of Gladstone, to look to the Liberal Party, with Chamberlain and Dilke as its men of the future, for this sort of legislation. Hence the Liberal victories of 1880 and 1885. But the Irish crisis, arousing strong national emotions and breaking up the Liberals, pushes Gladstone out and gives Salisbury six years of power…[In the 1890s] however, the electorate again thinks in terms of social reform and, although the Conservatives are by no means supine [inactive] or apathetic in this field, they do not do enough….'.

Blake, *The Conservative Party from Peel to Major,* 1997

■ **Activity**

1 Give examples which support Roberts' argument in Source 7 that Salisbury would allow social reform if it brought clear public benefit and electoral advantage?

2 Summarize Blake's argument in Source 8. Then comment on its validity in the light of the election results between 1880 and 1895.

3 Did Salisbury's caution on social reform do his party more harm than good?

Quotation

The more our Empire extends…the more we must urge on all who have to judge, that those things are matters of business and must be considered on business principles. The dangerous temptation…is that we should consider rhapsody an adequate compensation for calculation.

Salisbury in 1898 on the dangers of imperialism

Quotation

'Whatever happens is for the worst; and therefore it is in our interest that as little should happen as possible.'

'The use of Conservatism is to delay changes till they become harmless.'

Salisbury on the dangers of change

■ **Activity**   **KEY SKILLS**

Prepare a presentation for a class seminar, making the case for the Conservative Ascendancy being either mainly due to the weakness of the Liberals or to Salisbury's skilful leadership. Use the material in this chapter and at least one image for your presentation.

Imperialism and party politics

While Salisbury was Prime Minister, jingoistic imperialism reached its height. Newspapers and magazines were full of stories of imperial adventures and rivalries. Salisbury hated jingoism and was uneasy about imperialism (see the quotation in the margin) despite the fact that the British Empire grew very fast while he was Prime Minister. In a speech in 1898 he warned against 'rhapsody' (getting carried away) rather than 'calculation'.

He was in fact an economic imperialist. A larger Empire was needed, he told the House of Lords, because to 'keep our trade, our industries alive, we must open new sources of consumption in the more untrodden portions of the earth.' For this reason and for electoral advantage, he was happy to be thought an imperialist.

However, though the period from 1885 to 1900 was the golden age of imperialism, this does not appear to have given the Conservatives a significant advantage with the electorate. This was partly because some Liberal leaders like Rosebery, unlike Gladstone, were as imperialist in the 1890s as their Conservative counterparts.

The general election of 1900 was different. Salisbury held it when news of victories in the Boer War reached Britain. He let loose what he called a 'Jingo Hurricane' and played on the divisions amongst the Liberal leaders, some of whom were passionately against the war. The Conservatives won another landslide victory. Once the Boer War ended in victory in 1902, Salisbury retired.

Historical debate: Salisbury's legacy

Salisbury has had his fair share of critics, beginning with his bitter younger brother Eustace who believed that he looked on 'politics as a question of personal ambition rather principles'. Others, especially his Liberal opponents, believed him to be a cunning operator whose only interest was to keep power for his party and himself. The *Morning Post* newspaper described him as the 'Prime Minister of Despair'.

Historians have found him hard to assess. Some find him out of touch with his times. Here he was, the political leader of the fastest growing empire in the world and of an evolving industrial society, yet his gut instinct was to block change wherever he could.

Source 9

In an age of democratic politics centred largely on social issues, Salisbury seems to belong to a distant and antipathetic [unattractive] tradition, the last great aristocratic figure of a political system which died with Queen Victoria…a great whale irretrievably beached on the receding shore of the nineteenth century.

The historian Paul Smith,
quoted in Roberts, *Salisbury, Victorian Titan*, 1999

Others, however, make a strong case in Salisbury's defence. Under his leadership, they argue, Britain with the British Empire was the world's most powerful nation. He was the outstanding Foreign Secretary of the nineteenth century, effectively defending Britain's interests but avoiding war wherever possible. He was a brilliant Conservative leader whose tactical skills made it the dominant party of the final two decades of the nineteenth century. And on the nineteenth-century foundations which he and Disraeli laid, the Conservative Party dominated twentieth-century party politics.

Source 10

[Salisbury's] caustic, far-ranging common-sense, allied to an intellect as fine as that of any British Prime Minister and a talent for ruthlessness when the occasion demanded, made …him fully the equal of Gladstone and Disraeli.

Roberts, *Salisbury, Victorian Titan*, 1999

'Bob's your uncle': Balfour and the end of Conservative Ascendancy 1902–1906

Arthur Balfour succeeded Salisbury, his uncle, in 1902. Balfour owed much to his uncle. His father, James Balfour, a wealthy Scottish landowner, died when he was only seven and Salisbury became in effect his guardian. The Cecil family influence gained him the parliamentary seat of Hertford. Salisbury then made him his Parliamentary Private Secretary and took him to the Congress of Berlin in 1878. From 1886, he was a member of each of his uncle's ministries.

Balfour had many abilities. Highly intelligent, he wrote books on philosophy. He had an acute understanding about Britain's changing place in the world which led him to some sensible imperial and foreign policies (see Chapter 6). Charming yet ruthless, he was deft at finding compromises when his ministers seemed at loggerheads. However he had real weaknesses as a Prime Minister. He spent too long looking at both sides of a question. Too often he preferred a cautious compromise to giving a firm lead. A wealthy bachelor, cosseted by adoring sisters and nieces, he was cut off from the real world and, unlike his uncle, had no feel for the electoral mood. It was not entirely surprising, therefore, that in 1906 he led the Conservative Party to its greatest electoral defeat.

■ Activity

Salisbury's reputation
Read the quotations on page 75 and Sources 9 and 10.

1 List Salisbury's main achievements as a politician (do not forget his work as Foreign Secretary (see Chapters 2 and 6) and his imperial policies (see Chapter 5).

2 List his main failings.

3 Comment on Andrew Roberts' assessment (Source 10) which puts Salisbury in the same league as Gladstone and Disraeli.

Note

'Bob's your uncle'
The phrase, meaning a speedy and neat solution to a problem, entered the English language in 1902 when Uncle 'Bob' Salisbury speedily and neatly managed the succession of his nephew Balfour to the post of Prime Minister.

Quotation

The *Pall Mall Gazette*, Conservative in its politics, once described Balfour as 'shivering in philosophic doubt on the steps of a metaphysical bathing machine.'

Blake, *The Conservative Party from Peel to Major*, 1997

Balfour's government and Tariff Reform 1902–1905

Balfour was unfortunate that soon after he had become Prime Minister, the issue of Tariff Reform split the Conservative Party from top to bottom.

What was Tariff Reform? It was a scheme to transform the way in which Britain traded with the world. Trade between Britain and the British Empire would be protected from foreign competition by the placing of higher tariffs (customs duties) on non-Empire goods. Its supporters argued that trade within the Empire would flourish and both Britain and the Empire would grow richer. Britain's comparative industrial decline would be reversed and money generated for social reforms like old age pensions. Such protection, however, would mean the end of the free trade which had served Britain so well since 1846. This faith in free trade was deeply entrenched in all sections of British society.

Chamberlain and Tariff Reform

Joseph Chamberlain was the driving-force behind Tariff Reform. He was worried, as were many other politicians, about Britain's comparative economic decline. As Colonial Secretary, he was convinced that the Empire offered a way out of this decline. In 1902 Canada was keen to have a preferential tariff to protect Canadian corn exports to Britain. In return, Chamberlain suggested that the Canadians should offer preferential terms for British manufactured goods. Such a scheme obviously ran counter to the British free trade tradition, so the response he got from the Conservative leadership was mixed. Chamberlain then resigned from Balfour's Cabinet in 1903 so that he could lead a national campaign for Tariff Reform. In typical Chamberlain style, he created a pressure group, the Tariff Reform League and campaigned vigorously to make Tariff Reform official Conservative policy:

> ### Quotation
>
> Defending free trade was the greatest political struggle even in my long political life...Everything else pales into insignificance... We must be prepared to unite with anyone who will help and part company with anyone who will not.
>
> These comments by Lord Rippon, a senior Liberal peer, indicate the strength of opposition to Chamberlain's proposals

▲ Joseph Chamberlain, with habitual orchid and monacle.

> ### Quotation
>
> **Campaigning slogans on tariff reform 1903–1906**
>
> 'Tariff reform means work for all'
>
> 'Hands off the people's food'
>
> 'Your food will cost you more'
>
> 'Free Trade – the Big Loaf
> Tariff Reform – the Small Loaf'

> ### Source 11
>
> For my part, I believe in a British Empire, in an Empire which, although it should be one of its first duties to cultivate friendship with all the nations of the world, should yet, even if alone, be self-sustaining and self-sufficient, able to maintain itself against the competition of all its rivals. And I do not believe it a Little England which shall be separated from all those to whom it should in the natural course look for support and affection – a Little England which shall thus be dependent absolutely on the mercy of those who envy its present prosperity, and who have shown that they are ready to do all in their power to prevent its future union with the British race throughout the world.
>
> Chamberlain in Birmingham, May 1903

Balfour and Tariff Reform

Balfour did not himself believe in Tariff Reform but he realized that Chamberlain had much support within the Party. Consequently he adopted a position which supported additional tariffs in retaliation against those nations which were putting tariffs on British goods. This position of compromise did not in fact help Conservative unity and, on one famous occasion in 1905, he led his Party out of the House of Commons during a debate of tariffs lest their divisions became greater. The split was too great to be healed. In December 1905, Balfour decided to resign.

Source 12

WE PLEAD FOR THE WOMEN AND CHILDREN

Facts from the
Government Blue Book
1903

Average weekly wage for skilled labour	IN ENGLAND 42/- IN GERMANY 24/-
The price of wheat per quarter	IN ENGLAND 27/6 IN GERMANY 35/6
Hours of work per week	IN ENGLAND 48* IN GERMANY 72

FREE TRADE   PROTECTION

WHICH WILL YOU HAVE?
VOTE FOR

Hand Bill

AND
FREE TRADE

Source 13

Source 14

Both Liberals and LRC supporters could denounce the Chamberlain plan for Tariff Reform which from 1903 onwards became the leading political controversy of the time…[During the 1906 election] the tide ran strongly in the direction of Liberalism, especially in Lancashire, where Tariff Reform seemed to threaten the established foreign markets of the cotton trade.

Pelling, *A Short History of the Labour Party*, 1993

■ Think about

How do Sources 12 and 13 make the protectionist and anti-protectionist cases? Using Source 14 and your own knowledge, assess the part tariff reform played in the Conservative defeat of 1906.

Conservative defeat 1905–1906

Balfour resigned in 1905, hoping that the Liberals led by the inexperienced Campbell-Bannerman would split again over Irish Home Rule. However the Liberal leadership had done deals. The first was with Redmond, the Irish Nationalist leader, that he would not press immediately for a Home Rule Act. The second was in secret with the LRC that they would co-operate to defeat the Conservatives.

Consequently, when the country went to the polls in 1906, the Conservatives were in disarray. Tariff Reform split the leadership; Tariff Reform, the Taff Vale judgment (see p. 00) and 'Chinese slavery' lost them the working classes; the Education Act and 'Chinese slavery' the Nonconformists. There was also general feeling that they had been in power too long. The main task of the Liberals was to look united. This they did and their reward was an overwhelming victory, with 400 seats for the Liberals and only 156 for the Unionists (the Conservatives and Liberal Unionists combined).

■ Activity

People's voting behaviour
The historian Robert Blake makes this comment about the 1906 election:

'Until more work is done on psephological [voting] history, one cannot be at all sure about the causes of this collapse…It is hard enough to understand contemporary elections – with all the devices of opinion polling at our disposal. How much harder to discover the truth about elections long vanished into the dusty archives of the past.'

1 Debate this comment in the light of your knowledge of general elections between 1880 and 1906.

2 Which party won the last British general election and what appear to have been the main reasons for its electoral success?

3 Check out the results of the general elections of first 1970 and then 1992, both of which took the experts by surprise. Why was this?

■ Activity

Prepare to debate the question of whether Chamberlain did more harm to the Liberals in 1886 over Home Rule, than he did to the Conservatives in 1903 over Tariff Reform.

First consider the Home Rule crisis of 1886.
What part did Chamberlain play in prompting the Liberal split?
How damaging was it to the Liberals?

Then consider the Tariff Reform controversy.
What part did Chamberlain play in causing the split within the Conservative Party?
How damaging was it to the Conservatives?

■ Further reading

Robert Blake, *The Conservative Party from Peel to Major,* 1997
Richard Shannon, *The Age of Salisbury,* 1996
Andrew Roberts, *Salisbury, Victorian Titan,* 1999
P. Fraser, *Joseph Chamberlain, Radicalism and Empire,* 1966

■ Think about

Consider the attitude of this cartoonist of 1897 to Joseph Chamberlain's career. The four dogs are from left to right, the Liberal Unionists, Brum (Birmingham), Lord Salisbury (large) and Arthur Balfour (small). In the background is a 'Primrose dancer'.

▶ What part did each of the dogs play in Chamberlain's career? Explain the see-saw and the Primrose dancer. How valid a comment is the cartoon on Chamberlain's career to 1897?

Summary

- Though public opinion swung in favour of one party or the other, notably in 1886 and 1906, there were some long-term trends in voting behaviour. The upper and more of the middle classes voted Conservative, who also attracted the vote of about a third of the working class. The Liberals, therefore, needed the votes of the industrial and agricultural workers. Social reform and trade union legislation became increasingly important electoral issues.

- Two major party splits, of the Liberals over Irish Home Rule in 1886 and of the Conservatives over Tariff Reform in 1903, seriously harmed each of the two main parties. In both of them Chamberlain was a key player.

- The Conservatives were dominant for most of the period because the Liberals were disunited and Salisbury responded to the country's desire for calm at home and imperial success abroad.

- Salisbury was in many ways one of the great Prime Ministers of modern times, except that his pessimism about social change prevented desirable social reform to an extent that was harmful both to his country and his party.

- The main, among many, reasons why the Liberals won so great a victory in 1906 were their unity in contrast to the Conservative disunity over Tariff Reform (which was an unpopular policy anyway) and the Conservatives had been in power too long.

'JOEY'

In his wonderful Balance Trick, to be seen nightly at the St. Stephen's Circus, Westminster.

Chapter 5

The British Empire 1870–1914
The greatest empire in the history of the world?

Source 1

▲ Lord Curzon, Viceroy of India, on a tiger hunt with an Indian prince.

Source 2

In the Empire we have found not merely the key to glory and wealth but the call to duty, and the means of service to mankind.

George Curzon, Conservative MP and future Viceroy of India, writing in 1897

Source 3

▶ Expanding the Empire. Here British troops engaged in conquering Burma in the 1880s advance cautiously on what appears to be a well-defended temple compound.

Introduction

The British Empire, already large in 1846, had grown to be immense by 1914. It was far larger than that of any other nation. For most Britons it was a source of great pride. For governments, while it was, as Curzon said, a source of 'glory and wealth', it was not without its problems, as this chapter explains.

Key questions

- How did the British Empire expand between 1870 and 1914?
- Why did it grow so fast in these years?
- In what ways, and at what cost, did Britain maintain its control over its colonies?

First, some definitions. Imperialism means empire-building – when a powerful state aims to take control of areas and peoples beyond its borders against their will. It is a term used particularly about the empire-building across the world which European states undertook during the late nineteenth century. Imperialists were those people who led or supported the expansion of empires.

Britain's success 1870–1914

Britain was much the most successful imperialist power. When in 1897 Queen Victoria celebrated her Diamond Jubilee, 50,000 troops from all over the Empire processed through the streets of London and rows of warships, 30 miles in length, anchored off Portsmouth's Spithead to display Britain's naval might. Victoria's empire included 372 million inhabitants and extended over 11 million square miles. In comparison, the Roman Empire, which hitherto most Britons regarded as previously the pinnacle of empire-building achievement, had a mere 125 million inhabitants in an area of 2.5 million square miles. As the century drew to its close, more and more Britons shared the attitudes of Curzon and Rhodes. They were immensely and, in the eyes of most foreigners, smugly proud of their Empire.

Quotation

I contend that we are the first race in the world, and that the more of the world we inhabit the better it is for the human race.

Cecil Rhodes, Prime Minister of Cape Colony in South Africa

■ **Biography**

Cecil Rhodes (1853–1902)

Rhodes was the most imperialist of all imperialists. As a young man he made a fortune in South Africa out of diamonds and gold. He became Prime Minister of Cape Colony and used his wealth to conquer, in Britain's name, a large area of Africa that was called Rhodesia in his honour. His dream was to build a railway from the Cape in South Africa to Cairo in Egypt, the whole length of which would pass through British colonies. A ruthless man, always in a hurry, his conquests caused the deaths of many Africans and he helped to bring about the Boer War of 1902 (see pages 88–89).

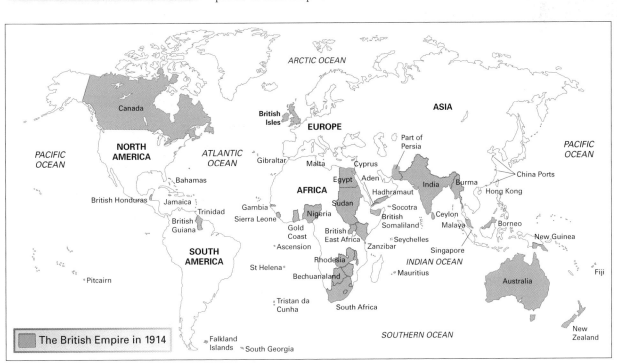

The British Empire in 1914

Before 1874: Why bother with colonies?

The British Empire began as a trading empire. From the sixteenth century British merchants set up trading stations scattered across the globe and the Royal Navy protected them. India was a particular source of wealth and soldiers. In addition, from the start of the nineteenth century Britons emigrated to settle in regions like Canada, South Africa, Australia and New Zealand.

Following the destruction of the French fleet at Trafalgar in 1805, the Royal Navy ruled the waves and her warships enforced across the world's oceans a 'Pax Britannica' or 'British Peace' which allowed international trade to flourish. Since this situation worked well for many years, most politicians opposed the cost and trouble which the conquest of new colonies would mean. As late as 1865 a parliamentary select committee could be found arguing against any further conquests in West Africa.

Disraeli and imperialism 1874–1880

Then came a substantial change. Between 1874 and 1914, the British Empire grew by another 90 million people and 4 million square miles. The reasons for this remarkable expansion are considered on page 85.

Disraeli was the first leader to make imperialism a central theme of his party's policy. In a famous speech in 1872 at the Crystal Palace, he presented to his audience an attractive vision of imperial power. It was part of Britain's role in the world to be a great imperial nation. He believed, correctly, that the glamour of empire-building would appeal to an electorate recently enlarged by the 1867 Reform Act.

The Suez Canal shares 1875

Of the measures he took as Prime Minister, Disraeli's purchase of the Suez Canal shares was probably the most important, since it started Britain's involvement in Egypt and the Suez Canal which was crucial to the growth of the Empire both in Africa and the Middle East.

In 1875 the Khedive of Egypt was bankrupt and the French government intended to buy his 40 per cent share in the Franco-British company which ran the recently completed Suez Canal. Since the Canal was a vital link to India and India was the most valuable part of the British Empire, Disraeli moved rapidly to raise the money to purchase the Khedive's shares for Britain.

THE LION'S SHARE.
" Gare à qui la touche !"

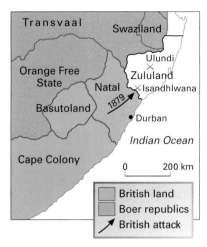

▲ Zululand, 1879–1881.

▲ Afghanistan, 1879

Victoria, Empress of India 1876

In 1876, by the Royal Titles Act, Disraeli persuaded Parliament to give Queen Victoria the title of Empress of India. It was an idea the Queen had liked for a number of years. The proposal ran into considerable opposition in Parliament and most newspapers at the time thought it ridiculous. However, as the years passed and Victoria played the part of the Queen-Empress with dignity, the title added to the glamour and vote-winning appeal of imperialism.

Another success was gaining Cyprus in 1878 as the reward for supporting Turkey against Russia in the crisis of 1877–1878 (see page 35).

Setbacks 1879

However, imperialism led to disasters in South Africa and Afghanistan. In both cases, aggressive 'forward' men on the spot went much further than the government in London intended. In South Africa, Sir Bartle Frere, the High Commissioner of South Africa, ignored instructions and provoked Cetewayo, Chief of the Zulus, into war. At Isandhlwana in 1879, the fierce and bold spear-wielding Zulu regiments ambushed and destroyed part of the invading British army. Not until 1881 did a bigger army finally win victory at Ulundi and add Zululand to the Empire.

The 1879 disaster in Afghanistan was the massacre of the British mission in Kabul. The mission was there because Lord Lytton, Viceroy of India, wished to lessen Russian influence in the region. He ignored instructions from London and forcibly deposed the Afghan ruler for being too pro-Russian and set up the mission to keep an eye on the Russian activity. Mutinous Afghan soldiers destroyed the mission and another British army had to be sent to Kabul to restore Britain's prestige.

Gladstone and imperial entanglements 1880–1885

Gladstone was deeply suspicious of imperialism. Britain, in his view should avoid 'needless and entangling engagements' which were often a waste of money. Imperial adventures also led to cruelty and exploitation. One of the themes of his Midlothian Campaign in 1879 was the immorality of Disraeli's imperial policy in Afghanistan, for example during a speech in Dalkeith in November 1879:

Think about

▶ What had happened in Afghanistan in 1879?

▶ What is Gladstone's main argument in Source 5 against British policy in Afghanistan?

▶ Would you expect this anti-imperialism to be a vote-winner?

(Remind yourself about Gladstone's Midlothian Campaign – see page 38.)

Source 5

Go into the lofty hills of Afghanistan, as they were last winter…You saw during last winter from time to time that from such and such a village attacks were made on British forces, and that in consequence the village was burned. Have you ever reflected on the meaning of those words?…The meaning of the burning of the village is that the women and children were driven forth to perish in the snows of winter…Is that not a fact which…rouses in you a sentiment of horror and grief, to think that in the name of England, under no political necessity, a war as frivolous as ever was waged in the history of man, should be associated with consequences such as these?

Remember that the rights of the savage, as we call him, remember that the happiness of his humble home, remember that the sanctity of life in the hill villages of Afghanistan among the winter snows are as inviolable in the eye of Almighty God as can be your own.

However during Gladstone's second ministry (1880-85) the British Empire grew faster than under Disraeli. That it did so caused Gladstone a deal of grief and some of the worst moments in his long political career. It also indicated that the forces driving British and European expansion in these years were too strong even for determined statesmen like Gladstone.

South Africa – the first Anglo-Boer War 1880–1881

The Boers (farmers of Dutch origin) of the Transvaal caused him his first difficulty. They had accepted British rule when the Zulus were a threat, but once the Zulus had been defeated in 1881, they demanded their independence. When Gladstone's government hesitated, the Boers declared their independence and destroyed a small British force at the Battle of Majuba Hill (1881). Gladstone's response, which was typical of his anti-imperialist thinking, was to grant the Transvaal its independence by the Pretoria Convention.

The occupation of Egypt 1882

Here Gladstone was both decisive in 1882, which won him considerable popularity, and indecisive in 1884/5 which temporarily made him the most unpopular man in Britain.

In 1882 he ordered the invasion of Egypt which, to all intents and purposes, turned that country into a British colony, though it remained in name a province of the Turkish Empire. He acted in this most un-Gladstonian way because a nationalist revolt appeared to be threatening not only the security of the Suez Canal but also the money which British and French investors (who included Gladstone himself), had lent to the Egyptian government and to the Suez Canal Company. Gladstone had hoped to invade jointly with the French or other European powers but they felt that the risks were too great. He also expected that this occupation of Egypt would only be temporary.

The Mahdi and General Gordon 1884–1885

There followed the worst crisis of his career. In 1884, in the Sudan (see map in margin) a Muslim religious leader, the Mahdi, successfully defeated Egyptian forces, led by British officers. Gladstone's government did not want to interfere in the Sudan but sent General Gordon there to bring Britons and Egyptians to safety.

Gordon was a bad choice. Instead of evacuating the Sudan, he allowed himself to be besieged by the Mahdi in Khartoum and waited for the British government to send an army to relieve him and take possession of the Sudan. An exasperated Gladstone refused for months to agree to the expense and danger that sending an army would entail. When at last he gave way to public opinion, he had left it too late. The relieving army got to Khartoum just two days after the Mahdi's forces had taken the town and killed Gordon.

Gordon may have disobeyed orders but in the opinion of most Britons, including Queen Victoria, he was one of the bravest of the brave whose life had been lost defending Britain's Christian honour simply because the Prime Minister had been unpardonably slow in ordering his relief.

With typical courage, some would say pig-headedness, Gladstone refused to respond to public outrage and ordered the relief force out of the Sudan, without attempting to punish the Mahdi. Later in 1885 he regained some popularity by threatening the Russians with war if they advanced any further into Afghanistan from the frontier (the Penjdeh affair).

▲ The Anglo-Egyptian Sudan in 1899, after its conquest by General Kitchener (see page 88).

■ Biography

Charles Gordon (1833–1885)

Gordon was an eccentrically religious soldier of great energy and strong if muddled views, who became a hero to his countrymen through his amazing adventures on the edges of the Empire, notably in China in the 1860s. The Egyptian government

employed him as Governor-General of the Sudan from 1877–1880. He was exceptionally brave and enterprising but not a good subordinate. 'Half-cracked' was how Gladstone's Secretary described him.

Historical debate

The reasons for the growth of European empires

The rapid growth of European empires, including the British Empire, is one of the most controversial episodes in modern history. There were many different causes: for example, the pressure of population growth in Europe, which led to mass emigration; the desire for wealth through trade and conquest; rivalries between the Great Powers; the Christian missionary impulse to convert and to 'civilize' the non-European world; the sheer excitement of exploration and adventure; the huge technological superiority which the industrial revolution gave to Europeans.

What historians tend to argue about is which is the most important cause. Here are some of the main interpretations.

● **That the main causes were economic**

This theory has been very influential with socialist and communist politicians. It was first put forward in 1902 by J.A. Hobson, a Liberal economist, who wrote a famous and highly critical study of imperialism during the Boer War. His main argument was that the British economy was not working as it should in the interests of the whole nation. Instead, what was happening was that certain businesses were over-producing and needed new markets in which to invest. A conspiracy of financiers drove imperialism forward. Lenin, the first communist dictator of the USSR developed Hobson's thesis. In Lenin's view, imperialism was the highest and last stage of capitalism. The capitalist nations had to take control of colonial markets to prevent their workers rising in revolution.

● **That the main causes were diplomatic**

Historians like D.K. Fieldhouse and A.J.P. Taylor have argued that national rivalries within Europe rather than economic developments were the main reason for imperial expansion. A.J.P. Taylor singled out Bismarck, the German Chancellor, as the diplomat who started the Scramble for Africa. His intention was to distract France from trying to recover the land she had lost to Germany in 1871 and to provoke Britain and France into quarrelling about imperial matters.

● **That the main causes were strategic**

The best-known 'strategic historians' are R. Robinson and J. Gallagher, whose *Africa and the Victorians* was published in 1961. They argue that on the whole British governments would have preferred simply to hold on to what they had and avoid imperial expansion. However, the need to defend their interests in Egypt and South Africa forced them into conquests. Such were the rivalries of the nations of Europe, and so technologically superior were they to their African opponents, that once the Scramble had begun it proved unstoppable.

● **That the main causes was financial – a specific concern for the City of London**

In 1993, P.J. Cain and A.G. Hopkins published an interesting variation of the economic interpretation. They argued that the 'gentleman capitalists' who ran the financial institutions of the City of London, and who were closely connected to the government, formed a very powerful group in Britain. They acted to make sure that imperial policies benefited their institutions and strengthened London's position as the world's leading financial centre, earning a great deal both for themselves and for Britain.

■ **Activity**

1 What kind of evidence would Hobson have used to support his economic interpretation?
   What kind of evidence would have persuaded Fieldhouse and Taylor that diplomatic causes were more important than economic causes in explaining the rise of the British Empire?

2 When Robinson and Gallagher stress the strategic causes for the growth of the British Empire, what do they mean?
   To what extent do events in
   (a) South Africa (see pp. 88–90) and
   (b) Egypt (see pp. 82–85) support their interpretation?

3 How much has the 1993 interpretation of Cain and Hopkins got in common with the 1902 interpretation of Hobson?

Britain's intervention in Egypt in the 1870s and 1880s
Why was it a turning point in the development of the British Empire?

Egypt's relationship with Britain

Britain never claimed that Egypt was part of the British Empire. Up to 1914, the formal ruler of Egypt was the Khedive who, in name at least, was a subject of the Sultan of Turkey. In reality, however, Egypt was effectively a British colony from 1882 since nothing of importance could happen there, especially in economic and financial matters, without the approval of Sir Evelyn Baring, Britain's Consul-General.

▲ The Prince of Wales visits Port Said, the northern entrance to the Suez Canal, in 1875. Note the variety of shipping, including a warship, the customs offices and warehouses and the Mediterranean in the background.

Other players in the Egyptian drama

France: The French had had, for many years, interests and influence in Egypt. The great French engineer, Ferdinand de Lesseps, had planned and supervised the building of the Suez Canal. Many Frenchmen had invested heavily in Egypt and expected the French government to protect their interests. They resented the growing British presence in the area. However they were having to recover from the devastating defeat by Prussia of 1870–1871 and usually aimed to avoid quarrelling with Britain.

The bondholders: These were the people, mainly French and British, who had invested their money in the Suez Canal Company and in loans to the Egyptian government. Among them was Gladstone. They wanted their money back and saw British intervention as the means of getting it. Financiers in the City of London worked hard on their behalf, as did newspapers like *The Times* and many MPs.

Egypt as a producer of cotton: Egypt produced cotton which Lancashire clothing manufacturers were keen to purchase. Khedive Ismail was an enthusiastic modernizer and the railway and harbour building projects which he had encouraged provided attractive contracts for British business. In 1880 Britain was taking 80 per cent of Egypt's exports and providing 44 per cent of her imports.

Colonel Arabi and Egyptian nationalism: Not surprisingly many Egyptians disliked the way Europeans, supported by the Turkish Sultan, were interfering in their affairs. Egyptian nationalism emerged between 1879 and 1882, led by Colonel Arabi, who demanded 'Egypt for the Egyptians'. The British invading forces of 1882 defeated Arabi's army at Tel-el-Kebir. Arabi himself was imprisoned.

The British refused to take Egyptian nationalism seriously before 1914. Gladstone described Arabi as 'the greatest villain alive', while Baring was of the opinion that to give power to an Egyptian nationalist 'would be only a little less absurd than the nomination of some savage Red Indian to be Governor-General of Canada'.

■ Questions

Britain's reasons for occupying Egypt
Consider the following:
● Britain's rivalry with France in North Africa
● The rights of the bondholders
● Egyptian cotton
● Fear of Egyptian nationalism.
List these in order of importance, giving your reasons. Does the illustration of the Canal suggest other reasons?

Source 6

Gladstone was still reluctant to take military action...but he was at variance with the majority of his [Cabinet] colleagues...So the line-up was overwhelming and Gladstone's ability to resist was weakened by his tiredness. For 1 July, after a continuous sitting on the Irish Crimes Bill from the Friday afternoon to 8.00 on Saturday evening, he wrote 'my share of the sitting I take to be 19 hours. Anxious Cabinet on Egypt...

The government acts in early July 1882

Source 7

What were our interests in connection with Egypt? They were first the Suez Canal; secondly our trade with Egypt; and thirdly, the subordinate but still important interest of the bondholders to whom Egypt was indebted.

A Liberal MP, JC M'Coan, in the House of Commons debate about invading Egypt 25 July 1882, recorded in Hansard

Timeline

1869 Opening of the Suez Canal. A private company owned mainly by European investors and the Khedive Ismail ran the Canal and made money from the tolls it charged.

1875 The Khedive went bankrupt; he was in debt, mainly to British and French bondholders.

1875 Disraeli buys Ismail's Suez Canal shares for the British government.

1876-82 Britain and France take 'Dual Control' of Egyptian finances.

1879 Britain and France force Ismail to resign; Tewfik, his son, succeeds.

1879-82 Egyptian nationalist unrest led by Colonel Arabi.

Source 8

Britain's advances in Africa were prompted by different interests and circumstances. Egypt was occupied because of the collapse of the Khedival regime. The occupation went on because of the French hostility which the occupation provoked...Britain's strength depended on the possession of India and preponderance in the East, almost as much as it did on the British Isles. Therefore her position hung above all upon the safe communication between the two...From start to finish the partition of tropical Africa was driven by the persistent crisis in Egypt. When the British entered Egypt on their own, the Scramble began.

Robinson and Gallagher, *Africa and the Victorians*, 1961

Source 9

Britain adopted a much more assertive policy towards Egypt than Robinson and Gallagher allowed...Gladstone was outmanoeuvred by the hawks in his government, headed by Hartington and Dilke, who were keen to shift the Liberals towards a strong foreign policy...British policy was assertive not because policy-makers were in the pockets of the bondholders, but because they recognised the need to defend Britain's substantial economic interests in Egypt...The other major consequence of the occupation of Egypt was to draw Britain into the Sudan.

Cain and Hopkins, *British Imperialism 1688–1914*, 1999

■ Questions

1 What do Sources 6 and 7 suggest are the main causes for

a) Britain's intervention in Egypt

b) Gladstone agreeing to this 'imperialist' action?

2 Re-read pages 80–85 and consider Sources 8 and 9. In what ways do Cain and Hopkins differ from Robinson and Gallagher? Would you describe Cain and Hopkins' interpretation as essentially economic, strategic or diplomatic?

3 Why do you think that Britain stayed in Egypt?

4 Why was Britain's intervention in Egypt a turning-point in the development of the British Empire?

Lord Salisbury as Prime Minister 1885, 1886–1892, 1895–1902

Unlike most Conservatives, Salisbury was not an enthusiastic imperialist. Despite this, he appointed as his Colonial Secretary, Joseph Chamberlain, one of the most aggressive imperialists of his generation, and, in his final years as Prime Minister, presided over the worst war in the Scramble for Africa, the South African War of 1899–1902.

Chamberlain's brand of imperialism 1895–1903

In 1895 Chamberlain was leader of the Liberal Unionists. When Salisbury gave him a choice of ministries, he showed no hesitation in opting for the Colonial Office. He believed that the Empire was of huge economic importance to Britain. From the Empire came cheap raw materials like gold and rubber, tea and coffee. Out of Britain came manufactured goods for profitable export. So he threw his great energies and organizing skills to strengthening and enlarging the Empire.

He later developed his imperialist ideas into a scheme for a more united empire where trade between members of the Empire would be protected by import taxes (tariffs) on foreign goods. 'Tariff Reform' would help all the members of the British Empire in an ever more hostile and competitive world. The main effect of his campaign for 'Tariff Reform' (see pages 77–78), however, was to split the Conservative Party.

With Chamberlain in charge, British colonial armies attacked rather than defended. In West Africa, they ended the independence of the Ashanti tribes. In the Sudan in 1898, led by General Kitchener, they destroyed the army of Khalifa, the Mahdi's successor, at Omdurman. The Sudan was renamed the Anglo-Egyptian Sudan and, to all intents and purposes, became another British colony.

Kitchener then advanced up the Nile to Fashoda to bar the progress of Major Marchand with a much smaller French force. The French government was outraged by the British insistence that the Upper Nile was theirs and for a few months in 1898 war seemed possible. However, so much stronger were the forces available to Kitchener, that eventually the French government ordered Marchand to withdraw.

The South African War 1899–1902

This war occurred mainly because Britain wanted the Rand goldfields. They had been discovered in 1886 and turned out to be the richest in the world. Unfortunately, they were in the Boer Transvaal Republic.

Successive British governments had toyed with the idea of persuading or forcing the Boer republics to join a British-dominated South African Federation, and the discovery of gold gave new life to such a scheme. As for Cecil Rhodes, Prime Minister of Cape Colony and the most ambitious imperialist alive, he wanted the goldfields for the Empire, by whatever means.

Leader of the Transvaal Boers was Paul Kruger, a farmer who had a deep-seated distrust of the British in general and Cecil Rhodes in particular. He expected war sooner or later and hoped that South Africa might be united under Boer rule. He used the wealth from the mines to purchase modern weapons and to build the Delagoa railway which would allow gold to be exported through Portuguese, rather than British, ports. Rhodes and

Hilaire Belloc on the machine guns which helped Britain to win colonial battles such as Omdurman:

'Whatever happens, we have got the Maxim gun and they have not.'

Source 10

MARCHEZ! MARCHAND!

GENERAL JOHN BULL (to MAJOR MARCHAND). "COME, PROFESSOR, YOU'VE HAD A NICE LITTLE SCIENTIFIC TRIP! I'VE SMASHED THE DERVISHES—LUCKILY FOR YOU—AND NOW I RECOMMEND YOU TO PACK UP YOUR FLAGS, AND GO HOME!!"

▲ A *Punch* view of the Fashoda crisis of 1898.

■ Think about

▶ Who are the two men in Source 10 and what is the standing one saying and why?

Chamberlain feared that the Transvaal, aided by Germany or France, might challenge the British position in South Africa. And South Africa, with its ports of Cape Town and Durban, was a vital staging post on a major imperial sea-route.

The Jameson Raid 1895

A particular difficulty for Kruger was the flood of foreigners (*Uitlanders*) into the Transvaal to mine for gold. Most were British so if they gained the right to vote, they might want a government which made them part of a British South Africa. Consequently, he refused them political rights, though taxing them heavily. Not surprisingly, the *Uitlanders* complained and Rhodes devised a plan, of which Chamberlain was aware, to use the grievances of the *Uitlanders* to seize the Transvaal for Britain. The *Uitlanders* would stage a rebellion in Johannesburg; Dr Jameson, one of Rhodes' closest associates, with a volunteer army paid for by Rhodes, would ride to their aid; and Kruger's government would fall.

The Jameson Raid, as it became known, took place in 1895. It was a shambles. The *Uitlander* leaders lost their nerve so there was no rebellion. Dr Jameson and his small band rode straight into the arms of a Boer force and surrendered with hardly a fight. Rhodes had to resign as Prime Minister of Cape Colony and he and Jameson had to face a parliamentary enquiry in London. Both took the blame for the raid of which Chamberlain denied all knowledge.

Milner and the *Uitlanders'* grievances

Chamberlain remained determined to annex the goldfields and the Transvaal. The *Uitlanders* kept complaining about their ill treatment by Kruger and British public opinion angrily supported them. Chamberlain sent Lord Milner to negotiate a better deal for the *Uitlanders*. Milner quickly decided that only force could make Kruger give up his independence. He negotiated so aggressively that Kruger decided that Britain was bent on war. Since the Boers' only chance of victory lay in a swift attack, it was Kruger who actually declared war in 1899.

The South African War 1899–1902

The events of the South African War (often called the Boer War) startled both Britain and the rest of the world. The two tiny Boer republics – the Orange Free State fighting alongside the Transvaal – very nearly defeated the world's largest empire in the first few months of the war. However, both major ports, Durban and Cape Town, remained in British hands and massive reinforcements arrived with new commanders, Generals Roberts and Kitchener. The fortunes of war quickly turned and by 1900 Roberts had taken both Johannesburg and the capital of the Transvaal, Pretoria.

Instead of surrendering, the Boers changed to guerrilla tactics. Britain had to bring in nearly 500,000 men and fought an ugly war. To reduce support for the Boer guerrillas, Kitchener moved Boer women and children into concentration camps, where as many as 20,000 died from disease. He had crops burnt and the countryside criss-crossed with barbed wire and blockhouses. Even so the Boers fought on until 1902. Only then, by the Peace of Vereeniging, the Boer Republics became part of the British Empire. Twenty thousand British troops died and thousands of Africans. The cost of the war was £200 million.

The Boer War was a turning point in the development of the British Empire. The first humiliating defeats, then the suffering on both sides and finally the

▲ Cecil Rhodes when Prime Minister of Cape Colony.

■ Biography

Alfred, Lord Milner (1854-1925)

Milner had a German mother and spent much of his early life in German. Highly intelligent, he did brilliantly at Oxford University where he became a convinced imperialist. He worked for Cromer in Egypt before becoming High Commissioner in South Africa. Once the war was won, he worked hard to revive the country, but he made many enemies and resigned in 1904. Lloyd George appointed him to his war cabinet in 1916 where he served with distinction.

■ Think about

▶ To what extent did Milner cause the Boer War of 1899-1902?

financial costs sobered up the feverish jingoistic imperialism of public opinion in the 1890s. European tensions made the political leaders look for peaceful rather than military solutions to imperial problems.

Controlling the Empire 1870–1914

Ultimately, like any empire, the British Empire relied on force. Its main military arm was the Royal Navy, the biggest in the world, with bases scattered across the oceans. There was also a small British and larger Indian army which were usually more than able to deal with any unrest.

India

India's size made it special: a sub-continent with a population of about 300 million people in 1900. It was also one of the earliest of British conquests. The 'jewel in the imperial crown', India's value to Britain was immense. It provided a huge market for British manufactured goods and its army of Indian troops and British officers, paid for out of Indian taxes, was an effective and cheap force for colonial wars.

Because India was so different, British rule there was different too. After the Rising (Mutiny) of 1857, the most senior Briton was the Viceroy, based in Calcutta. Though he was answerable to the British government in London, in India he had almost kingly powers, tempered by consultative assemblies. At his command was the Indian army, two-thirds Indian and one-third European.

About a thousand British civil servants ran India, answering to the Viceroy. Being a member of the Indian Civil Service (ICS) meant good pay, a pension on retirement, power, prestige and, usually, considerable job satisfaction. Entry was by competitive examination and the successful candidates were usually able. Alongside the Civil Service were the tax collectors. Land was the main basis of the Indian tax system.

> **Note**
>
> More and more Indians from the warlike north like the Sikhs and Gurkhas manned these armies and won a fine reputation for their fighting skills.

Source 11

It, with its associated army, political, educational and technical services…ran India with a high degree of both efficiency and devotion. At the same time, they were as a whole dedicated to maintaining things as they were. Their disbelief in Indian capacity was pronounced, distrust of Indian claims profound, and opposition to Indian encroachment in the higher services determined. The service was at once the strength and weakness of the British 'raj' in India, for while it served the needs of a static society to admiration, it was temperamentally unsuited to adapt itself to a changing world.

The strengths and weaknesses of the Indian Civil Service

> ■ **Think about**
>
> ▶ In what ways was the Indian Civil Service 'temperamentally unsuited to adapt itself to a changing world'?

The Viceroy ruled directly much of India but native Princes also governed large areas under his authority. After the Indian Mutiny, the Viceroys did their utmost to make the Princes feel valuable members of the Empire and to avoid interfering in their territories. With regard to Indian society generally, British policy after 1857 was to let things be, as long as the country was peaceful, trade flowed freely and taxes were paid. However, the government was active with public works. By 1900 it had created the best railway system in Asia. Extensive irrigation also substantially reduced the frequency and extent of famines.

Other forms of imperial control

F.D. Lugard was High Commissioner of Northern Nigeria from 1900 to 1906. He believed that too much direct rule by Europeans harmed African society. Direct rule by Britons, he maintained, should concentrate on law and order, trade and education. Otherwise, the British colonial government should rule, indirectly, through the traditional African chiefs. Lugard's ideas were influential in other tropical African colonies.

In Egypt from 1883, Sir Evelyn Baring (who became Lord Cromer) controlled the country's finances, and British officers led the Egyptian army. While appearing to rule, for example by appointing his own ministers, in reality the Khedive could take no major decisions without Baring's approval.

In South Africa, British armies and Boer commandos broke native resistance by violence during the nineteenth century. The white minority then stayed in power, partly by maintaining an effective army and police force, partly by restricting the movement of black Africans and their rights to hold land. Pass laws controlled the access of black Africans into cities and Cecil Rhodes' Glen Grey Act of 1892 rationed the amount of land available to black Africans in such a way as to force some of them to leave their homes to work in the mines or on white farms:

Source 12

The logic of the Glen Grey Act was to settle a limited number of African families on the land, and to make the others available as seasonal migrant workers either for farmers in the agricultural and pastoral regions, or for De Beers at Kimberley [Cecil Rhodes' diamond mines]…Those who enacted the Glen Grey legislation described it as 'a Bill for Africa', not merely a piece of local legislation. The Glen Grey Act offered a model of control over other African populations, in the interests of all major employers in the region.

Denoon and Nyeko, *Southern Africa since 1800*, 1984

By such means Britons controlled their Empire without too much difficulty during the nineteenth century, though early signs of anti-colonial nationalism appeared before the century was over. How this anti-colonialism grew and the British Empire collapsed after the Second World War is the subject of Chapter 17.

Summary

- At the end of the nineteenth century, the British Empire was the largest the world had ever known. It was founded on trade and defended by the most powerful fleet in the history of the world.
- Between 1870 and 1914 it expanded very fast, mainly in Africa but also in the Far East.
- Historians differ about the reasons for this expansion but economic needs and strategic concerns stemming from European rivalries were certainly important. Recent research emphasizes the fundamental importance of economic and financial considerations.
- Viceroys and High Commissioners supported by a navy, an army designed for colonial wars and dedicated British civil servants, often working in close co-operation with local princes and chiefs, kept the Empire under control with apparent ease, though in regions like India and Egypt, national movements were beginning to challenge British rule.

■ Further reading

M.E. Chamberlain, *The Scramble for Africa*, 1974*

James Morris, *The Pax Britannica Trilogy*, 1978*

R. Robinson and J. Gallagher, *Africa and the Victorians*, 1961

Bernard Porter, *The Lion's Share*, 1984

* Books particularly suitable for students

■ Think about

▶ In what ways was the Glen Grey Act 'a model of control over African populations'?

■ Activity

Study Sources 11 and 12. Answer these questions using the sources and your own knowledge.

1 What were the main similarities and differences between British rule in India and in South Africa?

2 What do you think most British members of the Indian Civil Service believed to be the main reasons for their work?

3 What were the main reasons for the Glen Grey Act in South Africa?

4 What light does your answer to Question 2 throw on the main reasons for the expansion of the British Empire between 1870 and 1914?

Chapter 6

Foreign policy 1890–1914
'Eat or be eaten'

▲ Summer 1914 and the Royal Navy shows off its might to its international rivals – not least Germany. The Spithead Review, Portsmouth.

'Eat and be eaten' is the great law of political as well as animated nature. The nations of the earth are divided into the sheep and the wolves – the fat and defenceless against the hungry and strong.'

Lord Salisbury in an article for the magazine
The Saturday Review

Introduction

In the 1890s Britain had many enemies, particularly France and Russia. Indeed, her successes as an empire-builder made her unpopular with most European countries. This unpopularity was at its worst during the Boer War of 1899–1902. The term 'isolation' – sometimes 'splendid isolation' – has often been used to describe Britain's position at this time. However, important changes took place between 1902 and 1914. Britain linked herself more closely to a number of nations, especially France, because she was worried by German aggression. In 1914, allied with her recent enemies France and Russia, Britain went to war with Germany. This chapter explains how and why these changes took place. It also explains why the Liberal government declared war on Germany, despite a great commitment to peace at all levels within the Liberal Party.

Key questions

- What were the main reasons for the enmity of (a) France and (b) Russia towards Britain between 1880 and 1902.

- To what extent was British foreign policy in these years dominated by imperial issues?

- How isolated was Britain in 1902 and how splendid was this isolation?

- How and why did Britain change its policies towards Europe between 1902 and 1914?

- Why did Asquith's Liberal government lead Britain into the First World War?

Influences on British foreign policy

A few key facts shaped British foreign policy during the nineteenth century. Britain was an island which, before the invention of aeroplanes, was easy to defend against any enemy as long as Britain had a strong navy.

She was also the world's leading trading nation with a large Empire. The prosperity and security of this Empire depended on continued peace and free trade.

Britain, therefore, aimed to have an unbeatable navy and to keep out of European alliances which might draw her into a European war. There were exceptions to that general rule, e.g. when one nation threatened to dominate the whole of the continent, as Napoleon had done from 1795 to 1815; or when a nation threatened a special British interest, as Russia did in 1854.

This concern about a single dominating European power made British governments determined that the nearest coastline to Britain – that of Northern France, Belgium and the Netherlands – should not come under the control of a major power; hence British guarantees to Belgium in 1839.

Salisbury's approach to foreign policy

Salisbury preferred to be his own Foreign Secretary. He combined the two posts until late in his career. Not until 1900 did he hand over the Foreign Office to Lord Lansdowne.

Salisbury was as pessimistic about foreign affairs as he was about home matters (see Chapter 3). 'Whatever happens will be for the worse, and therefore it is our interest that as little should happen as possible', he commented to a colleague in 1879. He realized that Britain could no longer dominate the world as she had a generation earlier and had to adapt to a world where economically the USA and Germany were increasingly powerful. He was very cautious. Though a strong defender of British interests, he believed that these were best safeguarded by a patient search for acceptable compromises, rather than by sabre-rattling. He once described his foreign policy as punting leisurely down the river of events, occasionally putting out the pole to avoid a collision with the banks. This analogy is much quoted but, though it gives a good impression of the appearance of British policy, it is misleading about Salisbury himself. He was anything but a leisurely Foreign Secretary. He worked incredibly hard, long hours and kept in frequent touch by personal letter with the other European leaders. While he was in office, the British Empire grew faster than at any time in its history. Yet, thanks to his skills and unceasing industriousness, he kept Britain at peace with all her European neighbours, immensely irritated though they were by her continuing imperial successes.

1886–1892 Salisbury and the European Powers

In 1886, Salisbury's major concern was the hostility of France, which considered that Britain's occupation of Egypt in 1882 was not only unjustified but a serious blow to French influence and prestige in North Africa. Having half-heartedly considered withdrawing British troops from Egypt and deciding against this, Salisbury set out to strengthen links with the Triple Alliance of Germany, Austria and Italy. The secret Mediterranean treaties of 1887, the first with Italy and the second with Austria, were the result. The treaty with Italy was mainly directed against France. Italy and Britain agreed to joint action to prevent the growth of French influence in North Africa. The one with Austria was mainly anti-Russian. Britain and Austria agreed to act together in the Balkans and the Eastern Mediterranean, should Russia try to expand in those areas. These treaties were known only to Lord Salisbury's Cabinet and to the Queen.

With Germany, Salisbury had an uneasy relationship. On the one hand he refused an offer from Bismarck of an alliance against France. In Salisbury's opinion, it offered Britain much less than Germany, and, anyway, one could never be certain what Bismarck was plotting. On the other hand, he agreed to exchange the North Sea island of Heligoland in return for Germany ending its claim to the island of Zanzibar, off the coast of East Africa.

To ensure Britain's continuing ability to keep free from European alliances, he increased naval building so that the British fleet remained at least as big as the combined fleets of her two main rivals (the 'two-power standard').

1895–1902 Caution in a hostile world

When he returned to power in 1895 after the Liberal interlude of 1892–1895, Salisbury was, if anything, even more cautious.

The world was becoming a more dangerous place. The young German Kaiser Wilhelm II, was pursuing a more aggressive policy, but in an unpredictable way, and France and Russia had signed a formal defensive alliance in 1894.

Worried by trends in Europe, Salisbury refused to be provoked by angry American gestures because of a boundary dispute between Venezuela and British Guiana. Like Palmerston, he accepted that the New World was an American sphere of influence and allowed the dispute to be settled by an international inquiry. He also withdrew, in 1901, Britain's claim to share with the USA the task of building the Panama Canal.

In the Near East, another massacre by the Turks, this time in Armenia in 1895, turned British public opinion against supporting the Turks against Russia.

■ Think about

Remind yourself of the geography of the eastern Mediterranean (see map on page 35).

The construction of the Suez Canal in 1869 had made the region particularly important to Britain since the quickest sea-route to India ran through the eastern Mediterranean and the Suez Canal. The security of the Canal was the main reason for the British occupation of Egypt. The Turkish Empire was weak and getting weaker. Russia was after Constantinople, while Italy desired colonies in North Africa. Austria wanted to hinder Russian expansion, while the French sought compensation in North Africa for the losses they had suffered in Egypt.

▶ Why do think Salisbury signed the Mediterranean treaties?

▶ Could Britain's essential interests in the region have been better defended?

Salisbury tried but failed to persuade the Great Powers to agree to put pressure on the Turkish government to reform. He refused to agree to an Austrian request that the Mediterranean agreements should be strengthened into a specific military alliance to defend Constantinople against a Russian attack. Austria then allowed the treaty to lapse.

The effect of these events was to make Britain's occupation of Egypt even more important to her position in the Eastern Mediterranean and to the defence of the sea-route to India. Salisbury therefore accepted that, to improve the security of Egypt, the Sudan should be conquered even though this would further damage Britain's relations with France. Consequently, in 1898, General Kitchener not only destroyed the Sudanese army at Omdurman but forced the French to withdraw from Fashoda (see page 88). Anglo-French relations fell to a new low from which they did not recover for another six years.

China and the final imperial Scramble

In the Far East, the European Scramble for empires had reached its final phase. The decaying Chinese Empire was the prize. With a population of about 400 million, it looked as if it would be the richest imperial prize of all. Britain, who had already established a strong presence along the vast Yangtze valley, favoured an 'open door' policy of encouraging free trade with China and avoiding an African-style carve-up by European powers.

Germany and Russia, however, were much hungrier. Germany was now pursuing a '*Weltpolitik*' to gain her 'place in the sun', the colonial empire which properly reflected her position as one of the world's most powerful nations. In 1898 she seized Kiaochow and much of the Shantung peninsula. Simultaneously, Russia was pressing into Manchuria. For her part, Britain gained the less important Weihaiwei.

In 1900 there was a desperate uprising in China against foreign involvement. This 'Boxer Rising' led to the murder of a German official and of thousands of Christian missionaries and their converts. In response, an international force occupied and looted Peking. The influence of Europeans in China increased further but without the European powers coming to blows.

The search for new allies

The activities of Russia and Germany in the Far East, followed by the massive international criticism of Britain caused by the Boer War, made some members of Salisbury's government anxious to find new allies. Some, notably Joseph Chamberlain and Lord Lansdowne, were keen to reach an understanding with Germany. Their efforts failed, however, because Germany was not prepared to act with Britain to oppose Russian expansion in the Far East.

Instead in 1902, Lansdowne signed an alliance with Japan. Both countries agreed to remain neutral if the other went to war against one other opponent but would come to the each other's aid, if either were attacked by a second opponent. Lansdowne believed Britain needed the alliance because the combined fleets of Russia and France in the Far East outnumbered Britain's, and Russia's Asian ambitions were a serious threat to the British Empire in Asia. For the Japanese government, the alliance with Britain was desirable because Russia was the most serious obstacle to Japan's expansionist plans for Korea and Manchuria.

■ Historical debate

Germany's '*Weltpolitik*'

The German government's decision in 1897 to pursue a 'Worldpolicy' led to the building of a new fleet and demands for colonies in Africa and Asia. Some historians, like F. Fischer, believe that *Weltpolitik* was a carefully considered policy which was the main cause of the outbreak of war in 1914 – an event which the German government welcomed. Others see it as vaguer: aggressive in an unpredictable way. The result was equally bad. France, Russia and Britain felt threatened, so moved closer together and increased their military spending. Germany then felt more encircled and more threatened, and so became even more aggressive herself.

▲ China c. 1890, the scramble for Chinese trade.

An end to splendid isolation?

Lansdowne himself regarded the Anglo-Japanese Treaty as marking a significant policy change. When he recommended the alliance to the House of Lords, he appealed to them not to let 'their judgements to be swayed by any musty formulas or old-fashioned superstitions as to the desirability of pursuing a policy of isolation'. The Liberal opposition also regarded it as a major change from the traditional principles of British foreign policy and condemned it as such. Salisbury himself had great reservations about it (see Source 3) but, as Lansdowne had the support of most of the Cabinet and he himself was about to retire, he let it happen.

Historians have disagreed about the significance of the Anglo-Japanese Treaty. These disagreements stem largely from their different interpretations of Salisbury's policy of 'isolation'.

Source 3

There is the isolation of those who are weak...and there is, on the other hand, the isolation of those who do not wish to be entangled in any complications and will hold themselves free in every respect... Our isolation is not an isolation of weakness; it is deliberately chosen, this freedom to act as we choose in any circumstances which may arise.

George Goschen First Lord of the Admiralty in 1896

Source 4

Salisbury, who had long despised and denounced what he called the 'sterile' and 'dangerous' policy of isolation, was stuck with a label for his non-aligned but heavily engaged foreign policy, which was far more complex, subtle and intelligent than crude isolationism.

Roberts, *Lord Salisbury, Victorian Titan*, 1999

Source 5

Salisbury appreciated how Britain was always intimately involved in the European balance of power and could not stand isolated, splendidly or ignominiously, apart from it...Isolation, or even a situation in which other Powers combined against Britain to strip her of trade and colonies, was in fact Salisbury's worst fear.... No Power that needed to protect its communications to India via the Mediterranean, and which had important outposts in Gibraltar, Malta, Cyprus and Egypt, could ever be entirely isolated from the antagonisms and power politics of the Continent...

'Lord Salisbury has no reason to think that England runs at present any special danger of being isolated', he reassured the Queen in 1888. The term 'isolation' was consistently used by him as something to be strenuously avoided rather than implying anything desirable let alone splendid.

Roberts, *Lord Salisbury, Victorian Titan*, 1999

Note

The origins of the term 'Splendid Isolation'

- On 9 and 10 January 1896, after the Jameson Raid crisis, *The Times* newspaper printed comments from the European press about how isolated Britain had become.
- In a debate in the Canadian parliament, a minister, George Foster, commented how 'the great Mother Empire stands splendidly isolated in Europe'.
- On 18 January, Joseph Chamberlain in an after-dinner speech said to loud cheers that 'the Empire stands secure in the strength of her own resources...in the abundant loyalty of her children from one end of the Empire to another'. A *Times* sub-editor attached the heading 'Splendid Isolation' to the report of Chamberlain's speech and the term then attached itself and has remained attached to Salisbury's foreign policy as a whole.

■ Think about

▶ Why was there so much talk in Britain about isolation between 1896 and 1902?

■ Questions

1 What does George Goschen mean in Source 3 when he speaks of isolation being deliberately chosen? Was it?

2 From Source 4 what do you think would have been Salisbury's attitude to the term 'splendid isolation'?

3 Why, according to Roberts, was Salisbury so determined to avoid isolation?

4 What measures did he take between 1886 and 1902 to avoid it? With what success?

Source 6

PARTNERS.

Britannia. "AFTER ALL, MY DEAR, WE NEEDN'T TROUBLE OURSELVES ABOUT THE OTHERS."
Colonia. "NO ; WE CAN ALWAYS DANCE TOGETHER, YOU AND I !"

■ Think about

▶ Look at Source 6, which appeared in *Punch* in 1901. It shows Britannia, Colonia, Germany, France and Russia. Britannia is saying 'After all, my dear, we needn't trouble ourselves about the others'.

▶ What does this cartoon suggest about *Punch*'s attitude to the international situation in 1901?

▶ Was it more or less isolationist than Salisbury?

■ Activity

In 1964, the historian Zara Steiner declared that 'Splendid isolation is a cliché which must be abandoned'. *The Historical Journal*

Draw up a table with two columns. In one, record all the evidence and specific examples you can find in this chapter and Chapter 5 which suggest that 'splendid isolation' is an appropriate description for the foreign policies pursued by Salisbury. In the other, record any examples or assessments of policy which suggest it is inappropriate.

How far do you agree with Steiner's opinion?

Document exercise: The significance of the Anglo-Japanese Treaty of 1902

Source A
The Treaty seen as revolutionary

The Treaty (since it increased British obligations through a formal agreement) was revolutionary, a departure... from the principles of Salisbury.

Temperley and Penson, 1938, quoted in Goodlad,
British Foreign and Imperial Policy, 1865–1919, 1999

Source B
An alternative view of the Treaty

The Alliance did not mean the end of British isolation; rather it confirmed it. Isolation meant aloofness from the European balance of power; and this was now more possible than before.

Taylor, *The Struggle for Mastery in Europe*, 1954

Source C
The effects of the Treaty: another historian's view

There is less certainty whether the Anglo-Japanese Alliance of 1902 should be regarded as marking the end of Britain's 'Splendid Isolation'. In one sense it obviously did. Britain had now abandoned her traditional policy of avoiding 'entangling alliances' in peacetime...On the other hand the alliance was restricted in scope: it was a regional pact, limited to the Far East. Historians, including A.J.P. Taylor, have therefore argued that the alliance did not impair Britain's freedom to maintain her isolation from her continental rivals. This is not quite accurate. In 1903, Britain as an ally of Japan, feared that she might become involved in a war against France, as an ally of Russia. The commitment to Japan acted consequently as a catalyst to the negotiations for an entente with France.

Lowe, *Rivalry and Accord International relations 1870–1914*, 1988

■ Examination-style questions

1 Comprehension in context
Explain what the 'principles of Salisbury' were in Source A.

2 Comparing the sources
How and why do the authors of Sources A and B differ in their interpretations of the significance of the Anglo-Japanese Treaty?

3 Assessing the sources
Explain the claim in Source C that the Anglo-Japanese Treaty had European consequences?

4 Making judgements
Using these sources and your own knowledge, explain whether you think that 'The Anglo-Japanese Alliance of 1902 should be regarded as 'marking the end of Britain's 'Splendid isolation.' (Source C)

Settling imperial issues with France and Russia

The Anglo-French Entente of 1904

Lansdowne's last major achievement as foreign secretary was the Anglo-French Entente, also known as the *Entente Cordiale*, of 1904. From this 'understanding' of 1904 developed the further fateful 'understandings' and military agreements, which would bring Britain into the European war of 1914. In 1904, however, it was, from the British side at least, an agreement aimed simply at reducing friction between the two countries on imperial issues. As Sir Eyre Crowe, a senior foreign office official, put it: '[It showed] the general tendency of British Governments to take advantage of every opportunity to approach more closely to the ideal condition of living in honourable peace with all other states.'

After the Fashoda crisis, French public opinion as reflected in the newspapers became extremely hostile to Britain. The British Press was hardly more pro-French. A much publicized official visit by Edward VII to Paris followed by a return visit to London by the French President Loubet and Delcassé, his Foreign Minister, in 1903 won over public opinion on both sides of the Channel.

The actual agreement (or Convention as it was in fact entitled) was signed in April 1904. The most important disputes it dealt with concerned Egypt and Morocco. In return for France giving Britain a free hand in Egypt, Britain did the same for France in Morocco. That Egypt ceased to be an international problem was a major gain for Britain. France's hostility to the British occupation since 1882 had forced the British government to look for allies in the Eastern Mediterranean. It had also limited the ability of the British governor, Lord Cromer (Sir Evelyn Baring), to carry out reforms, especially financial ones. In return, Britain was prepared to suffer some losses in Morocco which was an area where she had trading interests and, because of its position to the south of the Straits of Gibraltar, was strategically important to the sea-route to India.

The Anglo-Russian Entente of 1907

Three years later, a similar kind of agreement was made with Russia by the Liberal Foreign Secretary, Sir Edward Grey. Like the Anglo-French Entente of 1904, the aim was to end friction on imperial matters, which for Britain and Russia were all in Asia, Afghanistan, Tibet, and Persia. Russia was ready for this agreement because she had suffered a humiliating defeat by Japan in the Russo-Japanese War of 1904–1905. This defeat and the Anglo-Japanese Alliance ended Russian ambitions in the Far East. The Russian government turned its attention instead westwards towards Europe and the Balkans. There it faced opposition from Austria and Germany – hence the desire to end rivalries with Britain.

- As far as Afghanistan was concerned, The Russians agreed not to interfere and to leave it a British sphere of influence.

- As for Tibet, both nations agreed not to interfere, leaving China to re-conquer Tibet in 1910.

- Persia was the most important area. Russia had been pressing down on Persia from the north in search of a warm-water port. Britain's main concern was to prevent Russia reaching the sea, since this could create a new threat to her sea-route to India. Persia was divided into three (without consulting the Persians). The Russians gained a large northern zone, but with no access to the sea; the British a smaller zone in the east; and the rest was left neutral.

Note

Edward VII in Paris in 1903

Edward, who became king when he was 60, pursued pleasure, both respectable and disreputable, energetically. He loved travelling. He also loved France and spoke French fluently. When he first arrived on his Paris visit of 1903, mainly hostile crowds shouted 'Vive Fachoda' at him, but after some friendly, fluent and humorous speeches, they shouted 'Vive notre roi' instead.

Note

The Convention in fact dealt with disputes in a range of other areas too: Madagascar, Newfoundland, Siam, the New Hebrides and West Africa.

■ **Think about**

▶ Why was Britain prepared to accept losses in Morocco despite its strategic importance?

▼ The division of Persia, 1907.

Relations with Germany

Britain's natural ally?

In 1900, Germany appeared to many Britons as Britain's natural ally. Joseph Chamberlain wanted a combination of Britain, Germany and the USA to dominate and keep peace in the world. He described it as 'a new triple alliance between the Teutonic race and the two great branches of the Anglo-Saxon race'. Lansdowne too wished to give priority to Germany as a possible ally. 'We should use,' he wrote, 'every effort to maintain, and if we can, to strengthen the good relations between the Queen's government and the German Emperor.'

There were understandable reasons for these pro-German attitudes. After all, France and Russia were Britain's most serious rivals. The German Kaiser was the Queen's grandson. Though the German economy was growing faster than Britain's, Anglo-German trade was important to both countries. Britain purchased more goods from Germany than any other nation, while 20 per cent of Germany's imports came from the British Empire. World trade was growing so fast that there seemed room enough for both countries to prosper.

Britain was more tolerant towards the empire-building of Germany in Africa and China than towards France's or Russia's, because she considered it less threatening. Germany, however, interpreted Britain's friendly attitude as a sign of weakness rather than of strength.

The German naval-building programme

What made an Anglo-German alliance impossible was the German naval-building programme. This began in 1898 as part of the *Weltpolitik* of the Kaiser and his advisers. Germany could not be a genuine world power without a world-class navy.

Tirpitz, who became head of the German Admiralty in 1896, planned his new navy to challenge the Royal Navy. By the Navy Law of 1900, he aimed for a fleet of 38 new battleships. For Britain, this was a very worrying development since Germany already had one of the largest and best-equipped armies in Europe. Britain, in contrast, had a proportionately small army. (A large army was considered unnecessary as long as the Royal Navy controlled Britain's coastal waters.) If, however, Tirpitz succeeded in making his new fleet as strong as the Royal Navy, Britain would be under threat of invasion for the first time since the Spanish Armada.

The First Sea Lord and head of the Royal Navy was Admiral Sir John Fisher. He possessed colossal drive and determination and met the German challenge head on. He concentrated more of the navy in home waters and told his experts to design for him the most technically advanced battleship which would make Tirpitz' new fleet immediately out of date.

The result was HMS *Dreadnought*, completed in 1905. Though heavily armoured, *Dreadnought*'s high-pressure steam-engines gave it a top speed of 21 knots and made it the fastest battleship afloat. Its ten new 12-inch guns fired further than those of any rival. Consequently, it could catch and destroy any enemy ship without danger to itself.

The *Dreadnought* was a brilliant piece of engineering but it failed to deter the Germans. If the British could make dreadnoughts, so could they. Tirpitz had his own dreadnoughts designed, and accelerated his building programme. In 1908 he set a target of 58 dreadnoughts by 1920. Another problem for the British was

Note

The Kaiser and Britain

The Kaiser was a weak, complicated character with a love–hate relationship with Britain. His mother was Queen Victoria's eldest daughter, but he and Edward VII personally loathed each other. He greatly admired Britain, and was a frequent visitor. In return he wanted to be admired and respected by the British. Famous for his lack of consistency, he yet gave sustained support to Tirpitz' naval-building programme. He knew it upset the British but thought it would win their respect.

that if HMS *Dreadnought* made all other battleships obsolete, that included British ones too. Once rivals began producing their own dreadnoughts, Britain lost the big advantage in sheer numbers of ships, which she had created by the two-power standard.

Then followed a race to build the most dreadnoughts. In 1909 Fisher helped the journalist J.L. Garvin whip up a campaign to put pressure on a reluctant Liberal government to build eight dreadnoughts rather than four. 'We want eight and we won't wait' was the campaign's slogan and eventually Fisher got his eight. By now it was clear that the naval race was pushing Britain into a closer anti-German alliance with France, and the German government would not end the race. On the contrary, the Kaiser gave Tirpitz his enthusiastic support.

The last chance of ending this madness came in 1911–1912. The British government let it be known that it would settle for a battleship ratio with Germany of 16:10 rather than 2:1. In 1912 it sent Haldane to Berlin to discuss how tension between Britain and Germany could be lessened. Unfortunately Haldane's mission came to nothing because the German government insisted that there could be no agreement between the two countries unless Britain promised to remain neutral in a European war between Germany and France or Russia. Worse still, the mission caused Tirpitz to think that the British were wearying of the race and that, if he accelerated again, he could gain a decisive lead. So the race continued, despite talk by Winston Churchill, First Lord of the Admiralty, of a 'naval holiday' in 1913.

If the race had a winner, it was Fisher. By 1914 he was having super-dreadnoughts like the *Queen Elizabeth* built, which were oil-fired, more heavily armoured, faster still with more powerful guns. Tirpitz, who had had to accept cuts in navy funding in 1913 and 1914 so that the German army could be strengthened, opposed the war in 1914 because he knew that by then the Royal Navy had achieved a significant advantage.

Although the naval race played no direct part in the events that brought Britain into The First World War in the summer of 1914, it was the main reason why the British government and public had come to regard Germany as by far their most dangerous enemy.

Sir Edward Grey at the Foreign Office

Sir Edward Grey was Foreign Minister from 1905 to 1916. Few ministers have served at the Foreign Office for so long or in such difficult circumstances. Grey came from a famous Liberal family. He had served at the Foreign Office under Rosebery in Gladstone's last ministry and was the obvious candidate for the Foreign Office when the Liberals came to power in 1905. Quietly confident in his own judgement and respected by his colleagues, he directed foreign policy with little interference from the Cabinet.

Compared to Salisbury, Grey consulted his officials more frequently. The Senior Clerk from 1905 to 1912, later Assistant Under-Secretary, was Eyre Crowe. Though Crowe had a German mother and wife, he was strongly anti-German. He was convinced as early as 1907 that the German government was bent on dominating Europe, if necessary by force, and convinced Grey that it was vital for Britain to stand by France against German aggression. Equally anti-German were two Foreign Office chiefs, Charles Hardinge (1905–1910) and Arthur Nicholson (1910–1916).

■ Biography

Sir John Fisher (1841–1920)
Born in Ceylon and entering the navy at the age of 13, Fisher saw active service during the Crimean War, and in China and Egypt. He made his name as a gunnery expert and joined the Board of the Admiralty in 1892. In 1904 he reached the top as First Sea Lord, a position he held until his retirement in 1910.

Fisher was a man of exceptional boldness, energy and vision. His responses to the German naval-building programme were intelligent, dynamically executed and ultimately successful.

The government called him out of retirement in 1914. He had the satisfaction of the victory of the Falkland Islands in 1914 before resigning in 1915 over the disastrous expedition to the Dardanelles, which he had opposed.

■ Think about

Churchill summed up Britain's thinking about the naval race when he said that while the Royal Navy was essential to Britain, the German navy was for Germany a luxury.

▶ What do you think Churchill meant by this?
▶ How do you think Tirpitz might have responded?

Under Grey, the Foreign Office view was that if Germany had ever been Britain's natural ally, that time was past. It treated the Entente of 1904 less as an understanding and more as an alliance, and allowed secret military conversations between British and French officers to take place.

Trouble spot 1: Morocco

The Kaiser in Tangier 1905

In 1905 the German Foreign Office wanted to prove that the recent Anglo-French Entente was a feeble thing. It calculated that it could bully the French government and that Britain would leave France in the lurch. The Kaiser appeared in Tangier on horseback on 31 March 1905 and made a fiery anti-French speech. Morocco, he demanded, must be independent and he would defend German interests. An international conference must be called to settle Morocco's future.

A worried French government agreed to the conference, even though that meant the resignation of their Foreign Minister, Delcassé. The conference was held at Algeciras in 1906. Grey agreed with his officials that Germany must not succeed in humiliating France, so, far from leaving France in the lurch, Britain united all the delegates, with the exception of Austria, to back France against Germany. The conference agreed that France should control the Moroccan banks and police. Germany felt humiliated.

Agadir 1911

In 1911 there was unrest in Morocco. France sent in troops. This was in breach of the Algeciras agreement of 1906, so once again the German Foreign Office decided to be aggressive. It would 'thump the table', with the aim of making imperial gains at the expense of France. If Morocco was to remain French, then the French should hand over their Congo colony to Germany. On 1 July, the German gunboat *Panther* steamed into the Moroccan port of Agadir.

Britain treated this as another case of Germany attempting to bully France. On 21 July, Lloyd George made clear the position of the British government. Speaking at the Mansion House in London, he said: 'Britain would not tolerate being treated as if she were of no account in the cabinet of nations…Peace at that price would be a humiliation intolerable for a great country like ours to endure'.

The tension in the summer of 1911 was high, but agreement was eventually reached in November. France should have a protectorate over Morocco. In return Germany gained a small slice of the French Congo.

The consequences of the Moroccan crisis of 1911 were damaging. Once again Germany felt humiliated by the Anglo-French alliance. Her government felt increasingly hemmed in by her enemies and more ready to look to war in order to break out to gain her 'place in the sun'. A more anti-German government led by Poincare came to power in France. In Britain, while the government tried in vain to achieve better relations with Berlin through the Haldane mission, public opinion became even more anti-German.

▼ Morocco in 1912.

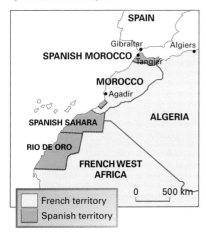

SPAIN

Gibraltar   Algiers

SPANISH MOROCCO Tangier

MOROCCO
• Agadir

ALGERIA

SPANISH SAHARA

RIO DE ORO

FRENCH WEST AFRICA

0   500 km

☐ French territory
☐ Spanish territory

■ Activity

German attitudes to Britain had changed significantly since 1900. With a partner, work out:

1 the reasons why Germany could reasonably regard Britain as her natural ally;

2 the reasons why Germany could by 1911 regard Britain as her enemy.

What was Germany trying to achieve in Morocco in 1905–1906 and in 1911?

What effects did these crises have on Anglo-German relations?

Trouble spot 2: The Balkans

Introduction

The Great Powers had solved the last Balkan crisis to their satisfaction by the Treaty of Berlin in 1878. Germany, Austria and Britain had combined to prevent Russia and her Balkan allies from making large gains at the expense of the decaying Turkish Empire.

However, the 1878 settlement had real weaknesses which soon became apparent. It assumed, wrongly, that the Turkish Empire could survive. It left Balkan nations like Bulgaria and Serbia unsatisfied. It did nothing to reduce Russian ambitions in the area. Between 1908 and 1914, the 1878 settlement fell apart with catastrophic results.

The Bosnian crisis of 1908

In 1908, a revolution led by the Young Turk movement seriously weakened the government of Sultan Abdul Hamid. The nations with interests in the Balkans all tried to use this crisis to strengthen their positions. Russia sought to open the Dardanelles to its navy; Austria, previously administering Bosnia on behalf of the Sultan, annexed it; Serbia, which wanted to unite with Bosnia, demanded an outlet to the Adriatic as compensation for Austria's annexation; Bulgaria proclaimed its independence; Crete demanded union with Greece.

Grey suggested a Great Power conference. Austria refused to participate and, supported by Germany, forced Turkey to agree to the annexation of Bosnia. When Russia appeared ready to go to war over Serbia's demand for compensation, Germany made it clear that she would support Austria. On this occasion, Russia backed down. In a similar situation in 1914, remembering this 1908 setback, she did not.

The Bosnian crisis was a temporary triumph for Austria and Germany. It left Serbia and Russia bitter and the Balkans more unstable. Britain became worried by the extent of German influence over both Austria and Turkey. An ambitious German plan to build a railway from Belgrade in the Balkans to Baghdad (close to the border of the Turkish Empire with Persia) caused the Foreign Office particular unease. After 1908, Grey's policy was to try wherever possible to prevent further conflict in the Balkans and to reduce German influence in Constantinople.

The Balkan Crises of 1911–1912

In 1911, Italy attacked and conquered the Turkish province of Tripolitania in North Africa. This setback to the Young Turk government in Constantinople proved, as in 1908, a trigger for other anti-Turkish risings in the Balkans. The Muslim Albanians rose in revolt and in 1912 the Bulgarians, Serbs and Greeks declared war on Turkey. In this First Balkan War, the Turks were defeated and driven back almost to the edge of Constantinople.

Grey acted decisively in this crisis. He persuaded the ambassadors of all the interested nations to meet under his chairmanship in London. By the Treaty of London in 1913, most of the gains made by the Balkan nations against the Turks were confirmed. However, rather than agree to Serbia taking over Albania and gaining an outlet to the sea, Grey supported the demand of Germany and Austria that the independence of Albania should be recognized and the Serbs thwarted.

Characteristics of the Balkans

'The Balkans' (Turkish for 'mountains') is the name given to a mountainous area of south-east Europe. It contains five main ethnic groups – Albanians, Greeks, Bulgarians, Turks, and Southern Slavs. The Southern Slavs include Serbs, Croats, Slovenes and Montenegrins.

The main religions are Orthodox Christian, Catholic Christian and Islam. The Muslim Turks conquered the whole of the previously Christian area in the fourteenth and fifteenth centuries and stayed in control for the next three centuries. However in 1830, the Greeks won their independence and, from then on, the various ethnic groups showed themselves ready to fight the Turks and each other to gain their independence.

Mountainous though the area is, it has few natural barriers and the ethnic groups are scattered. In the nineteenth century it was a trouble-spot mainly because the Great Powers of Russia, Austria and Turkey, propped up by Britain, had particular interests in the area. In the late twentieth century it became a trouble-spot again because of the deep-seated ethnic rivalries which surfaced with the death of Marshal Tito.

Grey's diplomacy kept the Great Powers at peace but not the Balkans. Barely a month after the signing of the Treaty of London, Serbia, Greece and Romania went to war against Bulgaria (the Second Balkan War). After two months, Bulgaria sued for peace and, by the Treaty of Bucharest, had to accept severe territorial losses. The main gainer was Serbia, whose army had proved the most effective in the two Balkan Wars and which now looked to act as the champion of the Slav minorities still within the Austrian Empire. So concerned was the Austrian government about the successes of Serbia that, in 1913, it briefly considered going to war immediately as a preventative strike against the bumptious Serbs.

After the London conference of 1913, there was no attempt by the Great Powers to meet again to consider the problems of the Balkans. The main lesson that Austria learnt from the events of 1912–1913 was that the Great Powers were unlikely to have the combined will to defend her interests against Serbia. Her best defence, therefore, was likely to be her own strength and, if Russia were to support Serbia, she would, as in 1908, have to turn to Germany. She did just that in July 1914, in response to the Serb backed assassination of the Archduke Franz Ferdinand. When the German response was to encourage an Austrian attack on Serbia, Grey could not prevent the escalation of this third Balkan crisis into a European war.

■ Think about

▶ Why do you think Grey acted as he did in response to the First Balkan War?

▶ Why was the Treaty of London so ineffective?

▶ Why do you think the Great powers did not meet again in response to the Second Balkan War?

▶ The Balkans in 1914.

■ Think about

Check the geographical position of Bosnia on the map. Most of its inhabitants were South Slavs. The Austrian Empire had a large Slav population, which showed signs of wishing to separate from Austria. It was in Bosnia that the Archduke Franz Ferdinand (heir to the Austrian throne) was assassinated by a Bosnian student assisted by Serbians.

▶ Why do you think Austria took possession of Bosnia from the Turks in 1908?

▶ Why were the Serbs so angry that they were able to get away with doing so?

■ Activity   KEY SKILLS

Discover through the internet and databases 6 substantial sources, including at least 2 foreign ones, on the origins of the First World War, and evaluate them in the light of your own knowledge. Then use them, with pages 100-107, in a written evaluation of the foreign policy of Sir Edward Grey.

When and why did Asquith's government decide to declare war on Germany?

Taken by surprise

The summer crisis of 1914, which led to the outbreak of the First World War, took the British government and British public opinion completely by surprise. Relations with Germany seemed better than they had been for some years. The two countries had reached agreements over problems in the Near East and Africa. Britain was clearly winning the naval race. The main worries of the government were the suffragettes, industrial strife and, above all, the situation in Ulster.

Grey did not realize immediately how dangerous the Sarajevo assassination was. That realization dawned when Austria decided nearly a month later to present her ultimatum to Serbia. Then, too late, he tried to repeat his 1913 success by organizing a Great Powers conference which would prevent a Balkan squabble becoming a European war. To the increasingly anguished appeals from Russia and from France between 24 July and 3 August to declare Britain's whole-hearted support for her Entente partners, he gave the coolest of responses. The Ententes, he said, were understandings not alliances and Britain had binding commitments neither to France nor to Russia. Grey took this non-committal line since the Cabinet was divided.

The debate within the Liberal government

The Liberal Party had a proud anti-war tradition which it inherited from Gladstone. War was a dreadful thing. Britain should use her influence to prevent war wherever possible by acting in concert with other nations. However, Britain should also steer clear of hostile alliances which might draw her into a war which was not of her making. There was, therefore, a strong impulse within the Liberal Party to stay neutral.

In the 11 nightmare days that divided the Austrian ultimatum to Serbia from Britain's declaration of war with Germany, three groups emerged within the Liberal Party.

- The first, which included Asquith, Grey and Churchill, realized from an early stage that Britain would have to go to war in support of France. They believed that a victorious Germany dominating Europe would be so dangerous to the vital interests of Britain and the British Empire that Britain had to fight alongside France and Russia.
- The second, which included ministers like Morley and Burns, insisted that Britain must remain neutral. They believed that the costs of war would be so great that Britain should stay out even if that meant a German victory. Both Morley and Burns resigned once they realized that the Cabinet was in favour of war.
- The third was much the largest and was made up of those who began by believing that war could and should be avoided but by 3 August had changed their minds. Within this group, Lloyd George was the most important figure.

Within the Cabinet, this is how the mood changed

As late as 27 July, Churchill noted that at least three-quarters of the Cabinet were determined not to be drawn into a European war. On 29 July, Grey tried but failed to get some general statement of support for France. On 31 July two Cabinet ministers, Morley and Simon, tried but failed to secure a declaration that under no circumstances would Britain go to war. Grey made it clear that he would resign if such a declaration were agreed.

Even though, on 1 August, Germany declared war on Russia, the Cabinet still hesitated. On 2 August the Conservative opposition went public in favour of war. Bonar Law, the Conservative leader, wrote to Asquith. 'It would be fatal to the honour and security of the United Kingdom to hesitate in supporting France and Russia at this present juncture.' Not until 3 August, however, did the mood of the Cabinet shift towards war. The Germans were marching into Luxembourg and would soon invade Belgium. The Cabinet agreed that Grey should appeal to Parliament to support Britain's entry into the war, which he did in a memorable speech. Apart from a handful of Liberal and Labour MPs, the Commons proved overwhelmingly in favour of war, as was public opinion.

What of Lloyd George?

The anti-war Liberals looked to Lloyd George to lead them. His sympathies were pro-French, but, at the beginning of the crisis, he believed that Germany favoured peace and he was worried that, should France and Russia manage to defeat Germany, a victorious Russia would be extremely dangerous to Britain's interests in Asia. Not until 3 August did he declare himself in favour of war and used the German invasion of Belgium as his justification. However, his lover Frances Stevenson, who was with him during the critical days, believed that 'his mind was made up from the first, that he knew we would have to go in, and that the invasion of Belgium was, to be cynical, a heaven-sent opportunity for supporting a declaration of war.'

Grigg, *Lloyd George: From Peace to War 1912–1916*, 1997

Military discussions with France 1906–1914

1906 Haldane's army reforms improve the ability of the British army to fight in a European war alongside France. British and French officers begin secret 'conversations' about fighting together against Germany.

1912–1913 Further military conversations lead to the agreement that, in the event of a European war, the British fleet should defend the Channel, the French the Mediterranean.

Consequently, if Britain stayed neutral in the event of a war between France and Germany, the French would face serious gaps in their defences, especially along their northern coast. The extent of these commitments was known only to Grey, Asquith and a few other ministers.

Timeline

1914

28 June Archduke Franz Ferdinand assassinated in Sarajevo.

23 July Austrian ultimatum to Serbia.

24 July Russia asks Britain to declare solidarity with Russia and France – British Cabinet divided, no commitment offered.

26 July Grey suggests a Great Power conference in London.

27 July Germany turns down the conference suggestion.

28 July Austria declares war on Serbia.

29 July Grey warns Germany not to count on Britain's neutrality and France not to count on Britain's support.

31 July Russia mobilizes. France asks if Britain will fight with them. British Cabinet still divided, no commitment given.

1 August Germany declares war on Russia and puts into action the Schlieffen Plan which meant a rapid attack on France through Belgium.

3 August Germany declares war on France.

4 August Germany invades Belgium and Britain declares war on Germany.

Source 7

THE NEW DIPLOMACY.

Advanced Democrat (to Foreign Secretary). "LOOK HERE, WE'VE DECIDED THAT THIS ISN'T TO BE A PRIVATE ROOM ANY MORE; AND YOU'RE TO PUT YOUR CARDS ON THE TABLE AND THEN WE CAN ALL TAKE A HAND."
Foreign Secretary. "WHAT, AND LET MY OPPONENTS SEE THEM TOO?"

Questions

1 In what ways had the 1904 Entente with France so changed its nature by 1914 that, privately at any rate, Grey knew that Britain was obliged to fight in support of France.

2 What was the Gladstonian tradition of foreign policy, which made so many Liberals unready to consider going to war in 1914?

3 Explain the position of (a) Asquith, (b) Morley and (c) Lloyd George.

4 What was the position of the Conservatives by 2 August?

5 In Source 7, the *Punch* cartoon, who are the Advanced Democrats and in what way are they critical of Grey's methods? Explain whether you think *Punch* is for or against Grey.

Historians disagree about the importance of the German invasion of Belgium

Source 8

Whatever other factors disposed towards British intervention, what brought almost all Liberals round to supporting the war was the German invasion of Belgium.

Clarke, *Hope and Glory, Britain 1900–1990*, 1996

Source 9

Both at the time and subsequently, the belief that Britain went to war for the sake of Belgium was a convenient myth, because to a nation which always likes to feel virtuous it made the decision more idealistic than it actually was....the moral claims of Belgium provided not the reason, but rather the pretext, for Britain's decision to intervene.

The reason for intervention was that the Cabinet, faced with the fact of a formidable German onslaught in the West, came round to the view that Britain's vital interests were threatened; and the Cabinet's view was shared by Parliament.

Grigg, *Lloyd George From Peace to War 1912–1916*, 1997

■ **Think about**

▶ Study Sources 8 and 9. To what extent do they contradict each other?

▶ What does Grigg mean by Britain going to war for the sake of Belgium being 'a convenient myth'?

▶ 'More standing up for brave little Belgium than self-interest'. Comment on this explanation for Britain's declaration of war on Germany in 1914.

Historical debate

Were Grey's strategy and tactics as Foreign Secretary between 1906 and 1914 in Britain's best interests?

Source 10

We felt that to stand aside would mean the domination of Germany; the subordination of France and Russia; the isolation of Britain; the hatred of her both by those who had feared and those who had wished for her intervention in the war; and ultimately that Germany would wield the whole power of the Continent. How would she use it as regards Britain? Could anyone feel comfortable about that question? Could anyone give to it truthfully in his heart anything but a sinister and foreboding answer?

Sir Edward Grey, *Twenty-Five Years*, 1925

Source 11

Profoundly pacific [in favour of peace], determined not to commit Britain irrevocably [without an escape route] he...warned Germany of the consequences of aggression. It was not his fault that his warning went unheeded...Grey pursued the policy of the balance of power consistently and far-sightedly...When the assassination of the Archduke Franz Ferdinand...set in train the events that led to war, Grey with moderation and skill managed to bring a Cabinet profoundly divided at the outset into almost unanimous acceptance of military intervention on the side of France.

Robert Blake in *The Encyclopaedia Britannica*, 1973

Source 12

Our diplomacy has not been guiltless. Secret arrangements, concealed from Parliament and even...from almost all the Cabinet, created, in spite of reiterated [repeated] denials, an obligation suddenly revealed...Yet, though the French knew of our obligations, Sir E. Grey refused, down to the last moment, to inform Germany of the conditions of our neutrality or of our intervention...

Bertrand Russell, one of Britain's leading philosophers, writes to the *Nation* magazine on 15 August 1914. Russell, *Autobiography Vol II 1914–44*, 1968

Bertrand Russell's criticisms of the effects of Grey's secret diplomacy were echoed by other politicians at the time and by later historians like Keith Wilson.

1 In Source 10, Grey gives one main reason for Britain going to war in 1914? What was it? Why was he so fearful for Britain if Germany came to dominate Europe? Do you think his fears were justified?

2 Blake (Source 11) and Russell (Source 12) disagree completely over Grey's handling of the July/August 1914 crisis. In what ways?

3 From your knowledge of the events of June to August 1914, when might Grey have had the most chance of persuading Germany to pause before going to war with Russia and France. Why did he not take such an opportunity?

4 Summarize Lloyd's defence of Grey in Source 13.

5 What were Grey's main strengths and weaknesses as Foreign Secretary between 1906 and 1914?

■ Further reading

John Lowe, *Rivalry and Accord, International Relations 1870-1914*, 1988*

Gordon Martel, *The Origins of the First World War*, 1996*

P. Hayes, *Modern British Foreign Policy, 1880-1939*, 1978

Zara Steiner, *Britain and the Origins of the First World War*, 1977

* Books particularly suitable for students

Source 13

In the year after 1914, Grey's diplomacy was often criticized. Some of the attacks came from German apologists, who in essence said that if they had known that England took the neutrality of Belgium seriously they would have respected it. This is not convincing: it was hard to negotiate with the German leaders about Belgium because they had already made an undertaking in a Treaty that they would respect it, and if they were ready to break the Treaty, they might also break any subsequent engagements they made. Grey was also criticized by the British Left. They wanted the country's policy to be peace-loving and upright...but they had two distinct objectives which were hard to reconcile; they wanted Belgium to be protected, and they did not want England to go to war. They overestimated England's place in the world: it was not at all certain that an English threat of war would have saved Belgium from invasion, and in any case Grey could deliver such a threat in a convincing way only by taking a bellicose [aggressive] attitude that the Left would have found very objectionable.

T.O. Lloyd, writing in 1970, attacks Grey's critics. Lloyd, *Empire to Welfare State, English History 1906–1967*, 1970

Summary

- Between 1886 and 1902, Britain's main enemies were France and Russia. In 1898 Britain and France came close to war over the Upper Nile region while there was an intense rivalry between Britain and Russia in Asia which continued to 1907.
- In these years of rapid imperial expansion by all the major European powers, British foreign policy was primarily concerned with defending her imperial interests.
- The Boer War from 1899 to 1902 had made Britain particularly unpopular and Balfour's government felt dangerously isolated in 1902. However, isolation was never British policy between 1886 and 1902, so the term 'splendid isolation', though often used, does not help our understanding of foreign policy in these years.
- Between 1902 and 1907 Britain formed alliances or understandings with Japan (1902), France (1904) and Russia (1907). Their initial aim was to strengthen the security of the British Empire. However, though Grey denied it, the Entente with France soon had a distinctly anti-German character.
- Asquith's Liberal government took Britain into the war against Germany because Asquith and Grey convinced their colleagues that a German victory over France and Russia, coupled with the new threatening German navy, would place in peril the position of Britain and the British Empire in the world. The invasion of Belgium united most of the Party and country behind them.

Chapter 7

The Labour Movement 1868–1906
A party for the workers

Source 1

A Labour Party Poster of 1910. By then Keir Hardie was the most famous socialist in Britain.

Keir Hardie gets the sack at the age of 9

In 1865, aged 9, Hardie, later to become Britain's first Labour MP, was working for a Glasgow baker. He got 3s 6d (18p) per week, working a 12 hour day with a 7 a.m start. He was the breadwinner for a family living in acute poverty because his father, a shipyard worker, was 'locked out' during an industrial dispute. His mother was in the last stages of pregnancy and his younger brother was dying from a fever. He was 15 minutes late for work two days running. The second time his employer called him to the dining room where he was breakfasting with his family and sacked him. For the rest of his life, Hardie remembered 'the great mahogany table…loaded with dainties' around which the employer's family sat.

Introduction

The industrial revolution had created a new urban working class. The Reform Acts of 1867 and 1884 gave millions of working men the right to vote. For many years most working men voted Liberal. Industrial conflict like the dockers' strike of 1889 helped both to strengthen the trade union movement and foster the sense of need for a separate political party. Socialists like Keir Hardie led the campaign for a separate Labour Party, which eventually emerged in 1906. Between 1918 and 1924, Labour replaced the Liberal Party as the main rival to the Conservatives. Central to the organization of the Labour Party and its main provider of funds was the trade union movement.

Key questions

- What economic and social changes contributed to the desire for a separate political party for working people?
- Why were the trade unions vital in the creation and growth of the Labour Party up to 1914?
- How important was socialism to the labour movement?
- Why was a separate Labour Party formed between 1900 and 1906 and how successful had it become by 1914?
- What effect had it on the other political parties?

The 1889 dock strike and Keir Hardie each has a proud place in Labour history. The dock strike was the largest and most famous of a number of strikes between 1888 and 1890 which sharpened the divisions between workers and employers and gave new power to the trade union movement. Keir Hardie was not only the first Labour MP but one of the earliest campaigners for a separate party for working people

The dock strike of 1889

The strike blew up out of a minor pay dispute at the West India Dock and spread rapidly across the Port of London. The main grievances of the dockers were that they were employed on a casual basis so had no job security and, when they were working, they were poorly paid. Soon 150,000 were on strike and Britain's largest port was at a standstill.

The strike was well organized by Ben Tillett, John Burns and Tom Mann. Great marches through the City of London helped to gain public sympathy. A gift of £30,000 from fellow unionists in Australia played a vital role when their strike fund was running low. Eventually they were victorious, gaining their 'dockers' tanner'', i.e. 6*d* (2.5p) an hour.

Keir Hardie 1856–1915

Keir Hardie was born in 1856 in Lanarkshire in Scotland, the illegitimate son of a farm servant. He had little education. His mother taught him to read using newspapers she had picked up in the street. A coal-miner from the age of 10 to 23, he managed to educate himself so effectively that he became a trade union organizer and journalist. He was a proud, passionate Christian idealist, determined to improve the position of the poor and downtrodden. A restless and ambitious visionary, he could inspire multitudes but was too much of an individualist to be a good team leader.

He began his political life as a Liberal but in the 1880s became convinced that the Liberals would never bring about the urgently needed improvements in workers' lives. After trying and failing to get elected as an independent working man in Mid-Lanarkshire, he succeeded in winning West Ham in London in 1892. He was one of the driving forces behind the creation first of the Independent Labour Party in 1893 and then the Labour Representation Committee (LRC) in 1900 (see Spotlight, pp. 114–115).

One of only two LRC candidates to be elected in 1900, he became the first Chairman of the Labour Party which was formed in 1906 when 29 LRC candidates were elected to Parliament. He was not a good Chairman and soon resigned. A keen supporter of female suffrage, he became a close friend and lover of Sylvia Pankhurst. He also worked hard to strengthen the unity of European socialist parties and to prevent war. The outbreak of war in 1914 and the enthusiasm with which the great majority of workers, in Britain and elsewhere, supported their belligerent governments depressed him hugely. He died the following year.

Growing class conflict 1875–1900

A separate Labour Party eventually emerged because working people came to see themselves more as a separate class with particular needs which the Conservative and Liberal parties could not meet and to which they were sometimes hostile. In the last quarter of the nineteenth century, changes took place which many working people found intolerable. They sharpened the divisions between the classes. The 1889 dock strike and Keir Hardie's career were in different ways reactions to these greater class divisions.

Between 1875 and 1900, the British economy slowed down. In contrast, those of the USA and Germany accelerated and British employers faced greater competition. At the same time the process of industrialization and the decline of British agriculture (see p. 68) pushed people from the country into towns. In 1851 the population divided roughly into 50 per cent rural, 50 per cent urban. By 1911 the proportion had changed to 20 per cent rural and 80 per cent urban. In 5 areas – Greater London, the West Midlands, South Lancashire, Merseyside and West Yorkshire – towns merged into conurbations of more than a million inhabitants.

Within these expanding cities, social class divisions became sharper. Trains and trams allowed the prosperous middle classes to move to the suburbs, leaving the inner cities to the workers. Working-class children usually attended board schools. Middle-class parents preferred Church or private schools. A distinct working-class culture emerged based on pubs, fish-and-chip shops, soccer and day-trips to seaside resorts like Blackpool.

Economic trends widened the gap between the classes. Though wages for people in employment rose between 1875 and 1900, the jobs available did not keep pace with the increase in the employable population. Consequently unemployment became a real problem. So did housing, especially in the inner cities. Two pioneering social surveys – by Charles Booth in London and Seebohm Rowntree in York – suggested that at least 30 per cent of the British population was living in poverty and made a wider public much more aware of the dire conditions in which many workers, employed as well as unemployed, were living.

Changes in the trade union movement

The trade union movement was crucial to the development of a separate political party whose priority was the betterment of the working class.

■ Historical debate

The 'Great Depression'?

Historians have debated how serious were the economic conditions of the late nineteenth century and sometimes you will find the term 'Great Depression' used about this period. There was without doubt a serious depression in agriculture (see p. 68) and a major financial crisis in 1886. The word 'unemployment' entered the English language in 1882 to describe a state of affairs in a new urban and industrial society which citizens of a more rural society had not noticed. At the same time much of British industry continued to grow vigorously so the term 'the Great Depression' is probably not a helpful one.

■ Biography

Charles Booth and Seebohm Rowntree

Booth was a wealthy shipowner who devoted the later part of his life to a detailed investigation of the lives of Londoners. With the help of a team of investigators, he researched and published in 17 volumes between 1886 and 1903 the *Life and Labour of the People of London*. It became famous for its coloured maps, which showed the extent of poverty street by street. Booth had originally intended to prove that socialist writers were exaggerating the desperate conditions of the London poor but found that the reality was far worse than he had expected.

What Booth did street by street in London, Seebohm Rowntree, the son of a rich chocolate manufacturer, did house by house in York. His *Poverty: a Study in Town Life* was published in 1901.

These books shocked public opinion and made politicians more ready to give priority to social reform.

■ Think about

▶ What did Tillett and Mann think the role of trade unions should be?

▶ How was this different from the aims of previous trade unions?

▲ Striking Matchgirls in 1888.

■ Think about

▶ How are the bargaining powers of employers and trade unions affected by trends in unemployment?

Nineteenth-century trade unions were entirely working class. Their membership grew; their organization improved; and they had funds which they were increasingly inclined to use for political purposes.

Between 1860 and 1880 the most powerful and politically influential trade unions had been the so-called 'new model' unions of skilled artisans like the Amalgamated Society of Engineers (ASE). Since employers needed the skills of their members so these unions had gained reasonable wages by negotiation rather than by striking. Their officials, whose wages were paid out of the comparatively high membership subscriptions, prided themselves on their respectability and most of them were happy to work with the existing political parties.

In the 1880s a different kind of trade union emerged like the Gas Workers and General Labourers Union formed by Will Thorne in 1889. The new unions differed from the 'new model' unions in two important ways. Firstly their members were drawn from among the less skilled and poorer workers. This meant that they were both larger and charged lower subscriptions. Secondly they used the strike weapon more swiftly. Their leaders like Ben Tillett, Thorne and Tom Mann were more militant and more influenced by socialist ideas.

These new unions took shape during the industrial strife of 1888–1890. This began in the East End of London when 1400 matchgirls at the Bryant and May factory struck for a fortnight. Though Bryant and May was a profitable firm, it paid its workers 5 shillings (25p) for a 70 hour week. Worse still, conditions in the factory were dangerous; in particular the phosphorous in the match-making process caused a serious condition nicknamed 'phossy jaw'. Their case gained much sympathetic publicity and the matchgirls won better pay and conditions. Will Thorne formed his Gas Workers' Union in March 1889. It soon had 20,000 members and demanded an eight-hour day. The employers gave in without a struggle. The dock strike followed soon after. As a result of these successes, trade union membership doubled between 1888 and 1891.

The 1890s: The reaction of the employers

British employers, fearful of international competition, were alarmed by the new militants' success. During the 1890s they co-operated with one another as never before and looked to the law-courts to defend them against the unions. William Collison organized a force of non-union labour, the National Free Labour Association, to help employers break strikes. The association flourished in periods of high unemployment and at one point had a membership of 850,000.

A Shipping Federation, formed in 1890 used non-union labour to undermine Tillett's dockers' union. A strike at Hull dock was completely defeated with naval gunboats protecting strike-breakers. By 1900 Tillett's union had only 14,000 members, a quarter of its 1890 membership.

In the Lancashire cotton mills in 1891 and the coalfields of Lancashire, Yorkshire and the Midlands, employers forced through pay cuts by co-ordinated lock-outs. The coal dispute, involving 300,000 miners and lasting three months, led to clashes between miners and troops, causing the death of two miners at Featherstone in Yorkshire. In 1897, the Engineering Employers' Federation won a crushing victory over the ASE, locking its members out for six months rather than agree to an 8 hour day.

Employers did not seem to be aiming to break the unions completely. Rather they sought methods of collective bargaining which would reduce strikes and lock-outs. They also preferred to bargain with the usually cautious senior union officials rather than with the more militant locals.

They also combined to influence parliamentary opinion by forming the Employers' Parliamentary Council. They wanted the law to weaken the capacity of unions to call strikes and to reinforce strike action by picketing. They were therefore delighted by an Appeal Court ruling – *Lyons* v. *Wilkins*, 1899, when a striker was convicted of peaceful picketing – which seemed to outlaw peaceful picketing, despite Disraeli's legislation of 1875–1876.

The employers' successes in the 1890s cancelled out many advances made by the new unionism and strengthened the case of those trade union leaders who argued that working people needed a separate parliamentary party. In 1900 the Labour Representation Committee was set up to work out how.

Keir Hardie played a crucial role in the decision to establish a distinct group in Parliament, and in shaping the kind of approach that the group should take in working for the interests of labour:

Source 2

It was Hardie personally who determined the major strategic decisions reached. Any attempt to restrict labour candidates to working men or socialists was voted down…Hardie carried the vital amendment that there should be set up 'a distinct Labour group in Parliament, who have their own Whips, and agree upon their policy, which must embrace a readiness to co-operate with any party which for the time being may be engaged in promoting legislation in the direct interests of labour.

Kenneth Morgan, Keir Hardie's biographer, on the formation of the LRC.
Morgan, *Keir Hardie*, 1975

The response of the Liberals

The 1884 Reform Act and the working-class vote

The crucial question was whether the Liberals could hold on to the rising numbers of working-class voters, especially in those constituencies, which after 1884 numbered a hundred or more where workers were in a majority. If it failed, and a separate Labour Party appeared which attracted the majority of working-class votes, the consequences for the Liberals were likely to be catastrophic, not only because the Conservative Party had a strong hold on the middle class but Britain's first-past-the-post electoral system made life hard for third parties.

In fact the pattern of party politics only changed slowly. Some workers, a minority, continued to vote Conservative (see p. 68). A greater number continued to vote Liberal. Many did not bother to vote at all. The number of working-class candidates rose only slowly because MPs remained unpaid.

One could argue that in some ways the Liberals did well in the 1880s and 1890s. Heavily industrialized constituencies continued to elect MPs known as Lib-Labs whose main interests were industrial matters but who would otherwise support Liberal policies. Nine Lib-Labs were successful in the 1886 election and one of them, Henry Broadhurst, briefly held government office as Under Secretary in the Home Office. The miners continued to return Lib-Lab MPs until 1909.

■ Think about

▶ Why do you think Hardie did not want membership of the Labour Representation Committee to be restricted to working men and socialists?

Note

Keir Hardie and Henry Broadhurst

Keir Hardie and Henry Broadhurst had no time for each other at all. At the annual TUC Congress in 1887 the young Hardie shocked the other delegates by his savage attack on Broadhurst who was Secretary of the Parliamentary Committee of the TUC. Hardie was particularly critical of Broadhurst's opposition to the principle of the eight-hour day but in his respectability and loyalty to Gladstonian liberalism, Broadhurst symbolized to Hardie all that was wrong with the traditional trade union leaders.

Quotation

Liberalism and, more particularly Liberal associations, have definitely declared against Labour.

Ramsay MacDonald writing to Hardie in July 1894

Local Liberal associations drive away working men

However, in many constituencies, Liberals failed to realize how vital to their long-term future working-class support would be. They behaved very stupidly by failing to adopt talented working men as candidates. Constituency associations were often dominated by local businessmen and by Nonconformist ministers who did not value independent-minded working men. As the historian R.K. Ensor has observed, Labour was given considerable help in its early struggles by the 'stupid and grudging attitudes of the local Liberal association' each run by a group of middle class people who had no use for 'a candidate without funds'. (*England 1870–1914*, 1936).

In 1888, for example, the Liberal association in Mid-Lanark turned down the local working man Keir Hardie, who then held an essentially Lib-Lab position, and called in from outside a wealthy Welsh barrister. In 1894 the Liberals in Southampton rejected Ramsay MacDonald. Such rejections were very damaging. Keir Hardie went on to do more than anyone to create a separate Labour Party while Ramsay MacDonald became the first Labour Prime Minister.

Another Liberal weakness was the ageing Gladstone. While the People's William was still held in enormous esteem by older working men, his obsession with Ireland and lack of commitment to social reform harmed his reputation with the younger generation.

Not surprisingly, therefore, Hardie and others set up the Independent Labour Party in 1893. Simultaneously the TUC grew more worried about the aggressive anti-union tactics of the employers in the late 1890s. As it could expect help neither from the Conservative government nor from weak Liberal opposition (and many aggressive employers were Liberals) it too saw good reason to encourage the creation of the Labour Representation Committee in 1900.

From the LRC to the Labour Party 1900–1906

In 1900 the LRC was extremely weak. It had no clear political programme. The only major unions that gave it active support were the Amalgamated Society of Railway Servants, the Boot and Shoe Workers and the two main printers' unions. Its funds were tiny – 10 shillings for every 1000 union members.

Immediately it then had to fight the 1900 general election. With hardly any organization and next to no money (it spent a grand total of £33) it saw only two of its candidates elected: Keir Hardie and Richard Bell. They did not make much of an impression for the LRC in Parliament since Bell was much closer politically to the Liberals than to Hardie, and there were also eight Lib-Labs who claimed to be able to speak for working men just as well as they could.

The Taff Vale decision (1901) and its impact

The fortunes of the LRC were transformed by the Taff Vale case. In 1900 the Amalgamated Society of Railway Servants had struck against the Taff Vale Railway Company in South Wales and had picketed its Cardiff stations. On the advice of the Employers' Parliamentary Council, the company sued the trade union for damages. In 1901, the House of Lords, the highest court of justice in the land, ruled in favour of the company. It restated the *Lyons* v. *Wilkins* judgment on picketing and ordered the trade union to pay £23,000 in damages. This was a bad blow to the unions and they realized that they had to increase their influence in Parliament. Between 1901 and 1903 all the big unions, except the miners, swung behind the LRC whose union membership rose from 376,000 in 1901 to 861,000 in 1903. The unions also agreed to increase LRC funds.

■ Biography

Ramsay MacDonald to 1914

J. Ramsay MacDonald, first secretary of the LRC (and Britain's first Labour Prime Minister – see Chapter 00) was Scottish, born of poor parents in Lossiemouth in 1866. Fiercely ambitious, he moved first to Bristol where he joined the local branch of the SDF and then to London where he became a leading member of the Fabian Society. He earned his living as Private Secretary to a London Liberal and hoped to become a Liberal MP. However the Liberal selection committee for Southampton turned him down as a candidate which caused him to abandon the Liberals for the ILP. There he again impressed by his grasp of issues and his administrative and organizational skills. He quickly won Keir Hardie's confidence, and was the obvious candidate for the post (unpaid) of Secretary to the LRC. What seemed to many at the time a thankless task proved a major step forward in his political career.

He proved a dedicated and efficient Secretary and, because of his position, was always at the centre of Labour politics. Elected to Parliament in 1906 for a Leicester constituency, he soon became one of the best Labour performers (not that the competition was very strong). In 1911, aged 44, he was elected Chairman (the effective leader) of the party, a post which he held until the outbreak of war in 1914.

Socialism

How important was it in the formation of the Labour Party?

Socialism

Socialism is the political philosophy which favours State rather than private ownership and control of the means of production; for example the ownership by the government rather than private shareholders of such things as a nation's mines railways, gas and electricity services.

The term was first used in the 1820s about thinkers like Robert Owen in Britain and Saint-Simon in France, who believed that a better society would come when people worked together co-operatively rather than in competition and the State had a responsibility to create social harmony by preventing unemployment and encouraging co-operative communities. Later writers went further and criticized private property as socially damaging. 'What is property', asked the Frenchman, Pierre Proudhon, in 1840. 'Property is theft', was his answer.

For the German Karl Marx and his collaborator Frederick Engels, the iron laws of history caused the property-owning middle classes to exploit the property-less workers. It was their ownership of property (the means of production) which allowed them to get rich by holding down the wages of workers. Eventually a revolution would come when the workers would triumph and the collective ownership of the means of production would lead to a better life for every one.

Marx's communism was the most extreme form of nineteenth-century socialism. And, internationally the most influential.

Source 3

Socialism, John, does not consist in violently seizing upon the property of the rich and sharing it out among the poor...Practical Socialism is a kind of national scheme of co-operation managed by the State. Its programme consists, essentially, of one demand, that the land and other instruments of production shall be the common property of the people, and shall be used and governed by the people for the people... What are the things to be done? We want to find work for the unemployed. We want to get pensions for the aged. We want to abolish the poor law system. We want to produce our own food so as to be independent of foreign nations. We want to get rid of the slums and build good houses for the workers...

But before we can accomplish any of these reforms we must have a public in favour of them, and a Parliament that will give effect to the Popular demands.

From 'Merrie England' by Robert Blatchford. Blatchford was a brilliant socialist journalist whose newspaper, the *Clarion*, was published in Manchester. 'Merrie England' was a collection of articles which he wrote to explain the essence of socialism to his readers. Published in 1894 it was hugely successful, eventually selling more than a million copies.

■ Activity

Read the descriptions of socialism here. Think about how the socialists differed from the Liberals in their views of the power and role of the state (see p. 143). Draw or plan a visual or cartoon representation of the differences between the two views.

The formation of the Labour Representation Committee (LRC) in 1900

The LRC came into existence as a result of an initiative from the Trades Union Congress (TUC). At its annual September meeting in 1899, it agreed by 546,000 votes against 434,000 to summon a special conference to make plans for labour representation in Parliament.

Most trade unionists were suspicious of socialism, especially continental versions like Marxism. Most union leaders were practical men interested mainly in getting a better deal for their members. The majority were Gladstonian Liberals and uneasy about radical changes. Convinced Marxists, like H. M. Hyndman, the Social Democratic Federation (SDF) leader, considered them hopelessly conservative.

This special conference was held in February 1900 in the Memorial Hall in Farringdon Street, London. 129 delegates attended and agreed to form 'a distinct Labour group in Parliament'. The conference then formed a committee, the Labour Representation Committee, to work out how to create such a group.

The main socialist groups in Britain in 1900

The Social Democratic Federation (SDF)

This was the earliest socialist group in Britain. Its founder was H.M. Hyndman who claimed that he was influenced by Marx's writings. It was strongest in London where it gave many people including young trade unionists like John Burns their introduction to socialism. However it was less effective than it might have been because of the domineering character of Hyndman, who was a product of Eton and Cambridge and managed to combine enthusiastic imperialism with his socialism. Hostile to the Liberal Party, Hyndman favoured the creation of a separate party for working people. Though it helped to create the LRC, it pulled out after only a year because it thought that the LRC was not socialist enough.

◀ Where the Labour Party began with the formation of the LRC in 1900 – the Faringdon Memorial Hall in London.

Source 4

Membership of the LRC

Organization	Members of LRC	Also provided
Trade unions	7	Most funding
ILP	2	1st Secretary: MacDonald
SDF	2	
Fabians	1	

■ Think about

▶ Why was the LRC set up?

▶ What was the balance within it of trade union and socialist interests?

The Independent Labour Party (ILP)

Founded in 1893, it was the brainchild of Keir Hardie. Its first meeting was in Bradford and it was determinedly provincial, unlike the SDF. Its major aim was 'to secure the collective ownership of the means of production, distribution and exchange', so it was strongly socialist. However to reassure the trade unions, it left the word 'socialist' out of its title and stressed its commitment to economic and social reform rather than radical political change.

However its early years proved disappointing. Its Central Executive had too many self-centred individuals to operate successfully and it lacked funds. In the parliamentary election of 1895, Hardie lost his West Ham seat and none of the other 27 ILP candidates was successful. Its main electoral achievements were in local elections, to school boards and town councils.

The Fabians

The Fabian Society was founded in 1894. It took its name from the Roman general Fabius who defeated the Carthaginian Hannibal by waiting patiently for long periods and then making swift and effective attacks. The Fabians were middle-class intellectuals like the dramatist Bernard Shaw and Sidney and Beatrice Webb whose marriage produced no children but numerous weighty sociological and historical publications. They agreed with Marx's analysis of the evils of capitalism (private ownership) but disagreed with him that socialism could only come by revolution. On the contrary, they believed that a socialist society would come to Britain gradually. By their writing and argument, their socialistic ideas would 'permeate' into policy making. In the long run, their ideas did permeate and were influential. However though they had a place on the LRC, their influence on the early Labour Party was small.

■ Activity

1 Draw up a chart with four columns to compare the SDF, Fabians and ILP in terms of their aims, members, methods, achievements.
What were the main differences between them?

2 Assess the importance of the socialists in the formation of a separate Labour Party.

The MacDonald-Gladstone agreement 1903

Another boost to the fortunes of the LRC came from a secret agreement between MacDonald and Herbert Gladstone, the Chief Whip of the Liberal Party. Both wished to see an end to the Conservative dominance of Parliament and agreed that where LRC or Liberal candidates stood a good chance of defeating the Conservatives if there was no third party, they would do their best to ensure that there was only either a Liberal or an LRC candidate standing against the Conservative so as not to split the anti-Conservative vote. Within the LRC only Hardie, apart from MacDonald, knew of the agreement.

In the short-term, it worked well for both parties. The next election took place in 1906 and the Liberals won a massive victory. At the same time the LRC won 29 seats. All 29 were working men. Seven were sponsored by the ILP, the other 22 by trade unions or other local labour organizations. Among them were Keir Hardie, Ramsey MacDonald and Will Thorne. Once assembled in Westminster, they renamed themselves the Labour Party.

Limited influence 1906–1914

A cork bobbing along on a Liberal tide?

The Labour successes of 1906 took the public by surprise. The emergence of an independent working-class party seemed likely to have great if unpredictable results. Arthur Balfour, the defeated Conservative Prime Minister, commented that the new Liberal Prime Minister, Campbell-Bannerman, would be so dependent on workers' votes that he would be like a 'cork bobbing along on a socialist tide'.

In fact the opposite turned out to be true. As the Fabian, Bernard Shaw pointed out, the Labour Party 'bobbed along on a Liberal tide'. The new Labour members were unable to make their presence felt in Parliament between 1906 and 1914 and probably had less influence in 1914 than they had had eight years earlier. Between 1909 and 1914, they faced heavy criticism by many of their supporters.

■ Think about

Read Peter Clarke's assessment of the electoral agreement between MacDonald and Herbert Gladstone in 1903 (Source 5).
▶ What do you think (a) the Liberals, (b) Labour gained from it?

Source 5

What made (this agreement) effective was the substantial ideological affinity between Liberals and Labour. For years the Liberal leadership had made approving but ineffective noises about encouraging working-class candidates. Now they were offered a job lot of about forty labour representatives – mainly comprising solid and sensible trade-union officials...all of them determined to get a fair settlement of labour legislation, but otherwise, almost to a man, imbued with a strong Liberal outlook.

Clarke, *Hope and Glory*, 1996

◀ Serious and respectable, Labour and Lib-Lab MPs at Westminster after their successes in the 1906 general election. Note Keir Hardie, seated fifth from the left and Ramsay MacDonald seated third from the left.

The reasons for the early weaknesses

The Liberal government had a huge majority and its own priorities; notably Home Rule for Ireland and the reform of the House of Lords. In addition, after 1908, Lloyd George and Churchill were pushing ahead with a major programme of social reform, which, though it was by no means the same as that which Labour MPs would have adopted, was so much better than nothing that it had to have their support.

Few of the new MPs became effective parliamentary operators. They were all working men with limited formal education and administrative experience. Most found the traditions of the Commons with its lengthy debates and complicated procedures off-putting.

Nor had the Party much unity. It was a coalition of ILP socialists and trade union officials and the latter had at least as much sympathy for the Lib-Labs as the socialists. It was uneasy with the idea of a leader so elected a Chairman on an annual basis.

Such was Keir Hardie's national and international reputation that he was elected Chairman from 1906 to 1908 but he was ill-suited to the task. His genius was for rallying support for great causes. His inspiration came in fits and starts and he was essentially a loner without the kind of personality and patience to coach an inexperienced party into becoming an effective parliamentary group.

He also forced on his Party another practice that weakened its effectiveness, the 'conscience clause'. When in 1907, he disagreed with a Party resolution on women's suffrage, he threatened to resign as Chairman. The response of the Party was to allow him to follow his conscience on this particular issue and to vote against Party policy. Other members were soon to follow his example so Party unity was difficult to sustain on controversial issues.

The most able MPs like Philip Snowden and George Lansbury were, like Hardie, prickly individuals. A contrasting personality was Arthur Henderson, the party's whip, on whom Hardie relied heavily to deal with the details of parliamentary business. When MacDonald became Chairman in 1911, Henderson took over as Party Secretary. Henderson was a patient and tactful man with real administrative abilities. His main weakness in the eyes of his colleagues was the closeness of his political beliefs to the Liberals.

The best year for the Labour Party was the first, 1906. They persuaded the Liberals to pass the Trades Disputes Act, which restored the legal position of the trade unions to what it had been before *Lyons* v. *Wilkins* and the Taff Vale cases. Peaceful picketing was legal and unions could not be sued for damages. Other early achievements were a Workmen's Compensation Act, a School Meals Act, a Medical Inspection Act and an eight-hour working day for miners.

Criticisms of the parliamentary party

The ILP soon found fault with the Labour performance at Westminster, in particular with its failure to put forward a distinctive programme, independent of the Liberals. It found a newsworthy spokesman in a young member, Victor Grayson, who fought and won the Colne Valley by-election as 'a clean socialist'. Once in Parliament, Grayson campaigned to free genuine socialists from the compromising 'Labour alliance' of the Parliamentary Labour Party with the Liberals. Another attack from the ILP came in the shape of the 'Green Manifesto' named after the colour of its cover, entitled *Let Us Reform The Labour Party*. 'Labour', it declared, 'must fight for Socialism and its own hand against BOTH the capitalist parties IMPARTIALLY.'

Simultaneously, the Party faced an attack from a different direction. 1911–1914 were years of serious industrial unrest (see Chapter 9) which the Liberal government found difficult to contain. However some the strike leaders were hostile to the Labour Party and to traditional trade union leaders. Influenced by syndicalist ideas, strike leaders like Tom Mann believed that that the unions should amalgamate and by strike action take control of the economy, by-passing the normal political process. While syndicalism attracted the more militant young socialists, its influence was limited. There were some union mergers, notably in the railway industry.

A positive side-effect of syndicalism was the creation of a socialist newspaper, the *Daily Herald*, in 1912. Its first editor was George Lansbury and it attracted rebels of all sorts on to its staff, including the brilliant cartoonist, Will Dyson.

THE MAN WHO WORKS THE PUMP: I'm beginning to think that I don't get my share of these Booms——
THE MAN WHO WORKS THE ORACLE: Maybe, my man, maybe—but remember the Slumps that come after—are we ungenerous to you then? No, sir; as far as is humanly possible we let you have the Slumps all to yourself!

The Osborne judgment 1909 and its effects

The Party suffered an unexpected setback in 1909. Then, MPs were not paid by the State, most Labour MPs were paid by the unions which charged a compulsory levy on their members. W.V. Osborne was a member of the Amalgamated Society of Railwaymen who voted Liberal and objected to paying the compulsory levy. His legal challenge eventually ended on appeal in the House of Lords where the Law Lords ruled for Osborne.

This was a devastating financial blow to the Labour Party and it took four years before the Liberal government fully put matters right. In 1911 it approved the payment of MPs (£400 per year), and, in 1913, it passed the Trade Union Act which allowed trade unions to levy money from their members for political purposes. Members who opposed the levy could contract out, but the onus lay on them to contract out rather those members in favour of the levy being asked to contract in.

As a result of the Osborne judgment Labour had to fight the two elections of 1910 in a situation of financial crisis and were even more dependent on their electoral pact with the Liberals. In January 1910 Labour won 40 seats and 42 the following December. Of these victories only two were won against official Liberal candidates.

The Labour movement outside Parliament

However, if the parliamentary party was in the doldrums, outside of Westminster Labour was much healthier.

Between 1906 and 1914 trade union membership rose from 900,000 to 1,500,000 and the membership of socialist societies like the ILP from 17,000 to 33,000. Vital for fighting elections were the local Labour parties and trade councils. Where in 1906 there had been only 83, in 1914 there were 158. A national agent, supported by two national staff and 20 local agents co-ordinated Party activities and built up Party networks in areas like Scotland where hitherto they had been weak.

Whatever the position in Westminster, the Party was in good shape to fight the next election which was expected in 1915. It would put forward at least 100 candidates and fight each seat without the need for an electoral pact with the Liberals.

Summary

- In the last quarter of the nineteenth century Britain became considerably more urbanized and industrialized and industrial workers more conscious of being a separate class whose interests were often different from and in conflict with those of other classes. People were more conscious and intolerant of poverty and unemployment.
- Trade unions changed in character. They grew in size and the leaders of the 'new' unions were often more militant than their predecessors. Because trade unions felt threatened by legal rulings like *Lyons* v. *Wilkins* and the Taff Vale judgments they supported a separate Labour Party which depended heavily on them for funds and leaders.
- The trade unions were much more important to the Labour Party than the socialist groups. Men like Hardie and MacDonald toned down their socialist beliefs lest they offended their trade union colleagues. None the less socialist ideas strongly influenced many Labour leaders, e.g. Hardie, MacDonald, Lansbury and Snowden and trade unionists like Burns, Tillett, Mann and Thorne.
- The LRC was founded in 1900 because the TUC was worried about the attack on its legal position by the employers' federations. It was at last ready to co-operate with socialist groups like the ILP which had been campaigning for a separate party since 1890.
- Though it had 42 MPs at Westminster in 1914, the Labour Party could not claim to be a powerful political force nationally in 1914 and seemed to be stagnating. In contrast, trade unions were growing rapidly and at local level Labour was thriving.
- The new party had as yet little effect on the other two parties. It seemed to threaten the Liberal Party but the electoral pact of 1903, while helping Labour, also assisted the Liberals in winning a huge majority in 1906 and in staying in power up to 1914. With the outbreak of war in 1914, normal politics was suspended until 1918 and historians cannot agree about how great a threat Labour posed to the Liberals in 1914 (see Chapter 9).

Note

Labour electoral fortunes 1906–1910

The increase in Labour seats between 1906 and 1910 was more apparent than real. Sixteen mining MPs, previously Lib-Lab, transferred to Labour in 1909, increasing the total to 45. Consequently the January 1910 election meant a loss of 5 seats. The evidence suggests that electoral support for the Labour Party stagnated or declined slightly between 1906 and 1914.

■ Activity

1 Look back at the list of reforms that Blatchford wanted in 1894 – in his Socialist programme' Merrie England' (Source 3)
How many of these had been achieved by 1914?

2 Reread the chapter considering the role of Keir Hardie.
What were his strengths and weaknesses as a leader?
What did he achieve?
How important was Hardie in the establishment of a distinct Labour Party?

■ Further reading

Paul Adelman, *The Rise of the Labour Party, 1880–1945*, 1996*

Clive Behagg, *Labour and Reform, Working Class Movements 1815–1914*, 1991*

Henry Pelling, *A Short History of the Labour Party*, 1961

Kenneth O. Morgan, *Keir Hardie, Radical and Socialist*, 1975

* Books particularly suitable for students

Chapter 8

Votes for women 1867–1928

8

Source 1

"THE ANGEL IN 'THE HOUSE;'" OR, THE RESULT OF FEMALE SUFFRAGE.
(*A Troubled Dream of the Future.*)

Source 2

No doctor can lose sight of the fact that the mind of woman is always threatened with danger from the reverberations of her physiological emergencies…It is with such thoughts that the doctor lets his eyes rest upon the militant suffragist. He cannot shut them to the fact that there is mixed up in the woman's movement much mental disorder.

Sir Almroth Wright in a letter to The Times in 1912

◀ A good example of 1880s middle class male attitudes, *Punch* June 1884.

Introduction

Female emancipation – the winning of those political and social rights which helped women towards equality with men – is one of the greatest changes in human history. It has been achieved only in the last two centuries. Winning the right to vote was a vital part of this global process with parts of the USA and Australia giving the lead with Britain not far behind. This chapter explains how, step by step in a long struggle, British women overcame male prejudice, such as that expressed in Sources 1 and 2, and won the right to vote on the same basis as men.

Key questions

● Why had the demand for women's suffrage become so strong by 1900?
● What were the main stages in the struggle of British women to win the right to vote on the same basis as men?
● Why did it fail up to 1914 but succeed partially in 1918 and totally in 1928?
● How important was the First World War in changing men's attitudes to women's suffrage?
● Which was the more influential organization, the NUWSS or the WSPU?

Why had demand for women's suffrage become so strong by 1900?

Women's roles in the nineteenth century

Nineteenth-century British society was profoundly unequal both in terms of class and gender. Women of all classes were seen as inferior to their menfolk. Their role was above all to marry and have children. If education was available, they received an inferior version to that of their brothers and one which was designed to fit them to their subordinate role. When they married, they promised in the marriage service to obey their husbands and their property became the property of their husbands. Without contraception, they spent a large proportion of their life in child-bearing, which was then a far riskier and potentially more life-threatening experience than it is today.

A middle-class woman would not be expected to work. In her mid-Victorian ideal form she would be a devoted wife and mother who ran the home with quiet efficiency, providing her breadwinner husband with the support he deserved.

For most working-class women, life was considerably tougher. While the upper and middle-class women could count on servants to do the physical housework, working-class women suffered the same subordination to their husbands but had also to care for their often large families in small homes without either servants or mechanical appliances to help them. Cleaning and washing were continuous backbreaking tasks. Such was the extent of poverty that many working-class women had to find employment where they would be paid less than men.

A double standard of morality existed. The ideal woman was homely, fragile, pure and free of the faintest hint of scandal. In contrast, men could drink at their clubs or bars and have a quiet fling or turn to prostitutes – as long as they were discreet about it.

■ Think about

▶ What are the details in Source 1 which show the attitude of the *Punch* cartoonist to female suffrage?

■ Further reading

There are many superb nineteenth-century women novelists – Jane Austen, Charlotte and Emily Brontë, George Eliot (born Mary Anne Evans) and Elizabeth Gaskell, for example – whose books give excellent insights into the experience of women of that time.

Reasons for changing attitudes – political philosophies

As the century passed, attitudes began to change. One cause was the political philosophies of liberalism and socialism. If, as liberals insisted, individual freedom mattered, then, sooner or later, people would realize that it mattered as much for women as for men. If, as socialists insisted, social justice mattered and no group should exploit another, then, sooner or later, people would no longer tolerate the extent to which men exploited women.

Millicent Garrett Fawcett (Source 3) was arguably the most influential women in the struggle to win the women's vote. Brought up a convinced liberal, part of her inspiration was the French Revolution of 1789.

Source 3

The whole movement of the emancipation [freeing] of women must be regarded as one of the results of the upheaval of the human mind of which the French Revolution was the most portentous manifestation [striking example]. The awakening of the democratic spirit, the rebellion against authority, the proclamation of the rights of man, were almost necessarily accompanied by the growth of a new ideal concerning the position of women.

Millicent Fawcett, *The Women's Suffrage Movement*, 1888

The Pankhursts who founded the Women's Social and Political Union (see pp. 128–129) were socialists, members of the Independent Labour Party, before they became militant campaigners for women's suffrage.

This did not mean that many convinced male Liberals, Gladstone and Asquith for example, did not remain strongly opposed to female emancipation, nor that convinced male socialists, trade union leaders for example, would not do their utmost to keep women out of the employment market and their wages lower than men's. What it did mean was that there were powerful ideas around in the second half of the nineteenth century which caused men as well as women to question the subjection of women to male authority.

Other causes of changing attitudes

Social and employment trends

Women were proving that they could succeed outside the home. Elizabeth Fry (1780–1845), for example, campaigned actively and successfully for the improvement of prison conditions. Florence Nightingale (1820–1910) became celebrated for her nursing reforms, while Elizabeth Garrett Anderson (1836–1917) overcame considerable male hostility to qualify as a doctor and run a successful hospital for women in London.

In the national drive for higher standards of education, women gained, both through new private schools for the well-off like North London Collegiate School and Cheltenham Ladies College, or the board schools established by Forster's Education Act of 1870. Thanks to the efforts of women like Emily Davies and Anne Clough, founders respectively of Girton and Newnham Colleges in Cambridge, university education became available – slowly – to women. Better-educated women asked more questions and would not accept unreasonable answers to questions like: why should men without education have the right to vote while they did not?

Timeline

1860–1894

1860s Langham Place group led by Barbara Bodichon and Bessie Parke begin campaigning for women's suffrage.

1867 J.S. Mill, acting on a request from Bodichon, presents a women's suffrage petition to Parliament.

1869 Municipal Corporations Act gives women the right to vote in local elections.

1870 Education Act gives women the right to vote for local school boards.

1870s Josephine Butler campaigns vigorously against the Contagious Diseases Acts.
Married Women's Property Acts give women greater control of their property.

1870s and 1880s Women's suffrage societies emerge all over Britain. Particularly strong in London and Manchester.

1874 Emily Davies founds Girton College, Cambridge.

1875 Anne Clough founds Newnham College, Cambridge.

1880s Conservatives found the Primrose League (1883) and the Liberals the Women's Liberal Federation (1887).

1884 Reform Act women's suffrage amendment defeated by 271 votes to 135.

1888 County Councils Act allows women both to vote and to stand as councillors in county elections.

1894 Local Government Act increases number of women able to vote in local elections.

■ Think about

▶ This early twentieth century poster comes from the library collection begun by Mrs Fawcett. What are the details which make clear the attitude towards women's suffrage of the artist who produced the poster?

■ Biography

Annie Besant (1847–1933)

Annie Besant was a most unusual woman whose capacity to shock respectable opinion was considerable. Before the 1877 prosecution, she had separated from her clergyman husband and declared herself an atheist. She then became a passionate socialist and organized a famously successful strike of London matchgirls in 1888. She developed a deep interest in religion and moved to India where her criticism of British rule caused her to be arrested, albeit briefly. She continued to campaign for an independent India until her death.

Note

The typewriter was invented in the USA in the 1860s and transformed business life between 1880 and 1900. While previously office clerks had usually been men, most typists were women.

Source 4

Employment opportunities improved steadily. More women became teachers, shop assistants and typists. Between 1851 and 1911, the number of women clerks rose from 2000 to 166,000. Some middle-class women resisted handing over their property to their husbands and a series of Married Women's Property Acts strengthened their position and increased their independence. Working-class women set up their own unions and campaigned against the low wages in the 'sweated' industries, like clothes making.

Contraception was not considered respectable before 1914 but it was increasingly discussed and practised, especially by middle-class couples. In 1877 Annie Besant and Charles Bradlaugh were prosecuted, unsuccessfully, for publishing a pamphlet on birth control. The publicity of the trial led to information about contraception becoming more easily available. Technological advance led to better condoms and, by the 1890s, barbers kept Durex, manufactured by the London Rubber Company, under their counters for their male clients. The cost of condoms, however, was comparatively high and, for working women, abortion remained a frequent means of birth control, though it was dangerous and illegal. Less time and energy spent on child-bearing gave women new opportunities; in particular to work, to study and to campaign.

Political activity

Throughout history, women had been active behind the scenes assisting their politician husbands. In the 1880s both major political parties formally established women's associations to help increase their popularity. The Conservatives' Primrose League was quickly followed by the Liberals' Womens' Liberal Federation. The former, which combined socializing with politics and had 500,000 members by 1891, was much more successful than the latter, which had 82,000 members in 1896.

Simultaneously, women were gaining the right to vote in local elections. In 1900 they made up 13.7 per cent of the local electorate. They could become members of school boards, Poor Law guardians and, from 1888, county councillors. By 1914, more than 1,000,000 women were voting in local elections and 1800 held elected office.

That they could not vote in national elections seemed for an increasing number of women (and men) incomprehensible and intolerable.

The beginnings of a national suffrage movement

The first steps 1832–1867

As early as 1832, the radical reformer, Henry Hunt, had proposed that unmarried women who met the property qualifications of the proposed Reform Bill should have the right to vote. In reply, Parliament made it clear that the suffrage was for men only. In 1839, the Chartists (working-class reformers) originally considered including votes for women in their reforming petition – but thought better of it.

The start of the sustained campaign for votes for women in general elections dates from the 1860s. Some mainly upper-middle-class women, led by Barbara Bodichon, formed the Langham Place group which published its own magazine, *The English Woman's Journal*. Other women's suffrage groups were formed outside London, those in Lancashire proving particularly active. In 1865 the Langham Place group persuaded John Stuart Mill, political philosopher and Liberal MP to try to have votes for women included in the 1867 Reform Bill (see pp. 28–29). Mill's reputation as a philosopher then and now is high and he wrote a powerful essay, 'The Subjection of Women', in support of female emancipation. However, he had little success in the 1867 Reform Bill debates; his amendment to the bill to include votes for women was lost by 73 votes to 194.

The campaigning continues 1867–1897

From then on, the women's suffrage groups tried almost every year to get a suffrage bill through the House of Commons but without success. Though they had many sympathizers amongst MPs, especially in the Liberal Party, Gladstone's opposition made success impossible. They were themselves weakened by disputes between London and Manchester, about whether or not to support Josephine Butler's campaign against the Contagious Diseases Acts and, above all, about whether to include married women in the suffrage proposals. This last issue was a problem, because only men with a property qualification could vote and married women had no property since that belonged to the husband. London cautiously favoured unmarried female property owners only, while more radical Manchester wished to include married women. Eventually a form of words was agreed which asked for votes for women on the same terms as men. The effect of this was to exclude married women but implicitly rather than explicitly.

The women's suffrage societies had high hopes when the 1884 Reform Bill was being debated, since their support among Liberal MPs seemed stronger than ever. However the Liberal leadership was unconvinced. Gladstone remained opposed in principle while the Party officials believed that more women would vote Conservative than Liberal. Consequently, to the outrage of the women's suffrage societies, their amendment was defeated by 271 votes to 135 while semi-literate male agricultural workers gained the vote.

After such a major setback, many campaigners lost heart. However, the Local Government Act of 1894 reinvigorated them, since it gave married women the same voting rights as unmarried propertied women. To allow more effective campaigning, most of the women's suffrage societies dotted across the country agreed in 1897 to the formation of the National Union of Women's Suffrage Societies (NUWSS) to co-ordinate their activities. Its first elected President was Millicent Fawcett (see pages 127–128).

■ **Biography**

Barbara Bodichon (1827–1891)

Barbara Bodichon was the daughter of a rich Liberal MP and a cousin of Florence Nightingale. Her father gave her the same education and inheritance as his sons. She married a French doctor, wintering with him in Algiers and spending the summer on feminist causes in Britain. She led the campaign for the first Married Women's Property Act of 1856 and helped to finance *The English Woman's Journal,* which proved very influential on women's issues.

■ **Biography**

Josephine Butler (1828–1906)

Josephine Butler came from a Northumbrian country family. She married a university lecturer and, after her five-year-old daughter had died tragically, devoted herself to feminist causes. She was especially concerned about the Contagious Diseases Acts which held women responsible for the large number of British sailors and soldiers who suffered from venereal disease and allowed the authorities to subject women to humiliating medical checks. She campaigned fiercely, sensationally and effectively, getting the Acts repealed in 1886.

The complications of party politics hinder female suffrage 1906–1914

If at any time between 1900 and 1914 there had been a free vote in the House of Commons about votes for women, a majority of MPs would probably have voted in favour. Women remained disenfranchised (without the vote) not because MPs were opposed to women's suffrage in principle but because of calculations of party advantage made by the party leaders. Remember that, despite the 1884 Reform Act, many men were still without the vote. If Parliament voted for female suffrage, it would be as part of another Reform Act which would add many more men to the electorate. Consequently, party managers had to estimate not just how the new women voters might vote, but also the millions of additional working-class men. To add to the complications, each of the political parties was divided on the principle of votes for women.

Note

The Conciliation Bill of 1911 had a majority. It failed to become law because the Liberal government did not give it enough time in Parliament for further debate.

■ Activity

Using the party voting figures (Source 5), make a bar chart to show how the votes of each party varied for each of the 4 parliamentary debates. Between 1911 and 1913, what were the trends in the voting of each of the parties? Why did the voting of:
● the Conservatives
● the Irish Nationalists
change so much?

Source 5

Party voting on women's suffrage between 1911 and 1917

	Con	Lib	Lab	Irish Nat	Total
1911 Conciliation Bill (see note in margin)					
For	53	145	26	31	255
Against	43	36	–	9	88
1912 Conciliation Bill					
For	63	117	25	3	208
Against	114	73	–	35	222
1913 Dickinson's Representation of the People Bill					
For	28	146	34	13	221
Against	140	74	–	54	268
1917 Representation of the People Bill					
For	140	184	30	33	387
Against	45	12	–	–	57

The Conservatives

If Disraeli had been 20 years younger, he would probably have been in favour of female suffrage. According to his biographer, Robert Blake, 'Disraeli was by no means unfriendly to the idea, anyway in principle. Indeed few people would have gained more than he by votes for women'. However, when John Stuart Mill proposed his amendment during the Second Reform Bill debate in 1867, Disraeli neither spoke nor voted on it. It was too far-reaching a step to be possible in 1867.

Other leading Conservatives were not against the principle of votes for women. Balfour and Bonar Law were in favour. So too were many local Conservative associations. However, most backbenchers, and some potential future leaders of the Party like Long and Curzon, were strongly opposed. So too were Party officials who believed that even if women did prove rather more ready to vote Conservative, they would be far outnumbered by the working-class men who would also be enfranchised for the first time and who would be likely to vote Liberal or Labour.

The Liberals

The Liberal position was the opposite of the Conservatives. While most Liberal MPs were in favour, their leaders tended to be lukewarm, or, in the case of Asquith, Prime Minister from 1908, hostile. From 1906 to 1910, when they had a huge parliamentary majority, female emancipation was never a priority and Party officials continued to believe that if women gained the franchise, more would vote Conservative than Liberal. After 1910, Asquith depended on the Irish Nationalist vote and he had no intention of risking Irish support by pressing ahead with a political initiative of which he strongly disapproved.

The Irish Nationalists

The overwhelming priority of the Irish Nationalists was to win Home Rule for Ireland. The two general elections of 1910 left them holding the balance of power in the House of Commons (see pp. 150–151), so that prize seemed in their grasp. Though many of them were privately in favour of female suffrage, they feared that any new suffrage measure would redistribute parliamentary seats at the expense of themselves. Anyway, they wanted to keep Asquith in power to secure Home Rule and they knew he was opposed to votes for women. Consequently, from 1912, they voted against women's suffrage and continued to do so until the Liberals passed the Home Rule Act in 1914.

Labour

The small Labour Party was from 1903 tied into an alliance with the Liberals (see p. 116). Its leadership was divided on the issue and there was a strong anti-feminist element amongst trade union leaders. However, a strong working-class campaigning group in the north-west eventually shifted opinion within the Party so that the 1913 Party Conference agreed to oppose any franchise bill which did not include votes for women. In the years immediately before the First World War, Labour was the only party in the Commons to support women's suffrage consistently.

This complicated party situation caused the political leaders to keep on putting off making a decision about women's suffrage.

Asquith's delaying tactics 1908–1914

Asquith took and held obstinately to a Gladstonian view of the issue. Women were naturally different from men and that made them unfit to take part in politics. Women in his opinion were not cut out for national politics because:

Source 6

the inequalities which democracy requires we should fight against are the unearned privileges and the artificial distinction which man has made, and which man can unmake. They are not those indelible differences of faculty [mind] and function [role] by which Nature herself has given diversity and rightness to human society.

Asquith speaking in the House of Commons from 1892 Hansard

However he was aware of the powerful feelings of many of his Party, including Cabinet ministers like Grey and Lloyd George who were in favour of votes for women. In 1910, therefore, he agreed to the setting up of an all-party Conciliation Committee to find a way of giving the vote to women on the same basis as men.

1897–1914
1897 National Union of Women's Suffrage Societies (NUWSS) founded with Millicent Fawcett as President (suffragists).
1903 Women's Social and Political Union founded, led by Emmeline Pankhurst and her two daughters Christabel and Sylvia (suffragettes).
1905 First suffragette militancy.
1907 The 'Mud' March (NUWSS).
1909 Government introduces forced feeding.
1910 Conciliation Committee set up to seek agreement between the parties on women's franchise.
1910 November Black Friday violent clashes between suffragettes and police.
1911–13 Various women's suffrage bills defeated by parliamentary manoeuvring.
1912 Suffragette militancy intensifies. NUWSS formally allies itself with Labour.
1913 'Cat and Mouse' Act. Emily Davison killed at the Derby horse race.
1914 Outbreak of the First World War. Suffragette campaign called off.

Another reason why Asquith was hated by the suffragettes was his weakness for young women. 'I think it disgraceful', one of them wrote in 1914, 'that millions of women shall be trampled underfoot because of the convictions of an old man who notoriously cannot be left alone in a room with a young girl after dinner.'

Then followed, between 1911 and 1913, a series of debates in the House of Commons, all of which ended in failure for women's suffrage. This was partly because of the party splits and manoeuvres described above, with the Conservatives and Irish Nationalists supporting Asquith against women's suffrage, and partly, in 1913, because the Speaker, James Lowther, refused on a technicality to let a women's suffrage bill be further debated. It seems likely that behind the scenes Conservative leaders leant on him. After Lowther had ruled against the Plural Voting Bill, Asquith noted in his diary:

Source 7

The Speaker's coup d'etat has bowled over the Women for this session – a great relief.

A year later, however, Asquith was adopting a friendlier tone. Talking to a group of East End working women and suffrage campaigners in 1914, he declared:

Source 8

On one point I am in complete agreement with you. I have always said that if you are going to give the franchise to women, give it to them on the same terms as men...(there is no reason for) giving to women a restricted form of franchise while you give to men an unrestricted form of franchise. If change is to come, it must be democratic in its basis.

Report in *The Suffragette* magazine, 26 June 1914

■ Think about

Having read this section on Asquith and Sources 6–8 consider his options between 1910 and 1914. He was against votes for women though most of his Party was in favour. His main priority was to get Home Rule for Ireland and to break the power of the House of Lords. How did he prevent the female suffrage issue from splitting his Party? If in fact he was changing his position in 1914, what actions of the women's suffrage organizations might have influenced him?

In normal times, the next general election would have been held in 1915. By then, some historians believe, Asquith would have withdrawn his opposition to votes for women, since he realized how damaging it was becoming to his Party. However, normal times ended in 1914 with the outbreak of the First World War. Parliament concentrated on how to win the war and postponed further consideration of domestic political issues like female emancipation until victory was won.

Not surprisingly, the longer the Liberal government stayed in power and did nothing, the more the frustrations and anger of the women's suffrage societies escalated. From 1905 to 1914 the votes for women campaign intensified. The campaigners divided into two main camps: the suffragettes and the suffragists.

The suffragists

Mrs Fawcett and the NUWSS

Millicent Fawcett was born Millicent Garrett, the daughter of a prosperous, quarrelsome Suffolk merchant and his highly religious wife. One of ten gifted children – Elizabeth Garrett Anderson was an older sister – she developed an early and strong interest in the women's suffrage movement. As a young woman, she was infuriated by the social attitudes which treated women as belonging to men, and decided that female suffrage was essential if these attitudes were to change. In her autobiography (Source 9), she describes an incident from her youth.

My two companions were talking, and presently took up the subject of a recent marriage in our immediate circle. The young husband and wife were estranged (living apart), and no one exactly knew the reason why. After pursuing this interesting theme for some time, one said to the other, 'I cannot see what she has to complain of. Look how he dresses her!' I fumed inwardly, but said nothing. I thought I would like to make that kind of talk impossible. I kept on thinking about it, and the shame and degradation of it, which seemed to be accepted by my companions as a matter of course. I did not know anything at that time about 'kept women', but 'look how he dresses her' was of its essence.

What I Remember by Millicent Fawcett, 1925

▲ Mrs Fawcett, c.1895, studious, calm but very determined.

At the age of 20 she married Henry Fawcett, a remarkable man who was not only Professor of Economics at Cambridge and a Liberal MP but blind. She worked as his political secretary and became an excellent economist in her own right. He died unexpectedly in 1884, leaving her as a 37-year-old widow. She devoted the rest of her life to political causes of which the suffrage was to her much the most important. Highly intelligent, a thorough organizer and fluent speaker, determined, energetic and attractive, she was President of the NUWSS from 1897 to 1919. She concentrated on the single aim, to win parliamentary suffrage on the same terms 'as it is, or may be granted to men'. She lived just long enough to see her hopes fulfilled in 1928, dying the following year.

The NUWSS greatly increased in numbers and effectiveness between 1902 and 1910. The number of local societies which it represented grew from 17 to 31 and it became more effective at putting pressure on parliamentary candidates. For example, before the 1906 election every candidate was questioned about his position on female emancipation.

The suffragettes

Emmeline and Christabel Pankhurst

The suffragettes were the creation of the extraordinary Pankhurst family, notably Mrs Pankhurst (Emmeline) and her eldest daughter Christabel who founded the Women's Social and Political Union (WSPU) in 1903.

Mrs Pankhurst was the daughter of a well-off Manchester business family. Both her parents were Liberal reformers and, at 14, she was attending women's suffrage meetings with her mother. When she was 21, she married Manchester's most radical lawyer, Dr Richard Pankhurst, who was himself active in the women's suffrage movement. During their marriage, they left the Liberals to join the Independent Labour Party. Richard died in 1898, when Emmeline was 40, with five children to care for. She then worked in Manchester as a registrar of births and deaths. A brilliant speaker, attractive in appearance and fashionable in dress, fearless and passionate, she loved being in the news.

Christabel, born in 1880, became her mother's deputy registrar and studied law at Manchester University. If her mother led the campaign and was the main speech-maker and fund-raiser (as much in America as in Britain) Christabel was the leader of the militant actions and increasingly the main organizer and policy-maker. An autocrat like her mother, she was as concerned about male sexual domination and sexual purity as about winning the vote.

Modern feminists understandably object to the habit of mainly male writers of commenting on the prettiness of women in the public eye when it is irrelevant to their work. However, Mrs Fawcett and the Pankhursts were considered attractive, and they believed that their cause was helped if they dressed well and looked good to men.

▶ Do you think judgements about their appearance are, therefore, historically relevant?

One reason why Mrs Fawcett and the Pankhursts took trouble with their appearance was the readiness of their opponents to make comments such as these:

'Women who wanted women's rights also wanted women's charms.'

'Women's Rights are Men's Lefts.'

'There are three sexes; masculine, feminine and Miss Becker' (a leading suffragist and ugly in the eyes of some men at that time).

▲ Making the headlines, as usual, Mrs Pankhurst being arrested outside Buckingham Palace, May 1914.

There was a particularly close bond between mother and daughter and together they founded the WSPU in 1903. Its motto was 'Deeds not Words' and its two chief aims were Votes for Women and Chastity (sex only within marriage) for Men. Much more openly than the NUWSS, the suffragettes were in revolt against traditional sex roles as well as seeking female suffrage.

As the following comments by contemporaries indicate, it was impossible to be neutral about the Pankhursts. People either loved or hated them. One of Emmeline's supporters wrote in 1908:

Source 10

She...was a mighty spirit in a fragile frame, endowed with superb courage, mental and physical, an indomitable will, natural dignity at all times and the keenest sense of duty. Her wonderful eloquence and beautiful voice appealed to all, and stirred all hearts with a desire to carry on the fight...To know her was to love her, and to love her was to follow her.

An American journalist who saw her when she was in the USA fund-raising asked:

Source 11

...can this frail woman have terrified Mr Asquith and caused an uproar in the House of Commons. Why she looks like a quiet housewife going shopping.

However, others regarded them as shallow. Here is the comment of Bruce Glaisier, who knew them through the Independent Labour Party and thought them a distraction from the work of spreading socialism:

Source 12

Really the pair (Emmeline and Christabel) are seeking not democratic freedom but self-importance...Christabel paints her eyebrows grossly and looks selfish, lazy and wilful. They want to be ladies and lack the humility of real heroinism.

And they had a remarkable knack of turning people once their closest friends against them. Teresa Billington-Greig was once one of their leading organizers but she became very disillusioned:

Source 13

What I really condemn in the militant tactics (of the Pankhursts) is...the crooked course, the double shuffle between revolution and injured innocence, the playing for effects and not for results – in short the exploitation of revolutionary forces and enthusiastic women for the purpose of advertisement.

■ Activity

Read Sources 10–13.

List the strengths and then the weaknesses of the Pankhursts as described in them.

Comment on the reliability of each of these sources.

How helpful are they in explaining the immediate success and ultimate failure of the WSPU?

Divide into two groups, one group taking a traditional nineteenth-century viewpoint, the other group a women's suffrage viewpoint. Pretend you are at a dinner party in 1908 where the conversation turns to the characters of the Pankhursts. Discuss, from opposing sides, the points you have outlined in the lists above.

Suffragette militancy and its effects

Militant tactics 1905–1908

Militants seek to create conflict to get their way and the suffragettes, in comparison with the suffragists, were militant. Their militancy had two main phases, 1905–1908 and 1908–1914.

In 1905 Christabel Pankhurst and her friend Annie Kenney heckled a Liberal minister, Sir Edward Grey, at a meeting in Manchester, unfurled a WSPU banner and were arrested. Christabel increased the shock to respectable opinion and the newsworthiness of the event by spitting at a policeman. They were both given a short prison sentence which kept them in the headlines.

For the next three years the suffragettes disrupted the meetings of senior politicians. Mrs Pankhurst was thrown out of the Ladies' Gallery in the House of Commons for interrupting a debate. Having been arrested for leading a march on Parliament, she was imprisoned for refusing to pay a fine. Other suffragette tactics included chaining themselves to railings, disturbing Mr Asquith on the golf course and organizing huge rallies.

The greatest rally was held in Hyde Park on 21 June 1908. Asquith had said that he would end his opposition to female suffrage if he could be convinced that most women wanted the vote. Christabel Pankhurst's response was to get 250,000 supporters to Hyde Park, the largest demonstration London had ever seen. Asquith remained unconvinced.

The suffragettes then turned to violence. In 1908, they threw stones through the windows of 10 Downing Street and when imprisoned went on hunger strike. They jostled ministers, including Asquith, damaging his car, and broke shop windows.

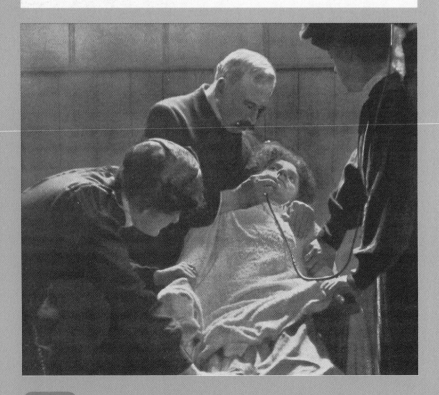

■ Biography

Annie Kenney (1879–1953)

Annie Kenney started work in a Lancashire cotton mill at the age of 10. She started a union and became a union official. She met Christabel Pankhurst in 1905 and became one of the most active WSPU militants. Courageous, self-educated and a witty and eloquent speaker, she was arrested many times, went on hunger strike and was a victim of the Cat and Mouse Act (see below)

Cat and Mouse Act

The government decided that it could not be seen to give way to violence and, at the same time, it did not want the bad publicity of a suffragette dying from hunger strike or of being physically harmed by forced feeding in prison. Consequently, in 1913, it brought out the Temporary Discharge for Ill-Health Act. It was soon nick-named the Cat and Mouse Act because it enabled the government to release prisoners whose health was failing in prison and immediately rearrest them when they got better. Also in 1913 Emily Davison was killed when she ran in front of the horses at the Derby, wrapped in a WSPU flag.

Her funeral, at which there were huge crowds, was the last great public demonstration of the suffragettes. Mrs Pankhurst was arrested under the Cat and Mouse Act for attending the procession.

◀ A suffragette being force-fed in prison in 1913.

Militant tactics 1908–1914

Such actions swung public opinion and many previously sympathetic MPs against the suffragettes. When on 18 November 1910 (Black Friday), Mrs Pankhurst led a deputation of 300 to the House of Commons, they were intercepted by the police and roughed up in a sexually aggressive way over a number of hours. Onlookers cheered the police and some took part in the assaults.

Though WSPU membership was now declining, the Pankhursts decided on greater violence. They made arson attacks on empty mansions and churches, placed a bomb in a house being built for Lloyd George and slashed one of the most famous paintings in the National Gallery, the *Rokeby Venus*. When imprisoned, some suffragettes went on hunger strike and had to be force-fed.

Emmeline and Christabel's highly autocratic leadership drove many former friends from the movement, including Mr and Mrs Pethick-Lawrence, its most effective fund-raisers.

Christabel moved to Paris and took up a stridently anti-male position, claiming that women were the sex slaves of men, between 75 and 80 per cent of whom were infected with venereal disease before marriage. She forced her sister Sylvia out of the WSPU for challenging this position.

▲ Emily Davison's funeral becomes a vast and moving suffragette demonstration.

Activity

Write a short report on Emily Davison's funeral (above), firstly as if you were writing for *The Suffragette* magazine and secondly for *The Times* newspaper.

■ Biography

Emily Davison (1872–1913)

Emily Davison gained a first class degree in English at Oxford and held a number of teaching posts before becoming a suffragette. She threw stones, was a pillar-box arsonist and once attacked a man on Aberdeen station, thinking, mistakenly, that he was Lloyd George. She was imprisoned eight times and forcibly fed frequently. After one forced feeding she tried to commit suicide. 'Deeds, not words' is written on her Northumbrian gravestone.

Note

The Bow election 1912

George Lansbury, Labour member for Bow resigned from his seat in the East End of London because he thought that his party was not giving female suffrage the priority it deserved, and fought the by-election solely on the 'votes for women' issue. Mainly middle-class WSPU women descended on Bow and upset Lansbury's local supporters by talking down to them about women's rights. They also refused to lend their cars for taking people to the polling stations because they would have been driven by men.

The NUWSS supports Labour 1912–1914

To begin with, relations between the NUWSS and the WSPU were reasonably good. Some women belonged to both organizations. The NUWSS appreciated the new vitality which the suffragettes brought to the women's movement and strongly criticized the government's tough actions against them. It also adopted similar tactics, organizing in February 1907 the famous Mud March, so called because the weather was poor and the road muddy, which created for that era the most unusual spectacle of 3000 women marching in the open air to the jeers of a mainly male crowd.

However, the NUWSS opposed the increasing militancy of the WSPU. From 1910, Mrs Fawcett was sure that it was turning opinion against votes for women. As she wrote:

Source 14

I do think these personal assaults abominable and above all extraordinarily silly. The PM's statement on the 22nd was not just exactly what we wanted but it was better than anything that had ever been offered to us before and was any rate good enough for *The Times* to say that if there is a Liberal majority (at the next election) it will be a mandate to grant suffrage to women. And then these idiots go out smashing windows and bashing ministers' hats over their eyes.

Letter to Lady Francis Balfour 1910

Some historians have agreed with her assessment:

Source 15

The evidence suggests that the politicians, voters, general public and active suffragists turned against the WSPU. Lukewarm suffragist ministers like Churchill and Birrell became antagonistic; and backbenchers turned out to oppose women's bills in growing numbers.

Pugh, *Women's Suffrage in Britain 1867–1928*, 1980

■ **Think about**

▶ How reliable a source on the impact of the suffragettes would you expect Mrs Fawcett to be?

Mrs Fawcett's response to the infuriating delaying tactics of the Liberal government was to persuade the NUWSS to help Labour candidates against Liberal ones at election time. This was a controversial policy within the NUWSS but in 1912 it established the Elections Fighting Fund Committee (EFF), headed by Catherine Marshall, to provide backing for Labour. In 1913–14 the EFF intervened in four by-elections. Though none were won by Labour, two were lost by the Liberals. Supporting Labour was in fact an extremely effective tactic since the Liberals knew that their future as a political party depended on Labour staying weak. By 1914, even Asquith seems to have realized that he could not delay much longer granting the franchise to women.

■ **Think about**

▶ Why did Mrs Fawcett decide that the NUWSS should support Labour from 1912 to 1914?

▶ It was a controversial policy. How successful was it?

Historical debate

For a long time accounts of the movement for female emancipation tended to emphasis the role of the suffragettes, paying little attention either to the activities of the suffragist movement or to their wider agenda. The contribution of the Pankhursts in particular was singled out.

This emphasis can be explained by looking at the way in which the history of female suffrage came to be written. In 1931 Sylvia Pankhurst wrote *The*

Prepare two presentations, one for a class of 13 year olds, and the other for history specialists of your own age, on suffragette militancy and the effect it had on parliamentary opinion between 1910 and 1914. Your material must include data drawn from the internet and include at least one example of an image and one of numbers.

Suffragette Movement, which portrayed the WSPU and her family as the main cause of the success of the female suffrage campaign. Hers was the standard interpretation for many years. More recent research, notably by Sandra Holton and Jo Vellacott, has provided a much better understanding of the role of the NUWSS. Holton, Liz Stanley and Martha Vicinus have shown that not only were there many women active in the WSPU other than the Pankhursts, but that for them it was a revolt against traditional sex roles, not just a campaign for the right to vote in general elections.

Document exercise: The contribution of the WSPU and NUWSS to female emancipation

Source A
A recent popular summary

The People's Century was published in 1995 by the BBC to support a documentary world history series about the twentieth century. It has half a page on women's rights including the following on Britain. It does not mention the NUWSS at all

> In Britain the first effective women's movement was launched in 1903: the Women's Social and Political Union. The suffragettes, as they were known, led a campaign to bring the issue of women's rights to the fore.

Hodgson, *The People's Century*, 1995

Source B
A historian challenges the traditional interpretation

The women's suffrage movement has been portrayed as being nearly moribund during the early years of the twentieth century until the Women's Social and Political Union brought new life to it. This view assumes the WSPU was responsible for obtaining women's suffrage, and places the NUWSS in the background. This interpretation underestimates the NUWSS' importance...although it was overshadowed by the more flamboyant WSPU, the NUWSS' transformation was one of the most significant developments in the suffrage movement between 1897 and 1910.

Smith, *The British Women's Suffrage Campaign*, 1998

Source C
A historian's view of the limitations of peaceful campaigning

Historians have sometimes argued that the militancy of the WSPU destroyed support for votes for women because it alienated sympathetic Liberal ministers. This is not so. Militancy may have been a convenient excuse to avoid giving the vote to women but it was not the real reason. The long peaceful campaign which had been waged before 1905 had not persuaded the House of Commons to pass legislation. Even, in 1910 when the WSPU called off its militant actions and adopted peaceful campaign tactics women were not granted the vote.

Bartley, *The Changing Role of Women 1815–1914*, 1996

IN THE HOUSE OF HER FRIENDS.

"TO THINK THAT, AFTER ALL THESE YEARS, I SHOULD BE THE FIRST MARTYR."

■ **Think about**

▶ Who is the figure in the foreground of Source D and the three figures behind her?

▶ What does it tell you about *Punch*'s attitude to the suffragettes?

■ **Examination-style questions**

1 Comprehension in context
In Source D, explain the roles of the 3 women and the cartoon's caption.

2 Comparing the sources
How do Sources A and B differ in their interpretation of the women's suffrage movement?
To what extent does Source C support Source A?

3 Assessing the sources
In what respects, if any, can Source D be considered a reliable source?

4 *Making judgements*
Using the sources and your own knowledge, explain how far you agree with the view referred to in Source B that 'the WSPU was responsible for obtaining women's suffrage'.

The impact of the First World War on female emancipation

Female employment

During the war, the number of working women in Britain rose by 1.3 million, nearly 30 per cent. Most of them worked in occupations directly related to the war effort – in munitions and other engineering factories, in agriculture and as nurses – and there were also new opportunities in transport and in clerical work. Their war-related work won women a good press and impressed politicians like Asquith but, in reality, their success in taking on industrial and agricultural jobs hitherto reserved for men frequently caused male resentment. For the most part, the trade unions kept their membership closed to women, and men continued to be paid at a higher rate. For example, when the government decided to give a cost-of-living bonus at the end of the war, men got 16s 6d per week while women got 11s. On the whole, women seem to have taken this state of affairs for granted. They were holding the fort in a great national crisis and would hand over to their menfolk when the war was over.

Sylvia Pankhurst (1882–1960)

Sylvia Pankhurst was two years younger than Christabel. A gifted artist who used her talents to produce many WSPU posters, she set up WSPU branches in the East End of London, was imprisoned many times for her suffragette activities and went on hunger strike. A pacifist and later a communist, she broke completely from her mother and sister in 1914.

The WSPU

The outbreak of war had an astonishing effect on Emmeline and Christabel Pankhurst. In the space of few days they swung from being violently against the government to becoming super-patriots. Germany they proclaimed to be a viciously male nation violating the more feminine Belgium and France. They called off their suffragette campaign and concentrated on calling British men to join up and British women to hand out white feathers to the cowards who stayed at home.

They played no part of any importance again in the women's suffrage campaign. The WSPU split and Christabel's younger sister Sylvia became the leader of an anti-war group with close links to the Labour Party.

The NUWSS

The war caused great tensions within the NUWSS. The first reaction of its leadership was to denounce the war and try to unite women to strive for a swift peace. Mrs Fawcett, however, quickly realized that for the NUWSS to support an international mainly female peace movement when the country seemed to fighting for its life against a powerful and aggressive enemy would be very damaging to the women's suffrage cause. Though many members of the NUWSS executive committee wanted to take part in an international educational campaign 'to keep public opinion sane' and encourage peace negotiations, Mrs Fawcett took an increasingly uncompromising patriotic position. The NUWSS executive committee suffered a bitter split in 1915. Though Mrs Fawcett continued as President, half the executive committee resigned.

Characteristically, Mrs Fawcett had chosen the best option for the female suffrage cause. If the NUWSS had given the impression that they were more pacifist than patriotic, it would have confirmed the argument of the anti-suffragists, that women's judgement could not be relied on in times of crisis like war.

The Speaker's Conference 1917

Female suffrage came back on the political agenda in 1916. Politicians were aware that 1915 would have been an election year. The case for votes for all men aged 21 and over, already strong, was made stronger by the introduction in 1916 of conscription (forced military service) for all adult men aged 18 or more. There was also a registration issue. Because so many men had left home to fight for their country and had been forced to stay away for long periods, the electoral registers were seriously out of date.

Once politicians started discussing male suffrage again, the women's suffrage societies came alive. They would not sit back and do nothing if the government thought it would give the vote to all men but still ignore women. Members of the NUWSS had been happy, as they put it, 'to bury the hatchet' at the beginning of the war, 'but they knew where it was buried and would, if occasion arose, dig it up'.

Faced with a divided Cabinet, Asquith once again decided to refer the problem to other people, this time to a Speaker's Conference. The Speaker was still the same Sir James Lowther who was still opposed to votes for women. However, he set up a balanced conference membership including Willoughby Dickinson and John Simon who had close links with the NUWSS. The conference came down firmly in favour of the principle of women's suffrage. However, it rejected the idea of equal suffrage with men, recommending instead that there should be an age limit for women of either 30 or 35. In addition, only women 'occupiers' (property owners) or wives of occupiers should have the right to vote.

Many suffragists were hugely disappointed with this outcome. It was, after all, far from the NUWSS principle of the votes for women on the same basis as men. They had friends in high places, like Lloyd George, who had replaced Asquith as Prime Minister while the Speaker's Conference was conferring, and the Labour leader Henderson who had a seat in the War Cabinet. None the less, they still faced strong opposition, notably within the Conservative Party, so Mrs Fawcett decided that the Speaker's Conference recommendations were the best that they could hope for in the circumstances. She refused to allow NUWSS members to campaign for a fairer deal and, instead, worked hard behind the scenes to make sure that the government did not delay in putting the proposals before Parliament.

Note

Mrs Fawcett said that this was the greatest moment of her life and a great victory celebration was held in London in 1918.

The Representation of the People Act 1918

The Conservative Party was split in various ways. Most back-bench MPs and Party officials were against. In contrast, many local associations which depended on women for their success, were in favour, as were some of the party's senior politicians, including Walter Long, Austen Chamberlain and the Party leader, Bonar Law. By the time the proposals came to be debated in the House of Commons, the Conservative leaders had overcome the objections of most of their followers. Consequently, on 19 June 1917, the House of Commons voted by 385 votes to 57 in favour of a clause in the Representation of the People Bill which granted the right to vote to most women aged 30 or over. The Conservative leaders also persuaded the many anti-suffrage Conservative lords not to defy the will of the Commons in this matter so the House of Lords also voted handsomely in favour, by 134 votes to 71.

Thus 8.4 million women gained the right to vote, 40 per cent of the electorate. It did not give the vote to all women aged 30 or over. By restricting the vote to those women who were also local government electors or married to local government electors, it excluded about 22 per cent of the age-group. Most of the excluded group were working-class or unmarried women in employment.

The final step 1918–1928

Perhaps the most striking thing about the 1918 Act was how little effect it had on the position of women in British society and politics. Male industrial workers got their jobs back. Women returned to domestic service. Men continued to be paid more than women for the same work and kept women out of unions. Nor did the appearance of 8.4 million new women voters do much to change party political practices. Women proved reluctant to stand for selection as MPs and, when they did, found selection panels reluctant to select them.

In the 1918 general election the Countess Markievicz won a Dublin seat but, as a member of Sinn Fein, refused to come to England. Consequently, Nancy Astor who was elected to a Conservative seat in Plymouth in 1919, became the first women MP to take her seat in Westminster. Twelve years later there were still only 15 women MPs out of a total of 650 and only one, Margaret Bondfield, had gained Cabinet rank. Though rather more women voted Conservative than men, the parties were slow to include women-friendly measures into their election manifestos.

Consequently when the suffragists pressed for women to have equal voting rights with men, the fears of the pre-1918 anti-suffragists that the female influence would transform politics and society for the worse had come to nothing. None the less the final step towards equal voting rights still had to fought for.

While in the 1920s the Labour Party and the divided Liberals favoured equal voting, the Conservative Party, which then was the dominant party, remained deeply divided. It still included numerous anti-suffragists among its back-benchers and, amongst its leaders entrenched opponents like Lord Birkenhead. Newspapers like the *Daily Telegraph* and *Daily Mail* told their readers that there were too many 'flappers' among modern young women, party-loving, sexually active and politically ignorant.

Overcoming opposition within the Conservative Party

However, Party officials realized that more women voted Conservative than men and that the Party was becoming increasingly dependent on women for fund-raising. From 1924 Balfour, Prime Minister, and Joynson-Hicks, Home Secretary, were convinced that equal voting was in the Party interest and set about overcoming internal opposition.

Outside Parliament, women's suffrage societies continued to campaign. The NUWSS had rechristened itself in 1918 the National Union of Societies for Equal Citizenship (NUSEC) and Eleanor Rathbone had succeeded Millicent Fawcett as President. It continued to put pressure on the three main parties through petitions and delegations. Less patient was Lady Rhondda's Six Point group, founded in 1921, which started marching again in 1926, an echo of the suffragettes.

1927 saw an intense debate within the Conservative Party about equal suffrage, with many MPs arguing for a minimum age of 25 for women. This, the leadership decided, would be a vote-loser so, in 1928, introduced the Representation of the People (Equal Franchise) Bill to the House of Commons. When the crucial vote was taken, 387 votes were in favour, 10 against.

All women aged 21 or over could now vote, which made women nearly 53 per cent of the electorate. Just how timid the 1918 Act had been is shown by this statistic – of the 3.5 million women who gained the vote in 1928, only 1.6 million were aged between 21 and 30, the remaining 1.9 million were 30 or more.

Historical debate: The influence of the war

'The Nation thanks the Women' was the slogan on newspaper billboards when Parliament voted in favour of female suffrage in 1918. The popular view was that by their efforts during the war, women had proved themselves worthy of the franchise.

Not all historians agree, however. Others argue that granting some women the vote did not reflect any new view of the role or worth of women. In fact the appearance of so many young, single, working women in the munitions industry in particular, had been regarded as a threat. By granting the vote essentially only to mature married family women, the Act represented a reassertion of traditional values.

Document exercise: The role of the war

Source A

A historian's judgement about women's war work

...it is naïve to think that the enfranchisement followed from changes in men's idea of the status of women; rather the crisis gave urgency to traditional notions...While hypocritically paying fulsome tribute to their war work, politicians had no intention of allowing the female majority to dominate the electorate or industry. Indeed, since the munitions girls were predominantly single, very young and working class, they appeared an unstable and disturbing element. Much preferable were the mature, married family women...This was the rationale for restricting the vote to women over thirty years, including married women. Enfranchisement came as the reaffirmation of traditional values as much as acceptance of new ones.

Pugh, *Women's Suffrage in Britain 1867–1928*, 1980

Source B

[Source C] brings out graphically the way in which women's participation in the war effort was deployed to support the case for women's suffrage.

Again the evidence on this point is abundant, and it seems tortuous in the extreme to deny it. Mrs Fawcett may be regarded as a more reliable authority than some latter-day historian; she was quite clear about the direct connection between women's war work and winning the vote. It is true that a small property qualification was retained for women, and that the vote was not granted to any woman under the age of thirty. But Mrs Fawcett and her colleagues recognized this as a tactical concession...She knew that the vital principle having been conceded....the vote would soon be given to women on the same terms as it was given to men...

Marwick, *Britain in Our Century*, 1984

Source C

Votes for Women was a suffragist weekly magazine.

Source D

A historian's view of the effects of the war on wider aspects of female emancipation

In the end, circumstances of war work were so circumscribed [limited] that although there was a change, and women made a substantial contribution to the war, the change did not endure, nor was it seen as changing women's nature as workers or citizens...profound cultural changes in the world of the woman worker or the 'girl', the 'mother' or the woman citizen awaited the changes in society and economy of the next world war, expansion of education and the development of welfarist politics that could begin to create institutions in the interests of women.

Thom, *Nice Girls, Rude Girls: Women Workers in World War I*, 1998

■ **Think about**

▶ Look at the cartoon on the cover of Source C.
▶ Who is the man in the black jacket and what is he doing?
▶ What, in the opinion of the magazine, should he have been doing?

■ **Examination-style questions**

1 Comprehension in context

Using Sources A and B and your own knowledge, explain on what terms women were first given the vote in general elections.

2 Comparing the sources

In what ways do the authors of Sources A and B disagree about the influence of war on female suffrage?

Is the argument of Source D about the effects of war on women closer to Source A or Source B?

3 Assessing the sources

How powerful a piece of evidence do you consider Source C to be as a support of the argument of Source B?

4 Making judgements

Using all the sources and your own knowledge, comment on the view that the First World War proved a major step forward in the emancipation of women.

Summary

The demand for women's suffrage had become so strong by 1910 for many reasons. Smaller families gave women more time to develop interests outside the family. New jobs like typing and shop work improved women's economic opportunities. Better education made more women aware of the basic principles of liberalism and socialism and more aware that these political ideals should encourage female emancipation. In the last quarter of the nineteenth century, women were able to vote in county council and school board elections so why not general elections.

The reasons for Parliament's delay up to 1914 were complicated and were as much the consequence of party calculations about matters quite different from the suffrage as the direct opposition to votes for women of political leaders like Asquith.

The suffragists succeeded in 1918 because the party political reasons for delaying in 1914 no longer existed and the suffragists made good use of the contribution of women to the war effort. They were also ready to accept an Act of Parliament that did not by any means give equality with men.

The First World War only helped female emancipation and female suffrage to a limited degree and much less than was once thought. The suffragists succeeded in 1928 partly because the case for equality was so strong and partly because the experience of 1918 to 1928 showed that votes for women did not transform party politics nor harm the prospects of the Conservative Party.

The WSPU hit the headlines between 1905 and 1914 and because of their militancy has always held the attention of non-specialist historians. In reality much of their militancy was counter-productive. Suffragists, like Millicent Fawcett, were the real heroines of the female suffrage struggle.

■ **Further reading**

Pauline Bruley, *The Changing Role of Women 1815–1914*, 1996 *
Harold Smith, *The British Women's Suffrage Campaign*, 1998 *
Martin Pugh, *Women's Suffrage in Britain 1867–1928*, 1980
Barbara Caine, *Victorian Feminists*, 1992
S. Holton, *Feminism and Democracy: Women's Suffrage and Reform Politics in Britain 1900–1918*, 1986
J. Liddington and J. Norris, *One Hand Tied Behind us: the Rise of the Women's Suffrage Movement*, 1978
*   Books particularly suitable for students

The last Liberal government 1905–1915
'I smell the blood of a plutocrat'

RICH FARE.

THE GIANT LLOYD-GORGIBUSTER : "FEE, FI, FO, FAT,
I SMELL THE BLOOD OF A PLUTOCRAT;
BE HE ALIVE OR BE HE DEAD,
I'LL GRIND HIS BONES TO MAKE MY BREAD."

Timeline

1899 Campbell-Bannerman becomes leader of the Liberal Party in opposition.
1905 Balfour resigns as Prime Minister; C-B takes over.
1906 General election. Massive Liberal majority.
1906–8 Liberal government frustrated by Conservative opposition in the House of Lords.
1908 Death of C-B, succeeded by Asquith.
1908 Old Age Pensions Act.
1909 Lloyd George's 'People's' Budget. Crisis over the House of Lords.
1910 January. General Election. Death of King Edward VII, who is succeeded by George V.
1910 December. General Election.
1911 Parliament Act.
National Insurance Act.
Ulster, industrial unrest and women's suffrage give the government many difficulties.
1914 Outbreak of the First World War.
1915 Asquith forms a war coalition government.

Source 1

◀ In this *Punch* cartoon of 1909, the ogre is Lloyd George, Chancellor of the Exchequer in the Liberal government, terrorising the rich (plutocrats) with his People's Budget of 1909 (see pages 150–1).

Source 2

It is better that you should have a party which combines every section and shade of opinion, taken from all classes of the community, rather than one which represents one shade of opinion alone or one class of the community alone.

Lloyd George stresses the classlessness of the Liberal Party in a very class-conscious age.
From a speech quoted in the *Manchester Guardian,* 7 November 1914

■ Think about

Study Source 2

1 Why do you think Lloyd George stressed the classlessness of the Liberals?

2 To which classes would he have accused the Conservative and Labour Parties of narrowly appealing?

3 How classless in reality was the Gladstonian Liberal Party in the 1890s?

Introduction

The Liberal Party regained power in 1905 and held it until 1915, when a wartime coalition was formed. As soon as it took power, its leaders showed that they were influenced by a political philosophy different to that of Gladstone. Unlike Gladstone, they gave high priority to social reform. The unelected House of Lords immediately provided them with determined opposition, which they only overcame after a long-drawn-out crisis lasting from 1909 to 1911 (see Source 1). They then had to deal with severe social unrest between 1911 and 1914. This government proved to be the last Liberal government. Between 1918 and 1924, it collapsed under pressure from both the Conservative and Labour Parties.

Key questions

● What was new about the 'New Liberalism'?

● Why was the House of Lords such a problem for the Liberal government between 1906 and 1910? How successfully did it deal with it?

● How much did this government achieve in the field of social reform and to what extent did the Liberal social reforms require a redefinition of the functions of the State?

● The Liberal government faced acute problems between 1911 and 1914. What were they and to what extent was it successful in dealing with them?

● How strong was the Liberal Party in 1914, especially in comparison with Labour?

The Liberal government of 1905

The Liberal government of 1905–1915 was led first by Sir Henry Campbell-Bannerman from 1905 to 1908 and then by Herbert Asquith from 1908 to 1915. It was one of the most gifted and effective of the twentieth century. It included David Lloyd George, the man who more than any other Briton helped to win the First World War, and, Winston Churchill, the man who did more than any other Briton to win the Second World War. In 1906, the former was in his 40s, the latter in his 30s, and together they proved a dynamic partnership pushing forward progressive social reforms. Other excellent ministers among many were Richard Haldane (see p. 149) and Sir Edward Grey (see p. 117).

Campbell-Bannerman was a wealthy Scots property-owner, who had been a member of Gladstone's last government. A lazy man who loved the good life and had no enemies, his main achievement was to unite the warring factions of the Liberal Party between 1899 and 1905 so that, after 20 years in the political wilderness, the Party was once again in a position to win power. He was also a good judge of character and without malice. Though Asquith, Haldane and Grey together plotted unsuccessfully to remove him from the leadership in 1905, he rewarded them all with senior ministries. Asquith he made Chancellor of the Exchequer, Grey became Foreign Secretary and Haldane got the War Office.

C-B, as he was known, was Prime Minister for barely two years and in poor health. He died 17 days after his resignation in April 1908. His greatest achievement as Prime Minister was the Trades Disputes Act of 1906. He ignored the advice of his Cabinet and civil servants and gave to the trade unions the legal position they were seeking after the setback of the Taff Vale judgment.

▲ A 'Spy' cartoon of Herbert Asquith in 1904, when he was then the rising star of the Liberal Party.

Herbert Asquith

During C-B's illness, Herbert Henry Asquith had been in effect leader of the government and succeeded him without competition. He was born in 1852 near Leeds in Yorkshire, the son of a mill-owner who died when he was only eight. Highly intelligent, Herbert moved to London to live with relatives. Educated at the City of London School and Oxford University, he gained a first class degree in classics and became President of the Union. After 10 years as a barrister, he was elected Liberal MP for East Fife in the 1886 election. He quickly made his mark in Parliament as an impressive debater and joined Gladstone's Cabinet in 1892 as Home Secretary.

He suffered a personal tragedy in 1891 when his wife Helen died of typhoid, leaving him with five young children. Three years later he married Margot Tennant, 12 years his junior and one of the stars of London high society. She preferred to call him Henry, bore him five children and remained famous for her stylish parties.

In 1908, Asquith was at the height of his powers. He had a mind which Churchill described as 'opening and closing like the well-oiled breech of a gun'. His intelligence gave him a grasp of the business of government unequalled since Gladstone. His debating skills enabled him to dominate the House of Commons. In Cabinet, he was an efficient chairman who gave his gifted ministers plenty of freedom but, when necessary, could ensure collective decisions were made. By temperament he was cautious and patient. 'Wait and see' was his motto but, having waited and watched, he could move swiftly once he was clear about the right direction. Unlike Lloyd George and Churchill, he did not have a passionate addiction to politics and enjoyed the social life which Margot arranged. His love of good wine was well known in Parliament! He was an outstanding peacetime Prime Minister but unsuited to the dangerous dramas of war (see Chapter 10).

The New Liberalism (also see Spotlight p.144–5)

One reason why the Liberals had been out of power for so long was that Gladstonian Liberalism had lost its appeal to many sections of the electorate. Gladstone had stood for political freedom, an end to privilege, low taxation and crusading on moral issues like the Bulgarian atrocities. He was uneasy about the radicalism of Chamberlain and his demands for social reform. Even if he had come to accept the need for social reform, Gladstone's commitment to low government spending and to keeping the powers of the State within strict limits would have hampered any reforming programme.

By 1908, however, many leading Liberals, notably Lloyd George and Churchill, were greatly influenced by the political philosophy of New Liberalism which redefined liberalism so that it could give a high priority to social reform.

The leading thinkers of the New Liberalism were the economist J.A. Hobson and the sociologist L.T. Hobhouse. Their friends referred to them as the two Hobs. Hobson had a new economic philosophy. In his view, uncontrolled free trade was not working as well as once it had. The present problem with the British economy was under-consumption. Imperialism made a few businessmen and adventurers very rich but the great mass of the population was too poor to spend enough on goods to ensure the greater profitability of British industry. This 'under-consumption' would be ended if the State intervened to reduce unemployment and poverty. Other economists like Alfred Marshall and A.C. Pigou also provided the Liberals with other arguments to justify a major reform programme.

Note

Asquith's drinking

During the Parliament Bill debates in 1911, Churchill wrote to his wife: 'On Thursday night the PM was very bad and I squirmed with embarrassment. He could hardly speak and many people noticed his condition. He entrusts me with everything after dinner...I like the old boy and admire both his intellect and character. But what risks to run!'

Note

A reminder about 'laissez-faire' and 'collectivism'

'Laissez-faire' was the political philosophy of mid-nineteenth-century Liberalism. The phrase means 'Let be' or 'Leave alone' and indicates that individuals would be freer and society better if the functions of the State were as few as possible. In practice this meant low taxation (Gladstone wanted to abolish income tax) and a strong belief in the virtue of individual self-help rather than of government hand-outs.
'Collectivism' challenged the individualism of 'laissez-faire' in the late nineteenth century. Collectivists who ranged from New Liberals to communists argued that society was more than just the individuals within it and community needs might well need to take precedence over individual ones, especially if the riches of the few were harming the poor majority. Governments should act in the collective interests of their citizens. In practice this meant more taxation and the acceptance that an important function of government was to pass laws and spend money on the 'welfare' of all its citizens.

National efficiency

The early defeats in the Boer War and the poor physical condition of many of the soldiers caused politicians to talk about the need for greater national efficiency. Rosebery tried in 1902 to make 'national and imperial efficiency' a priority for the Liberals rather than social reform but C-B had no time for the idea.

Hobhouse lectured in philosophy at Oxford until 1902 when he joined the staff of the *Manchester Guardian*, the leading progressive newspaper of the time. He knew Sidney and Beatrice Webb well. Like them, he believed the problems of poverty which Booth and Rowntree had described could only be reduced by State action. He argued working-class poverty was the result of wealth being unfairly distributed.

His solution was a new departure for liberalism, known as collectivism, which prescribed that governments should take action to distribute wealth more fairly throughout society for the collective benefit of that society. Consequently, New Liberals proposed that governments should use taxes in a most un-Gladstonian way to benefit the poorer sections of society through social reforms.

The New Liberals differed from socialists in two main ways. Firstly they refused to accept that conflict between the classes was inevitable. On the contrary, well-designed social reforms should reduce conflict. Secondly, they did not anticipate the government needing to take control of the means of production, like the mines, railways and iron works.

Politicians like Lloyd George and Churchill realized that it was vital to the Liberals to prevent the Labour Party gaining a greater hold on the working-class vote. For them, New Liberal thinking helped them design programmes of social reform which would appeal to working people. They also needed to offer a clear alternative to the Conservatives' Tariff Reform scheme which proposed to reduce unemployment by protecting British industry and to fund social reform by the money raised by the customs duties (tariffs) on foreign goods.

The main phases of the Liberal government

It had three phases.
- Phase 1 lasted from 1906 to 1909 when the government achieved much less than it intended because of the opposition of the Conservative-dominated House of Lords.
- Phase 2 lasted from 1909 to 1911, the years of crisis surrounding the People's Budget of 1909 and reform of the House of Lords.
- Phase 3 lasted from 1911 to 1914, years of acute difficulty at home and abroad, ending with the outbreak of the First World War.

Phase 1 Limited by the Lords 1906–1909

Balfour was determined in 1906 that

'the great Unionist [Conservative] Party should still control whether in power or opposition, the destinies of this great Empire'.

(An interesting reflection on the relevance of general election results!)

In the House of Commons in 1906, the Liberals had the largest majority since the Reform Act of 1832 and could steam-roll through that House any policy they wished. However, since the House of Lords had the powers to block any Commons bill and the Conservatives had an overwhelming majority in the Lords, the Leader of the Opposition, Balfour, was in fact in a very strong position. The Lords had already shown their power in 1893 when they had thrown out Gladstone's Home Rule Bill by a majority of 10 to 1. Though the Grand Old Man had wished to make his final crusade one that would reform and reduce the power of the Lords, he could not carry the rest of the Party with him. Once the Conservatives were back in power in 1896, the Commons and Lords again acted in harmony.

Balfour, with the Marquess of Lansdowne, the Conservative leader in the Lords, decided on a simple strategy in 1906. They would let any genuinely popular bill sent up from the Commons become law but would block any which seemed to them narrowly Liberal, even if it had been part of the programme put forward by the Liberals during the 1906 election campaign.

The New Liberalism

Source 3

We have long been accustomed to look upon the poverty of London as exceptional, but when the results of careful investigation show that the proportion of poverty in London is practically equalled in what may be regarded as a typical provincial town, we are faced with the startling probability that from 25 to 30 per cent of the town populations of the United Kingdom are living in poverty.

Seebohm Rowntree on the extent of poverty in Britain in 1901.
Rowntree, *Poverty: a Study of Town Life*, 1901

Source 5

All expenditure which succeeds in improving the part benefits not that part alone but the whole community, and this is why all sections [of society] may justly be called upon to share the cost of measures which in their direct and immediate application touch only on the well-being of the poorer.

Herbert Samuel (1870–1963) on government spending. Samuel was another of Asquith's gifted Cabinet (and later Liberal leader) and very much a 'New Liberal'. Samuel, *Liberalism*, 1902.

Source 4

▲ Poverty in the East End of London. This photo appeared in the *Illustrated London News* in 1889. Note the numerous children, the chickens and the washing.

■ Questions

Poverty and New Liberalism

Study Sources 3 and 4. To what extent were the 'New Liberals' influenced by writers like Rowntree and scenes like that in Source 4?

■ Questions

Taxation and New Liberalism

Study Source 5.

1 What did New Liberals consider to be the use of taxation. Were taxes a bad thing?

Study Source 6.

2 Explain the reference to JB and £6,000,000 surplus. What is the attitude towards taxation of the *Punch* cartoonist?

3 Is this attitude closer to that of Gladstone or of the New Liberals?

Source 6

THE PATIENT ASS.

THE INCOME-TAXED ONE MURMURETH. "I DON'T GRUMBLE, BUT—I *SHOULD* LIKE JUST A LITTLE TAKEN OFF."

Source 7

The way Hobhouse put it was to say that the task of liberalism in the nineteenth century had been the achievement of political democracy; in the twentieth century, it would be social democracy. There were senses of 'socialism', therefore, which were acceptable to Liberals, and certainly labour, representing a special case of the maldistribution of wealth in the community, ought to be part of the Liberal coalition.

Peter Clarke, a historian writing in 1996. Clarke, *Hope and Glory*, 1996

◀ The Patient Ass. This *Punch* cartoon appeared in 1896.

■ Questions

New Liberalism and Socialism

Study Sources 7, 8 and 9.

1 What were the main similarities and differences between New Liberalism and Socialism?

2 You could set these out in a chart, or try to illustrate them in cartoon or poster format.

Source 8

Socialism seeks to pull down wealth; liberalism seeks to raise up poverty. Socialism would destroy private interests; liberalism would preserve private interests in the only way they can be safely and justly preserved, namely reconciling them with public right.

Churchill in 1911 on the differences between liberalism and socialism

Source 9

New Liberalism provided the intellectual arguments for the welfare reforms with which the Liberal governments of 1906–14 laid the foundation of an interventionist welfare state. By continuing to focus primarily on the individual, however, it did not solve what was rapidly becoming the main problem for liberalism at the turn of the century: mass society. Liberalism was never fully at ease with the world of the masses, and never understood the collective and defensive response that the constant insecurity of working-class life evoked.

Alan Sykes, a historian writing in 1997. Sykes, *The Rise and Fall of British Liberalism 1776–1988*, 1997

The Lords' blocking tactics

As a result of the Conservative strategy described on page 143, in 1906, the Lords passed the Trades Disputes Bill, which did not seem to them narrowly Liberal, but blocked an Education Bill, which they considered to be proposed simply to please the Nonconformists. The unelected Lords were not only overwhelmingly Conservative but Anglican too, so they blocked this Education Bill, not just in 1906, but in 1907 and in 1908. Much the same happened to a Plural Voting Bill which the government first got through the Commons in 1906. Its sensible intention was to limit the right of people who owned more than one property in different constituencies to only one vote. The Lords, however, threw it out since it would have hurt the Conservatives more than the Liberals.

1907 was no better. Four bills which aimed to reform land-holding in Scotland and Ireland as well as England were either blocked or so changed as to be valueless.

Asquith, Lloyd George, Churchill and the first reforms

None the less, despite the very considerable problem posed by the Lords, the Liberal programme of reform began to take shape. The key figures were Asquith, Chancellor of the Exchequer to 1908 and then Prime Minister, Lloyd George, President of the Board of Trade to 1908 and then Chancellor of the Exchequer, and Churchill, President of the Board of Trade from 1908. Asquith's role was to decide that a programme of social reform should be a government priority; to appoint the ministers to define the programme and turn it into laws and to make the funds available for the new laws to be effective. He also was mainly responsible for old age pensions (see page 147).

▲ A remarkable pair – Lloyd George (on the left), then Chancellor of the Exchequer, and Churchill, then Home Secretary, make their way to the House of Commons on budget day in 1910.

Lloyd George's early career 1863–1905

The most dynamic and effective minister of this Liberal government and one of the most constructive yet controversial politicians in British history was born David George in 1863. His father was an elementary school head teacher but died when his son was only a year old. David was brought up by his uncle Richard Lloyd in the village of Llanystumdwy in Carnarvonshire, north Wales. His uncle ran a small shoe-making business and was one of the better-off villagers. He was Welsh-speaking, a deeply religious Nonconformist and convinced Liberal. He and his nephew became very close. To indicate how much he owed his uncle, David George as an adult liked to be known as David Lloyd George.

At school he managed both to be mischievous and to impress his teachers. At the age of 14 he left school to join a firm of lawyers in Porthmadog and by the age of 21 he was a qualified lawyer with a firm of his own and four offices in Carnarvonshire. His reputation grew as a young man with quick wits and sympathy for the underdog, for the Welsh against the English, for the Nonconformists against the Anglicans. With his heart set on a political career, he wrote for the local press and toured the area speaking in favour of temperance.

His local reputation as a Radical Liberal who spoke with passion and humour continued to grow and, in 1890, he won the by-election of Carnarfon Boroughs with a tiny majority of 18 votes. He was to remain its MP for the next 54 years. In his first nine years in Parliament, he was a back-bencher whose main interests seemed to be Welsh affairs.

In 1899 he became a national figure by declaring that the Boer War was both unnecessary and immoral. Such a public stand was very courageous since the country was in a feverish jingoistic mood. He was assaulted in Bangor. His effigy was publicly burnt in his home town of Criccieth and, in Birmingham in 1901, he had to be smuggled out of the back of the Town Hall when a mob estimated at 30,000 attacked the front.

However this 'Pro-Boer' stand did him no harm within the Liberal Party either nationally or locally, and he further improved his reputation by leading a skilfully organized Nonconformist campaign in Wales against the Conservatives' Education Act of 1902.

Lloyd George at the Board of Trade 1905–1908

Here he proved that he was a man who could get things done. He headed a department of 750 and was responsible for industry, commerce and transport. Aided by able and sympathetic civil servants, reforms began to flow.

A Merchant Shipping Act (1906) improved working conditions and safety regulations for British sailors and for foreign ships using British ports. A Census of Production Act (1906) provided the means to gain better information about trends in industrial production. A Patents and Designs Act (1907) protected British designers against foreign copiers. Perhaps his greatest achievement at the Board of Trade, however, was the creation of the Port of London Authority. This merged a number of inefficiently competing private companies into a single organization to plan the development of Britain's largest port, so that it could hold its own against other rival European ports like Hamburg and Rotterdam. In these years Lloyd George demonstrated his skills as a negotiator. He aimed to talk issues through with possible opponents and listen to their concerns before drafting his proposals. He also managed to settle two major industrial disputes – the first on the railways in 1907 and the second in the shipyards in north-east England in 1908.

Old age pensions 1908

The need for old age pensions stemmed from the fact that the poor as well as the rich were living longer. How they should be cared for in the new urban environments of the industrial world was a question with which many governments across the world were grappling. Many European nations had already decided that the State must provide old age pensions. Thanks to Joseph Chamberlain, they were firmly on the British political agenda. The scheme, which Lloyd George introduced in 1908, and for which he took the credit, was essentially the work of Asquith who, in his last budget as Chancellor of the Exchequer, had set aside funds for its introduction. It did not look particularly generous since it gave 5 shillings (25p) per week to people aged 70 or over. It was, however, very popular for it ended the fear of old people living in poverty that they would end their lives in the workhouse. It also represented a watershed in British social legislation. The Old Age Pensions Act of 1908 gave old people their pension as a right, to which they had to contribute nothing. It was paid for out of general taxation.

Churchill's early career

Churchill was eight years Lloyd George's junior. He was born in Blenheim Palace in Oxfordshire into one of the country's most aristocratic families. His grandfather was the Duke of Marlborough, his father Lord Randolph Churchill (see p. 72) and his mother Jennie, the daughter of a New York businessman. An adventurous and boisterous boy, he neither liked nor thrived at Harrow and

Collecting old age pensions for the first time in January 1909.

Note
The popularity of old age pensions

Old age pensions were immediately popular and associated closely with Lloyd George.

Many old people could not believe that they were getting them free and brought flowers and fruits from their gardens as a way of saying thank you to the civil servants who gave them their pensions.

This is not really surprising if you remember that a pensioner who was 70 years old in 1909 would have been growing up in the 1840s and 1850s when 'laissez-faire' and 'self-help' were dominant.

his father decided that he should go into the army. He graduated from Sandhurst in 1895, the year of his father's tragic death, and joined the 4th Hussars regiment.

His army career was brief and brilliant and he managed to combine it with the writing that made him famous. He reported the Cuban War of Independence for the *Daily Graphic,* and 1897 found him with his regiment in action on the North-West Frontier of India. The letters he wrote from there, about his experiences, were published with the help of his mother in the *Daily Telegraph*. In 1898 he was with Kitchener's army at Omdurman and charged with the 21st Lancers through the Dervish lines. His *River War* of 1899 vividly described this campaign.

Standing as a Conservative candidate in 1899 he failed to win a by-election in Oldham so went off to South Africa to report the Boer War for the *Morning Post*. He became a national hero by first rescuing an ambushed armoured train and then escaping from a Boer prison. After his return in 1900, he was able to improve his precarious income by lecture tours in Britain and the USA and to win the Oldham seat in the 1900 general election.

Churchill was now 29, a young man of strong opinions, considerable self-confidence and ambition. He was not a conventional Tory by any means and when Chamberlain launched his Tariff Reform campaign, he decided to change sides. On the 31 May 1904, when he entered the House of Commons, instead of turning to the left to join the Conservative benches, he bowed to the Speaker and turned right to sit down next to Lloyd George. Within days he was delighting the Liberals and upsetting many old friends with savage personal attacks on Balfour and Chamberlain.

His reward in 1905 was the post of Under Secretary for the Colonies, and, in 1908, Asquith promoted him to succeed Lloyd George at the Board of Trade. By now he had fully absorbed the main ideas of the New Liberalism. In a speech in Glasgow in October 1906, he declared that the 'whole tendency of civilization was towards the multiplication of the collective functions of society...increasingly and earnestly it must concern itself with the care of the sick and aged, and, above all, of the children...I look forward to the universal establishment of minimum standards of life and labour, and their progressive elevation as the increasing energies of production may permit.'

Quotation

He is really a spoilt child with the brain of a genius.

Hobhouse on Churchill in 1912

Churchill at the Board of Trade 1908–1910

Here he had two main achievements. The first was the setting-up of labour exchanges (1908). These were places where men out of work and employers could register their requirements. This was a sensible measure which central government could do more efficiently than any other body. The second was

■ Think about

▶ How 'collectivist' (see page 143) was the setting up of labour exchanges?

◀ The Camberwell Green Labour Exchange in 1910.

the creation of Trades Boards (1909). These Boards investigated the so-called 'sweated industries' where wages were very low and the workers unprotected by a union. They had powers to prosecute any employer who was found to be paying his workers at a level below that laid down by the Board of Trade.

The achievements of other reforming ministers

Such were the personalities and achievements of Asquith, Lloyd George and Churchill that other ministers tend to be overlooked. For example, Haldane, the Secretary of War, transformed the British army from one which could only fight small colonial wars into one which, in the event of a European war, could be moved swiftly across the Channel and fight effectively alongside France. At the Home Office, Herbert Gladstone was very effective, carrying out a number of reforms, including a Workman's Compensation Act (1906) which extended compensation to another 6 million workers.

Phase 2 The years of crisis 1909–1911

Despite these numerous reforms, Liberal spirits were low in 1908. Two years on from their thrilling victory of 1906, they and their supporters felt that they had achieved far less than they had expected. In their opinion, the Lords were not playing the parliamentary game; if they were not actually breaking the letter of the Constitution, they were certainly breaking its spirit. They were seriously weakening the ability of the elected government to govern as it wished. In 1908, acting on behalf of the brewing industry which paid considerable amounts of money to the Conservative cause, the Lords blocked a Licensing Bill which yet again had come through the Commons with a large majority. The Liberals were at a loss as to what to do. By-elections were running against them and trade was bad. Balfour, the Conservative leader, looked well placed to win the next election.

However, Liberal fortunes underwent a great revival between 1909 and 1911, starting from the unlikely position of an acute financial crisis. In response to Germany's naval-building programme (see p. 99), the Admiralty demanded eight of the newest Dreadnought battleships, the last word in naval technology and colossally expensive. The Cabinet tried to compromise on four but had to give way to a jingoistic campaign whipped up by the Press – 'we want eight and we won't wait'. To make matters worse, Asquith had miscalculated the number of old people eligible for pensions for whom additional funds had to be found. Consequently, Lloyd George as Chancellor of the Exchequer, faced in 1909 the task of finding an extra £15 million from somewhere. By the standards of the time, this was an enormous sum, more in fact than the Conservatives had to find at the height of the Boer War in 1900.

The People's Budget

This is what Lloyd George did in his budget of 1909. He increased income tax and death duties on the estates of the wealthy. He created a super tax for the very rich, and introduced a tax on land. He also increased the taxes on tobacco and alcohol. Financially it was a sensible budget since it found the money required. Politically it was brilliant, since it hit Conservative landowners the hardest in order to safeguard the Liberal social reform programme which was designed to benefit the great majority of the population. 'This was a war budget,' Lloyd George declared, 'for raising money to wage implacable war against poverty and squalidness.' His far-reaching budget and fighting talk produced a massive political crisis which was to last for the next two years.

Note

'We want eight and we won't wait'

This campaign was mainly the creation of James Garvin, editor of the *Observer*. He was famous for his fiery articles and was strongly anti-German. He was actively helped by Admiral Sir John Fisher, who supplied him with the technical information that he needed. Garvin also secured the backing of the Conservative Party to his campaign.

■ **Activity**

Source 10 on the next page gives you an example of the speeches made by Lloyd George in support of his People's Budget.

1 Think how the Conservatives would have responded to the measures proposed in the budget and to the arguments used to support them.

2 Draft a speech that might have been made by a Conservative peer in response.

Spotlight

'Peers against the people' The Parliament Act crisis 1909–1911

Timeline

1909 March Budget prepared by Lloyd George and approved by the Cabinet.

April Lloyd George presents budget to the House of Commons.

Summer/Autumn Conservative opposition builds up, Liberal ministers, notably Lloyd George and Churchill, tour the country criticizing and ridiculing the Lords.

November Budget approved by Commons, then rejected by the Lords by 350 votes to 75. Asquith calls a general election.

1910 January General election. Results: Lib. 275, Cons. 273, Irish Nat. 82, Lab. 40.

March Asquith proposes how the House of Lords should be reformed.
1909 budget goes through both the Commons and the Lords.

May Death of Edward VII.

Summer Constitutional conference to try to find a compromise.

Autumn Asquith persuades the new King, George V, to create if necessary up to 500 new lords sympathetic to the Liberals, if the Conservatives keep up their opposition to reform.

December Second general election. Result: Lib. 272, Cons. 272, Irish Nat. 82, Lab. 42

1911 August After furious debate, Lords approve the Parliament Act by 131 votes to 114.

Think about

▶ Read Source 10. Lloyd George was one of the finest public speakers of his generation and this was one of his best efforts. Why was it such a good speech?

The 1909 budget and the Lords

There is no evidence that the Liberal leaders expected the House of Lords with its Conservative majority to throw out the budget. When it did, they were delighted. 'At last, with all their cunning, their greed has overcome their craft. We have got them at last!' declared Lloyd George.

Generations of historians have been very critical of the decision of the Conservatives to block the 1909 budget. R.C.K. Ensor in his *England, 1870–1914* (1936) described it as 'almost incredible', while Robert Blake in his *Conservative Party from Peel to Major* (1997) thought it 'insane'.

They seem to have made this bad misjudgement for a number of reasons. The first was their realization of how much was at stake. If they let Lloyd George succeed, their chosen route to economic progress, to social reform and to greater popularity with the electorate, Tariff Reform (see pp. 77–78) would lose its appeal. If the Lords lost their power to block Liberal plans, Home Rule for Ireland, the Liberal policy most loathed by the Conservatives, would quickly become law. The second was their anger about the manner in which Lloyd George and Churchill mocked them. The third was their belief that somehow they were able to read the popular mood and the people would never allow them to be weakened. The fourth was their confidence that they would get away with it; that Asquith was bluffing when he said that he would ask the King to make enough Liberal lords to finally overcome their opposition. Twenty years or more of having their own way had made them foolishly arrogant.

Source 10

A fully-equipped duke costs as much to keep as two Dreadnoughts – and they are just as great a terror – and they last longer...Let them realize what they are doing. They are forcing a revolution, and they will get it...The question will be asked whether five hundred men chosen accidentally from among the unemployed, should override the judgement – the deliberate judgement – of millions of people who are engaged in the industry which makes the wealth of the country. That is one question. Another will be: who ordained that a few should have the land of Britain as a perquisite [something to enjoy]? Who made ten thousand people the owners of the soil, and the rest of us trespassers in the land of our birth? Who is it who is responsible for the scheme of things whereby one man is engaged through life in grinding labour to win a bare and precarious subsistence for himself, and, when, at the end of his days he claims at the hands of the community he served a poor pension of 8 pence a day, he can only get it through a revolution, and another man who does not toil receives every hour of the day, every hour of the night, whilst he slumbers, more than his poor neighbour receives in a whole year of toil?... The answers are charged with peril for the order of things which the peers represent.

Lloyd George speaking in Newcastle 9 October 1909

Reforming the Lords

Asquith's leadership during the crisis

Asquith was at his best. He knew what he wanted and kept his nerve. When many of his Cabinet became nervous about Lloyd George's boldness, Asquith backed Lloyd George. When the Irish Nationalists, who after the general election of January 1910 held the balance of power were unhappy with the budget, he skilfully won them round with the promise of Home Rule. When Edward VII died, he did not rush the new King, George V, into a difficult decision about creating new peers. He bided his time and eventually got the royal decision he wanted. He then let Balfour and the House of Lords know he was not bluffing and the Parliament Act was passed. Perhaps the only serious criticism that can be made of him was that he missed the opportunity to make the House of Lords more representative of the country, but there was not great demand even from within the Liberal Party for more radical reform.

Source 11

The Lords will not be allowed to touch a Bill if the Speaker says it is a Money Bill.
A Bill passed by the Commons in three successive sessions should pass into law whether the Lords consent or not.
The length of Parliament should be shortened from seven to five years.

Asquith's Resolution of 21 March 1910

Source 12

We have reached a fateful period in British history. The time for words is past, the time for action has arrived. Since the House of Lords – upon an evil and unpatriotic instigation (scheme) – as I must judge it – have used their veto to affront the Prerogative (right) of the Crown and to invade the rights of the Commons, it has now become necessary that the Crown and the Commons, acting together, should restore the balance of the Constitution and restrict for ever the Veto of the House of Lords.

Churchill in the House of Commons 1910 during the debate on reducing the powers of the House of Lords

Balfour's leadership

This was lamentable. He could not make up his mind. 'He blew hot,' it was said of him, 'he blew cold and then ceased to blow at all'. At the height of the crisis, he went off to Germany for a health cure. The Conservative press started a BMG (Balfour Must Go) campaign and he resigned as Party leader in November 1911.

Note

'Hedgers' and 'Ditchers'

Despite the reforming parties having clear majorities in the two elections of 1910, the Lords did not give in easily. Until the last moment it seemed as if the 'ditchers' – those who would die in the last ditch, refusing to compromise – would win the vote and force the King to create those extra Liberal peers. However, Lord Curzon, argued that the Party's best interest lay in giving way and keeping its majority in a House of Lords which could still delay Liberal bills, and persuaded enough peers to allow the Parliament Bill to become the Parliament Act. Those who voted with Curzon were known as 'Hedgers'. Some 'ditchers' never forgave Curzon for what they regarded as his treachery.

Note

The three main changes to the Parliament Act, when it finally became law in 1911, were those of Asquith's Resolution (Source 11).

■ Questions

Read Sources 10, 11 and 12.

1 What was the strategy of the Liberals once the Conservatives made it clear that they would use the House of Lords to block the Budget?

2 Study the section headed Reforming the Lords.
(a) Summarize Churchill's comments (Source 12).
(b) Explain what the powers of the House of Lords were before 1911
(c) Explain how the Parliament Act changed them.

3 Why did the Lords behave the way they did?

4 What were the various consequences of the crisis of 1909–1911

The National Insurance Act 1911

The Parliament Act made possible the last and most important social reform of this government, the National Insurance Act of 1911.

It had two parts. Part 1 was to insure working people against ill-health. It was modelled on a scheme already in operation in Germany. Workers whose income was below the limit for paying income tax paid 'a flat rate' of four pence per week; their employer paid three pence and the State two pence. With this 'nine pence for four pence' insurance premium, a worker having to stay off work because of illness would receive 10 shillings per week and the services of a doctor who was on an insurance panel.

All Lloyd George's skills as a negotiator were needed to gain the agreements needed to make this an effective reform.

There were arguments about who the government would approve to act as insurers. Eventually Lloyd George agreed to a wide range of organizations acting as insurance agents. His decision to allow trade unions to act as approved insuring societies considerably strengthened these organizations. The Act included a maternity payment of 50 shillings but, because of opposition from the insuring organizations, benefits for widows and orphans were dropped.

There were also longer and sharper arguments with the doctors. For some months, their equivalent of a trade union, the British Medical Association (BMA) seemed hostile to the scheme. However, Lloyd George increased the fees that doctors would receive from taking part in the scheme and medical opposition evaporated.

The Labour Party would have preferred the whole cost to be paid for out of taxation with no contribution from the worker but Lloyd George won their support by agreeing to the payment of MPs.

Part 2 of the Act dealt with unemployment and had originally been designed for Churchill by a civil servant, William Beveridge, at the same time as the labour exchanges (see p. 148). Workers in industries like shipbuilding, construction and engineering, in which unemployment swiftly rose and fell, paid a weekly premium. In return they would get unemployment pay of 7 shillings per week for 15 weeks if laid off.

Part 1 of the Act was not immediately popular. Employers were seldom happy about their forced contribution. The same was true of many workers about their compulsory four pence contribution. Fine ladies joined mass meetings with their servants to protest about having to lick insurance stamps. However, it came to be accepted by the three major parties and by the population as a whole.

In contrast Part 2 was immediately popular and, in 1914, the government was considering extending it to other trades.

What was new about the National Insurance Act was this. It accepted that the State had responsibility for improving people's lives, especially the lives of the poorest workers. At the same time it insisted that people needed to take some responsibility for themselves. Hence the combination of contributions from the State, the employer and the individual. While, to begin with, the benefits in the 1911 Act were small and available only to a limited section of the population, its principles became an important feature of British social legislation for the rest of the twentieth century.

■ **Biography**

William Beveridge (1879–1963)

Beveridge is often described as the man who designed the British 'Welfare' State.

Born in India, he quickly impressed with his intelligence and had an impressive career as a student at Oxford University. At the age of 24 he became a sub-warden of Toynbee Hall in London's East End which was a centre for bringing privileged students in touch with industrial conditions. He soon became an expert on unemployment. He became director of labour exchanges in 1909,

Between the wars he held senior university posts and was appointed during the Second World War to plan the social services of peacetime Britain. His famous Beveridge Report was published in 1943 (see p. 256).

As the following sources illustrate, historians have debated both the motives behind the National Insurance Act and its significance.

Interpretations exercise: Social reform, Lloyd George and New Liberalism

Source A

One historian's view of Lloyd George's motives

To what extent did Lloyd George propose social reforms in response to the emergence of the Labour Party and in order to forestall its future growth? He was certainly aware that the Labour Party was using the need for social improvements in order to attract recruits. He also knew that the Liberal Party could not merely assume the allegiance [support] of working-class voters. In an important public speech in 1906 he argued that if the government failed to address social problems Labour would indeed become 'a great and sweeping force in this country – a force that will sweep away Liberalism.'… Nevertheless, at this time in his career, Lloyd George remained confident that Labour could be retained as a junior partner in a progressive alliance aimed at the Conservatives. The major political incentive to take up the cause of Liberal social reform was the continuation of Chamberlain's tariff reform campaign…[which] offered a constructive vision of improved imperial defence, greater national prosperity, more security of employment and higher standards of living.

Constantine, *Lloyd George*, 1992

Source B

An alternative view of Lloyd George's main motives

The issue of New Liberalism has…assumed immense importance in the debate that has focused on the rise of labour and the decline of Liberalism…It has been argued that L.T. Hobhouse, J.A. Hobson and David Lloyd George attempted to retain working-class support for the Liberal Party by offering a variety of social reforms and compromises to the working classes that became known as the New Liberalism. It is further argued that their prime concern was to reconcile the demand of labour with the need for Liberal Party unity.

Laybourn, *Modern Britain since 1906*, 1999

Source C

Another historian explains where Lloyd George got his ideas from

More than anyone else, he [Lloyd George] was responsible for giving the New Liberalism a real purchase in Edwardian politics; yet he had no more read his Rowntree or his Hobhouse in 1908 than he had actually read the Reports of the Royal Commission on the Poor Law in 1909 when he airily began citing them in his speeches. Talking to Rowntree or to Hobhouse or to others who had read them gave to Lloyd George more in half an hour than anything he got from book learning.

Clark, *Hope and Glory*, 1996

■ Examination style questions

1 What does Clarke (Source C) mean when he writes that 'Lloyd George was responsible for giving New Liberalism a real purchase in Edwardian politics…'

2 In what important way does Constantine (Source A) disagree with Laybourn (Source B) about the main reason for the Liberals' social reform policies?

3 Using the sources and your own knowledge, explain whether you agree with the view that the Liberal social reforms of 1906–1911 were introduced simply in order to forestall the future growth of the Labour Party.

Document exercise: The significance of the Liberal social reforms

Source A

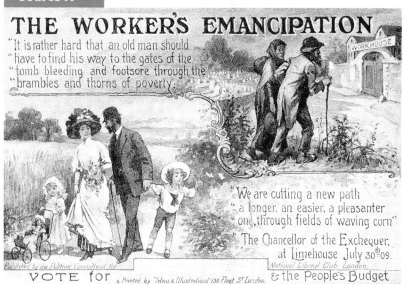

THE WORKER'S EMANCIPATION

"It is rather hard that an old man should
"have to find his way to the gates of the
"tomb bleeding and footsore through the
"brambles and thorns of poverty.

WORKHOUSE

"We are cutting a new path
"a longer, an easier, a pleasanter
"one, through fields of waving corn"
The Chancellor of the Exchequer,
at Limehouse July 30ᵗʰ 09.

Published by the Political Committee of the   *National Liberal Club London.*

VOTE for   *& Printed by "Ideas & Illustrations" 130 Fleet St London.* & the People's Budget

◀ A Liberal election postcard of 1910. Note the workhouse in the top right hand corner and the space for the local candidate's name on the bottom line.

Source B

A historian's account of reactions to the social reforms

...there was widespread suspicion [among working people] of the policies and action of Liberal and other politicians. The grounds for this suspicion were that they were too limited, 'too intrusive' and a threat to working class independence. But these views were not universal and probably diminished over time. Many poorer people, though, were grateful for the amelioration [improvement] of hard lives. It is reasonable to conclude that very many people would have preferred, as an ideal, regular work, wages sufficient for a decent life, however defined, allowing them sufficient surplus to save for hard times and perhaps even to choose to pay for their children's education, their own health or health care, leaving the State the minimal role of providing services which the individual could not.

Thane, 'The working class and State welfare',
Historical Journal 27/4, 1984

Source C

Another historian assesses the significance of the National insurance Act

The entire [National Insurance] Act was a considerable departure in British social legislation, though so much of Part 1 was borrowed from German experience that it showed no great claims to originality.

Lloyd, *Empire to Welfare State. English History 1906–1967*, 1970

Source D

An alternative view of the significance of Liberal measures

A 'social service state', in which minimum standards were assured, was beginning to emerge by 1914, although this minimum was not yet universally available. The true 'welfare state', embracing the idea of the optimum (the best) rather than the minimum, lay forty years in the future. But the principle of provision through insurance was already established. This contrasted to the socialist method, advocated by Keir Hardie in opposition to Lloyd George, of financing benefits through graduated taxation. Ramsay MacDonald accepted the contributory principle in 1911, and the 1945 Labour government followed MacDonald, not Hardie, when it created the present-day Welfare State.

Read, *Edwardian England*, 1980

Another verdict on the significance of the reforms.

One of the longest running controversies in twentieth century historical studies is over the scope and status to be attributed to the social reforms of the Edwardian era: do they deserve to be regarded as forming the origins of the modern Welfare State or were they the continuance of a late-Victorian tradition of minimal piecemeal reform?...Without doubt there is room for legitimate debate among historians, but in my view these reforms fall within a limited, filling-the-gaps tradition, bearing no more than the faintest distant relationship to the idea of a comprehensive Welfare State.

Marwick, *Britain in Our Century*, 1984

■ Historical debate

The Strange Death of Liberal England

George Dangerfield's book was published in 1936. It has a memorable title and is vividly written. He argued that so serious were the problems faced by the Liberals and the country after 1909 that liberalism was finished and parliamentary democracy in great danger. The First World War prevented revolution but liberalism was past recovery; hence its collapse between 1918 and 1924. Dangerfield exaggerated the danger of revolution but his thesis that liberalism was fatally wounded before the First World War has aroused lively controversy among later historians (see Chapter 11)

■ Examination-style questions

1 **Comprehension in context**
For what reasons does the poster (Source A) suggest that the workers should vote Liberal in 1910?

2 **Comparing the sources**
To what extent do Read (Source D) and Marwick (Source E) disagree about the nature of the Liberals' social reforms?

3 **Assessing the sources**
To what extent does Source B confirm the message of the Liberal poster (Source A)?

4 **Making judgements**
Using the sources and your own knowledge, explain how far you agree with the view expressed in Source C that the National Insurance Act was 'a considerable departure in British social legislation'.

Phase 3 Years of difficulty 1911–1914

1911–1914 industrial unrest

In the years leading up to the First World War, the country was disrupted by a series of major strikes – to such an extent that some writers, notably George Dangerfield in his *Strange Death of Liberal England* (1936) believed that, but for the war, there would have been social revolution. There was a major coal strike in south Wales in 1910–1911, and one of dockers and railway workers in 1911. In 1912, which saw another major coal strike and another London dock strike, 41 million days were lost in strikes.

The causes of unrest

These were mainly economic, despite the influence of syndicalism on some of the union leaders (see p. 118) Though the country as a whole was getting richer, and some of the rich were very rich, most working people did not feel part of that prosperity. On the contrary, there was little unemployment and inflation was taking prices higher while wages remained stable. In the 13 years from 1900 to 1913, real income (that is income allowing for inflation) rose only 0.4 per cent each year. That compared poorly with the 1.2 per cent of the 1890s and the 3.5 per cent of the 1880s. Many workers were actually getting poorer and the waves of strikes were needed to get their real wages back to 1900 levels.

Some employers angered their workers by making them work harder without extra pay. Some coal owners argued that they had to demand more of their miners because the government had forced them to accept the eight-hour day. Railway owners also justified requiring more of their workers because the government was now regulating freight rates and preventing increases which it considered excessive.

Sir George Askwith, the government adviser on industrial affairs described the situation in 1913:

Source 13

There is a spirit abroad of unrest, of movement, a spirit and a desire of improvement, of alteration. We are, in fact, in as quick an age of transition as there has been for many generations past....When you come to certain standards of wages and livelihood and find that particular things that you particularly use rise greatly in price, it affects the amenities of life and the margin of life to such an extent that there is disenchantment and a desire to keep to that standard which may have been achieved...In addition you have in this country for some years past what I may call political equality....if a man has got educated up to the view of considering himself politically equal to another man, he is far more anxious to achieve a greater amount of equality...That shortly sums up some of the reasons why there is unrest, unrest that nobody can be surprised at, and which is bound to continue.

Another cause may have been the growing size and confidence of trade unions. In 1910, the TUC had 1,648,000 members, in 1914, 2,232,000, a 35 per cent increase. This rise was partly due to non-unionized workers deciding that membership would help them in these difficult times and partly because the National Insurance Act of 1911 included trade unions among the 'approved' societies which could provide insurance.

These were big and bad-tempered events which caused suffering and anxiety. The summer of 1911 was the hottest for a generation which made matters worse. Alarmed by the international crisis begun by the Agadir incident (see p. 101) the government used soldiers to maintain law and order and keep essential services running. In August 1911, serious rioting occurred in Llanelli in the South Wales Coalfield which included looting. The rioters stoned the troops sent to restore order. Shots were fired and two bystanders killed.

Since the Liberal Party claimed to be the party of both the employers and the workers, the Liberal government found it difficult both to take sides and also to stay out of the disputes. Lloyd George's negotiating skills helped to bring the 1911 railway strike to an end. In contrast Churchill, rather unfairly, gained a lasting reputation as a minister who was too quick to bring troops into industrial disputes. The government also continued its move away from 'laissez-faire' by passing in 1912 the Minimum Wages Act which set up Boards in the coal-mining districts to fix, district by district, minimum daily rates of pay.

1912 was the worst year for industrial unrest, though another 10 million days were lost because of strikes in 1913, when three large unions – the National Union of Railwaymen, the Miners' Federation and the Transport Workers' Federation (which included the dockers) – agreed to assist each other in industrial disputes. If they struck together, the combined numbers of this 'triple alliance' were such that it would have been virtually a general strike. 1914 started quietly with few labour disputes but the government was bracing itself for another storm of industrial strife. Instead, in the light of the national emergency brought by the outbreak of war with Germany in August 1914, industrial peace descended.

■ Think about

Study Source 13.

▶ What does Askwith mean by 'as quick an age of transition as there has been for many generations past'?

▶ What does he believe to be the two most important causes of the unrest?

▶ How useful a source is this on the causes of industrial unrest between 1911 and 1914?

▶ What other sources would be particularly useful to historians studying the causes of this civil unrest?

Note

Dangerfield made considerable use of Askwith's diaries for his *Strange Death of Liberal England* (see page 155).

▶ Striking railwaymen on the march, London 1911.

■ **Think about**

▶ How important were the railways to British society in 1911?

▶ What else does Source 14 tell you about early twentieth-century transport?

▶ Why were these men striking?

■ **Think about**

▶ Hardie's view that strike action was no substitute for political action. Why did he believe that these waves of strikes were damaging to the Labour Party?

Note

Lloyd George and Frances Stevenson

His liaison with Frances Stevenson increased Lloyd George's dodgy reputation. Frances was a friend of his daughter Mair and trained as a teacher. She met Lloyd George when she was giving private lessons to his younger daughter Megan and, in her own words, 'had her judgement swept aside' by his magnetism. She became his secretary and mistress, bore him a child and stayed with him for the rest of his life. He promised her that he would marry her when his wife Margaret died and fulfilled this promise in 1943, two years before he died.

Both Lloyd George and Frances Stevenson were strongly criticized for their relationship. In defence of them both, it is worth pointing out that his wife, Margaret, refused to move from her home in Criccieth and had no interest in his political career.

Source 14

The Labour Party and industrial unrest

The industrial strife of 1911–1914 was a great challenge to the Labour Party since, on the one hand, it was very sympathetic to the grievances which caused the conflicts; but on the other, it thoroughly disapproved of the tension and violence of the industrial disputes which did nothing to improve Labour's electoral popularity.

Kenneth Morgan, Keir Hardie's biographer, describes well the difficulties which the industrial conflicts posed for the Labour leader:

Source 15

He [Keir Hardie] was instinctively sympathetic to the workers' cause. He well understood the growing unemployment, the decline in real wages, the population pressures, the squalid living conditions that had brought the strikes about. He also recognized the massive combines and cartels (employers working closely together), with their resultant sharpening of the conflict between capital and labour...On 15 November 1910 he clashed bitterly with Winston Churchill, the Home Secretary, about police brutality during the Tonypandy disturbances [industrial unrest in south Wales]...In one notorious episode [in 1911]...two railway workers were shot down and killed. Hardie replied with a searing pamphlet 'Killing no murder'...and laid the blame...entirely upon the army to whom the government had given a free hand to suppress industrial violence, whatever the human cost.

On the other hand, he was disturbed by some of the forms the industrial protest took. He deplored all attempts to agitate for the unions' demands in a violent manner...Further, efforts to transform the nationwide industrial struggle into localized campaigns for syndicalism or workers' control were totally against Hardie's commitment to disciplined, coherent class action. The strike was no substitute for political action. Workers should strive to control the State, not destroy it, and the Labour Party was their predestined instrument.

Morgan, *Keir Hardie*, 1997

More crises 1911–1914

The Marconi scandal 1912

The reputation of the government and of Lloyd George in particular took a severe knock in 1912. In comparison with many of his political colleagues, Lloyd George was far from wealthy and one of his ambitions was the desire to be really rich. In 1912 he bought 1000 shares in the American Marconi Company for £2 each, on the advice of a Cabinet colleague, Rufus Isaacs. Soon the shares had doubled in value. Rufus' brother Godfrey was a director not only of the American Marconi Company, but of the linked English Marconi Company too. Recently the Liberal government had given a big contract to the English Marconi Company. Other leading Liberals were involved and the media found out. Asquith appointed a Select Committee to investigate the issue. It did no more than criticize the ministers involved for 'want of frankness' and the government easily survived a vote of censure in the Commons.

Lloyd George does not seem to have thought that he had done anything wrong. However, many people, including some old friends, thought that, for someone holding the post of Chancellor of the Exchequer, he had behaved foolishly and, without Asquith's firm support, he might have had to resign.

Female suffrage 1910–1914

The problems which the Liberal government faced over women's suffrage are described in Chapter 8. What effect they had on the popularity of the government is hard to judge. On the one hand, the violence of the suffragettes clearly turned opinion both inside and outside Parliament against the immediate granting of votes for women. On the other, Asquith's obstinate and prejudiced opposition to change persuaded many otherwise Liberal women to turn to Labour as their best hope for suffrage reform and may well have stayed loyal to Labour when they won the vote in 1918. Furthermore, the measures which the government used to deal with suffragette violence, like the Cat and Mouse Act (see p. 130) were clearly illiberal and unlikely to improve the Party's electoral popularity.

Home Rule for Ireland

This was the government's priority between 1911 and 1914. Reform of the House of Lords allowed the Liberal government at last to make Home Rule a reality and the Home Rule Act was passed in 1913. It was one thing, however, to pass a Home Rule Act in London and quite another to make it effective peacefully in Ireland. Chapter 3 explains in detail what then happened.

As far as the popularity of the Liberal Party in England is concerned, Asquith's 'wait and see' policy meant that there was no civil war over Ulster and appeared in the summer of 1914 to be bringing both Redmond's Irish Nationalists and the Ulster Unionists to the realization that a peaceful settlement could be achieved if each side were prepared to compromise on the details of partition. That compromise could not be found by the time the First World War started and events during the war made compromise impossible. If Asquith had been more decisive, insisted on a partition earlier and achieved a settlement before the outbreak of war, the history of Ireland might have been quite different.

▲ A poverty-stricken mother waits with her children to see what the local poulterer has left over at the end of the day (1889).

■ Think about

Look at Sources 16 and 17 and consider the extremes of wealth in late Victorian Britain.
▶ Why did such differences exist?
▶ How far have they now been reduced?

▲ The upper classes show themselves off to each other at Ascot (1911).

The Liberal electoral prospects in 1914

The next election was due in 1915. Voting intentions a year in advance are hard to predict now and were harder then but the Liberal leadership in 1914 were in no way downhearted.

The Labour Party had performed feebly in Parliament and seemed much in need of a Liberal alliance if it were to maintain, let alone improve on its 42 seats.

The Conservative Party was in a mess. It was still split over Tariff Reform. Its new leader Bonar Law had a cold and rather forbidding image and his total commitment to the Unionist cause in Ulster was not a vote-winner.

The major uncertainty for the Liberal leadership about the 1915 election was the Irish vote. Since 1886, 80 or more Irish Nationalists had voted loyally with the Liberals in order to gain Home Rule, and Irish Nationalist support had been, since the January election of 1910, the difference between the Liberals governing and being in opposition. By the Home Rule Act, there would be 42 Irish MPs but how would they vote, now they had achieved Home Rule? They might continue to vote Liberal out of gratitude but on education, licensing and tariffs, they were closer to the Conservatives.

All in all the Liberal Party seemed to be in as good an electoral state as it had been in 1910 and some distance away from electoral disaster.

Summary

- The Liberal leaders, particularly Lloyd George and Churchill, were influenced by the 'New Liberalism'. These ideas marked a break with the traditions of Gladstonian Liberalism. They represented a move away from laissez-faire towards collectivism and encouraged policies of social reform. There is no doubt that the New Liberalism was influential but how influential is a matter of debate between historians.
- The effectiveness of the Liberal government was badly affected by the blocking tactics of the House of Lords between 1905 and 1909. The Liberal government dealt skilfully with this problem. By the People' Budget of 1909, it provoked the Lords into total opposition and then used popular support to reduce the powers of the Lords by the Parliament Act of 1911.
- This was one of the most vigorous reforming governments of modern British history. Its social reforms considerably extended the functions of the State, though the extent to which they amount to the foundations of the 'Welfare State' is a matter of historical debate.
- Particularly difficult problems faced the Liberal government after 1911 – notably the campaign for female suffrage, the Home Rule crisis in Ireland and industrial unrest. The coming of the First World War makes it virtually impossible to judge how successful the government would have been in the long run in dealing with these problems in normal peacetime conditions.
- How strong the Liberal Party was in 1914 is a matter of intense debate among historians (see Chapter 11).

Questions

The government faced a number of problems including:
(a) the demand for health insurance
(b) the demand for old age pensions
(c) pressure from the suffragettes
(d) antagonism from the House of Lords

1 Explain how any of these two issues caused problems to the Liberal government from 1906 to 1914.

2 Compare the success of the Liberal government from 1906 to 1914 in dealing with at least three of these problems.

Activity   KEY SKILLS

Synthesize all the sources on pages 152-159 to explain why, despite its social reforms, the years 1910-1914 were so difficult for the Liberal government.

Further reading

Donald Read, *Edwardian England*, 1980
R. Jenkins, *Mr Balfour's Poodle, Peers v. People*, 1952
M. Pugh, *Lloyd George*, 1988
J. Grigg, *Lloyd George, 3 vols*, 1973-85
M. Freeden, *The New Liberalism*, 1978

Chapter 10

The First World War and its effects
Catastrophe

▲ This painting of 1918, entitled 'The Mule Track', by Paul Nash brilliantly captures the horrors of a First World War bombardment.

Source 2

If I were fierce, and bald, and short of breath,
I'd live with scarlet majors at the Base,
And speed glum heroes up the line to death.

From *Base Details* by Siegfried Sassoon

Introduction

Britain did not want to go to war in 1914. The war she had to fight turned out to be far more destructive and lasted much longer than anyone had dared imagine before it started. Though Britain emerged on the winning side, the war had many damaging consequences and the post-war period of adjustment was extremely difficult. This chapter concentrates on Britain's part in the war in Europe and its effects on British politics and society.

Key questions

- What were the main strategic issues of the war?
- Why did it prove to be so destructive?
- Why did it last so long?
- Why did Britain and her allies emerge victorious?
- What were the main effects of the war on British society?

1914: A war of movement

The Western Front, 1914–1917.

The Germans expected their carefully planned advance on Paris through Belgium to win them a quick and decisive victory. However, as agreed during the pre-war Anglo-French military conversations, the small British Expeditionary Force (BEF), 100,000 strong, entered Belgium to fight alongside the French. It first met the enemy in Belgium near Mons but was swept back with the French by the surging German advance. The instinct of the British commander, Sir John French, was to desert his French colleagues and head for the safety of the Channel ports. However, General Kitchener, ordered him to keep in contact with his French allies. Consequently, the BEF marched furiously south to take part in the Battle of the Marne (see small map).

The part it actually played was decidedly odd. The main German armies were wide apart and struggling to hold off the counter-attacks of the French. The BEF found itself advancing into the gap between the German forces and experienced few casualties. The Germans then decided that their strategic position was fragile and retreated. As they reached the River Aisne, they discovered that by digging trenches they could, with their machine-guns, hold off their pursuers fairly easily. The British and French then tried without success to prevent them from extending their defensive line to the Channel.

The Battle of the Marne, September 1914.

Note

The Allies and the Central Powers

The Allies: Britain, France and Russia
The Central Powers: Germany and Austria-Hungary
Fighting with the Allies were Serbia, Italy (1915), Romania (1916) and the USA (1917)
With the Central Powers, Turkey and Bulgaria (1915)

This manoeuvring led in mid-October to British and German troops meeting and fighting in the first battle of Ypres (see main map). The Belgian town was held for the Allies but with such high casualties that the BEF was effectively destroyed. The British war effort now depended on Kitchener's new volunteer army, much larger but less well trained.

1915–1916 A war of attrition

The word 'attrition' means 'wearing down'. It describes the strategy which most of the generals adopted on the Western Front. If there were to be no quick victories, then the enemy would have to be worn down. In practice, attrition meant immense and frequent bombardments by heavy artillery. These were followed by infantry assaults on the enemy trenches. If these did not achieve a breakthrough (which they seldom did) then it was hoped that the enemy's losses would be heavier than one's own and, eventually, he would ask for peace. Hence the long list of offensives on the Western Front and their almost unbelievable numbers of casualties. 'Easterner' strategists like Churchill planned to achieve victory without 'attrition' by concentrating on Eastern Europe, defeating first Turkey, then Austria-Hungary. Disaster at Gallipoli in 1915 greatly lessened their influence.

The war at sea

The assumptions of the pre-war admirals turned out to be as false as those of the generals. The splendid and expensive Dreadnought fleets, instead of meeting in some equivalent of the Battle of Trafalgar, skulked in harbour for most of the war. The admirals had failed to notice that the new technology of submarines and mines had made their Dreadnoughts out of date almost as soon as they were launched. There was only one major indecisive clash, in 1916, in the North Sea off Jutland.

So a war of attrition also came to be waged at sea. It hit both Britain and Germany hard. German submarines (U-boats) sank ships bound for British ports, carrying food and other supplies. Unrestricted U-boat warfare, i.e. the sinking of all ships, not just British ones, nearly starved Britain into surrender in 1917, until the introduction of convoys greatly reduced the rate of sinkings. For their part, the British blockaded Germany by mining the North Sea, putting pressure on neutral countries to end their trade with Germany and intercepting ships approaching German ports. This blockade grew steadily tighter. By 1917, there were severe shortages and food riots.

Peace feelers 1916–1917

As the carnage continued, there were a number of attempts to start peace talks – President Wilson in 1916, Lord Lansdowne in Britain and the Archduke Charles of Austria-Hungary in 1917. European socialists called for a peace without conquests and damages. They also suggested a peace conference at Stockholm. The British government opposed the idea, causing Henderson, the Labour leader, to resign from the War Cabinet.

There were many reasons why no serious peace talks took place before 1918. For almost the whole length of the war, the German government believed that victory was likely. It had no intention of giving up Alsace and Lorraine, to which it intended to add part of Belgium. The French could not abandon Alsace and Lorraine nor the British Belgium. Moreover, by 1917, Britain and France had committed themselves to the self-determination of people subject to the Austrian Empire, which was a serious obstacle for the Austrian government.

Facts and figures

Major offensives on the Western Front, showing British casualties

1914	Ypres	60,000
1915	Loos	50,000
1916	The Somme	400,000
1917	Passchendaele	350,000

Note

Gallipoli and the Easterners

The 'easterner' strategy was an imaginative one. This was the plan. Compared to Germany, the Turkish Empire and Austria-Hungary were weak, so:

- Seize the Gallipoli peninsula to the south of Constantinople.

- Take Constantinople.

- Link with Russian forces and, by a co-ordinated attack defeat Austria-Hungary.

- Germany would then have to make peace.

Unfortunately, the attack on Gallipoli was an appalling bungle. Allied troops had to be withdrawn having failed to get off the beaches. Winston Churchill, whose plan it was, resigned from the government and the 'westerners' led by generals like Haig kept a grip on strategy. Victory would be won, they insisted, by a breakthrough on the Western Front.

▲ German sailors on the conning tower of their U-boat on the look-out for more victims.

Anyway, the important leaders like Lloyd George in Britain, Ludendorff in Germany and Clemenceau in France insisted on total victory.

1917–1918 Allied victory

Wars of attrition need more than strong armies if they are to be won. Also required are the economic means to keep providing the men and weapons which such wars devour. Having started with an army of only 150,000 men, by 1918 the British Empire had mobilized more than 9,000,000, first through volunteers and then through conscription. In 1918 a large and well-equipped British army was bearing the brunt of the final German onslaught.

The first of the Great Powers to be broken by attrition was Russia, in 1917. That same year the German leaders had decided on the unrestricted U-boat warfare, which was effective against Britain, but ran the risk of bringing the USA into the war against them. They believed that they had to starve Britain into surrender before the British blockade caused a revolution in Germany. Once Britain surrendered, France would give up too and Germany would then have control of Europe well before the USA could send troops across the Atlantic.

Since the U-boat gamble failed, Germany had no option but to seek a decisive military victory before the American troops arrived in France in any strength. Between March and July 1918, Ludendorff launched a series of offensives which on a number of occasions appeared to be close to breaking through to Paris. In this crisis, the British and French governments appointed the French general Foch to overall command of the Allied forces. In fact Foch only influenced the course of the battles in a limited way, but he was able to move the Allied reserve armies more flexibly than before to close the gaps which Ludendorff had opened.

The Allied line held. By September there were a million American troops in France. Then the Central Powers suddenly collapsed. An Allied army advancing north from Salonika in Greece triggered off revolts which caused the Austrian Empire to sue for peace. Though by now the German army was in retreat, it was retreating in good order. Nonetheless, the German government knew that its position was hopeless. It approached President Wilson to negotiate peace terms on the basis of the Fourteen Points he had announced in January 1918. Internal revolutions then swept away the old German government. Against this chaotic background an Armistice was signed and fighting ceased on 11 November.

Why did Britain and her allies emerge victorious in 1918?

In simple terms, the alliance of Britain and the British Empire, France and the USA proved too strong for that of Germany, Austria-Hungary and Turkey. The military and economic strength of the USA was the critical element. The US government declared war on Germany because it was provoked by Germany and also it calculated that it had too much money invested in Britain and France to allow a German victory.

Nonetheless Britain's contributions to victory were considerable. The naval blockade of Germany was increasingly effective. The British army fought with resolution and growing expertise. It kept the war going long enough to enable the American army to get to France. The government of Lloyd George was dynamic, resourceful and wholly committed to victory. It managed to mobilize and concentrate enough of the resources of Britain and the Empire to make victory possible and then sustain popular support through difficult times to ensure that victory was won.

▲ 'Our monster tanks' reads the caption of this 1917 photograph 'break the belts of barbed wire and completely surprise the Hun at Cambrai'. In fact, tanks played only a small part in the First World War but were to transform completely land warfare in the Second World War.

■ Think about

▶ Could victory have been won without such heavy casualties?

Consider:

● In 1918, Ludendorff's troops nearly broke the Allied lines. The bombardment by heavy artillery was more accurate. Specially trained troops moving fast in small groups made surprise attacks on those parts of the line they had found to be the weakest.

● In the Second World War, trenches provided no adequate defence against tanks. There were tanks in the First World War but they were unreliable and the generals did not work out how to co-ordinate them effectively with the rest of their armies.

● A revised 'easterner' strategy. If Gallipoli (1915) was a disaster, Salonika (1918) was a triumph, though after years of stalemate.

Haig's qualities as a general

Historical Debate: How good a general was Field Marshal Sir Douglas Haig?

Haig commanded the largest army in the history of his country and led it to victory over a German army which was by any standards a formidable fighting force. During the war, whatever politicians like Lloyd George might think of him, his reputation with the King, with his fellow soldiers (for the most part) and with the British public was good. This reputation was sustained by his diaries and by the verdict of the British Official History of the War, which to a large degree confirmed Haig's interpretation of the war as set out in his diaries. There he appears as an experienced no-nonsense professional who knew what he was doing, though he sometimes had to make difficult choices in demanding circumstances. In such circumstances he could count on the aid of the Almighty. His task was often made harder by ill-informed and unscrupulous politicians like Lloyd George and untrustworthy foreigners, mainly the French.

For many years, this version of Haig's skills as a general was the usual one, as the following three sources show.

Source 3

Punch was a weekly magazine that was very popular with the British middle classes between 1850 and 1950. It produced its *History of the Great War* in 1919, which contained the following poem about Haig:

'And howsoe'er at times the battle sways
The army's trust in your command increase
Patient in preparation, swift in deed
We have in you the leader we need.'

Source 4

It is a simple historical fact that the British generals of the First World War did not fail in their duty. It was not a British delegation that crossed the line with a white flag in November 1918. No German army of occupation was stationed on the Thames…Behind Haig's bristling moustaches and the granite jaw was a surprisingly high degree of broad-minded flexibility, unexpected adaptability to change, (and) readiness to accept and use novelties.

Terraine, *Haig, the Educated Soldier*, 1960

■ Biography

Sir Douglas Haig (1861–1928)

Haig fought in the Sudan (1898) and South Africa (1899–1902). A cavalry specialist, he was very ambitious and secured some useful friends in high places, notably King George V. He was promoted to senior posts in India before returning to England in 1912. On the outbreak of war, he was effectively second-in-command of the BEF to Sir John French and succeeded the latter when he was sacked in 1915. Despite the enmity of Lloyd George, he kept his command for the rest of the war. Then a grateful country made him an Earl and gave him £100,000, a huge sum for those days. He died in 1928.

▲ Haig looking resolute for the photographer in 1917.

Source 5

Haig was a simple and humble man of great character. Unshakeable in purpose, far-seeing and determined, he had under his command at the time the largest British army which had ever taken the field, with complicated problems of supply, organization and training. He had to deal with politicians who did not always support him…He had difficulties with the French, to whom he was always loyal in his pursuit of victory.

The Encyclopaedia Britannica 1974 edition.
The Encyclopaedia Britannica was first published in 1768 and in the course of two centuries aimed to provide its readers with reliable up-to-date information on all important matters by having its entries written by experts.

In contrast, since 1960, historical opinion has tended to be very critical of Haig.

Source 6

Oft-quoted is his memo of 1915 to the War Council:

> The machine-gun is a much over-rated weapon and two a battalion is more than sufficient.

And the fact that by 1918, the average number of machine-guns per battalion was 43!

Source 7

Another quotation frequently repeated in relation to Haig and other British generals of the First World War comes from a conversation after the war between Ludendorff and colleague General Hoffman.

> Ludendorff: The English soldiers fight like lions
>
> Hoffman: But don't we know that they are led by donkeys.

Source 8

I could hardly believe that my ears were not deceiving me. He spoke in the rosiest terms of our chances of breaking through. I had been all over the ground and to my mind the eventuality was impossible.

Lt-Col Alan Brooke, on Haig's briefings before the Battle of Passchendaele, 1917

Haig in action: Passchendaele 1917

Haig was confident that he could break through the German line, advance along the Belgian coast, swing behind the German lines and win the war.

> 'Everything went wrong. The drainage system of Flanders broke down, as had been foretold. To make matters worse, it was the rainiest August for many years. Men struggled forward up to their waists in mud. The guns sank in the mud. The tanks could not be used. Haig had declared his intention to stop the offensive if the first attack failed. He did not do so. The futile struggle went on for three months. The British advanced in all four miles. Three British soldiers were killed for every two Germans.'

Taylor, *English History 1914–45*, 1965

Source 9

[Haig insisted that the] massed linear advance was to remain basic…What Haig should have been working towards, as the French and Germans had perceived…were flexible barrages, infiltration methods and training in small groups. Haig's orders demonstrate that all these were beyond his grasp.

The critical historian Denis Winter on Passchendele.
Winter, *Haig's Command*, 1991

■ Questions

1 Study Sources 3, 4, and 5. What do they consider to be Haig's outstanding qualities as a general?

2 Study Sources 6, 7, 8, and 9. Summarize what seem to be their main criticisms of Haig as a general.

3 Compare Source 4 (John Terraine) with Source 9 (Denis Winter). To what extent do they agree and disagree?

4 What was Haig trying to achieve at Passchendaele? What success did he have?

5 From the information on these pages and your own knowledge, how good a general do you think Haig was?

6 Had he much choice about the way he used his troops?

Source 10

◀ Machine-gunners surrounded by the mud and water of Passchendaele in 1917.

The effects of the war on British politics

At the start of the war, the Liberal government tried to continue without much change. 'Business as usual' was its motto. Only a few of its own supporters opposed the war. It had the full backing of the Conservatives. Though Ramsay MacDonald had resigned as Labour leader in protest against the war, the new leader, Arthur Henderson, and most trade unionists also offered their warm support. The only major change to the government was to bring in Lord Kitchener as Secretary for War.

The parties agreed that the general election due in 1915 should be postponed until the war was over. The reality of wartime 1915 was the Gallipoli disaster and a scandal over the apparent shortage of shells for the Western Front. These crises persuaded Asquith to form a coalition government, bringing into the Cabinet the Conservatives Bonar Law and Balfour. Lloyd George moved to the Ministry of Munitions where he quickly gained the reputation for getting things done.

War needs caused the government to extend considerably State controls. Businesses were controlled to ensure the production of weapons; skilled workers' privileges ended so that unskilled men and women could do specialist war work. Worried that workers were unproductive because they were drinking too much, the government raised the price of beer, had it diluted and forbade pubs to open in the afternoons. Tight censorship of the Press was introduced in 1914, conscription in 1916 and rationing in 1918. It raised income tax a number of times. At the end of the war the rate was 6 shillings (30p) in the pound.

By 1916, when there was little sign that the war was being won, the Press and politicians began to grumble about Asquith's leadership. 'Wait and see' may have worked well in peacetime, but it was not a recipe for winning wars. In particular, he dithered about introducing conscription. At the end of 1916 some complicated plotting ended up with Lloyd George replacing Asquith as Prime Minister and started a personal antagonism which was to help destroy the Liberal Party.

However, Lloyd George was a vastly better war leader. Dynamic, imaginative, determined and persuasive, his confidence that the war could be won was infectious. He wanted the best people to help him and cared little about their party political opinions. To run the war, he created a small cross-party War Cabinet – himself (Liberal), Bonar Law, Curzon and Milner (Conservative) and Henderson, (Labour). Businessmen and trade unionists were called in to run vital ministries like Shipping and Labour. He appointed many new personal assistants to help in the war effort and had temporary accommodation built for them close to 10 Downing Street (the garden suburb). Between 1916 and 1918 he spent little time in Parliament.

He brought the Admiralty under his control in 1917, when he insisted on the introduction of the convoy system. He failed, however, with the army. He would have liked to have got rid of Haig but the latter had the support of the Conservatives and the King, and could not be budged. The British war effort suffered from the mutual distrust of the Prime Minister and the Commander in Chief.

At the end of the war, Lloyd George's personal popularity had never been greater. However, between 1916 and 1918 he had made many enemies within the Liberal Party and had become heavily dependent on the Conservatives. As far as their fortunes in peacetime were concerned, the Conservative and Labour Parties did well out of the war, the Liberals badly as Chapter 11 explains.

■ Think about

▶ Why was it particularly hard for a Liberal like Asquith, who had served under Gladstone, to provide the kind of leadership which so great a war required?

Note

The Maurice debate

In May 1918, Sir Frederick Maurice, a friend of Haig, wrote a letter to *The Times* accusing Lloyd George of lying to the House of Commons about the strength of the British army. Asquith used this to set up a debate in the House of Commons which was essentially a vote of confidence in Lloyd George's leadership. Lloyd George triumphed in the Commons, by using figures, apparently from Maurice himself, to prove that he had not lied. However, the figures he presented to the Commons were suspect and, almost certainly, he knew that. The Maurice debate was another important stage in the break up between Lloyd George and Asquith.

The social and economic consequences of the war

These were widespread and far-reaching.

On the negative side, 750,000 men were dead, another 1,500,000 were permanently affected by the effects of wounds or gas. A generation of parents and loved-ones had to bear a burden of grief without precedent in British history.

The economic effects on Britain were also very damaging. U-boats had sunk 40 per cent of British merchant shipping. To keep the war going, Britain had lent around £1,800,000,000 to her allies and borrowed about £850,000 from the USA. In the chaos of the inter-war years, she got few of her loans back, while remaining indebted to the USA. Consequently, Britain never regained her pre-war international financial predominance. Some of her overseas markets, which had been closed to her during the war, were lost to the neutral competitors who had taken them over.

On the credit side, the war boosted democracy. In 1918 virtually all men and women over 30 gained the vote (see Chapters 7 and 8). It created a new demand for education which was partially met by Fisher's Education Act of 1918, which raised the leaving age for compulsory, full-time education to 14. Unskilled working men found work and were paid at better rates. Their health improved as did that of their families.

Wars usually boost technologies which then can be adapted to peacetime use. the First World War was no exception. Aeroplane design improved quickly during the war and the first regular passenger air service was opened between London and Paris in 1919. Radio technology also advanced by leaps and bounds during the war. By 1922 the BBC was broadcasting to the nation.

Recent historians have tended to suggest that the consequences of the First World War were not as far-reaching as contemporaries and earlier historians have made out. Women would have won the vote any way, they argue. The loss of life was not that disruptive because fewer people emigrated. If women outnumbered men in the 1920s, they outnumbered them before 1914, so the change was only marginal.

What cannot be ignored is the death, destruction and sheer horror of the war and its impact on the national mood. During the nineteenth century most Britons had looked forward to the future with confidence. They had, for the most part, a real if simple belief in progress. That confidence was shattered as a consequence of the 1914–1918 war. The attempts by national leaders to solve the acute problems of the 1920s and 1930s were characterized by a caution, a nostalgia for pre-1914 certainties and a determination to maintain peace at any price which were an important, direct and harmful consequence of the four ghastly years of the Great War.

■ Think about

▶ If you had been living in 1918–1919, in the light of the damage and suffering caused to Britain between 1914 and 1918, what attitude would you have wished Lloyd George to take towards Germany at the Versailles peace negotiations?

▲ Thanks to the technological advances of the war, a 'must' for the modern home of the 1930s, an Amphion 6 wireless of 1931.

Document exercise: Lloyd George as war leader

Source A

Lloyd George leads a revolution in government

Lloyd George's accession to power in December 1916 was more than a change of government. It was a revolution, British-style. The party magnates [bosses] and whips had been defied. The backbenchers and the newspapers combined in a sort of unconscious plebiscite and made Lloyd George dictator for the duration of the war. Balfour said: 'If he wants to be a dictator, let him be. If he thinks that he can win the war, I'm all for letting him have a try.' Lloyd George was the nearest thing England has known to a Napoleon, a supreme ruler maintaining himself by individual achievement. A detached observer wrote at the end of the war: 'The effects of the change in direction two years ago may be compared to the substitution of dynamite for a damp squib.' The dynamite exploded. There were new departments of state; new men; new methods of control and regulation; and a new form of cabinet government. The explosions were sporadic. Lloyd George was not a man of plan and system. When faced with a difficulty, he listened to ideas of others and saw, in a flash, the solution.

Taylor, *English History 1914–1945*, 1965

Source B

Decisive intervention in the shipping crisis, March 1917

Lloyd George made his inquiries [about the losses to U-boats], consulting junior officers secretly and in defiance of custom. He learnt that, out of the 2,500 ships [that the Admiralty claimed sailed each week], 2,400 were in the coasting trade; only 100 ships a week had to be protected against attacks on the high seas. The Admiralty had insisted that merchant seamen were incapable of sailing in convoy; Lloyd George showed that they were already sailing the Channel in convoy. At the end of April, the War Cabinet let it be known that the convoy system was going to be imposed on the Admiralty; on 30 April Lloyd George and Curzon took the Admiralty over for the day, saw that the convoys would be organized, and arranged for the creation of a naval general staff...this was one of the decisive interventions of the war.'

Lloyd, *Empire to Welfare State. English History 1906–1967*, 1970

Source C

A reassessment

Critics and admirers alike considered that the system of government instituted by Lloyd George in December 1916 represented a watershed in British constitutional history. To some he was the Man Who Won the War, to others simply a dictator...

...to some extent the impression of Lloyd George as a dominating war leader is superficial exaggeration, the inevitable result of the excessive publicity he received, indeed cultivated, from the Press; reputation is a poor guide to the realities of administration. Nor were Lloyd George's methods always novel ones; he is often credited with techniques which were practised regularly, if discreetly, by his predecessors... [Lloyd George's] habit was to wake up early and plough into the pile of official papers which were placed by his bedside, so by breakfast he had mastered the contents and skimmed through much of the London and provincial press. Hankey [Secretary to the Cabinet] confirms earlier ministerial experience in emphasizing that the Prime Minister's supreme virtue lay in a capacity to obtain and use good advice.

Had he experienced defeat on the Western Front, as seemed likely for a time in 1918, he and his system would doubtless have been held up to execration [bitter criticism] as Asquith's has often been...As Premier, his chief contribution to victory lay in his success in the maintenance of food supplies, the allocation of manpower, the stimulation of production and the preservation of shipping. As a result, Britain won the war of attrition...[However] Lloyd George could hardly be given credit for the military victory, if such it was.

Pugh, *Profiles in Power, Lloyd George*, 1988

■ Examination-style questions

1 Comprehension in context

Explain why the establishment of the convoy system was 'one of the decisive interventions of the war' (Source B).

2 Comparing the sources

To what extent does Martin Pugh (Source C) disagree with AJP Taylor's assessment of Lloyd George (Source A)?

3 Assessing the sources

How useful is Source A as an explanation of popular opinion of Lloyd George during the war?

4 Making judgements

Using these sources and your own knowledge, comment on the statement that 'more than any other Briton, Lloyd George was the man who won the war'.

Summary

- For Britain, the main strategic questions of the war were as follows.
    1 Once the Germans had dug their trenches across Belgium and northern France, how could they be driven out?
    2 Who were right, the 'westerners' or 'easterners'?
    3 As the stalemate continued, how could the government best mobilize all the resources of the nation, economic and social as much as military, to win this 'total' war?
- The war proved so destructive because the new technology of war – massive armies, barbed wire, machine guns, heavy artillery and trenches – made defence much easier than attack. However, the military leaders had been trained to fight short wars of rapid movement, which would be won by continuous attack. Once the trenches were dug and the barbed wire and machine-guns were in place, they had the greatest difficulty finding an alternative to the frontal assaults on the trench lines which caused so many casualties.
- It lasted so long because most of the time Germany was winning. The government believed that victory would lead to the German domination of Europe, which she had been seeking before war began. Because German troops occupied Belgium and parts of France, the Allies could not seriously consider making peace unless Germany was prepared to retreat from these areas, which she was not.
- The Allies emerged victorious because the combined military and economic forces of Britain, the British Empire and France, backed eventually by the USA, proved more durable than those of the Central Powers. The German leaders also made some foolish mistakes, the most serious of which was to resume unrestricted U-boat warfare in 1917.
- The consequences of the war were profound – and complicated, so historians disagree about precisely what they were. The war certainly had important effects on Britain's economic position, wage rates, the fortunes of the three main political parties, female expectations and attitudes to war and to the idea of human progress.

■ Activity   KEY SKILLS

Summarise Sources A-C on page 168. Then, using pages 162-169, prepare a presentation which critically appraises Lloyd George's effectiveness as a war leader. Include the main points from your summary of the sources and at least one image to illustrate a complex point.

■ Further reading

There are very many first-class books on the First World War:

On the war itself:
A.J.P. Taylor, *An Illustrated History of World War I*, 1963
Alan Clark, *The Donkeys*, 1960
Trevor Wilson, *The Myriad Faces of War*, 1988
Denis Winter, *Death's Men*, 1978
On the Consequences of the war:
Arthur Marwick, *The Deluge*, 1965

Chapter 11

The decline of the Liberal Party 1906–1935
'Hit by a bus'

Source 1

▲ At the peak of his career. Lloyd George for Britain as one of the 'Big Three' at Versailles in 1919, watches the German representative sign the Peace Treaty. Lloyd George is closest to the German, with first Clemenceau for France and Wilson for the USA on his right.

Quotation

In the 1918 general election, Lloyd George's coalition government won an overwhelming victory.

'Lloyd George can be Prime Minister for life if he wants', commented Balfour, a leading Conservative.

A different comment came from Walter Long, another senior Conservative: 'George thinks he won the election. Well, he didn't. It was the Tories and he shall soon begin to find that out!'

■ Think about

The importance of parties

Lloyd George lost the support of the official Liberal Party organization.

Joseph Chamberlain, another powerful political figure, never got quite to the top of the tree because he first left the Liberals in 1886 and then split the Conservatives in 1906.

The 'Gang of Four', all senior Labour politicians, who broke with the Labour Party in 1981 and founded a new party, the Social Democrats (SDP), failed in their attempt to 'break the mould of British politics'.

▶ What are political parties and why do they usually prove stronger than any individuals, however gifted or popular those individuals may be?

Introduction

In 1919 as the illustration on page 170 shows, Lloyd George was a national and international hero. The 'Welsh Wizard' had won the war. Most people would have agreed with Balfour that he was much the best politician in the country and that he could go on being Prime Minister as long as he wanted. However, it was Walter Long, not Balfour, who turned out to be right. Lloyd George, the Liberal who rivalled Gladstone in terms of real constructive achievement, was, by the end of 1918, under the control of the Conservatives. In 1922 they were able to destroy his political career. What happened to Lloyd George between 1916 and 1922 lies at the heart of the decline of the great Liberal Party, from its triumph in the 1906 election, when 400 MPs returned to Westminster, to the sad insignificance of 1935 when just 21 huddled around the ageing Lloyd George. In the crises of the 1920s and 1930s, it was Labour who provided the real opposition to the Conservatives and in the second half of the twentieth century was the alternative party of government.

This chapter considers how this change happened and the main reasons for it. How important in the decline were the actions of men like Lloyd George and Asquith, his Liberal rival? Were there larger forces at work, which would have destroyed the Liberals anyway?

Key questions

- What were the main stages in the decline of the Liberal Party?
- To what extent was it losing ground to Labour between 1906 and 1914?
- Were the effects of the First World War more damaging to it than to other parties?
- How significant a factor in its decline was the rivalry between Asquith and Lloyd George?
- In what ways do historians disagree in their explanations of the decline of the Liberal Party?

Historical debate: When and why did the Liberal Party go into irreversible decline?

Historians disagree on two related questions. The first is whether the Liberal Party was dying before 1914. To put it another way, had the Labour Party achieved so strong a hold on the working-class vote by 1914 that it was bound to drive the Liberal Party into third place, whether or not Britain had gone to war in 1914?

The second disagreement concerns the importance of the events of the First World War – particularly the Lloyd George-Asquith split – in the decline of the Liberal Party. If war had ended with Lloyd George as the undisputed leader of a united Liberal Party, would the Party have declined at all, let alone so fast?

In an important contribution to the debate, Trevor Wilson (Source 13. Page 180) uses a vivid image to clarify the key issues. The Liberal Party, he suggests, should be seen as an individual who seems in pretty good health, but has recently not been well. Before his doctor can make a diagnosis, he is run over by a bus and soon dies. Did the injuries caused by the bus kill him? Or was he already dying? Or was it a combination of the injuries from the accident on top of his earlier illness that proved fatal? The bus represents the First World War; the previous illness represents the problems faced by the Liberal Party before 1914.

This chapter is divided into three sections to help you understand what is quite a complicated debate among historians. It is structured around the image of the person being knocked down by a bus.

- Section 1 considers how ill the person was. How serious were the weaknesses of the Liberal Party before 1914?
- Section 2 measures the damage done by the bus. What effects did the First World War have on the Liberal Party?
- Section 3 describes the patient's lingering death and asks why he died. What happened to the Liberal Party after 1918 and what were the main causes of its decline?

Each section includes examples of the evidence which historians have used in the debate about the decline of the Liberal Party and some extracts from some historians who have contributed most to the debate.

Section 1 How ill was the patient before 1914?

Outline of events

Before you tackle this section, it will be worth your while reminding yourself about the origins of the Labour Party in Chapter 7, and about the Liberal government before 1914 in Chapter 9.

General election results 1906 to 1914

Party	Jan/Feb 1906 Turnout 83%		Jan/Feb 1910 Turnout 87%		Dec 1910 Turnout 82%	
	No. of seats	% of vote	No. of seats	% of vote	No. of seats	% of vote
Liberal	400	49%	275	44%	272	44%
Cons.	157	43%	273	47%	272	44%
Labour	30	5%	40	7%	42	6%
Irish Nat.	83	0.6%	82	2%	84	3%

In the first general election of 1910, the Liberals lost 125 seats (from 400 to 275) and their share of the votes cast dropped by 5 per cent (from 49% to 44%), nonetheless, the Liberals had no difficulty in staying in power, since, with support from the Irish Nationalists and from Labour, they had a majority of more than 100 over the Conservatives. This margin they kept in the second election of 1910, which was called because of the crisis over the future of the House of Lords (see pp. 149–151).

Between 1906 and 1914, the Liberal Party appealed to the electorate on a wide range of issues. It was the party of free trade and of Nonconformity, concerned to maintain international peace through negotiation. It was against privileges, notably those of the House of Lords. Totally committed to Home Rule for Ireland, it was also increasingly the party of social reform and progress. Its leaders – Asquith, Lloyd George, Churchill, and Grey – were, by any standards, very able and outshone their Conservative and Labour rivals.

Consequently, the Liberal Party attracted voters from all social classes. The promise of Home Rule secured the Irish vote and the combination of free trade, international peace and social reform both persuaded many working-class voters to vote Liberal and held the new Labour Party in an informal progressive alliance.

The four years from 1910 and 1914 were full of violent crises (see Chapter 9) – suffragette disturbances, industrial strife, near civil war in Ireland. Historians cannot agree whether or not these problems prove that the Liberal Party was already in serious decline. The Liberal leaders certainly did not think so. They believed that they had a good chance of a fourth successive victory in the next

Note

The Liberal loss of seats 1906–1910

The two-party first-past-the-post system tends to cause swings in parliamentary balances which exaggerate moves in public opinion. Two examples illustrate this:

- In 1906, the Conservatives had just 157 seats, compared with 402 in 1900. The fall in their percentage share, however, was only 7 per cent, from 50 per cent to 43 per cent.
- Between 1945 and 1951, the number of Labour seats fell from 393 to 295, yet its actual share of the vote went up by 1 per cent.

The fall in the Liberal vote between 1906 and 1910, which represented a 5 per cent drop in popularity, was therefore less of a setback than the 125 drop in seats would suggest, particularly since the Conservatives had been badly split in 1906 and fought an unusually poor campaign.

If you compare the proportion of the votes cast in the two 1910 elections, you will see that the Liberals improved their share of the vote but lost two seats. In contrast, the Labour share dropped marginally but the party gained two seats.

■ Activity

Recent election results

1 What were the results of the last two general elections?

2 How did the position of the parties change
 a) in the number of seats won
 b) in the proportion of votes cast?

3 What was the turnout at each election?

election, which was due in 1915. They did not think that the Conservatives had obvious election winners in their main policies – Tariff Reform and 'no surrender' over Ulster. As for the Labour Party, they knew that its parliamentary performance was poor and that many of its MPs owed their seats to the unofficial Liberal-Labour pact.

There was one straw in the wind, however, which encouraged Labour. In 1909, the Miners' Federation of Great Britain had transferred its considerable support from the Liberal to the Labour Party. With trade union membership increasing fast, this was a trend which the Liberals needed urgently to counter.

How ill was the patient? Some historical interpretations

George Dangerfield, in his book *The Strange Death of Liberal England* (see p. 155), believed that the Liberal Party was dying in the years before 1914. So too do a number of more recent historians who have concentrated on the changing nature of British society between 1870 and 1914 and the way in which the organizations of the Liberal and Labour parties related to this changing society. They have concluded that the Liberal Party was unable to adapt to these changes. In particular, it could not meet the expectations of the new industrial working class, which was aware of itself as a separate class. Consequently, Labour came into being as a party whose main reason for existence was to meet working-class needs. This Labour Party became part of the culture of the working class so, as this class gained greater economic strength through the trade unions, and voting power through the Reform Acts of 1884 and 1918, it was bound to replace the Liberal Party as the main opposition to the Conservatives. The new class structure existed well before 1914, as did the links between the new Labour Party and the working class. Hence, by 1914, the Liberal Party was already doomed. Sources 2 and 3 are good examples of this interpretation.

■ Think about

In some mining areas, most voters were miners. This meant that the Miners' Federation of Great Britain (MFGB) had great influence in at least 15 constituencies and a strong voice in the TUC. It had been staunchly Lib-Lab, reformist and anti-socialist. However, in 1909 it lost patience with the Liberals because of their slowness in granting an eight-hour day to miners and transferred its support to Labour.

▶ Which section of the Liberal Party would have been uneasy about the idea of an eight-hour day?

■ Think about

Research methods

▶ Where do historians go to find evidence for voting patterns and for attitudes to political parties?

▶ What do you think were the main sources used by McKibbin (Source 2) and Bernstein (Source 3)?

▶ What additional sources do Clarke (Source 4) and Tanner (Source 5) appear to have used?

▶ In what ways has this influenced their interpretations?

Source 2

This organization [of the Labour Party], particularly in the constituencies, was itself only the political side of an industrial organization that had grown rapidly in the late 19th and early 20th centuries. Almost everywhere, the proliferating trades councils became the local agencies of the Labour Party…

Why was it Labour, and not the Liberal Party, which benefited from these changes? The answer is to be found in the nature of the relationship between the Labour Party and the trade unions on the one hand, and between the trade unions and the industrial working class on the other. Since the Labour Party was inextricably linked with the unions, it, like them, followed the main line of British economic development. Because it had no life apart from the unions it gained electorally from their growth.

McKibbin, *The Evolution of the Labour Party 1910–24*, 1974

Source 3

Even if there had been no war, the Liberal Party was not in a strong position to retain the support of the working-class electorate in a political world which was moving towards class politics. Liberalism was a set of beliefs which assumed harmony between capital and labour. It was not equipped to defend the interests and redress the grievances of a labour movement which was hostile to capital...There were limits beyond which most Liberals would not go on issues that really mattered to the workers, like the right to work and a national minimum wage. It should not cause surprise that the Liberals were out of touch with the aspirations of the workers. Both in Parliament and the constituencies, the Liberals were a party of the middle class. If the emergence of class politics meant that the workers wanted a party whose priority was the concerns of the poor and the working class, then they would have to look elsewhere.

Bernstein, *Liberalism and Liberal Politics in Edwardian England,* 1986

However, other historians, have looked at the electoral results in detail in different parts of Britain and arrived at very different conclusions. In their opinion the patient was very far from dead.

Source 4

...the first quarter of the twentieth century saw two sorts of change in British politics. The first sort centred on the emergence of class politics in a stable form; the second sort upon the effective replacement of the Liberal Party by the Labour Party. But the first...does not in any simple way explain the second. For one thing the chronology is wrong. By 1910, the change to class politics was substantially complete. That from Liberalism to Labour had not really begun. Nor were there signs that it must begin. It was no light thing to overturn one party and make another to put in its place. At the beginning of the second decade of the twentieth century it looked as if both Labour and Liberalism would be subsumed in progressivism. It seemed that social democracy was bound up with the prospects of the Liberal Party.

Clarke, *Lancashire and the New Liberalism,* 1971

Source 5

[Before 1914] Labour had not developed the ideological/political strength to support an expansionist strategy. It had not created a solid 'class' vote, based on cultural units which were common to working-class voters. It had not even the uniform support of trade unionists. The assumption that it did is based upon inadequate theory and partial empirical [evidence-based] analysis. In reality, electoral politics followed a pattern in which past political and current economic interests combined to create an extremely uneven electoral map. The distribution of support was such that it was comparatively strong where the Liberal Party was weak, and unable to seriously rival it in most Liberal areas.

The Labour Party was not on the verge of replacing the Liberals in 1914...The Liberal Party stood for prosperity, improvement and security.

Tanner, *Political Change and the Labour Party 1900–18,* 1990

■ Think about

Class
▶ What precisely does Bernstein in Source 3 mean by 'middle' and 'working' class?

▶ To what extent did and do people vote according to the class to which they belong?

Regional differences
▶ According to Source 5 where was Labour comparatively strong, and where was it weak?

▶ In what other ways were regional influences strong in the distribution of support for British political parties?

■ Questions

Study Source 2.

1 What were the trade unions and trades councils?

2 How important does the author of Source 2 consider them to be in the rise of the Labour Party at the expense of the Liberals?

Study Source 3.

3 To what extent does the author agree with Source 2?

4 What additional reasons does he give for the decline of the Liberal Party?

Study Sources 4 and 5.

5 Explain in what ways they agree with each other about the health of the Liberal Party before 1914.

6 In what ways do they disagree with Sources 2 and 3?

Study Source 6.

7 What is the main point that Hardie is making in Source 6?

8 How useful to historians are his views of the comparative strengths and weaknesses of the Liberal and Labour parties in 1910?

9 Is his view closer to that of Sources 2 and 3 or Sources 4 and 5?

Keir Hardie, one of the founders of the Parliamentary Labour Party had his own views on the state of health of the Labour Party in 1910:

Source 6

The younger members of the Liberal Party have driven the cabinet to a point which has severely strained the loyalty of the Whig (traditional) element. The result of this will be that a halt will be called to social reform measures, and this in turn will sour the advanced section of the Party, which in turn is bound to come over to us. It is impossible for the Radical section of the Liberal Party to turn it into an advanced movement.

Keir Hardie writing in the *Christian Commonwealth* newspaper, 16 February 1910

Section 2 The dangerous bus: the war

Drifting under Asquith 1914–1915

Though only two Cabinet ministers actually resigned from the government when it decided to declare war on Germany, most of the Cabinet and the Party accepted the decision uneasily. The Party adapted badly to the different approach needed for governing during a war, especially when the war turned out to be a lengthy war of attrition. Amongst the Liberal MPs was a small group resolutely opposed to the war which campaigned for a fair peace, the end of secret diplomacy and international disarmament. Another group, which included Alfred Mond and Addison, believed that the Party had no choice but to concentrate all its efforts on winning the war, even if this meant reducing people's individual freedom; i.e. acting illiberally. They soon lost confidence in Asquith as a war leader and attached themselves to Lloyd George.

Without a strong leader to rally them, most Liberal backbenchers remained uneasy and depressed. They had to agree to the passing of the Defence of the Realm Act (DORA) which gave the government new wide powers to use as the war effort required. They also had to accept censorship of the Press, internment of aliens and the doubling of income tax. Furthermore, the government postponed putting into effect until the war was over two measures to which the Party was strongly committed, the Disestablishment of the Church of Wales and Home Rule for Ireland.

Kitchener, whom Asquith had appointed as Secretary of State for War, had great success in persuading men to sign up as volunteers. He realized earlier than most that the war would last years rather than months and planned to recruit millions rather than thousands. Otherwise the appointment was not a good one. Kitchener was out of his depth among politicians and communicated poorly with them. He despised them. Most of them felt the same way about him. Consequently, there was no effective co-ordination of the war effort. Kitchener directed the army, Churchill the navy. Asquith considered that his task was to let them get on with it.

The Conservatives were even more unhappy than the backbench Liberals. They had supported wholeheartedly the declaration of war in August 1914 and Bonar Law, their leader, had agreed to avoid raising controversial domestic issues as long as the war lasted. They had little confidence in the ability of the Liberal government to wage war effectively and felt that, in such an acute national crisis, their leaders should be more involved in the decision-making.

■ Biography

Dr Christopher Addison (1869–1951)

Addison entered the Commons as a committed Liberal and became one of Lloyd George's most loyal and effective supporters. It was he who rallied more than 100 Liberal backbenchers behind Lloyd George rather than Asquith – a vital move in securing Lloyd George's success. He was Minister for Reconstruction in the 1918 coalition but was sacrificed by Lloyd George under pressure from the Conservatives. He later joined the Labour Party and from 1930–1931 was Minister of Agriculture.

Matters came to a head in May 1915. Nowhere was the war going well. The newspapers, especially Northcliffe's *Times* and *Daily Mail*, were gunning for Asquith. On 14 May *The Times* had published an article which blamed the government for a shell shortage on the Western Front. The following day, the First Sea Lord, Sir John Fisher, resigned after months of argument with Churchill over the Gallipoli campaign, which was lurching towards disaster. Asquith's response to this crisis was a typically clever example of political manoeuvring which saved his position for 18 months. It did nothing, however, to address the real issues of how to win the war and regain the nation's confidence.

Coalition 1915

What he did on 18–19 May 1915, very swiftly and consulting only a handful of colleagues, was to form a coalition government, bringing in eight Conservative leaders and Henderson to represent Labour. Asquith claimed that he decided on a coalition because he had 'come to the conclusion that the continued prosecution of the war requires what is called a broad-based Government'.

Cynics then and historians since have argued that Asquith formed the 1915 coalition mainly to remain Prime Minister. He was also aware that he had as yet no agreement with the Conservatives about postponing the next general election. This election was due in the next few months and Asquith was doubtful whether a divided and demoralized Liberal Party could win it. Bonar Law, the Conservative leader, and his senior colleagues were pleased to join the new coalition, though disappointed that the Liberals held on to most of the top posts. The Conservative leaders now had the chance to play their part in the war effort and, having been out of power since 1905, to gain some valuable political experience. Now they were part of a coalition government, they agreed that there was no need for a potentially divisive general election.

Liberal backbenchers were shocked when they heard about the coalition. They did not want it and were furious that Asquith had ended their government without consultation. It took all his powers of persuasion to get them to accept the change.

The formation of a coalition in 1915 was a significant step in the decline of the Liberal Party. Its backbenchers remained demoralized while the Conservatives and Labour made good use, for party purposes, of their share of power.

1916 The fall of Asquith (see also pages 178–179)

The coalition of 1915 did little to improve the way the war was managed and nothing for Asquith's popularity. The success of the coalition was Lloyd George, who, as Minister for Munitions, transformed the production of shells and weapons. Instead of having to complain about shortages, the army eventually had more than it asked for.

Otherwise most news was bad news. Easter 1916 saw a revolt in Ireland. The Somme slaughter started in July. Meanwhile, the issue of conscription divided the coalition. For Asquith and many Liberals, forcing men to fight rather than to rely on their volunteering was a step too far for their liberalism to tolerate. Asquith delayed many months before agreeing to conscription and angered the Conservatives and Lloyd George's supporters, who regarded it as an urgent if regrettable necessity.

By November, Lloyd George feared that the war would be lost while Bonar Law knew that his backbenchers were close to revolt over the running of the war. Secret negotiations then began (see Timeline on p. 178) which ended on 7 December when Lloyd George became Prime Minister.

Note

Lord Northcliffe during the war

Lord Northcliffe (1865–1922) was a larger-than-life character who made politicians nervous. He was the most successful newspaper publisher in the history of the British press. He created popular newspapers when he founded the *Daily Mail* in 1896. By 1914 he was also owner of *The Times*, which was then much the most politically influential of the quality press.

He was also a megalomaniac who wanted power as well as influence. He campaigned to get rid of Kitchener and Asquith. Lloyd George managed him by giving him politically harmless jobs and sending him on missions, such as a war mission to win support in the USA in 1917.

He died in 1922 after a complete mental breakdown.

Note

Bonar Law and Lloyd George

Bonar Law could hardly have been more different from Lloyd George. A melancholy Scot whose melancholia was increased by the early death of his wife and the loss of two sons in the war, he seemed a dull dog beside the brilliant Welshman. However they had a mutual respect which made them a most effective combination between 1916 and 1922. It was Bonar Law who kept the Conservative backbenchers loyal through the six years of coalition. His loss of confidence in Lloyd George was an important cause of the latter's fall in 1922.

■ Think about

▶ What impression of the new Prime Minister is the *Punch* cartoonist aiming to give to the readers in December 1916? Why do you think he chose this image?

THE NEW CONDUCTOR.
OPENING OF THE 1917 OVERTURE.

The Lloyd George coalition

Lloyd George won the war but he could not win back the Asquithians. Since he had to make do without all the experienced Liberal ministers, his coalition government was dominated by Conservatives. The War Cabinet of five, which made the big decisions, consisted of one Liberal (himself) , three Conservatives (Bonar Law, Milner and Carson) and one Labour (Henderson).

Though Asquith took care through 1917 and much of 1918 to avoid criticizing the new government, many of his followers, who fiercely hated Lloyd George, took on an opposition role. The high point of their opposition was the Maurice Debate of May 1918 (see p. 166) when they were joined by Asquith who proposed a vote of no confidence against Lloyd George. Time, therefore, sharpened rather than healed the Liberal split. Lloyd George tried to secure his own position by creating a new 'National Liberal' organization. He built up a large personal fund for political use by the sale of honours (see p. 182). He also purchased the *Daily Chronicle* to counteract the mainly pro-Asquith Liberal press.

Meanwhile, the Labour Party was growing stronger. Trade union membership rose considerably during the war. Arthur Henderson, the Labour leader, as well as sitting in the War Cabinet, reorganized the national party through the War Emergency Workers' National Committee. He also brought in middle-class intellectuals like the Webbs to develop the party's policies for the post-war world. Lloyd George made a bad mistake in 1917 in the manner in which he handled Henderson's request to attend the proposed international peace conference at Stockholm. Humiliated by the so-called 'doormat' incident, Henderson resigned from the War Cabinet and joined the long list of Lloyd George's unforgiving enemies.

Note

The 'Doormat' incident 1917

Lloyd George opposed sending British representatives to Stockholm and put Henderson's proposal to the rest of the War Cabinet which discussed it while keeping Henderson outside, as if 'on the doormat'. The rest of the Cabinet agreed with the Prime Minister, and an angry Henderson resigned.

The fall of Asquith, 1916

How did it happen? Why did it cause such bitterness?

Timeline

November Lloyd George and Conservative leaders start secret talks.

25 November Bonar Law suggests a new War Committee chaired by Lloyd George to run the war, with Asquith staying on as Prime Minister. Asquith rejects this idea.

1 December Lloyd George again suggests this War Committee to Asquith and asks Bonar Law for his support.

3 December Bonar Law tells Asquith that the Conservatives would resign from the coalition unless something was done. Asquith agrees to the War Committee proposal.

4 December Liberal ministers in the coalition tell Asquith they are most unhappy with the proposal. Asquith changes his mind and withdraws his agreement.

5 December Lloyd George resigns. Asquith resigns too and dares Lloyd George or Bonar Law to form a government. King George V asks Bonar Law to try but he will only do so if Asquith will serve under him. Asquith refuses. Bonar Law recommends Lloyd George to the King.

7 December Lloyd George becomes Prime Minister. All the Liberal ministers leave the government with Asquith and refuse to serve under Lloyd George.

In 1917 and in 1918 Asquith turns down Lloyd George's offer of ministerial posts.

Source 8

▲ The painter Neville Lytton portrays the hopeless waste of the Somme battle. The failure of the offensive on the Somme strengthened the critics of Asquith's leadership.

Source 9

I fully realize the frankness and loyalty with which you have put forward the proposal...But under present conditions, and in the form it is presented, I do not see my way to adopt it...

As to Lloyd George, you know as well as I do both his qualities and his defects. He has many qualities that would fit him for the first place, but he lacks the one thing needful – he does not inspire trust...Here again there is one construction, and one only, that could be put on the new arrangement – that it has been engineered by him with the purpose, not perhaps at the moment, but as soon as a fitting pretext could be found, of his displacing me.

Asquith replies on 26 November to Bonar Law

Source 10

If the PM refuses to accept it, then there will be a smash. The only weak spot is Bonar Law, who cannot make up his mind to strike. If D strikes alone, it will mean him forming an opposition, but if he and Bonar strike together it will mean the smashing up of the Government. Asquith has great influence over Bonar and is using it to his full advantage. D says that the PM is devoid of all principles except one–that is retaining his position as Prime Minister.

Frances Stevenson 30 November 1916. Bonar Law and D (David Lloyd George) had sent their War Committee proposal to Asquith

The change of leader and the Liberal Party

The consequences of this crisis were good for Britain but disastrous for the Liberal Party. While Britain at last gained a war leader who could invigorate the nation and lead her to victory, the Liberals split. All the Liberal ministers left the coalition in sympathy with Asquith, who also kept the support of the majority of Liberal backbenchers and control of the Party. Lloyd George's controlling majority in the Commons was massive but it mainly consisted of the Conservatives, Labour and only about 100 Liberals. Once the war was won, what would he do?

Source 11

I have received your letter with some surprise. On Friday I made proposals which involved not merely your retention of the Premiership, but the supreme control of the War, whilst the executive functions, subject to that supreme control, were left to others. I thought you then received these suggestions favourably. In fact you yourself proposed that I should be Chairman of this Executive Committee, although as you know, I never put forward that demand…Today you have gone back on your own proposals.

I have striven my utmost to cure the obvious defects of the War Committee without overthrowing the Government. As you are aware, on several occasions during the last two years I have deemed it my duty to express my extreme dissatisfaction with the Government's method of conducting the War…We have thrown away opportunity after opportunity, and I am convinced, after deep and anxious reflection, that it is my duty to leave the Government.

> Lloyd George replies on 5 December to Asquith's letter telling him that he had changed his mind about the War Committee proposal.
> Lloyd George, *War Memoirs*, Vol. 1, 1938 (2 vols)

Source 12

Please forgive me if I venture to ask you to consider if it is at all possible for you to accept a post in office in a Lloyd George ministry. Do not think I underrate the magnitude of the sacrifice I am suggesting. But at this time it really is of vast importance that you should do so. Nothing else can preserve the unity of the country or the respect of Europe.

> Lord Cecil a leading Conservative writes to Asquith on 6 December

■ Questions

Read Source 9 and the Timeline:

a) What was Bonar Law's proposal?

b) Why would Asquith not accept it?

c) What is his opinion of Lloyd George?

1 Read Source 11:

a) What is the main purpose of Lloyd George's letter

b) What are his two main criticisms of Asquith?

c) How does he try to defend himself against the charge of wanting himself to be Prime Minister?

2 Read Source 12. Why does Lord Cecil believe that:

a) Lloyd George should take over as Prime Minister?

b) Asquith should serve under him?

c) Why do you think Asquith refused?

3 Compare Sources 9 and 11 and the Timeline:

a) Why should one expect Source 10 to be biased (see page 157).

b) How good an analysis of the situation on 30 November is Source 10.

c) Why does Frances Stevenson consider Bonar Law so important?

d) What is her main criticism of Asquith?

4 Asquith and his followers never forgave Lloyd George for what they considered his unscrupulous plotting in 1916. How much plotting actually went on and to what extent to you consider that Asquith's problems were to a large extent of his own making?

Historical debate: Trevor Wilson and the dangerous bus image

The argument that being struck by a bus is the most likely explanation for the death of Liberalism, i.e. that the worst damage was done during the First World War is expressed persuasively by Trevor Wilson. The following extracts are all taken from his book *The Downfall of the Liberal Party* (1966).

Source 13

Extract 1: Nor in purely electoral terms was there any sign that Labour was supplanting the Liberals. In the general elections of 1910 and the by-elections from 1911 until the outbreak of war, Labour fared abysmally in contests with the Liberals...By and large, the Labour parliamentary party still existed in 1914 by Liberal indulgence – that is, because the Liberals deemed it advantageous to give Labour a free run against the Conservatives in certain seats.

Extract 2: To make clear the view taken here about when the Liberal Party 'reached the point of no return' it may be permissible to resort to allegory. The Liberal Party may be compared to an individual who, after a period of robust health and great exertions, experiences symptoms of illness (Ireland, Labour unrest, the suffragettes). Before a thorough diagnosis can be made, he was involved in an encounter with a rampant omnibus (the First World War), which mounted the pavement and ran him over. After lingering painfully, he expired. A controversy has persisted ever since as to what killed him. One medical school argues that even without the bus he would soon have died; the intimations of illness were symptoms of a grave disease which would soon have ended his life. Another school goes further and says that the encounter with the bus would not have proved fatal had not the victim's health already been seriously impaired. Neither of these views are accepted here. The evidence of them is insufficient, because the ailment had not yet reached the stage where their ultimate effect could be known. How long, apart from the accident, the victim could have survived, what future (if any) he possessed cannot be said. All that is known is that at one moment he was up and walking, and at the next he was flat on his back, never to rise again; and in the interval he had been run over by a bus. If it is guesswork to say that the bus was mainly responsible for his demise, it is the most warrantable guess that can be made.

Extract 3: The outbreak of the First World War initiated a process of disintegration in the Liberal Party which by 1918 had reduced it to ruins...the onset of war jeopardized the existence of a party whose guiding principles were international conciliation, personal liberty, and social reform. On the fateful 4 August 1914, Christopher Addison, a junior member of the Liberal government, foretold his party's demise which, with one variation or another, was to be repeated many times in the following years. Addison was talking to Sir John Simon...about possible resignation from the government, and Simon said that he was reluctant to see too many ministers resign because that would necessitate a coalition government, 'which would assuredly be the grave of Liberalism'. Addison gloomily replied that in the opinion of most Liberals, and certainly himself, Liberalism was in the grave already.

■ Think about
Extract 1
▶ What does Wilson mean by his claim that 'the Labour parliamentary party existed in 1914 by Liberal indulgence'?
▶ Do you think his view is closer to those of Sources 2 and 3 or 4 and 5.

■ Think about
Extract 2
▶ How would you sum up Wilson's arguments for rejecting the view that the Liberal Party was dying in 1914?

■ Think about
Extracts 3 and 4
▶ How useful is the evidence of Christopher Addison for the decline of the Liberal Party?
▶ Why was he so gloomy about the future of the Liberal Party in 1914?
▶ What was it about Liberal principles that made government in times of war so difficult for a Liberal government?

Extract 4: For a Liberal administration to lead Britain into war and to direct a wartime administration seemed almost a contradiction in terms. Its task of international pacification had automatically disappeared. And it had little hope of preserving intact those principles and practices identified with liberalism: free trade, protection of minorities, the 'pacification' of Ireland, liberty of individuals and voluntary service in the armed forces. Yet once a Liberal government began to modify its ideals under stress of war, how long would it be before the Liberal position was abandoned altogether and that of the Conservatives adopted?

Extract 5: For the Liberal Party this (the fall of Asquith and the creation of the Lloyd George coalition in 1916) constituted a shattering defeat – even though some excellent Liberals considered it necessary for the success of the war…Towards the new, basically non-Liberal regime, which Lloyd George had formed, it was difficult for Liberals to behave … with sympathy. Now not even success in battle would make any difference. Indeed every step the Allies advanced towards victory brought catastrophe closer to the Liberal Party…'

Wilson, *The Downfall of the Liberal Party 1914–35*, 1966

■ Think about

Extract 5

▶ Why does the author consider the fall of Asquith such a shattering defeat for the Liberal Party?

▶ Explain his comment that 'every step the Allies advanced towards victory brought catastrophe closer to the Liberal Party.'

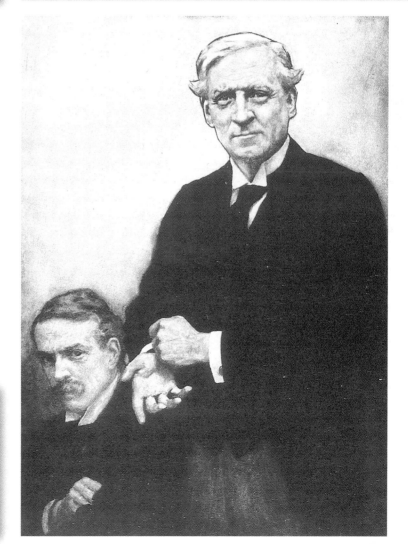

▶ Happier days in 1910. Asquith is Prime Minister and Lloyd George is Chancellor of the Exchequer.

■ Activity   KEY SKILLS

1 Summarize Trevor Wilson's explanation for the decline of the Liberal Party.

2 Write a critical appraisal of Wilson's explanation from the viewpoint of MacKibbin and Bernstein (Sources 2 and 3)

Section 3 Mortally wounded? 1918–1922

General election results 1918–1924

December 1918 (The 'coupon' election at the end of the war)
Turnout 57%

Party	No. of seats	% of the vote
Coalition (Lloyd George Liberals + Conservatives)	523	53%
Asquithian Liberals	36	13%
Labour	57	21%
Sinn Fein	73	5%

Party	November 1922 Turnout 73%		December 1923 Turnout 71%		October 1924 Turnout 77%	
	No. of seats	% of vote	No. of seats	% of vote	No. of seats	% of vote
Liberal	115	28%	158	30%	40	18%
Cons.	344	39%	258	38%	419	48%
Labour	142	30%	191	31%	151	33%

Lloyd George realized that if, after the war, the country returned immediately to normal party politics, the prospects for the Liberals generally and himself in particular were dire. His solution was to try to keep the coalition going. He therefore persuaded the Conservative leaders that the coalition should call a general election before the end of 1918. They did not expect the war to be over by then (the rapid collapse of the Central Powers took everyone by surprise) and intended to use the wartime mood to gain massive electoral support for the coalition government. Having won the election, he would lead the new government to bring the war to a speedy end and then tackle the problems of peace.

With the Conservative leaders, he did a deal whereby his Liberal supporters would not have to face Conservative opponents (and vice-versa) in their constituencies. The Conservatives were happy to co-operate. Their leaders, notably Bonar Law, Balfour and Austen Chamberlain, worked reasonably harmoniously with Lloyd George and recognized his leadership flair. They believed that the country still needed the unity of a coalition government to 'win the peace'. Following the success of the Communists in Russia in 1917 and the socialist risings in Central Europe in 1918, they also feared that socialism might triumph in Britain too, especially as the 1918 Reform Act had added millions of working men as well as women over 30 to the electorate. Continuing the coalition under Lloyd George seemed as good a defence as any against the spread of socialism.

To all the approved coalition candidates Lloyd George and Bonar Law wrote a letter of endorsement. This letter was received by 159 Lloyd George Liberals, mainly on the basis of their attitude to the coalition since 1916. Asquith referred sneeringly to this letter as a 'coupon' and the election of 1918 became known the 'coupon election'.

It went very much to the coalitionists' plan. They won 523 seats, of which 136 went to Lloyd George's Liberals. Labour was held to 57 while the Asquithian Liberals were smashed, winning only 36. Asquith himself lost his seat, as did many of his senior colleagues. However, the most striking feature of the 1918 election was the success of the Conservatives. Of the coalition seats they had won 400. What was even more worrying for Lloyd George was that many of his coalition Liberals would not have won their seats had a Conservative stood

Note

Lloyd George and the sale of honours

For generations British politicians had given honours to relations, friends and the rich who could help them and their parties. Large individual donations to party funds were and remain part of political life. Lloyd George was simply cruder in the way he encouraged honours to be bought.

Agents let it be known that a knighthood could be had for £12,000, a baronetcy for £40,000. A peerage cost more. Some really shady characters were honoured. As a result, Lloyd George gained a large political fighting fund which he kept for his own use, but he further damaged his reputation and helped towards his downfall in 1922.

against them. Consequently, he and his followers were henceforth heavily dependent on the good will of the Conservatives.

1922–1924 disaster

Yet despite this desperate situation, the Liberals would not put aside their past disagreements. A by-election victory brought Asquith back to Parliament as bitter against his old colleague as ever. His followers were, if anything, more bitter still.

The 1922 election

They were in no fit state to fight an election. Yet this is what they had to do in 1922, when Conservative backbenchers surprised their leaders and the nation by voting to end the coalition and get rid of Lloyd George (see pp. 191–192). Divided and in disarray, the Liberals ended in third place with 115 seats behind the Conservatives, led by Bonar Law, with 344 and Labour with 142.

The British electoral system is harsh on third parties. If the Liberals were to make a comeback, they would have to end their differences once and for all. They also needed some new distinctive policies which would appeal to the post-war electorate. Most of their pre-war policies had dated badly. Ireland had moved past Home Rule (see pp. 61–62) and no Irish MPs would come again to London to sustain the Liberals against the Tories. Nonconformity was on the wane, so causes like disestablishing the Church of Wales were obsolete. The reform of the franchise was nearly complete and, though Britain was still an unequal society where the many enjoyed unfair privileges, Labour was making itself the champion of equality. Labour also presented itself as the real heir to the Gladstonian tradition of a peaceful and moral foreign policy.

Labour and Conservative

In fact, Labour was making an attractive case to the working-class electorate which the 1918 Reform Act had made much stronger. It attracted middle-class voters too, including former Liberal MPs like Addison. Labour's starting point was a better deal for working people; to be achieved through a minimum wage, improved working conditions, a greater control of industry in the national interest and higher taxation to accelerate social progress, especially in health and education. Its party organization had been reformed. The trade unions came up with the necessary funds for fighting elections. Its leaders had a vision for the future.

The Conservatives, in contrast, were not in the least visionary but they offered from 1922 an increasingly clear and reassuring message to the electorate. They were the patriotic and imperial party. Where possible, they would return the country to the best of the pre-war times. They were cautious in a world full of dangers. With Stanley Baldwin as their leader, they aimed to convey decency and a commitment to social improvement.

Liberal and Labour 1923–1924

Since the Asquithians (or 'Squiffites') did less badly than the Lloyd Georgeites in the 1922 election, Asquith stayed on as Party leader. He was now 70 and did little more than recycle old ideas. However in 1923, Baldwin offered him an apparent lifeline by deciding to call an election on the protection versus free trade issue (see p. 194). Free trade was still a vote winner and the Liberals knew how to argue the free trade case.

The significance of the Fourth Reform Act of 1918

Since this added nearly 5 million men to the voting registers as well as women over 30, this was clearly an important measure. However, historians disagree about its electoral effects.

Some argue that because the men who gained the right to vote were mainly working class, the 1918 Act was another boost to Labour at the expense of the Liberals.

Others disagree. They argue that the men who gained the vote were not obviously of any class; rather men who were not householders. They were likely to be those still living at home, of any class.

In the 1923 election, though they still came third, they polled much more strongly, gaining 158 seats. Labour won 191 and the Conservatives 258. Most of the Liberal gains had been at the expense of the Conservatives. They continued to fall back against Labour in the industrial areas.

Now Asquith made what many historians regard as his last great mistake. He offered general support to a minority Labour government without securing any commitment about what kind of policies it should follow. Lloyd George's advice was to make any support conditional on a radical but not socialist programme of social reform for which the Liberals could take some credit if it were successful or blame Labour if it failed. Asquith's decision allowed the Labour leader Ramsay MacDonald to form a government without any obligation to the Liberals.

MacDonald was not grateful in the least. On the contrary, his priority was to do everything possible to weaken the Liberal Party so that it was driven into third place permanently without hope of recovery. Then Labour could take on the Conservatives with a real chance of success. In the short period of his first ministry, 1923–1924, MacDonald showed that a Labour government was respectable, trustworthy and entirely independent of the Liberals. In the general election of 1924 (see pp. 196), public opinion polarized, with disastrous results for the Liberals. The Labour share of the vote increased, though it lost 40 seats. The Conservatives benefited from a massive switch of Liberal votes; they won 419 seats, a gain of 161. The Liberals lost 118, holding on to just 40.

A Conservative poster for the 1923 election.

■ Think about

Look at the way Source 14 portrays Lloyd George. Why did the Conservative leaders so distrust him?

Note

The circumstances of the 1924 election

In September 1924, the Conservatives criticized the minority Labour government for failing to prosecute a Communist journalist for 'inciting to mutiny'. Simultaneously, the Liberals voted against Labour because of the terms negotiated for a treaty with the Communist USSR. The Labour government then resigned. A few days before polling day, the Conservatives published a forged letter, supposedly from the Russian Communist Zinoviev, which encouraged the workers of Britain to join in the international class struggle against the capitalist rulers. It is hard to measure the influence of this forgery and the extent to which fears of Communism influenced voter behaviour. While the labour vote held firm, there was a massive shift of Liberals to the Conservative Party. Perhaps many Liberal voters felt the need for security and the Conservatives seemed a better bet than the present muddled Liberals.

A Lingering Death 1924–1935

General election results 1929 to 1935

Party	May 1929 Turnout 76%		October 1931 Turnout 76%		November 1935 Turnout 71%	
	No. of seats	% of vote	No. of seats	% of vote	No. of seats	% of vote
Liberal	59	24%	37	7%	21	7%
Cons.	260	38%				
Labour	287	37%	52	31%	154	38%
National			521	61%	429	53%

Note

Of the 37 Liberals elected in 1931, 33 were elected with support from the MacDonald–led, but mainly Conservative, coalition.

1924 was really the end of Liberal fortunes. In 1926 Asquith at last resigned the leadership. Lloyd George succeeded him and made one last concentrated effort for the 1929 election. The Party was united as it had never been since 1916. His political fund meant that the election campaign was generously financed. He had some sensible policies to meet the challenge of unemployment. To most voters, these efforts were irrelevant since the crucial struggle was between the two larger parties. The Liberals did better but still ran a poor third with only 59 seats.

In the crisis of 1931, most Liberal MPs led by Sir John Simon allowed themselves to be swallowed up in the National government. In 1935 there were only 21 independent Liberal MPs left.

Interpretations exercise: The death of liberalism

Source 15

▲ A Labour poster for the 1924 election.

Source A

Scott's view of Asquith in 1921

What struck me most was his immobility. He had not moved – did not really know about things... he had not seen de Valera [the Irish leader] and knew nothing of his real temperament and outlook. Again thought nothing of Austen Chamberlain [then leader of the Conservative Party], wholly ignoring his sterling qualities and setting him down as a poor creature. So also of [Lloyd George], he could see no good in him or anything he did. All the time he laid down the law with great positiveness. Altogether a somewhat querulous and very old man.

Maclean, [a leading Squiffite] said that he had evidence that he was not gaining but losing ground in the country. He had missed a great and unique opportunity by his failure to make any figure in Parliament since his return. Was it, I asked, consideration for him [Maclean had been leader while Asquith was out of Parliament] or indolence? Something of both, said Maclean, but evidently he thought that the first was only a cover for the second.

C.P. Scott was a committed Liberal, the editor of the *Manchester Guardian* and very influential with Liberal politicians. He knew both Asquith and Lloyd George well.
Scott, *Political Diaries 1911–28, 1922*

■ Think about

▶ How does the Labour poster use *The Daily News*, a Liberal newspaper, for its own purposes?

▶ In what ways did Ramsay MacDonald's first Labour government weaken the Liberal Party, though it only lasted a few months?

Source B

Herbert Gladstone, Director of Liberal Headquarters writing about the 1918 election results

The results of the 1918 election broke the Party, not only in the House of Commons, but in the country. Local Associations perished, or maintained existence in name only. Masses of our best men passed to Labour. Others drifted to Conservatism or independence. Over and over again our remnants in the constituencies declined even to hold meetings. In the election of 1922, many constituencies actually refused to fight, even though candidates and funds were available.'

Source C

A historian's explanation for the Liberals' poor results

Why did the Liberals not fare better in 1929? All the features which a political party needs for victory seemed to be present: unity, a sense of purpose, enthusiasm, personalities, money, organization.

A party often reaps the benefit, or suffers the damage, not from its actions in the immediate past but from what happened years earlier. The actual rights and wrongs of Asquithians or Lloyd Georgeites simply passed electors by...The one impression which was left on the minds of ordinary voters was that the Liberals were having a long and savage running fight which seemed to have no meaning, no beginning and no end...

The personal record of Lloyd George was a very dubious asset. Liberals could, and did, argue that in the war he 'got things done'. But could men who had written in 1926 of Lloyd George that 'confidential relations are impossible in one whose instability destroys confidence' expect to carry much conviction three years later when they declared that he was the best possible leader for the nation? And when Lloyd George made sweeping promises about conquering unemployment, even though those promises were upheld by serious professional economists and others, men were all too inclined to recall the disappointments and the real, or alleged, broken promises of the coalition. For all his genius, and for all his concern for the poor and downtrodden, a vast number of people both inside and out side the Liberal Party utterly mistrusted him as a man.

Douglas, *A History of the Liberal Party 1895–1970*, 1971

Source D

A Liberal, Lord Lothian's assessment of liberalism in 1931

From a party point of view, liberalism is in an almost hopeless position so long as Baldwin is leader of the Conservative Party and Arthur Henderson, a leading figure in the Labour Party. Both are democrats, liberally minded, supporters of disarmament and the League of Nations...We have, therefore, no future by just talking what may be called the general principles of liberalism and criticizing certain aspects of the government's policy. Apart from the stalwart remnant of the old guard, the mass of voters will tend to vote for one or the other of the two major parties, which at any rate have some hope of coming into power and are both, today, liberal minded.

■ Examination-style questions

1 **Comprehension in context**
Study Source A. According to Scott, what were Asquith's main weaknesses as a leader in 1921? Was he or Lloyd George most to blame for the Liberals' decline? Study Source B. Why were the pre-war Liberals no longer appealing to the electorate?

2 **Comparing the sources**
Study Sources C and D. How far do the two sources differ in their explanations of the decline in the support for the Liberal Party?

3 **Assessing the sources**
How useful a source do you think Source A is for assessing Asquith? Comment on the value of Source B for studying the morale of the Liberal Party.

4 **Making judgements**
'The decline of the Liberal Party during the inter-war years was caused principally by the emergence of the Labour Party as a more relevant and attractive alternative to the Conservative Party.'
With reference to the sources, and using your own knowledge, assess the validity of this view in the context of other explanations of the decline of the Liberal Party in this period.

Summary

- There were 6 stages in the decline of the Liberal Party between 1906 and 1935. **1** – 1910–1914, when Asquith's government faced acute social difficulties, including industrial strife. **2** – 1914–1916 when the Party, still led by Asquith, struggled to give effective leadership in the war. **3** – 1916–1918 when Lloyd George replaced Asquith and the Party suffered a bitter split. **4** – 1918–1922 when Lloyd George's dependence on the Conservatives split him further from Asquith's supporters with disastrous results in the 1922 election, when the Liberals came in third behind Labour. **5** – 1922–1924 when the Party tried to reunite under Asquith and break out of the third party situation. A failure of strategy towards the Labour minority government of 1923–1924 led to a further disastrous setback in 1924. **6** – 1924–1935 when, despite Lloyd George's efforts, the Party made little improvement in 1929 and by 1935, had drifted into insignificance.

- Historians disagree about the extent to which the Liberals were losing ground to Labour before 1914. In terms of performance in elections and by-elections, the Liberals were holding their own. At the same time, however, trade unions were getting stronger as were Labour organizations at a local level. There were considerable variations from locality to locality in the comparative strength of the Liberal and Labour parties.

- The First World War was much more damaging to the Liberals than to the other parties. They fared poorly as the governing party during the first part of the war. They suffered an extremely damaging leadership split. In contrast the Conservatives gained experience of government through the coalition and came to appear a sounder party of government than the Liberals. Labour were also involved in managing the war effort. Trade union membership doubled. Party organization improved. The Party leaders developed attractive policies for the post-war years.

- The rivalry between Lloyd George and Asquith was a major factor in the decline of the Liberal Party. It started in 1916 and rumbled on until Asquith resigned as leader of the Party ten years later. It was particularly damaging between 1916 and 1922 when it prevented the Party from deciding how it might adapt to the post-war world.

- The main disagreements amongst historians are about what were the most important causes for the decline of the Liberal Party. They disagree in particular about the related issues of 1) the relative strengths of the Labour and Liberal parties in 1914 and 2) how damaging the First World War was to the Liberal Party.

■ Further reading

Paul Adelman, *Decline of the Liberal Party* , 1995

*Robert Pearce, *British Domestic Politics 1914–35,* 1992

T. Wilson, *The Downfall of the Liberal Party 1914–35,* 1966

R., McKibbin, *The Evolution of the Labour Party 1910–24,* 1974

G.L. Bernstein, *Liberalism and Liberal Politics in Edwardian England,* 1986

See also the 'Further reading' section of Chapter 8 (p. 139)

Chapter 12

The inter-war years: Conservative, Labour, National
Rule by pygmies?

Source 1

BRITAIN'S FIRST LABOUR CABINET.

▲ Britain's first Labour Cabinet in 1924.

Source 2

Waiting with the other members of the Cabinet to meet the King for the first time, Clynes reflected: As we stood waiting for his Majesty, amid the gold and crimson of the Palace, I could not help marvelling at the strange turn of Fortune's wheel, which had brought MacDonald the starveling clerk, Thomas the engine driver, Henderson the foundry labourer and Clynes the mill hand to this pinnacle.

J.R Clynes, the Deputy Leader of the Labour Party in his Memoirs

Introduction

The most outstanding economist of his generation, John Maynard Keynes, wrote in 1919:

> ## Source 3
>
> In this autumn…we are at the dead season of our fortunes…We have been moved already beyond endurance, and need rest. Never in the lifetime of men now living has the universal element in the soul of man burnt so dimly.
>
> Keynes, *The Economic Consequences of the Peace,* 1919

Keynes reflected the exhaustion that Britain and Europe faced at the end of the First World War and the sense that before them loomed a steep mountain to climb. The tasks facing Britain's rulers were as daunting as any their predecessors had faced in peacetime. Though Britain had won, the damage that the country had suffered was great. Yet the people's expectations for a better future were high. The defeat of the Central Powers and the revolutions which had followed that defeat had created new and unpredictable situations in Europe, which asked new questions about Britain's international role. Uncertain too was the future of Britain's main political parties. Britain's coalition government would continue after the war but what would happen when it broke up?

This chapter deals with home affairs in Britain during the inter-war years. Though the course of party politics took some complicated twists and turns, the Conservatives were the dominant party, with Labour twice taking power for brief spells. In the eyes of later politicians and many historians, the 1920s and 1930s were gloomy years when few of the hopes at the dawn of peace in 1918 were realized and the problems both at home and abroad too often defied solution. The politicians of the time seemed second rate, without the energy and vision to find new solutions to what were, in fact, new problems. This chapter will help you to assess that judgement.

Key questions

- How did the Conservative Party achieve political dominance in Britain in the inter-war years?
- How successful a Prime Minister was Stanley Baldwin?
- How effective were the Labour governments of 1924 and 1929–1931?
- What reputation does Ramsay MacDonald deserve as Labour leader?
- How fair is it to describe the leadership provided by British politicians during the inter-war ears as 'the rule of pygmies'?

The coalition government 1918–1922

The general election of December 1918 gave the coalition a massive majority in the House of Commons of about 400 seats. Lloyd George continued as Prime Minister. His most senior colleagues in the Cabinet were all Conservatives. Austen Chamberlain held the post of Chancellor of the Exchequer, Lord Curzon that of Foreign Secretary and Lord Birkenhead that of Lord Chancellor. Also in the Cabinet, with less demanding posts, were Balfour as Lord President of the Council and Bonar Law, in declining health but as influential as ever, as Lord Privy Seal. Liberals held posts where they could make a positive contribution to the task of peacetime reconstruction. Addison was Minister of Health, which included responsibility for housing. H.A.L. Fisher was Minister for Education. Another reforming Liberal, Edwin Montagu was Secretary of State for India.

■ Biography

J.M. Keynes (1883–1946)

Keynes appears a number of times in this chapter. Born in 1883, he was educated at Cambridge University and taught Economics there for much of his life. However, he became involved in national policy making when he was in his early 30s. Keynes was a member of the British delegation at Versailles but resigned in disgust at what he regarded as the economic folly of reparations. His highly critical *The Economic Consequences of the Peace* (1919) made him famous.

What made him the most influential economist of his generation, not just in Britain but internationally, were the ideas he worked out from his study of unemployment in the 1920s and 1930s. These ideas he published in his *General Theory of Employment, Interest and Money* (1936). He argued that the orthodox policies which British and other governments used in times of economic depression – balanced budgets, cutting government expenditure – often made matters worse rather than better. Instead he argued that, when there appeared a danger of an economic depression, governments should increase spending. In that way, economic growth would continue and unemployment would be avoided.

After the Second World War, most Western countries followed Keynes' advice and enjoyed economic growth and low unemployment. During the economic crisis from 1929–1931, he suggested to the government ideas for managing the economy which would probably have lessened the harm of the slump. However, they were not yet fully worked out nor was the government ready to listen.

The new Parliament has gained an unfair reputation of being full of 'hard-faced men who had done well out of the war'. In fact the number of men with a business background increased marginally, as did the number of trade unionists and middle-class professionals. The influence of the landed classes was less, which reflected the economic pressures, mainly from higher taxes, which the war had placed on owners of large estates. An unusual number of landowners put their estates on the market between 1918 and 1921. Often they split them and sold out to their tenant farmers.

Immediate problems

There was a frenzied quality about these four years. Lloyd George and Curzon were frequently out of the country, first negotiating the long, complicated and difficult peace settlement at Versailles, then at other conferences tying up the loose ends of Versailles or discussing new diplomatic problems (see Chapter 14).

Simultaneously, the Prime Minister had to give as much time and attention as he could spare to Ireland, which was in a state of barely suppressed revolt. In the 1918 election, Sinn Fein, committed to Irish independence, had won 73 of the 81 Irish seats. They refused to come to the London parliament and set up their own assembly, the Dail, in Dublin. Chapter 3 describes how Lloyd George eventually negotiated an Irish settlement in 1921.

Then the army had to be demobilized. The soldiers naturally wanted to come home at once. However, there were more than 4 million of them and the economy, which had been geared up to concentrate on wartime priorities, needed to adapt to the different requirements of peacetime. The government at first tried to demobilize those skilled workers most needed for the peacetime economy. However logical this policy seemed to be to government ministers and their civil servants, it made no sense whatever to the soldiers, especially those who had been in His Majesty's Service the longest and believed, with some justification, that they were losing out in the job market to those back at home. Mutinies threatened, so Churchill, the Secretary for War, ordered that the first to be demobilized should be those who had served longest.

As a result, many returned home not to work and a decent wage but to unemployment. In order to cushion their hardship if they failed to find work, the government gave them an out-of-work donation. This came on top of the unemployment insurance, which had been extended to more industries during the war. Then, in 1921, after a short frantic post-war boom, the economy sharply declined and unemployment soared. The government agreed that unemployed workers could go on drawing benefits even though these were not covered by national insurance contributions. These payments were called officially 'uncovenanted' benefits, though most people referred to them as 'the dole'. Dole payments survived, as did mass unemployment, throughout the inter-war period.

If Versailles, Ireland, demobilization and unemployment were not problems enough, the government found itself facing industrial conflicts as bad as those of 1911/12. In 1919, 35 million days were lost in strikes, 27 million in 1920 and 86 million in 1921. These conflicts, their causes and consequences are considered in more detail in the following chapter. The Prime Minister was heavily involved in negotiations with the trade union leaders. He had some successes, notably with the railwaymen in 1919, but he antagonized the miners who believed that he went back on a promise to nationalize the mines.

Note

Anger about demobilization

So annoyed did 2000 Guardsmen get in 1919 that they ignored their officers and marched from their camp in Shoreham to Brighton through cheering crowds to make a protest to the Mayor. He received them kindly and said that he would see what he could do. Nothing seems to have come of their protest.

Attempts at reconstruction

For two years the government pushed ahead with the task of reconstruction. Even before the war had ended, Fisher had got through Parliament his Education Act of 1918. This raised the school-leaving age to 14. It also gave larger grants to local authorities to improve teachers' salaries. In contrast to elementary schools, secondary schools remained fee-paying. However, the government increased the number of scholarships available to those attending these schools, and also encouraged local authorities to provide free part-time education for those pupils who left elementary schools at the age of 14.

The most important reconstruction initiative, however, came through the Ministry of Health, where Addison aimed to provide those 'homes fit for heroes' which the coalition had promised during its election campaign. Here an idealistic minister was unlucky. Addison was determined to build new houses of a decent quality. His method was to provide subsidies to local authorities. The problem was that the money became available at the height of the post-war boom, when construction costs were unusually high. Those houses that were built often proved too expensive for the heroes for whom they were intended. There was much disillusion and anger against the Ministry of Health. Under pressure from his colleagues, Lloyd George agreed that Addison must go.

The 'Geddes Axe'

The boom ended suddenly in 1921. Many Conservatives believed that government spending was far too high and looked back with nostalgia to the low-tax, low-spending days of before the war. 'Anti-Waste' campaigners, who invented the inefficient and spendthrift civil servants, Dilly and Dally, won two by-elections in June 1921. The Cabinet therefore decided to appoint a committee with a strong business element, chaired by Sir Eric Geddes, to discuss possible cuts with the Treasury. These cuts were duly identified and, in 1922, the government swung the 'Geddes Axe'. They abolished five government departments that had been set up during the war and cut spending on the army and public health. They also ended the housing subsidies to local authorities. The worst cuts of all were suffered by education. Fisher's hopes of reducing class sizes in elementary schools came to nothing. More than a quarter of these schools had classes of 60 or more in 1922. He had aimed to reduce them all to 50 or less. As for his 14–18 part-time continuation schools, these were suffocated at birth.

The fall of Lloyd George

By 1922, the knives were out for Lloyd George, not from his Conservative colleagues in the Cabinet, but from their backbenchers. Their anger against the Prime Minister had many causes. He had returned from Versailles without even getting the Kaiser to trial, let alone hanged. They bitterly opposed the reforming policies of Montagu in India and of Milner in Egypt. They considered that in Ireland Lloyd George had sold out to the nationalist terrorists. They hated his dictatorial style; his degrading of the honours system; the manner in which he rewarded his cronies. What particularly concerned party organizers like Sir George Younger was the Prime Minister's known ambition to create a centre party of moderate Conservatives and Lloyd George Liberals, which, under his continued leadership, would keep Labour out of power for the forseeable future.

■ Activity

List first the achievements of the coalition government between 1918 and 1922; then the problems it faced. In the circumstances, how well did it go?

Quotation

'Lloyd George knew my father, my father knew Lloyd George'

was an often repeated saying, summing up the resentment felt for the way Lloyd George promoted his friends.

Younger could see no advantage to the Conservative Party from staying in the coalition. In by-elections, the coalition Liberals were faring disastrously and 'independent' Conservatives were beginning to stand against the official coalition candidates. However, he knew that even though the idea of a centre party would badly split the Conservative Party, some Conservative leaders like Birkenhead and Austen Chamberlain were still attracted to the idea. When George Younger learnt that Austen Chamberlain supported Lloyd George's idea of continuing the coalition and fighting an early election, he wrote to his deputy, Sir Robert Sanders:

Source 4

The fat is properly in the fire if our mandarins [top people] persist in the policy which they appear to have adopted...I am to see Austen tomorrow afternoon, and shall let him distinctly understand that such a policy amounts to an inevitable split in the Party; ... and that also the Party ought to be given the opportunity of expressing its view before anything is finally settled. He may not like it but I shall insist upon it.

Almost the last straw was the so-called 'Chanak' incident. As part of the Versailles Settlement, the Treaty of Sevres had given part of the Turkish mainland around the city of Smyrna to Greece. A nationalist revolution in Turkey had brought to power an army officer, Mustapha Kemal (later known as Atatürk), who immediately set about driving out the Greeks. Britain had naval forces in the area and, when Kemal advanced on Chanak, Lloyd George gave orders to the naval commander, Harrington, to turn back the Turks, by force if necessary. He did so without fully consulting his colleagues. He also misread public opinion. Whatever the rights and wrongs of the dispute, few Britons wanted to be at war again. Bonar Law, now in retirement, better reflected the national mood when he sent off an anonymous letter to *The Times*, saying that 'We cannot act as the policeman of the world.' Harrington avoided a conflict by ignoring Lloyd George's instruction. Instead he negotiated an agreement with Kemal which was acceptable to the British government. To the Conservatives, however, Chanak was further evidence that the Prime Minister was increasingly a liability.

Things came to a head in October 1922. Lloyd George had the idea of a swift election to win for the coalition another five years of government. He tested the idea out on Austen Chamberlain, who had succeeded Bonar Law as Conservative leader. Chamberlain agreed and thought that he could bounce the Party into accepting it. Many of his colleagues, however, were aghast. Chamberlain then called a special meeting of the Party at the Carlton Club, intending to win support for the continuation of the coalition.

On the morning of the Carlton Club meeting, news came through that an 'independent' Conservative had won a by-election at Newport. Labour had come second, the coalition Liberal third. At the meeting the relatively unknown Stanley Baldwin made a powerful attack on Lloyd George, but the most influential speech against continuing the coalition came from Bonar Law, who indicated that if need be he would be prepared to resume the leadership of the Party. The meeting voted 185 to 88 to end the coalition. Lloyd George resigned the same day.

Note

In 1922, Austen Chamberlain took over from Bonar Law as Conservative Party leader. He was committed to the coalition and found himself in embarrassing public argument with Younger, his Party Chairman. It was said of Chamberlain – 'He always played the game and always lost.' He was an ideal second-in-command and in this situation, it was Younger who prevailed.

■ Think about

▶ Why do you think Chamberlain believed that the coalition should continue?

Greek minority areas
British controlled zone
Turkish advance
Movement of populations

▲ The Chanak incident 1922.

A *Punch* cartoon from 1922.

■ Think about

The Conservative break with Lloyd George.

▶ Study Source 5. Who is the dog? Explain Austen Chamberlain's comment.

Study Sources 6 and 7.

▶ What was Baldwin's main reason for wanting to end the coalition? What other criticisms of Lloyd George would you expect him to have included in his speech?

▶ Bonar Law clearly respected Lloyd George. Why then did he believe that the time had come to end the coalition?

▶ Why do you think that most historians consider his speech more influential than Baldwin's?

Historians now believe that most Conservative MPs had already made up their minds to part with Lloyd George before they listened to the speeches. What do you think were the most important reasons for their attitude?

■ Think about

▶ Do great statesmen have to be good people?

Alexander the Great came to think that he was a god. He also murdered one of his closest friends in a drunken brawl.

Henry VIII was a strong English king but a monstrous husband.

The US President J.F. Kennedy won a golden reputation before his assassination in 1963, but in private was a serial adulterer.

THE DOG THAT BROKE HIS LEAD.

Mr. Lloyd George. "CALL OFF THAT DOG OF YOURS, AUSTEN."
Mr. Chamberlain. "I'M NOT QUITE SURE THAT HE'D DESCRIBE HIMSELF AS MY DOG."
Mr. Lloyd George. "WELL, ANYHOW, IF YOU DON'T CALL HIM OFF I'M GOING HOME."

Source 6

Lloyd George is a dynamic force, and it is from that very fact that our troubles, in my opinion, arise. It is owing to that dynamic force, and that remarkable personality. That the Liberal Party, to which he formerly belonged, has been smashed to pieces; and it is my firm conviction that in time, the same thing will happen to our party…

Stanley Baldwin on Lloyd George

Source 7

As to Mr Lloyd George, whoever else may speak with disrespect of him, I never will. We may differ from him, and during the whole course of my co-operation with him I could see quite plainly that the time might come when we would differ; but that difference would never make me think that he did not render a service to this country in the war for which the country can never sufficiently thank him (applause). Mr Lloyd George cannot look on the Unionist [Conservative] Party with the same sort of feeling that I have. In the nature of the case, although I am sure he does not deliberately try to do it (I am quite sure of that), if it were broken I do not think it would break his heart (laughter).

Bonar Law

Lloyd George: an assessment

Lloyd George was 59 when he resigned in 1922. His immediate reaction was of relief. He had been in office continuously for 16 years and felt in need of time to rest and reflect. Neither he nor his opponents believed that he would never hold office again. However, without a secure party base he could not find a way back and, though he remained an MP for another 23 years, the rest of his career was an anti-climax.

History treats Lloyd George much more generously than did British public opinion in the 1920s. If you consider what he achieved rather than how he behaved, his record is remarkable. He was the creative social reformer from 1906 to 1914; the man who more than anyone brought the over-mighty Lords to heel between 1909 and 1911; the invigorating Minister of Munitions of 1915; above all, the man who won the war between 1916 and 1918; but also the tough but imaginative negotiator who, in 1921, found to the apparently intractable Irish problem a solution which was to survive for 50 years. The peoples of Britain, Ireland and the wartime Allies benefited greatly from his political genius. Many Liberals blame him for destroying the Liberal Party but Asquith was more guilty than he. The Conservatives threw him out because they feared his dynamism. Yet, in reality, Britain in the 1920s and 1930s was sadly in need of dynamism such as his.

His weakness lay in his personality. As A.J.P. Taylor puts it:

Source 8

He was the most inspired and creative British statesman of the twentieth century. But he had fatal flaws. He was devious and unscrupulous in his methods. He aroused every feeling except trust. In all his greatest acts, there was an element of self-seeking. Above all there was no stability. He tied himself to no men, to no party, to no single cause.

Taylor, *English History 1914–1945*, 1965

He had a sharp wit and a cruel tongue. Of Sir George Younger he said in 1922 that 'he would not be bullied by a second-rate brewer.' But the second-rate brewer pulled him down.

1922–1924: return to the two party system

The end of the coalition led to three elections in quick succession, during which time the Liberal Party faded into the background leaving the other two parties struggling for power. The Conservatives, led by Bonar Law, won the first election in 1922, but Law, dying of cancer, resigned after just eight months. His successor, Baldwin, failed to win in December 1923 and the first ever Labour government, led by Ramsay MacDonald, then took office. The third, which followed the resignation of MacDonald in October 1924, secured a large majority for Baldwin's Conservatives, who were then able to hold on to power for a full five-year term. This was the sequence of elections which destroyed the Liberal Party.

Law's government was inexperienced since some coalition ministers like Chamberlain and Birkenhead refused to join. Curzon stayed on as Foreign Secretary and Baldwin became Chancellor of the Exchequer. In the short Law ministry, the most important event was Baldwin's visit to the USA to try to negotiate as favourable a deal as he could over the repayment of Britain's war loan. He did not get a particularly good deal and then made it virtually impossible for the government to renegotiate better terms by carelessly announcing the negotiations to the Press before discussing them with the Cabinet. Bonar Law was not best pleased but the rest of the Cabinet supported Baldwin, who later succeeded him.

Baldwin's first ministry 1922–1923

Hardly had he become Prime Minister than Baldwin decided to call an election on the controversial issue of Tariff Reform – a policy in which he still believed, despite all the problems which it had caused the Conservatives since 1903 (see pp.77–79). Baldwin's family owned an ironworks near Worcester and Baldwin was convinced that Tariff Reform was the best policy to protect traditional British industries in the tough economic conditions and high levels of unemployment that the country was experiencing in 1923. At the time, his decision seemed rash. Baldwin seems to have calculated that it would unite his party after the arguments over the coalition. He also expected Lloyd George to suggest a protectionist programme and wished to take the wind out of his sails.

■ Activity

Identify each specific claim that A.J.P. Taylor makes about Lloyd George (Source 8)
e.g.
● He was inspired
● He was creative
● He was devious etc.

Look back over all you have read about Lloyd George. For each claim try to find at least one specific example or piece of evidence that would support it.

Are there any claims for which you can find evidence that challenge Taylor's view?

Note

George Curzon

Curzon, ex-Viceroy of India, was a possible successor to Bonar Law and was amazed and upset when Baldwin was preferred. He had much more experience and was more intelligent and hard-working. However, he was also vain and thin-skinned. He never quite lived down the malicious poem penned about him when he was an Oxford student:

'My name is George Nathaniel Curzon,
I am a most superior person,
My cheeks are pink, my hair is sleek,
I dine at Blenheim once a week.'

(Blenheim was the home of the Duke of Marlborough.)

In the short term, the calculation failed. Lloyd George was not in fact planning to go protectionist and the Liberals managed to fight a reasonably united pro-free trade campaign. The election was lost.

1923–1924 the first Labour government

Labour was now in power because it had become a formidable political force. There were many reasons for this success. The Party was securely based on, and more than adequately funded by, an established trade union movement. During the war, the coalition governments had involved Labour leaders like Henderson, Barnes and J.R. Clynes in leading the war effort, which gave them important experience and confidence. The Party reorganization which Henderson had master-minded had enabled the Party to put candidates in most constituencies in 1922.

The heart of its electoral support were the industrial working classes and, for them, the leadership identified key policies of immediate relevance to post-war circumstances. These were based on four main principles which the Party had approved at its annual conference in 1918:

- A minimum wage and a standard 48-hour working week
- The democratic control of industry – including the nationalization of key industries (Clause 4)
- A new approach to taxation – tax the rich heavily to pay for defence and social improvements
- Investing in the common good – financial surpluses to be spent on educational and cultural improvements for the benefit of all

> **Note**
>
> **Clause 4**
>
> Clause 4 was the most clearly socialist of these principles and was to cause continuous tension between the left-wing members of the Labour Party who believed passionately in the nationalization of key industries like coal and the railways and the moderates who were cooler and worried that nationalization would lose votes. By the 1970s it was clearly a vote-loser but not until the 1990s did the modernizers of that decade get it considerably watered down.

The post-war leadership was strong and clear-headed. Between 1922 and 1931, Ramsay MacDonald was leader. In Henderson he had a capable and hard-working right-hand man. Also in the leadership team were Clynes, J.H. Thomas and Philip Snowden.

They realized that their political success depended on their being able to convince the electorate that they were moderate, not revolutionary, more social reformers than socialists and certainly not Bolsheviks. They turned down regular requests from the British Communist Party for a formal link and, while pursuing a foreign policy which emphasized international co-operation and disarmament, tried to avoid appearing to have a special relationship with the Soviet Union. This would have been electorally damaging. Public opinion was strongly anti-Bolshevik and the Conservatives took every opportunity to suggest that Labour was really a Bolshevik wolf in sheep's clothing (as events in 1924 would prove).

Ramsay MacDonald's leadership in the 1920s

Because of the events of 1931 (see pp. 200–201) Ramsay MacDonald became a hated figure in the Labour movement and his historical reputation has suffered generally. However, in many ways he was just the right man to lead Labour in the 1920s. He was 47 when he became Prime Minister with already impressive achievements to his credit. More than anyone other than Keir Hardie, he was the maker of the Labour Party before 1914 (see pp. 113–117). Though he had resigned as leader because of his opposition to the war and then suffered great abuse for continuing his opposition, he also gained respect within the movement for his principled stand. Once the war was over, his belief in the need for maintaining the peace through international disarmament and collective security brought him back into harmony with the rest of the Party and he was re-elected to the leadership in 1922.

He was a moderate. He was impressive in appearance and appeared to speak from the heart. An experienced journalist and author, he had also proved himself as an efficient administrator and effective chairman. Above all, he had the skills and personality both to lead committed Labour supporters but also to appeal to the middle ground of floating voters without whose support Labour would never become a governing party with a secure majority. Through his commitment to international peace, social reform and free trade, he and his colleagues turned Labour into the 'progressive' party in British politics, and were able to attract influential converts from the Liberals – like Haldane, Addison and Trevelyan, all of whom eventually became Labour ministers.

The first Labour ministry 1924

MacDonald's aim was simple. It was 'to gain the confidence of the country'. This would be done by avoiding any radical measures and demonstrating that the government was safe in Labour's hands.

MacDonald was his own Foreign Secretary as well as Prime Minister. Snowden, who was a convinced free-trader in the Gladstonian mould, became Chancellor of the Exchequer and Henderson Home Secretary.

In 10 months, the government could not achieve much on the home front. Snowden presented a respectable, balanced, free-trade budget and Wheatley launched an ambitious programme of council house building. In foreign affairs MacDonald immediately looked the part of an experienced international statesman, and also gained some real successes.

Because of delays in the repayment of reparations, France had occupied the Ruhr industrial area of Germany. This had caused a serious diplomatic and economic crisis. MacDonald organized and chaired a conference in London at which France and Germany agreed the terms on which France would leave the Ruhr. He visited the League of Nations and made clear his commitment to the ideals of the League, to disarmament and collective security. He recognized the legality of the USSR, and offered a loan and a preferential trading deal.

This Russian deal gave the Conservatives and Liberals the opportunity to attack Labour as being too soft on the Bolsheviks. They continued this attack when the government decided not to go ahead with the prosecution of a communist journalist, J.R. Campbell, for an article which a law court might have decided was an incitement to mutiny. This trivial affair blew up out of all proportion. MacDonald handled it clumsily. The Liberals joined the Conservatives to vote Labour out. The 'Red Scare' continued during the election campaign of November 1924 with the publication of the Zinoviev letter (see p. 184).

Despite losing the 1924 election, MacDonald was pleased with the results of his first ministry. The Party had achieved its main aim. In the election, the Labour vote had increased and the Liberal Party was broken.

Baldwin as Prime Minister

Baldwin is one of the great puzzles of modern British political history. He led the Conservative Party for 14 years, longer than anyone else except Winston Churchill and Margaret Thatcher. For most of those years he enjoyed great public popularity – but it is hard to know exactly why.

▲ MacDonald with Henderson. Despite the great contributions each made to the success of the Labour party, they never really got on. This photo was taken in 1929 when MacDonald had at last given Henderson the post he wanted, Foreign Secretary.

Born in 1867, he was a slow political starter. In his thirties he was running the family ironworks and he did not become an MP until he was 41. He did not make a mark on the Party. It was only through Bonar Law's influence that he became President of the Board of Trade in 1921.

Baldwin was undoubtedly lucky in the way events turned out in 1922–1923. Austen Chamberlain and Birkenhead refused to serve under Bonar Law, so Baldwin became not only Chancellor of the Exchequer, but Law's second-in-command in the Commons. Then Law's sudden death enabled him to become Prime Minister.

A bitter Curzon described him as 'of the utmost insignificance'. Compared to many of his colleagues, he was not particularly clever, or hard working; nor was he ambitious. However, as one of his closest colleagues, Neville Chamberlain, observed, he was less simple than he made out. What there is no doubt about is that he was a thoroughly decent, generous man who was impossible to dislike. Perhaps he gave the Conservative Party what it wanted after the dramas of coalition, and the country what it wanted after the violence and exertions of the war. Whether that was what either needed is a different question.

Baldwin's second ministry 1924–1929

The major issues with which the government had to deal were economic. To the surprise of almost everyone, Baldwin appointed Churchill, who had not yet fully rejoined the Conservatives after his two decades as a Liberal, as Chancellor of the Exchequer. Churchill continued with his career of continual controversy by restoring the pound to 'the gold standard'. This meant raising its value by 10 per cent, which probably increased the country's economic problems, though not by as much as his critics then and since have argued. Britain's economic difficulties and the General Strike of 1926 are described in the next chapter.

The most successful minister was Neville Chamberlain who had chosen to go to the Ministry of Health, rather than the Exchequer, because he was confident that at Health he could get more done. His confidence was well-founded since he managed to put through Parliament 21 separate Acts. The most important effects of this legislation were that:

- Nearly a million new houses were built
- Maternity and child welfare clinics began to be provided
- A radical reform of local government was achieved which ended the Poor Law by dividing the responsibilities of the Poor Law Guardians between local government departments
- Local government funding through the rates was supported by a fairer system of 'block grants' from central government

Three other achievements of this government were the founding of the BBC in 1926; the establishment of the Central Electricity Board to create a national electricity grid; and the passing of the Equal Franchise Act of 1928 which lowered the voting age for women to 21, at last making the franchise equal for men and women.

Source 9

PEACE ABROAD
REDUCED COST OF LIVING
WIDOWS PENSIONS
IMPROVED EDUCATION
EQUAL FRANCHISE
OLD AGE PENSIONS
ORPHANS PENSIONS
RATING REFORM
800,000 HOUSES
PURE FOOD & MILK

The CONSERVATIVE SUN-RAY TREATMENT

▲ A Conservative poster from the 1929 election which lists the achievements of Baldwin's government. However, the 'Conservative Sun-ray treatment' had done nothing for the unemployed, which is one reason why the Conservatives lost the election.

Document exercise: Baldwin's leadership

Source A

A skilful political operator

He seemed, though he was not, an ordinary man…His simple exterior concealed a skilful political operator. Lloyd George, after bitter experience, called him 'the most formidable opponent I ever encountered' – no mean tribute. Baldwin played politics by ear. He read few official documents, the papers not at all. He sat on the treasury bench [the government front bench in the House of Commons] sniffing the order paper, cracking his fingers, and studying the House of Commons in its every mood.

Taylor, English History 1914–1945, 1965

Source B

A defender of simple British decency

Conservatives always did best when they had an internal enemy whom they could depict in some 'Un-English way', and in the form of the Labour Party they now had such an object. Difficult though it was to depict MacDonald…as the equivalent of Lenin, Labour's adoption of 'socialism' allowed the necessary smoke and mirrors to be deployed. Against this alien ideology, simple honest British decency was the first, and Baldwin's only, line of defence.

Charmley, A History of the Conservative Politics 1900–1966, 1996

Source C

An effective communicator

Baldwin captured the spirit of the age: the widespread desire for tranquillity at home, peace and disarmament abroad, and a return wherever possible to pre-war verities. He also made effective use of the two new forms of mass communication, the radio broadcast and cinema newsreel.

Ball, The Conservative Party and British Politics 1902–51, 1995

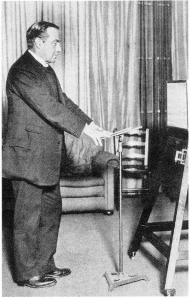

▲ Baldwin in his element, broadcasting to the nation in 1924.

Source D

A peacemaker

In 1925 Stanley Baldwin opposed the end to the union political levy which allowed trade unions to fund the Labour Party. He declared:

We are not going to press our political advantage home at a moment like this…We stand for peace. We stand for the removal of suspicion in the country. We want to create a new atmosphere, a new atmosphere in a new Parliament in a new age, in which people can come together…We abandon what we have laid our hands to. We know that we may be called cowards for doing it…But we believe we know what at this moment the country wants…I know…that will be the feeling of all those who sit behind me…And I have equal confidence in my fellow countrymen…Although I know that there are those who work for different ends from most of us in this House, yet there are many in all ranks and all parties who will re-echo my prayer: 'Give peace in our time, O Lord.'

THE WORCESTERSHIRE LAD

Farmer Bull: "WELL DONE, STANLEY : A LONG DAY AND A RARE STRAIGHT FURROW."

▲ A cartoon from *Punch*, May 1937.

■ Think about

▶ *Punch*'s attitude to Baldwin. The caption under the cartoon reads: 'Farmer Bull: well done Stanley: A long day and a rare straight furrow.' Explain the reference to 'a straight furrow'. To what extent does this help to explain Baldwin's popularity?

Note

The first woman MP to take her seat in the House of Commons was Nancy Astor, in 1919. An American by birth, she married the wealthy Waldorf Astor and, when he moved to the House of Lords, fought and won for the Conservatives the Plymouth constituency he had previously held. She was well known as a conscientious MP for 26 years and as hostess at Cliveden, the Astor's mansion overlooking the Thames.

■ Examination-style questions

1 Comprehension in context

Source E, was published by *Punch* magazine when Baldwin retired. What qualities of Baldwin does the cartoonist wish to convey?

2 Comparing the sources

a) Study Sources A, B and C. In what ways do they (a) agree and (b) disagree about Baldwin's strengths as a politician.

b) Study Source D. Does it better confirm the view of Source A or Source B?

3 Assessing the sources

To what extent do Sources A, B, C explain why both Baldwin's political contemporaries and later historians have had such difficulty in assessing his abilities?

4 Making judgements

Using these sources and your own knowledge, explain why for most of the period between 1924 and 1937 Baldwin was Britain's most successful and popular politician.

MacDonald's second ministry 1929–1931

In the 1929 election, Baldwin's campaigning slogan was 'Safety First'. Labour reminded the electorate in its 'Labour Faces the Nation' programme that it was a responsible moderate reforming party. Having achieved a majority of 21 over the Conservatives, though not an overall majority since Lloyd George's Liberals held 59 seats, MacDonald returned as Prime Minister. He had a similar ministerial team to that in 1924, though now he let Henderson have the Foreign Office. Margaret Bondfield, the first woman in Britain to join the Cabinet, was Minister of Labour. Four months after Labour took office, the Wall Street Crash triggered the worst economic depression of modern times. Few governments around the world could weather it. MacDonald's could not.

In comparison with its competitors, the British economy had struggled through the 1920s, Because her old-established 'staple' industries, like textiles and coal, were less competitive, British levels of unemployment were high by international standards. Successive governments essentially tried to find a way back to the better days of before 1914: balance the budgets; encourage free trade; restore international business confidence. Churchill's return to the gold standard was an element of this policy. Snowden for Labour did not disagree with him on this; his main criticism of Churchill was that his budgets were not adequately balanced.

The Wall Street Crash

The Wall Street Crash led to a collapse of world trade, a massive increase in unemployment across the world and an international banking crisis as banks tried to recall money lent in better days. In the summer of 1931 the Labour government faced an exceptional crisis. Unemployment, already in 1929 the major national problem, was getting substantially worse, while the international banking crisis threatened the Bank of England and London's position as one of the world's great financial centres. The consequence was the collapse of the Labour government, the creation of a National government and a bitter split of the Labour Party, which was to keep it out of power for 14 years. The next page shows the sequence of events leading to the Labour split.

- 1929: the Macmillan Committee on Finance and Industry set up to enquire into whether British financial systems could be improved to lessen unemployment.
- February 1931: May Committee set up to advise government about making economies. Chaired by Sir George May, it was dominated by businessmen.
- May 1931: Macmillan Committee reports. Its membership had included Keynes and Bevin from the TUC. To its main report were added various 'reservations' which suggested a devaluation of the currency and a more managed economy. These suggestions, though sensible, add to the nervousness of the money markets about the stability of the pound.
- 31 July: May Committee reports. It calculates that £120 million is needed to balance the budget, recommending that £24 million should be found through taxation and £96 million by cuts in government spending. These cuts would include a 20 per cent cut in unemployment relief.
- Early August: the run on the pound continues. The Cabinet debates what to cut. Because he has no overall Commons majority, MacDonald also has to consult the other party leaders.
- 19 August: Labour are close to agreement on cuts of £56 million. TUC strongly opposes cuts. The Conservatives want £78 million.
- The run on the pound intensifies. No one will consider devaluation so the Bank of England has to seek a loan from New York.
- 23 August: the Cabinet learns that New York loan is dependent on cuts of £76 million. In the Cabinet, 11 support MacDonald who advises accepting the conditions, 9 are opposed. MacDonald advises King George V that the Cabinet is split and that he will have to resign. The King asks him to consider forming a National Government.
- 24 August: MacDonald meets with the King, Baldwin and Samuel (Liberal leader while Lloyd George is undergoing an operation). He agrees to form an all-party National Government and returns to Downing Street to announce this to a dumbfounded Cabinet, who were assuming he had resigned.
- August/September: Snowden and Thomas join the National Government. Most of the Party, along with the TUC, follows Henderson and Clynes into opposition. Henderson is elected leader and MacDonald is expelled from the Party.

Document exercise: MacDonald in 1931 – traitor to the people's cause or courageous patriot?

Quotation

Keynes described the May Committee Report as: 'The most foolish document I have ever had the misfortune to read'.

Most economists and historians now agree with Keynes. May greatly exaggerated the budget deficit and therefore the problem which the government faced. Unfortunately, MacDonald, Snowden, and the money markets thought that the May Committee knew what it was talking about.

■ Think about

▶ What alternative did the government have to cuts?

▶ What would the present government do if a depression was looming and unemployment was increasing? (See also p. 270)

▶ What were people like Keynes and Ernest Bevin of the TUC advising?

▶ Why did the government take no notice of them?

▶ Why did it feel so strongly that it must avoid devaluing the pound?

Source A

Putting country before class

He emerges as a greater and, at the same time as a more attractive man, than he has generally been thought to be; the hostile view of him which became almost universal, at any rate in the Labour movement, after the split of 1931 seems to me to emerge as myth rather than history…All his life MacDonald fought against the class view of politics, and for the primacy of political action as against industrial action; for him, the logical corollary [consequence] was that the Party must be prepared, when necessary, to subordinate the sectional class of the unions to its own conception of the national interest.

Marquand, *Ramsay MacDonald*, 1977

Source B

Beatrice Webb considers MacDonald

He is no longer intent on social reform – any indignation he had at the present distribution of wealth he has lost; his real and intimate life is associated with non-political aristocratic society, surrounded with the beauty and dignity that wealth can buy.

Cole (ed.), *Beatrice Webb's Diaries*, 1952

Source C

WE MUST THINK OF OUR SAVINGS AND OUR HOME THAT'S WHY I'M VOTING FOR THE NATIONAL GOVERNMENT

▲ A National government election poster from 1931.

Source D

The view of MacDonald's secretary

It is evident that MacDonald never really accepted the socialist faith of a classless world, based on unselfish service.

The members of the Labour Cabinet naturally assumed on the Sunday night, 23 August, Mr Baldwin would be asked to form a government. But it is significant that MacDonald had something quite different in view. Without a word of consultation with his Cabinet colleagues, without even informing them of his intentions to set up a National Government with himself as Prime Minister, he proceeded to carry out his long thought-out plan...

The impression left on the minds of those who had heard that speech (on the Monday morning) was that the whole thing had been arranged long before and that while in Cabinet...they had been making panic-stricken efforts to balance the Budget, the whole thing had been humbug and make-believe.

MacNeill Weir, *The Tragedy of Ramsay MacDonald*, 1938

Source E

A reappraisal of MacDonald's actions

There is no evidence that MacDonald had any real thought of coalition with the Tories until his government submitted its resignation to the King, late on Sunday 23 August 1931. That very evening, he announced his intention of leading his stricken party into opposition, and confirmed this to his daughter...But, by the time he went to bed, there were hints that he might be changing his mind. Several factors played their part in turning the scale. The unbridgeable gaps in Labour's ranks over the proposed cuts in unemployment benefits; the refusal of Bevin and the TUC to countenance any meaningful cuts at all; a...visit to George V which brought a powerful personal appeal from the King to MacDonald's sense of patriotism; the urgings of Neville Chamberlain and others that MacDonald's leadership was vital to ensuring foreign confidence in the new administration – all these...played their part.

Morgan, *Labour People*, 1992

■ Examination-style questions

1 **Comprehension in context**
What events of 1931 would have led to Source C?

2 **Comparing the sources**
In what ways does Source E differ from Source A in the explanation offered for MacDonald's behaviour?
Why is this difference important to MacDonald's reputation?

3 **Assessing the sources**
How reliable are Sources A and B as evidence to explain MacDonald's action during the August crisis?

4 **Making judgements**
Using these sources and your own knowledge, explain whether you think MacDonald was more a courageous patriot than a traitor to the people's cause.

The National government 1931

The new National government had a small Cabinet with just 10 members – four Labour, four Conservative and two Liberal. MacDonald stayed on as Prime Minister, as did Snowden as Chancellor of the Exchequer. Baldwin was effectively Deputy Prime Minister as Lord President of the Council and Neville Chamberlain came back to his preferred post as Minister of Health. The leading Liberal was Sir Herbert Samuel who became Home Secretary.

Its first action was to make the cuts to secure the New York and other loans. Snowden raised taxes and made cuts of £70 million. He reduced unemployment benefits and the salary of employees in public services by, on average, 10 per cent. However the crisis went from bad to worse. When sailors of the Atlantic fleet at Invergordon learnt that some of them were facing cuts of more than 10 per cent, compared to the admirals 7 per cent, they refused to go on duty. The news of this 'Invergordon Mutiny' was telegraphed around the world and there was another run on the pound. This time the government could not arrange additional loans and the nightmare which the National Government had been formed to prevent happened. Britain went off the gold standard and the pound slipped below the previous fixed rate of 4.86 dollars first to 3.80 and then to 3.40. After the initial shock, people discovered that the heavens had not fallen in. On the contrary, the weaker pound made it easier to balance the budget because it encouraged exports and discouraged imports.

The 1931 election

The Cabinet then decided to go to the country. They asked for a 'doctor's mandate' to nurse the sick nation through a dangerous crisis. As far as MacDonald was concerned, he no longer had a political future except as part of a National Government and the Conservatives were happy to work with him through the crisis. They also believed that they would do well in the election. They were right. The nation rallied to the National Government and to the Conservatives within it. Of the 556 seats that went to National candidates, the Conservatives won 473. Labour did very badly, gaining only 52. It fought a bitter but muddled campaign. Their opponents criticized them for running away from responsibility and MacDonald and Snowden made them out to be little better than Bolsheviks.

Neville Chamberlain, Chancellor of the Exchequer

The most effective member of the government was Neville Chamberlain, who took over from Snowden as Chancellor of the Exchequer. In his six years as Chancellor he proved himself careful but ready to try new measures. An early step, of which his father Joseph would have been proud, was to introduce a general tariff of 10 per cent. In 1932, he made further spending cuts and added a tariff on tea. Low interest rates made possible a boom in house building, which helped to pull most of Britain slowly out of depression. Though wages had fallen for many workers, the cost of living had fallen more. The lower cost of living also partly cushioned the effects of the cuts in unemployment benefits.

In 1934, Chamberlain cut income tax and partially restored public pay to its pre-1931 level. 'The first chapter of Great Expectations has succeeded Bleak House', he said. In 1935 he was able to restore fully public salaries. For most of the country, better times had arrived.

For the unemployed, however, the bad times continued. An Unemployment Act of 1934 set up a national Unemployment Assistance Board (UAB) which paid out 'the dole' on a uniform basis using a means test. The means test was extremely unpopular, as was the fact that UAB rates were in some areas less than those the local councils had given previously. Also in 1934, by the Special Areas Act, two commissioners were given £2 million to try to revive industry in those areas where unemployment was worst, like Tyneside and South Wales. They were not able to achieve much.

MacDonald, whose powers began to weaken embarrassingly, handed over to Baldwin in 1935 who won the election of that year convincingly, though Labour's support improved. In turn, Baldwin decided to retire in 1937. Chamberlain, who had been waiting for years to succeed him, and would have been happiest driving forward social and administrative reform at home, inherited instead the alarming all-consuming problem of how to deal with Hitler (see Chapter 14).

Edward VIII and Mrs Simpson 1936

The new king, Edward VIII, who succeeded his father in January 1936, posed Baldwin his last major problem before retirement. A rather weak and foolish bachelor of 41, Edward was deeply in love with, and in the constant company of, Wallis Simpson, a witty attractive American who was living apart from and divorcing her third husband. Although the newspapers knew about the affair, they did not report it. There would, therefore, have been no crisis if the lovers had been content to continue their relationship as an affair. They were not. Mrs Simpson gained her divorce in October and Edward assumed that she would become his Queen.

Source 10

Baldwin made it equally clear that she would not. He was sure that neither the established Church of England nor respectable opinion would tolerate a divorcee on the throne. Edward must decide between the throne and Wallis. Baldwin skilfully consulted first the Cabinet and then the leaders of the Dominions of the British Empire and gained their agreement that Mrs Simpson could not become Queen. Up to 1 December, the crisis had been behind closed doors but then the news broke. A small number of MPs tried to persuade the King to stay but Baldwin had read public opinion correctly, insofar as Parliament and the national press represented it. (On the streets, though, there was noisy support for the King). Edward, however, had made up his mind that his choice was 'the woman he loved' and abdicated on 11 December. He left the country for the continent and Wallis. His brother succeeded him as George VI.

■ **Think about**

▶ Baldwin and Britain's political leaders were hostile to the idea of Wallis becoming Queen. If the King had very little real power, why was there such powerful opposition to the marriage?

▶ Edward, King no longer, honeymooning with Wallis in a French chateau in 1937.

Rule by pygmies: a valid interpretation?

▲ An unemployed Tynesider surveys the empty docks and waterway, which until the 1920s had throbbed with activity and provided thousands of jobs.

The initial verdict of historians

The 1920s and 1930s can seem dreary years. They are sandwiched between two world wars; and the outbreak of the second seems an appalling mistake after the terrible experiences of the first. The political, economic and diplomatic difficulties of these decades proved, as often as not, unmanageable to the politicians of the time. In comparison, the periods both before 1914 and after 1945 seem much more constructive. There were problems but governments like that of Asquith from 1906 to 1914 and Attlee from 1945 to 1951 responded to them constructively, determined to make Britain a significantly better place by their efforts.

Later politicians and historians have been hard on the likes of MacDonald, Baldwin and Chamberlain. Churchill described the thirties as 'the years which the locusts have eaten'. In 1940, three young Labour supporters wrote a passionate criticism of their recent rulers. 'Guilty Men' they called them in their pamphlet and the name has stuck. The phrase Devils' Decade is often used to describe the 1930s. 'Rule by pygmies' is the tag given to the period in the 1950s by the historian C.L. Mowat, who wrote an excellent study of the period in 1955.

Where were the equivalents to Disraeli and Gladstone, to Salisbury, Asquith and Lloyd George, to Churchill, Attlee and Bevin?

■ Questions

1 Study Source 12. What does Charmley mean when he says in the third paragraph that 'it appeared that Keynesian economics had provided the "philosopher's stone"'? (see p. 223).

2 What are the two main points that Charmley makes in defence of the National government?

3 The scene in Source 11 might seem a powerful criticism of the National government. How might the author of Source 12 answer the criticism?

4 Study Sources 13 and 14. How far do they agree with each other in their assessment of Baldwin?

More recent historians are more charitable

Source 12

Because the Churchillian account of the 1930s as 'the years which the locusts have eaten' has been so influential, it has been assumed that Baldwin was a failure…(this does not) stand up to examination. The 1930s was a decade of global instability, and international disorder which was reflected in and caused by domestic upheavals: Japan became more militaristic; the fascist dictatorship installed by Mussolini became more adventurous and provided a model for other European nations, most notably Germany, to copy…Spain dissolved into a bloody civil war…Britain came nowhere near revolution. When this record is compared with that of other parts of the world it gives some indication of the success enjoyed by Baldwin; if the main task of Conservatism is to preserve the constitutional order against the forces of change and decay, then it was achieved here under the most adverse circumstances…

In the more comfortable circumstances of the 1950s and 1960s when it appeared that Keynesian economics had provided the 'philosopher's stone' which would deliver full employment and ever-increasing standards of living, it was quite the fashion to slate the National Government for not doing something more about unemployment…from the vantage point of the late 1990s, when the unemployment figures are so high that they are subject to constant massage, such complacency is less natural…[The international context for a Keynesian approach did not exist] Indeed it might be argued that by promoting a climate in which money was 'cheap' and labour costs low, the [National] government did as much as it could to promote the right climate for economic recovery.

Charmley, *A History of the Conservative Politics 1900–1966*, 1996

Source 13

Later on…rulers and ruled exchanged accusations. According to one version, the rulers were 'Guilty Men', at best incompetent, more often deliberately deceiving the British people. Churchill described Baldwin as putting 'party before country'. According to their version, much formulated by Baldwin himself, the fault lay with 'democracy' which was reluctant to make exertions, sacrificing the future for the sake of the present…Both accusations missed the truth. The statesmen were incompetent, probably more so than usual. Baldwin made this a virtue. 'I always make mistakes', he said in 1935. Equally English people showed little enthusiasm for a dynamic leadership, even if it were offered to them.

Taylor, *English History 1914–1945*, 1965

Source 14

Baldwin represented with singular accuracy the mood of a nation wearied by war. He was peace loving at a time when Britain hated the memory and dreaded the prospect of war. He was insular at a time of political isolationism, conciliatory in an age of compromise. He was easy-going at a time when his fellow-countrymen wanted nothing so much as to be left alone. If he misconstrued the European situation, so did most others. If he evaded realities, the nation was glad to follow.

Blake, *The Conservative Party*

■ Activity

You are going to assess for yourself the fairness of some of the labels applied to the 1920s and 1930s. As well as looking at the actions and decisions taken by Britain's leaders, you will need to take into account the constraints imposed on them by the British electorate and the international context. As you assess the judgements made by historians at different times, you also need to think how their views may have been distorted by hindsight, or inappropriate comparisons with other periods.

1 Read the sources here and look back over the chapter as a whole. You may want to work in groups, each considering a particular ministry. Draw up a chart to summarize:

Positive achievements	Political failures	Mitigating factors (Constraints on what could be done)	Distorting lenses (Factors which may affect historians' perspectives of these events)

2 Using this information, explain whether you consider the description 'Rule by pygmies' is a fair assessment of the political leaders of the inter-war years. This could be done as a debate.

3 Think up your own epithets (descriptive phrases) to provide the most accurate description of the period.

Conservative ascendancy 1918–1939

Coalitions and National Governments can obscure the fact that for 18 years out of 21, the Conservative Party was the largest in the House of Commons. Lloyd George may have been Prime Minister for 4 of those years and MacDonald for another 4, but both were to a large extent the prisoners of their Conservative supporters.

Circumstances more than design brought the Conservatives to power. The war and 1916 split between Lloyd George and Asquith gave Bonar Law and his colleagues their first boost. The changes to the constitution of Ireland between 1918 and 1922 lost the Liberals about 80 parliamentary seats, while the Conservatives gained the Ulster Unionists. Then in 1931, with the Liberals broken, Labour split. The strengths of the Conservatives were their unity and their ability to respond to the public desire for a quiet life. Bonar Law came up with the slogan 'tranquillity' and set the tone for inter-war Conservatism which Stanley Baldwin effortlessly sustained. Neville Chamberlain added limited social reform and undoubted administrative efficiency.

Sir Oswald Mosley and the British Union of Fascists

In 1930, Mosley, then aged 34, was one of the most promising young British politicians. Starting as a Conservative MP in 1918, he joined the Labour Party in 1924 and was a minister in MacDonald's 1929 government. An impressive speaker with a lively mind, he was sure that the economic problems of the 1920s needed new solutions. In 1930, he tried to convert the Labour government from free trade towards a more planned economy, in particular towards carefully directed government spending to encourage the expansion of industry. When the government rejected his proposals, Mosley resigned from the Cabinet and tried to win the support of the Labour Party rank and file. When he failed with them (by quite a narrow margin) in 1931 he left to found his own New Party, which he intended to develop as an alternative to socialism.

In 1932, he visited and was impressed by Mussolini and his blackshirted fascist private army. On his return to Britain, he replaced his New Party by the British Union of Fascists. Mosley convinced himself that the future of Britain and Europe would be fought over by fascism and communism. There could be no comfortable democratic middle ground. His blackshirts were anti-communist and anti-Semitic. For a brief moment in 1934, he gained the support of Lord Rothermere's *Daily Mail*. Any respectable backing he might have gained was lost, however, when, at a meeting at the Olympia stadium in London in 1934, his supporters severely manhandled some hecklers.

Between 1934 and 1937, the BUF stirred up anti-communist and anti-Semitic feeling in the East End of London and the industrial cities of Lancashire and Yorkshire. Sometimes they gained up to 25 per cent of the poll in local elections but never made any headway nationally. The government significantly weakened it by the Public Order Act of 1937, which forbade the wearing of uniforms for political purposes and gave the police powers to ban demonstrations which might lead to disorder. The BUF then withered away. Fascism was never a serious internal threat to British democracy.

Hyde Park in 1936. Mosley responds to the salutes of his female supporters.

Source 15

Summary

- The Conservative Party dominated British party politics mainly because of the weakness of their opponents. The Liberal split of 1916 helped them to a parliamentary majority between 1918 and 1923. The Labour split of 1931 allowed them to dominate the National coalition from 1931 to 1939. Simultaneously, Baldwin's calm, patriotic approach, along with some social reform, proved attractive to the electorate.

- Baldwin must be rated, superficially, a successful Prime Minister. He was, after all, Prime Minister three times and made a major contribution to the Conservatives' electoral success. However, though his decency and gift for compromise may have kept Britain a comparatively conflict-free society in the inter-war period, his inability to do anything to reduce unemployment and his slowness to appreciate the dangers posed by fascism, places a real question-mark against his record.

- The Labour government of 1924 did well in a short time. It achieved its key aim, which was to establish its respectability, and made a good impression in foreign affairs.

- Ramsay MacDonald's reputation has been unfairly harmed by the crisis of 1931 during which he was more the victim of exceptionally difficult circumstances than the selfish betrayer of the working class. If he had died in 1930, he would be regarded as the best leader the Labour Party has ever had.

- MacDonald, Baldwin and Chamberlain do not immediately compare well with the political leaders of the pre-1918 and post-1940 eras. Until recently, most historians would have regarded the description 'rule of pygmies' as essentially correct if harshly expressed. Recent historians tend to acknowledge their positive qualities, and their appeal to the British public of the time, and to explain their poor record of achievement by reference to the circumstances in which they found themselves.

■ **Further reading**

*Paul Adelman, *The Rise of the Labour Party*, 1996

*Stuart Ball, *The Conservative Party and British Politics*, 1995

Robert Pearce, *British Domestic Politics 1918–39*, 1992

C. Cook, *The Age of Alignment: Electoral Politics in Britain, 1922–29*, 1975

D. Marquand, *Ramsay MacDonald*, 1977

Chapter 13

Economic and social issues 1918–1939
Hungry years for some, but by no means for all

◀ Welsh miners with their families outside their terraced homes in 1931.

▼ New detached homes in the suburbs of South London, plus two of their well-dressed middle class occupants, in 1935.

Introduction

Recurring themes throughout the previous chapter were industrial tension and economic difficulties: in 1919–1920, a record number of days were lost through strike action; in 1921, the Geddes Axe mutilated Fisher's Education reforms because the government was convinced of the need for cuts; the greatest challenge to Baldwin's second ministry was the General Strike; the economic crisis of 1931 broke MacDonald's government. This chapter concentrates on these economic problems and describes how working people and governments responded to them. As the pictures opposite show, the effects of the problems varied greatly. The traditional industrial areas like south Wales suffered enormously, the suburbs of the south-east not at all. On the contrary, many regions of Britain experienced beneficial economic and social change. The 1930s have often been described as 'the hungry thirties'; the accuracy of this interpretation is assessed at the end of the chapter.

Key questions

- What were the main economic and social problems faced by Britain in the inter-war years?
- What was the nature and extent of the industrial and other conflicts in these years? How successfully did the government deal with them?
- What steps did the government take to reduce the problems of unemployment and how successful were they?
- How much did British society change in these years?
- How hungry were the thirties?

Boom and bust in the twenties

It was sections of the so-called staple industries of coal, iron and steel, textiles, and shipbuilding that had the most difficult time. The leaders of Britain's industrial revolution, they had been established in the regions of the natural resources of coal and iron ore and imported supplies of cotton – in the north of England, south Wales, and central Scotland. Less affected, often not affected at all, were new industries like motor vehicles, chemicals and electrical goods. Their factories tended to be to be electrically powered and set up in the Midlands and the South, rather than in the traditional industrial areas. On the whole, the staple industries shrank in the inter-war years while the newer ones grew vigorously.

International competition had put the staple industries under pressure before the First World War. As other nations industrialized, these industries could never maintain the lead they had achieved during the nineteenth century – a lead achieved simply because Britain had been the first nation to industrialize. However, the exceptional requirements of the war economy, gave the staple industries – especially shipbuilding – a considerable if short-lived boost. Because of the need to repair the damage done by the war, the boom lasted until 1920.

It came to an abrupt end in 1921 and the staple industries were hit fast and hard. The coal industry faced stiff competition from mines in the USA, Germany and Poland, often working in larger units with more modern methods. To make matters worse, alternative fuels like oil and electricity were becoming available. In 1913 British coalfields had produced 287 million tons annually; 20 years later in 1933 the comparable figure was only 210 million tons.

The collapse of the textile industry was even more dramatic. The severest competition came from Japan and India. Between the wars, the Lancashire cotton industry lost most of what had been its best market – India and the Far East. There would have been some loss however modern and well-managed British factories might have been, but in many cases the Japanese seem to have had more modern machinery and better marketing methods, as well as cheaper labour.

The problems of British shipyards were as great as those of the cotton mills. Once the war damage was repaired, the world needed fewer ships than in 1913. Competition from foreign shipyards was intense and British yards were slower to adjust to the trend from steam to oil–powered ships. In 1913, British yards built 1,930,000 tons of shipping. In 1933, the worst year of the 1930s slump, they only produced 133,000 tons.

The experience of the iron and steel industries was more mixed. An overall decline in the 1920s was partially compensated for by a reviving demand for steel for new industries like motor vehicles in the 1930s. There were mergers and some modernization of plant. Stewart and Lloyds at Corby, for example, was an international leader.

Primarily because of these difficulties in the staple industries, unemployment soared, as soon as the post–war boom ended. Between December 1920 and June 1921, it doubled from 1 to 2 million. This was nearly 17 per cent of the workforce. Between 1921 and 1939, the average annual unemployment rate averaged about 14 per cent. Only once, briefly in 1927, did it dip below 10 per cent. The country had never experienced anything like it. Between 1886 and 1913, the average rate had been closer to 5 per cent.

Industrial conflict

Severe industrial conflict began soon after the war ended, again on a scale beyond Britain's previous experience. In 1919, 35 million days were lost in strike action, 86 million in 1921. (The worst year by far before 1914 had been 1912 with 41 million days lost). The causes were various but the most important was a rapid increase in prices – 25 per cent in the 2 years between 1919 and 1920 – with which wage increases failed to keep pace. Men returned from the war in a more assertive mood and with higher expectations. A record number of workers, about 8 million in 1921, were members of unions which were better organized and, through a series of amalgamations, larger and more powerful.

Politicians and the newspapers worried about revolution. They were scared by the success of the Bolshevik Revolution in Russia and the vigour of communism in other parts of Europe. A Communist Party was founded in Britain which took instructions from Moscow and, in 1919, during a strike on Clydeside, extreme socialists flew the red flag from Glasgow City Chambers. There was also a riot between the strikers and the police. This so alarmed the government that they sent 12,000 troops with six tanks to keep the peace.

In reality, British trade union leaders were profoundly unrevolutionary. They concentrated on gaining better wages and working conditions for their members. In 1914, miners, railwaymen and transport workers had formed themselves into an apparently formidable 'Triple Alliance'. Of these three big unions, the most aggrieved and determined was the Miners' Federation, which had more than a million members. The government had partially nationalized the mines during the war. The miners' leaders wished nationalization to

Note

Red Clydeside

The Labour MPs of Glasgow and the industrial towns of the Clyde valley were, on the whole, fiercely left wing, and frequently critical of the moderation of the Labour leadership. The best known of them was James Maxton, a magnificent public speaker, who was also a powerful figure within the Independent Labour Party (ILP) which also became very critical of Labour's moderation in the 1920s.

■ **Think about**

▶ Why do you think the government felt so alarmed despite the moderate stand of most trade union leaders?

continue. They believed that only through nationalization would the industry be modernized and achieve better safety standards. They also wanted to bargain for their members at a national level, rather than locally with hundreds of separate private companies. With the support of the Triple Alliance and threats of strike action, it persuaded Lloyd George to appoint a Commission, chaired by Sir John Sankey, to inquire into the problems of the industry.

The Sankey Report was mainly sympathetic to the case made by the Miners' Federation. It noted the high profits made by the industry during the war, most of which had gone to the owners rather than the miners, whose housing conditions were a national scandal. It was also critical of the way the industry had been organized before the war with 1500 separate mining companies. The Commission recommended wage rises and shorter hours. On the casting vote of its chairman, it also recommended nationalization. The government agreed to the wage rises and shorter hours but not immediately to nationalization. Lloyd George gave the impression that he was in favour of nationalization but said that his government needed more time to discuss its details. He was probably playing for time since he had little chance of getting his Conservative colleagues to agree to such a radical piece of State intervention.

Eventually, in 1921, the government handed the mines back to the owners. Boom had given way to bust. The price of coal fell by half while the miners suffered pay cuts. At the beginning of April, the country braced itself for a major industrial conflict. The Triple Alliance seemed united. The miners threatened to strike and the railwaymen and the transport workers to support them. Lloyd George declared a state of emergency and negotiated energetically with the miners' leaders. He suggested a temporary settlement and managed to split the leadership. On Friday, 15 April 1921, the miners struck but found themselves on their own. The leaders of the railway and transport unions did not believe that the situation justified the total disruption of the country and were not sure that their members would respond solidly to the strike call. That Friday went down in trade union history as 'Black Friday'.

In 1925, the mine-owners again faced renewed difficulties. Following the international agreement known as the Dawes Plan the French had withdrawn from the Ruhr and Germany had restarted its coal exports. In addition, Churchill had reintroduced the gold standard (see p. 197), which made exporting more difficult by raising the value of the pound. The mine-owners decided that, to protect the industry, they must lengthen miners' working hours and cut their wages. The TUC made clear to both the mine-owners and to the government that, this time, the mineworkers could rely on the support of the TUC.

Baldwin's government decided to buy time and appointed another commission, this time chaired by Sir Herbert Samuel, to find a solution to the dispute. On another Friday, nicknamed Red Friday, the government agreed to pay a subsidy to the owners for nine months so that they could postpone the imposition of longer hours and lower wages.

The Samuel Commission recommended that the industry should be reorganized, that the government subsidy should end, that a temporary wage cut should take effect until the reorganization had taken place but hours should not be lengthened. The mine-owners showed little interest in reorganization and modernization and went ahead with the wage cuts. The Miners' Federation led by the fiery A.J. Cook would not consider any cut in wages, however temporary. 'Not a minute on the day, not a penny off the pay', was his battle cry and he rallied his members with a call for a 'war to the death'.

Quotation

Vernon Hartshorn, Labour MP and representative of the miners on learning that the government would not carry out the nationalization of the mines as recommended by the Sankey report:

'We have been deceived, betrayed, duped.'

■ Think about

The solidarity of the coal miners was always strong. If they were called out on strike they came and would be slow to accept defeat.

▶ What were the characteristics of coal mining that made miners more 'solid' than, say railwaymen or transport workers?

Quotation

Lord Birkenhead who was leading the government's negotiation team remarked that he thought that

'the miners' leaders were the stupidest men in the country until he had the misfortune to meet the owners.'

While some trade unionists and, on the other side, some members of the government wanted a showdown, most of the TUC General Council and Baldwin, the Prime Minister, did not. It seemed to them very dangerous, with results that were unpredictable and could be very harmful.

However, both sides handled the negotiation poorly and muddled into conflict.

The events of the General Strike

It lasted nine days. Trade union support was solid. Public transport stopped completely. No newspapers appeared, except the *Daily Mail* which was printed in Paris. There was some vandalism and violence. 3000 strikers were arrested but no one died.

However, not everything came to a halt. The government knew it had to win and was well prepared. It had an emergency scheme which divided the country into ten areas, each with its own civil commissioner. By the Emergency Powers Act, it was able to take over essential vehicles, fuel and buildings. The movement of essential supplies by road, which often made use of the army, was particularly well organized. It built up ample stocks of coal and took over the power stations to keep gas and electricity supplies running. In London, Hyde Park was closed to the public and used as a milk depot. The middle classes rallied to the government. Businesses stayed open, come what may, and booked rooms in nearby hotels for their staff. Office staff crammed together in private cars or walked to work. Volunteers drove buses, with some success, and tried to do the same, less successfully, with locomotives.

In the propaganda war, the government had the better artillery. Without newspapers, the two sides produced their own propaganda. Churchill devoted his abundant energies to editing the *British Gazette* and Baldwin was able to make masterly use of the BBC.

Timeline

2 May: The TUC was to meet the Cabinet in a last minute bid to save the situation. Muddled communication meant that the Cabinet was kept waiting.

9pm: Meeting began. Cabinet was very irritated, so no immediate agreement. TUC negotiators went to talk with miners.
Cabinet received news of a strike at the *Daily Mail*, and assumed (wrongly) that the General Strike had begun.

Later: TUC delegates returned to find Cabinet had broken off negotiations and gone to bed.

4 May General Strike began.

A scene from the General Strike – a bus, with a police escort, leaves its depot, which is guarded by the army.

The Propaganda War

Headlines from the *Daily Herald*'s single sheet produced daily by volunteers:
'Justice for the Miners: Labour's One Aim'. 'If it be war, so be it'. 'Blame rests on the Government'. 'Beware the Wireless! the Government controls it'. 'Bishops call for Justice, Mercy and Humanity'.

Those from the *Daily Mail*, printed in Paris, were rather different. 'The Pistol at the Nation's Head'. 'Great Menace to a Free Press'. 'For King and Country'. 'No Fumbling'. 'Surrender of the Revolutionaries, A Triumph for the People'.

Source 4

At his room in the Treasury [he was then Chancellor of the Exchequer], Churchill collected material which he felt should have a place in the paper, giving prominence to those aspects of daily life where the Strike was proving least effective. He also marked as 'not recommended for publication' details of serious shortages of flour and sugar, of the overturning and stoning of trams that were still running, and of an incident of looting where the police had to use their truncheons.

Churchill at work on the British Gazette

The recently founded BBC, was in a difficult position. If it were completely impartial, the government might take it over. It therefore gave Baldwin, but not his opponents, freedom of the air. At the same time, however, it provided listeners with accurate news about the Strike, calmly reported.

In contrast, the General Council of the TUC had neither the will, nor the resources, nor the organization to make it work. It found co-ordination with the miners difficult. As Source 5 shows, the Labour Party kept its distance:

Source 5

MacDonald was in a difficult position over this episode, for public criticism of the miners and those who had embarked on the Strike would only serve to isolate the moderate Parliamentary Party further from the industrial wing…He steered clear of the Strike as best he could, for he saw it as potentially damaging to the Party's reputation…Once the dispute was over he set out his views [in the *Socialist Review*]: 'The General Strike is a weapon which cannot be wielded for industrial purposes. It is clumsy and ineffectual…I hope that the result will be a thorough reconsideration of trade union tactics.

Watts, Ramsay MacDonald, 1998

■ **Think about**

Study Source 5.

▶ Was MacDonald more in sympathy with Baldwin, or with the General Council of the TUC?

▶ Why do you think most of the Labour Party leadership stayed quiet during the Strike?

Nothing had been done to prepare public opinion. The TUC even let a sympathetic newspaper like the *Daily Herald* strike, so that it lost a useful means of explaining its position. Its special strike newspaper, the *British Worker* was no match for the *British Gazette*.

Once the TUC realized that the government would not give way, it looked for an honourable settlement of the dispute which it knew it could not win and the longer it continued the more costly a drain it would be on union funds. When Sir Herbert Samuel suggested that he would be prepared to help find a solution, it speedily started talking to him. Samuel proposed a brief renewal of the 1925 subsidy, a return to work on the old rates of pay and starting negotiations again on wage cuts and reorganization.

As they muddled into the dispute, so the General Council of the TUC leaders muddled out of it. Samuel always made it clear to them that he was talking to them unofficially and could in no way guarantee that the government would accept whatever he agreed with the TUC. However, the General Council agreed to his proposals, the Samuel Memorandum, and hoped that Samuel could persuade the government to accept it. The Council then convinced the miners' leaders that Samuel's persuasion would work and called off the strike on 12 May.

Different groups of workers went back to work at different speeds. Some were victimized by their employers. The government had won a complete victory and refused to agree to the Samuel Memorandum. The miners stayed on strike for months until, because their families were facing starvation, they returned to work on their employers' terms.

Document exercise: Revolutionary in intent?

Source A

◀ A cartoon from *The Daily Graphic*, 28 April 1926. A.J. Cook, the miners' leader is against the wall being told off by John Bull.

■ **Think about**

▶ Given that the government was so determined not to lose, what would the TUC have had to have done to make the Strike more effective?

▶ If the TUC had succeeded and the General Strike had ended with the miners victorious, what would have been the likely consequences?

■ **Think about**

▶ Where does the sympathy of *The Daily Graphic* lie?

▶ What was it, in effect, advising the miners to do?

Source B

Baldwin's view on 6 May 1926 of the challenge the Strike presented

The General Strike is a challenge to Parliament and is the road to anarchy and ruin.

Source C

The TUC General Council's claim about their aims

TUC statement 7 May 1926
The General Council does not challenge the Constitution...the sole aim of the Council is to secure for the miners a decent standard of life.

Source D

Press views – of a revolutionary movement

For King and Country
A general strike is not an industrial dispute. It is a revolutionary movement intended to inflict suffering upon the great mass of innocent people in the community and thereby to constrain the government...This being so, it cannot be tolerated by any civilized government, and must be dealt with by every resource at the disposal of the community...We do not wish to say anything hard about the miners. As to their leaders, all we need say at the moment is that some of them are (and have declared themselves) under the influence of people who mean no good to this country.

Editorial in the Daily Mail (printed in Paris) 3 May 1926

Source E

A historian's assessment of the political implications

The general strike of 1926 was certainly not a revolutionary act, neither was it a simple industrial dispute. Only if the government had intervened by additional subsidies or by coercing the coal owners could the difficulties of the coal industry have been solved in some way other than at the expense of the miners. The general strike, therefore, was a political strike and needed to be pursued as such if it was to make any progress...Yet no attempt was made either by the TUC or the Labour politicians to mobilize public opinion behind a demand that the government, having partly created the problem, must take responsibility for solving it...The difficulty was that, although MacDonald and the Labour Party had a theoretical commitment to nationalization as a solution, they thought that this was too advanced a demand in the existing political situation.

Morris, The British General Strike, 1973

Quotation

The Workers Weekly 1926

'The response of the workers was beyond all praise; the leadership was beyond contempt.'

■ Examination-style questions

1 Comprehension in context
Study Sources B and D.
Why does Baldwin see the General Strike as the road to anarchy and ruin and the *Daily Mail* describe it as a revolutionary movement?

2 Comparing the sources
How far do the authors of Sources D and E disagree in their interpretation of the nature of the strike?

3 Assessing the sources
How useful is Source A for historians of the General Strike?

4 Making judgements
Using all the sources and your own knowledge, explain to what extent you consider that the General Strike was revolutionary in its intentions.

The consequences of the General Strike

The miners lost badly. So did the coal industry. The much-needed re-organization did not take place and the industry became even less competitive internationally.

The trade union movement lost too, at least in the short and medium term. The Trades Disputes Act of 1927 made sympathetic strikes illegal and required trade union members to give their individual authorization to the political levy. The membership of trade unions dropped to below 5 million in 1927. The number of strikes also fell.

Within the TUC, there was much debate and ill-feeling about who was to blame for the failure and moderates like Ernest Bevin and Walter Citrine gained the upper hand. Bevin looked to improve things for his members through collaboration with the employers, and this approach often gained a positive response from business leaders like Sir Alfred Mond, head of ICI. Thanks to this moderate approach and the combination of reasonableness and firmness which union leaders like Bevin demonstrated, trade unions remained a powerful element in British politics and economy. As soon as Churchill became Prime Minister, he appointed Bevin Minister of Labour.

As for the political parties, Labour, perhaps surprisingly, gained rather than lost. MacDonald judged public opinion correctly when he decided that it would have disapproved of the Labour Party supporting the General Strike so Labour benefited from not getting involved. It benefited further because the public seems to have felt that the Conservatives were too harsh in the manner in which they used their victory. Not only did they pass the Trades Disputes Act but they reduced unemployment benefit and made it harder to get. It was Labour who won the 1929 election.

The 1930s

Unemployment worsens

The world economic crisis of 1929 to 1931 turned unemployment from a serious to a desperate problem. In 1928 and 1929, about 10 per cent of the workforce were unemployed; in 1931 and 1932 about 22 per cent. Though the level fell slowly through the 1930s, it was still at 13 per cent in 1938. For the old staple industrial areas like Jarrow or the mining villages of the Rhondda valley, the result was that the majority of workers were jobless with the older men having no chance of re-employment. (See Spotlight on pages 218–219).

The costs in human unhappiness were immeasurable. Instead of hope and confidence came demoralization, apathy and sometimes despair. Many observers noted the signs. With little to do and nothing to spend, people came to look shabby and ill. Men in particular slouched around on street corners.

Obviously the unemployed were among the poorest in the land. Seebohm Rowntree calculated that up to 70 per cent of the families of the unemployed were living below the poverty line. The Pilgrim Trust, which used a harsher measure still, found 30 per cent and noted that an extra child often pushed families under the line.

Source 6

A medical officer reported to the Trust 'that the principal effects of prolonged unemployment on the health of the unemployed men themselves were a subtle undermining of the constitution through lack of physical exertion...insufficiently varied diet, and worry; and the emergence of abnormal psychological conditions characterized by disabling fears and anxieties...We have a number of striking examples of local men who had been apparently normal in work, but who had 'gone to pieces' after being unemployed for several years.'

Pilgrim Trust, *Men Without Work*, 1938

■ Think about

Coping with unemployment

▶ If a Rhondda Valley miner lost his job in the 1920s, what difficulties would he have faced in finding another job? How would he have spent his time 'on the dole'?

▶ Unemployment has not disappeared. If today someone were made redundant, what difficulties would s/he face in finding another job?

▶ Is it as hard to survive unemployment today as it was in the 1920s and 1930s?

Key term

GDP or Gross Domestic Product is the annual measure of the wealth of a nation in terms of the value of the goods and services which it produces. It is used to indicate the level of a nation's economic activity.

JEAN BERTE COLOUR PROCESS

▲ 'She admires his Austin 7' is the caption of this 1931 advertisement.

Families economized on heating and food. Begging increased. Londoners were entertained by unemployed Welsh miners singing for pennies. Those who found the change the hardest were the many skilled workers, who, when in work had enjoyed decent wages.

While on many measures the overall health of the nation improved during the thirties, the health of many families in the unemployed areas deteriorated. In 1932, the average rate for infant mortality was 65 per 1000, in the cotton town of Oldham it was more than 100, in an estate in the north-east it was 134.

A similar difference emerged for women dying in childbirth. The chances of dying in childbirth for pregnant women in the south-east of England were half those of women in south Wales.

But not for everyone – the affluent 1930s

However Britain and the majority of the British people were becoming better off. Between 1922 and 1938, Britain's Gross Domestic Product (GDP) grew at an average of 2.1 per cent per annum. This was very similar to the growth rates of the second half of the nineteenth century (2 per cent in 1856–1899) and better than the years before the war (1.1 per cent in 1900–1913). The rate of growth was faster in the 1930s than in the 1920s, reaching nearly 4 per cent per annum between 1932 and 1937. In comparison with Europe, while Britain lost ground in the twenties, she held her own in the thirties.

A range of new industries played an important part in this growth. Motor vehicles led the way. In 1924, the USA was the world's main manufacturer by a wide margin. France was Europe's largest producer with 145,000 vehicles, followed by Britain with 116,000 vehicles. By 1937, British production had tripled to 379,000 and Britain had taken the lead in Europe, followed by Germany with 277,000. The main manufacturing centres were Birmingham (Austin) and Oxford (Morris).

Electrical engineering was another successful new industry. It grew at between 4 per cent and 5 per cent per annum throughout the inter-war period. The creation of the Central Electricity Board in 1926 and of the national grid gave a considerable boost to the industry. In the 1930s electricity consumption per head of population increased by 70 per cent. Here Britain and France led Europe and were not far behind the USA. Where there were 730,000 consumers in 1919, there were nearly 9 million in 1938.

The wireless industry flourished. The wireless manufacturers created the British Broadcasting Company in 1922 to provide programmes that would encourage people to buy their product. This became the British Broadcasting Corporation (BBC) with a government charter and financed by a licence fee in 1927. The erection of a powerful transmitting station at Daventry in 1925 gave reasonable reception to most parts of the country. By 1938, about 2 million radios (as wirelesses had become known) were sold each year and their price had fallen from £30 in 1920 to about £7. Other electrical goods which found a mass market were vacuum cleaners and electric irons.

New industries such as these had accounted for 14 per cent of British industrial production in 1924. By 1935 this proportion had increased to 20 per cent. Over the same period, the proportion of the staple industries had fallen from 37 per cent to 28 per cent.

Spotlight

Red Ellen and Jarrow 'the town that was murdered'

About Jarrow

Jarrow is now part of the Tyneside conurbation, lying on the River Tyne between Newcastle and the sea. In the nineteenth century it was a prosperous industrial town, thanks largely to Sir Charles Palmer who had built shipyards and steel works which, up to 1920, provided work for most of the men in the town. In 1934, when Palmer's yard was sold off and closed down, 8000 people, many of them skilled workers, lost their jobs. Unemployment in the mid-1930s was running at 68 per cent. Encouraged by their Labour MP, Ellen Wilkinson, the townspeople decided to march the 500km to London to ask the government for help. A group of 200 men was chosen to set off on the Jarrow Crusade.

Source 7

On 28 Feb, 1930, the first public statement was made regarding National Shipbuilders Security Ltd. Its purpose was defined as being to assist the shipbuilding industry by purchase of redundant and obsolete yards....

In the early summer of 1934 it was announced that Palmer's had been sold to NSS. The death warrant of Palmer's was signed. The reason for Jarrow's existence had disappeared overnight.

Why was Palmer's Yard sold? It certainly was not an obsolete yard. One of the biggest firms in the industry and one which had invariably secured a fair share on competitive tenders cannot be classified as obsolete. It had one of the finest sites in the country...Financial weakness, not technical inefficiency, decided the fate of the company...Sold by NSS to a demolition firm, work was commenced to clear the site. Oxy-acetylene burners made short work of the steel girders. Cranes crashed to the ground, the machine shops emptied and their numerous chimneys vanished... Shipbuilding is exiled from Jarrow.

Wilkinson, *The Town that was Murdered*, 1939

Victor Gollancz and the Left Book Club

The publisher Gollancz founded this 'club' in 1936 when he was communist. He wished to strengthen the Left nationally and internationally against the threat of fascism. It produced two books a month for its members. Their authors wrote about topics of the time from a strong left-wing slant. John Strachey and Harold Laski, who were both at the time communist sympathizers, helped Gollancz choose the books.

The Left Book Club was a great success. Before long it had 60,000 members, ten times as many as the British Communist Party, from which Gollancz was soon to part company. It provided inspiration to the rising generation of Labour leaders.

Source 8

◀ Ellen Wilkinson in 1944.

■ Questions

What problems did Jarrow face in the 1930s?

Study Sources 7 and 10.

1 What was Ellen Wilkinson's connection to Jarrow?

2 What does Morgan mean when he describes her as 'uniquely identified with the passions of the thirties'?

3 Why does Wilkinson believe that Palmer's shipyard should not have been closed?

4 In her opinion, what was its chief weakness? How might that, in her opinion have been put right?

5 What would you expect to be the strengths and weaknesses of *The Town that was Murdered* as evidence of the problems of Jarrow in the 1930s?

Source 9

▲ Ellen Wilkinson with the Jarrow marchers in 1936 on the last leg of the march from Luton to London

Source 10

Ellen Wilkinson made the role of women in high politics credible and effective as no one had done before. As a trade union organizer, as a journalist and international propagandist, above all as an inspirational orator…she placed an unforgettable imprint on the mind of the British Left.

She was uniquely identified with the passions of the thirties…above all with the moral outcry against mass unemployment and poverty. Her leadership of the march from Jarrow, the town she represented in Parliament, and her remarkable Left Book Club volume, *The Town that was Murdered*, had a dramatic, perhaps decisive impact on the public conscience, long before the new egalitarian passions of the Second World War.

The Historian Kenneth Morgan's assessment of 'Red Ellen'.
Morgan, *Labour People*, 1987

Source 12

The great demonstrations in which unemployed workers marched to London to try to convince Parliament of the sufferings of south Wales and Jarrow had relatively little effect. The government appeared resigned to high unemployment and the decline of the traditional industries…Coal-mining and shipbuilding constituencies were likely to vote Labour in any case.

An alternative view
of the impact of the march.
Lloyd, *Empire to Welfare State.*
English History 1906–1967, 1970

Source 11

…the Jarrow crusade definitely brought a new consciousness of the plight of industrial Britain to the prosperous south.

A historian's assessment of the significance of the march.
Marwick, *Britain in Our Century*, 1984

■ Think about

▶ Why does Morgan (Source 10) consider Ellen Wilkinson such an important woman politician?

■ Questions

Study Sources 9, 11, and 12.

1 What impression do you think the marchers in Source 9 were aiming to give?

2 To what extent to Sources 11 and 12 contradict each other?

3 Is the interpretation of Source 10 about the significance of the Jarrow march closer to that of Source 11 or Source 12?

Signs of affluence

Britons in work in the 1930s found that their standard of living went up by about 15 per cent. This was not because wages rose but because the cost of living fell.

Vivid evidence of increasing affluence for most, though not all, was the housing boom. Between the wars, 4 million houses were built. In 1939, one in three families lived in houses built since 1918. About half were private developments, especially in the south east (see p. 208), the rest were council houses for rent. Both kinds were built to new standards – baths, hot water, and proper kitchens. In the mainly private sector estates in the suburbs, each home would also have a decent garden.

Other developments reflected the fact that more people had more spending money. Most towns would have their Woolworths and their Marks and Spencer. New magazines, like *Woman's Own* in 1932, appeared which included features on clothes and consumer durables.

Entertainment was revolutionized by the cinema. In 1934, there were 4300 cinemas in Britain with attendance running at 20 million per week. Many were large, being able to seat an audience of 1000, some were huge like the 4000 seaters in Glasgow and Croydon. Four big companies – Gaumont-British, the Associated British Picture Corporation, Odeon and Granada – had gained control of the market by the 1930s. Though there was a British film industry, Hollywood already dominated and audience surveys usually showed that American films were preferred. Cinema tickets were so cheap that even the unemployed could afford them. Of the unemployed youth of Liverpool and Glasgow, 80 per cent went to the cinema at least once a week. 'The pictures (cinema) is my first choice,' an unemployed Londoner told a researcher in 1932, 'because they make you think for a little while that life is alright.'

▲ Frocks and fiction – *Women's Own* in 1937.

◀ A barmaid on her day off in 1939 checks what's on at the cinema

Government economic and social policies

Governments of the inter-war years still believed, as had their nineteenth-century predecessors, that more harm than good would come from a government interfering in the economy to try to reduce unemployment. They were the last British governments to take this view.

The economic policies the inter-war governments were decided mainly by the Chancellor of the Exchequer of the time, advised by officials of the Treasury. The advice to governments from the Treasury were based on four main principles:

● Governments should balance their budgets. They should not spend more than they raised through taxation. If governments overspent and had to borrow to finance that extra expenditure, damage would be done to the economy as a whole.
● Governments should aim to spend as little as possible and to keep taxes as low as possible. The more people were taxed, the less they would have to spend and the less they had to spend, the less the economy as a whole would grow.
● Free trade benefited Britain and, indeed, the world. The less governments interfered in the flow of trade between nations, the more trade would expand and the more prosperous the world would become. Free trade encouraged competition and competition made businesses more efficient. Britain had a particular interest in encouraging free trade as she was still one of the world's leading trading nations.
● Since the British currency, sterling, was so important to international trade and since fixed exchange rates benefited international trade, the value of the pound sterling should be fixed and devaluation avoided.

Austen Chamberlain, who was Chancellor of the Exchequer in Lloyd George's Coalition government from 1918 to 1922, accepted these principles. The 'Geddes Axe' of 1921 made cuts in government expenditure to balance the budget, as boom turned to slump.

Philip Snowden, Labour Chancellor in 1924 and again from 1929 to 1931, was entirely persuaded of the correctness of the Treasury view. He was most insistent that his budgets balanced even in the 1931 crisis.

Churchill, Chancellor in Baldwin's government from 1924 to 1929, was honest about his ignorance of economics. He confessed that when his Treasury advisers were advising him about financial technicalities, he often felt that they might as well have been talking in Persian. However, since he had no doubt that they were at least as expert as anyone else in the world, he had no anxieties about acting on their advice.

The return to the gold standard in 1925

Churchill's most important decision was made in 1925. He put the pound sterling back on 'the gold standard' at the 1914 exchange rate of £1:$4.86. The thinking of the Treasury and of Montagu Norman, Governor of the Bank of England, went like this. Before 1914, London had been the hub of the financial markets of the world. The gold standard and the fixed exchange rate had given stability to world trade and strengthened London's position. Britain had gone 'off gold' in 1919 because of the exceptional conditions created by the war. Since then the British economy had been in difficulties. Once Britain went back onto gold, the Treasury believed, improvements would follow. Other nations

Note

Montagu Norman

Norman, the son of a merchant banker, was Governor of the Bank of England from 1920 to 1944. He was highly orthodox. He believed that the nation's finances were best left to experts such as himself. He came up against Keynes and Bevin during the Macmillan inquiry of 1929 to 1931 and made it crystal clear that, in his opinion, there was absolutely nothing that could be done to solve the unemployment problem and that he was not prepared to give any alternative serious consideration.

would follow Britain's example and fix their own currencies at a sensible level in relation to the pound. The stability of a fixed exchange rate would make life easier for businessmen. If it meant that British industry had to face tougher competition, there was no harm in that. Perhaps British industry needed to modernize and perhaps British wage rates were too high.

The return to the gold standard did not have the effects which Churchill and the Treasury hoped. It may have helped London as an international financial centre but the £1:$4.86 exchange rate over-valued the pound and made exporting more difficult. Unemployment did not lessen; on the contrary, it increased.

We have seen how the economic crisis of 1931 forced Snowden to take Britain off the gold standard. The value of the pound fell to $3.40, a devaluation of 30 per cent. Perhaps unsurprisingly, the Treasury became more flexible in its advice. Neville Chamberlain, Chancellor from 1931 to 1937, made greater use of tariffs and flexible interest rates, though the extent to which they helped the economic recovery remains unclear.

However, as far as taking measures to help unemployment, government and Treasury thinking hardly changed. In their view, workers were made redundant because their company was failing and could not produce what the market required, either because the goods were no longer needed or because they were too expensive. If the company could adapt and produce goods the market required then it would succeed and re-employ its workforce. If however it closed, then the workers would need to find work in a company that was competitive. In stable free trade conditions, which allowed companies to compete fairly, failing companies would be balanced by successful ones and unemployment should not last long.

Consequently, there was nothing that governments could do directly to reduce unemployment. Their responsibility was to create the best conditions for market forces to work with the greatest efficiency; then businesses would expand and be able to take on more workers. As Chamberlain put it: 'the quickest and most effective contribution which any government can make towards an increase in employment is to create conditions which will encourage and facilitate improvement in ordinary trade.'

However, rising concern in the 1930s about continuing large-scale unemployment persuaded Chamberlain, through the Special Areas Act of 1934, to make available £2 million for special projects in the most depressed areas to create employment. Some workers were helped to move to other towns where there was work; others were retrained. Some parks were tidied up, some swimming pools built. If it was a move in the right direction, it was far too timid. It achieved little and its frustrated commissioners resigned in 1936.

Social policies

As for social policy, as we have seen in Chapter 11, governments accepted that they had an active role to play as long as costs were kept low. They made sure that through unemployment benefits, those out of work and their families did not actually starve. Pensions were increased. Subsidies helped the housing boom. Some local authorities made limited improvements to their health and education services.

■ Think about

Communities heavily dependent on a single employer

Some towns are heavily dependent on a single large company for employment. Related businesses develop to serve those employees. If such a company goes bankrupt because of reduced demand for the goods it produces, the whole community tends to be affected.

▶ In such circumstances, is there anything that a government should do?

▶ Or should such a town 'seek its own salvation'?

Were there feasible alternative policies?

Most politicians and their financial advisers, not just in Britain but throughout the industrial world, did not believe that any satisfactory alternative policy existed. In Britain, however, Maynard Keynes was developing an alternative and British governments knew that he was. From 1919, Keynes was in the centre of affairs and impossible to ignore. His *Economics of the Peace* damning the Versailles Settlement of 1919 was followed in 1925 by *The Economic Consequences of Mr Churchill* damning the return to the gold standard. He played an important part in drafting the Liberal election manifesto of 1929 which recommended an ambitious programme of public works, and was a member of the Macmillan Committee from 1929 to 1931 (see pp. 200–201).

Keynes argued that the traditional Treasury principles did not work any more. The problems which were creating the high levels of unemployment were too great for a free market to solve. The government, therefore, had to try new policies. Among the various ones Keynes proposed were large-scale public works, lower interest rates, tariffs (temporary) and in August 1931 devaluing the pound. Keynes' most important point was that governments should not make cuts when the economic situation deteriorated, rather they should spend themselves and encourage the public to spend by lower interest rates. This could well mean greater government borrowing in the short-term but it would lead to continuing economic growth and low unemployment.

In 1930, while he was still a member of the Labour Party, Mosley tried to convert the Party to a programme of public works, greater direction of industry and higher pensions to encourage public spending. Snowden and MacDonald remained unconvinced. The TUC also believed that new approaches must be tried. Like Keynes, Ernest Bevin had been a member of the Macmillan Committee. Through its General Council it argued fiercely against Snowden/MacDonald proposals for cuts in August 1931. Its alternative package devised by Bevin was influenced by Keynes and included devaluation, temporary protection and higher taxation on the rich. This, too, Snowden and MacDonald ignored.

Keynes focused his thoughts into his hugely influential book, *General Theory of Employment, Interest and Money* which was published in 1936. For 30 years after the Second World War most governments of the Western world went Keynesian. They became much more active in managing the economy and did not hesitate to use government spending powers to head off depressions.

The inter-war years were years of unparalleled depression so historians of the inter-war years blamed the British governments of the 1920s and 1930s for not heeding Keynes' advice. However, in the last quarter of the twentieth century, the Keynesian approach worked less well. Inflation became a serious problem and unemployment returned to the levels of the twenties.

More recent historians argue that the Treasury officials may not have been so wrong after all. Furthermore, they argue, in 1931 Keynes' ideas were not fully developed and they were so different that they would have been exceptionally difficult to put into practice.

■ **Think about**

Economic trends and unemployment

Keynesian policies seemed to have ended the problem of large-scale unemployment between 1945 and the 1970s. However between 1979 and 1982, Britain suffered a severe slump which to the number of unemployed to over 3 million.

An even sharper slump in 1990–1 again took unemployment figures back to 10 per cent, reminiscent of the interwar years.

The eighties and nineties were similar to the thirties in other ways. The north suffered more than the south and the slumps were followed by vigorous recoveries, which again were more vigorous in the south than in the north.

▶ What are present levels of unemployment in Britain?

▶ How Keynesian is the present government in its approach to managing the economy?

■ **Activity**   **KEY SKILLS**

On 31 May 1931, the May Committee (see pages 199–200) reported to the government. It recommended a range of cuts in government spending. Write two different comments on the May Committee's recommendations, in the form of:
1 a confidential letter from J.M. Keynes to an economist friend
2 a leader in the *Daily Mail* (a Conservative newspaper)
Use pages 189, 199–205 and 209–223 to help you.

Historical debate: the hungry thirties

Among the most powerful images of the inter-war years are the hunger marches and the derelict shipyards (see pp. 219 and 204). For the Labour Party, which came to power in 1945, unemployment was a great evil that should never be allowed to recur. It was the memories of the sufferings which high unemployment had caused that provided an important motive for the creation of the Welfare State (see pp. 260–262). So, it was the prevailing opinion of the immediate post-war years that the 'guilty men' who had appeased Hitler, the pygmy rulers who had let the nation drift without guts or vision, had allowed unemployment to make the thirties 'hungry'. Is this image historically valid?

Document exercise: The hungry thirties

Source A

Inspections by the Ministry of Health, south Wales 1929

The primary object of our visit...was to ascertain whether as a result of unemployment in the coalfield the physical condition of the population was such as to call for special action...The first question to which it was obvious that we ought to direct our attention was that of any variation to be observed in the rates of mortality in south Wales...indicating new conditions exceptionally injurious to health. No such indications are forthcoming from the general death rates...there has been no unusual mortality from epidemic diseases...On the criterion of infant mortality...there are no figures which...give rise to anxiety...As regards what are termed 'deficiency diseases', there is no evidence of the existence of scurvy, and the only form belonging to this category which appeared to have shown signs of increase was rickets...in some areas, mothers, especially young mothers, suffer to an unusual extent from languor (tiredness) and anaemia.

Ministry of Health, *Investigation in the coalfields of south Wales*, 1929

Source B

'Work at last'

Source C

Observations from a journey through England

The traditional historic England; the industrial England of the nineteenth century; and 'the new post-war England, belonging far more to the age itself than to this particular island. America, I suppose, was its real birthplace. This is the England of arterial and by-pass roads, of filling stations and factories that look like exhibition buildings, of giant cinemas and dance halls and cafes, bungalows with tiny garages, cocktail bars, Woolworths, motor-coaches, typing, factory girls looking like actresses, greyhound racing and dirt tracks, swimming pools and everything given away for cigarette coupons.

On his journey, the author J.B Priestly became aware of three different 'Englands'. Priestly, *English Journey*, 1933

◀ A Strube cartoon from the *Daily Express*, 1936.

Source D

Wal Hannington of the NUWM – observations of poverty

Take a look at a funeral procession in South Wales these days...the miners, who in times of good trade always had a preference for smart serge suits, would turn out in their best apparel and bowler hats and present an extremely respectable appearance. But not so today. A funeral procession in the Rhondda Valley bears the mark of extreme poverty. The few serge suits which can be seen can be marked out by their cut as pre-war or immediate post-war, because for years no new clothes have been bought.

Hannington, *The Problem of the Distressed Areas*, 1937

Source E

The assessment of an economic historian

Not only was there a significant increase in real incomes and real wages but, partly as a result of this improvement and together with the extension of community services, the nation generally was better fed and clothed, and was housed in better conditions than those prevailing before the war. The statistics again point to an improvement in the national health and physical well-being of the population.

Aldcroft, *The Interwar Economy: Britain 1919–1939*, 1970

■ Examination-style questions

1 Comprehension in context
Study Source B. What is the message of the Strube cartoon? In what ways is it a Keynesian message?

2 Comparing sources
How far does Source C support the conclusions reached by Aldcroft in Source E?

3 Assessing the sources
How useful are Sources A and D to historians studying economic and social conditions in Britain in the 1930s?

4 Making judgements
Using these sources and your own knowledge, comment on the view that, 'the hungry thirties is a wholly misleading description of the 1930s'.

Summary

- The main economic and social problems were in the areas of traditional staple industries which for many reasons became less competitive. In the 1920s many companies failed and unemployment levels rose quickly. The world depression made these problems worse in the 1930s. The social consequences of unemployment, like poverty and ill-health, were acute.

- The worst industrial conflicts were in the 1920s. At the heart of them were the miners who wished for better pay and conditions and for the mines to be nationalized. This conflict came to a head in 1926 with the General Strike, which ended with a determined government prevailing over an uncertain and poorly prepared TUC. This defeat and high unemployment made unions ready to compromise. There were fewer industrial conflicts in the thirties.

- All governments, including the Labour ones, believed that governments could do little to reduce unemployment. They reorganized the methods of paying unemployment benefit so it was more uniform across the country. However, they only kept it at a level just high enough to prevent people from actually starving. They were prepared to humiliate the unemployed, through the means test, in order to keep costs as low as possible.

- Most of Britain, however, was growing richer and this affluence brought more and better homes and home conveniences, the greater application of electricity, motor vehicles, more shops and greater choice within them. Cinema and the radio changed the way people relaxed.

- For millions in the depressed areas, the thirties were hungry and hopeless. For the rest of the country where the majority of Britons lived, it was an increasingly comfortable decade.

■ Further reading

*Rex Pope, *The British Economy since 1914*, 1998

*Robert Pearce, *British Industrial Relations and the Economy 1900–39*, 1993

D.H. Aldcroft, *The Interwar Economy, Britain 1919–39*, 1970

John Stevenson and Chris Cook, *The Slump*, 1977

Chapter 14

British foreign policy 1919–1939 The failure of collective security and appeasement

Source 1

▲ Appeasement at its height, the Munich Conference in September 1938. Chamberlain, with Mussolini the Italian dictator to his left stands opposite Hitler (with the swastika armband).

Source 2

No conqueror has returned from a victory on the battlefield adorned with nobler laurels than Mr Chamberlain from Munich yesterday…he has not only relegated an agonizing episode to the past; he has found for nations a new hope for the future.

The Times 1 October 1938

Source 3

We shall today level no reproaches at those who have forsaken us in our hour of direst need. History will pass judgement on the events of these days.

The Czech government, 21 September, on learning that Britain and France would not support its resistance to Hitler's demands for the Sudetenland

Introduction

Of all the tragedies of human history, none have surpassed the Second World War and the Nazi atrocities associated with it. Subsequent generations have had and will continue to have the greatest difficulty in understanding how they could have happened, particularly so soon after Europe had experienced the horrors of the First World War. What were the political leaders of Europe doing? Why could they not find the means of resolving their differences peacefully? If Hitler was bent on war, why could not the other major European powers unite to stop him before it was too late? Since Britain, apart from Germany, was much the strongest of the nations of Western Europe, and was the country to whom the rest of the continent looked for a lead, then it could be said that she played a central role in this failure. Not surprisingly, historians argue vigorously about the nature of and justification for the foreign policies which Britain pursued in the inter-war years.

Key questions

- From the British point of view, how satisfactory a peace settlement was the Versailles Treaty of 1919?
- To what extent did British governments pursue foreign policies of 'collective security' and 'appeasement' between 1919 and 1939?
- How and why did international conditions in the 1930s differ from those of the 1920s?
- How much was 'appeasement' essentially the policy of Neville Chamberlain and to what extent was he responsible for its failure?
- How have historians differed in their interpretations of British foreign policy between 1933 and 1939?

The Versailles settlement

Bringing peace to Europe in 1919 was an enormous undertaking. Four years of war had caused not only millions of deaths and great damage, but it made the victors and well as the vanquished bitter and vengeful. The Austrian and Turkish Empires had collapsed. Russia was engulfed in civil war. Revolutions stalked Central and Eastern Europe. To this chaos, the Versailles peacemakers tried to bring some order.

The judgement of many contemporaries, and of historians, is that even allowing for the immensity of their task, they did not do well and that failure sowed the seeds of the next war.

The main reason for their failure was that the three Great Powers that mattered, the USA, France and Britain, came to Versailles with different priorities. These differences were not resolved in the terms of the settlement, nor, more seriously, in the decisions taken about how to maintain the settlement and secure international peace in the future.

The different priorities operated even before the war ended. The German government had approached President Wilson of the USA for an armistice based on his Fourteen Points, which the Germans judged correctly, would give the best chance of a lenient peace. However, in the feverish days of November, disorder spread through the German cities and the will of the German armed forces to continue fighting dissolved. Haig and Foch were able to include in the Armistice terms that the German navy should be handed over to Britain and that French troops should occupy the Rhineland. Worthy as the Fourteen Points might be, Britain and France, having slogged their way to a hard-fought, bloody and draining victory, clearly had their own particular goals in mind.

Note

The Versailles settlement consisted of 5 separate treaties.
1 Treaty of Versailles with Germany.
2 Treaty of St Germain with Austria.
3 Treaty of Trianon with Hungary.
4 Treaty of Neuilly with Bulgaria.
5 Treaty of Sèvres with Turkey. War between Greece and Turkey quickly made the Treaty of Sèvres redundant. The Treaty of Lausanne (1923) settled that war.

The details of the reparations payments were not fixed until 1921 at £6,600 million (see p. 228).

President Wilson of the USA was committed to a just peace based on his Fourteen Points. Central to his hopes that this should prove to have been a war to end all wars, was a new institution, the League of Nations, which would provide the place for the discussion and resolution of international problems. Clemenceau, the French President, represented the French at Versailles. Germany had attacked his country without provocation. Part of northern France had been occupied and fought over for four years. Of the victorious Allies, it was the French who had suffered proportionately the greatest loss of men and severest damage to property. Clemenceau, therefore, expected full compensation for the damage done and permanent security against another attack by Germany.

Lloyd George for Britain was pulled in two directions. He realized that much of what Wilson said made sense. There could never be a secure peace in Europe unless the Versailles settlement was clearly founded on fair and just principles that the defeated as well as the victors recognized as fair and just. At the same time, he came to Versailles having recently won an election. The catch-phrases of the election campaign had been 'Hang the Kaiser' and 'Make Germany Pay'. The electorate expected the Germans to be dealt with harshly.

Consequently, during the negotiations, Lloyd George was sometimes on the side of moderation towards Germany, sometimes on the side of toughness. For example, on the one hand, he threw his weight successfully against the French proposal that the Rhineland should be separated from Germany and that the Saar should become French; on the other, he took a tough position on reparations, insisting that war pensions as well as actual physical damage should be included. This insistence probably tripled the sum demanded, which was eventually fixed at £6,600 million.

◁ Europe according to the peace treaties, 1919–20.

The main weaknesses of the Versailles settlement

Because of the different priorities of the main negotiators and the sheer range of problems to be solved, the settlement included compromises which soon proved unworkable.

Its five most serious weaknesses were these:

1 It united Germany against it bitterly and permanently. The new German government only signed the Treaty because it had no choice. It regarded it as outrageously harsh in comparison with the Fourteen Points, on the basis of which it had agreed to the Armistice. It found particularly unacceptable the losses of its eastern territories to Poland, being held guilty of causing the war and the huge sum of reparations which it considered unpayable. German bitterness was increased by the readiness of the Versailles peacemakers to allow self-determination to all the peoples of Central and Eastern Europe except the Germans, and the lack of any substantial moves towards disarmament by the victors, although Germany was now defenceless.

2 At the same time, the settlement failed to give France, or indeed other nations, security against the time when a revived Germany would be seeking to revise the Treaty. Wilson and Lloyd George persuaded France not to require harsher measures against Germany by promising to guarantee the frontiers of France in the future. However, they broke that promise. Congress refused to ratify the Treaty so destroying Wilson's promise. Then Britain, who had made her guarantee conditional on having American agreement, withdrew her guarantee as well.

3 The settlement of Eastern Europe, as you can see from the map opposite, created a number of small nations between Germany and Russia. Before long, those two Great Powers would regain their strength and Germany at least would be looking to recover the territories she had lost. The weakness of these new nations was increased by the existence within them of discontented minorities, notably Germans in Czechoslovakia and Poland.

4 Reparations might have been payable if they had been fixed at a lower figure. Keynes suggested a figure of £2,000 million. German resistance to paying the £6,600 million slowed the economic recovery of Europe and maintained tension in Europe until 1929 when the Young Plan did reduce them to about a third of the original level (close to Keynes' proposal of 1919).

5 The US Congress failed to ratify the Treaty and also refused to join the League of Nations. This meant that the world's most powerful nation with economic interests throughout the world was isolating herself from the organization that her President had spent so much effort in creating. Also missing from the League were Germany and the Soviet Union. These absentees obviously weakened the League's authority.

British attitudes to the Versailles settlement

While the negotiations were still continuing in France, criticisms of the Treaty began to be made. Keynes resigned over the reparations issue. 'The negotiations', he said, 'were a tragic farce' and 'the Prime Minister is leading us all into a morass of destruction.' Keynes was not alone. When the Treaty was finally signed and sealed, one of the senior advisers of the British delegation, Sir James Headlam-Morley, admitted that, 'taken as a whole the terms of the Treaty were unworkable'.

Source 4

PEACE AND FUTURE CANNON FODDER

THE TIGER. "Curious! I seem to hear a child weeping!"

▲ This brilliantly prophetic cartoon by Dyson appeared in the *Daily Herald* in May 1919.

■ Think about

Look at Source 4 about the Versailles peace negotiations.
▶ Who are the men and why is the child weeping?

Keynes' *Economic Consequences of the Peace* was published in December 1919 and attracted much attention in Britain and the USA. Other experts had their say too. Before long the prevailing view in Britain was that the Treaty was dangerously flawed. Its main weakness was that it was too harsh on Germany, not just in the matter of reparations but also with regard to her boundaries. This view was shared by both Conservative and Labour politicians who tended, therefore, to enter into negotiations with Germany in the 1930s with a guilty conscience. As a result, they underestimated German aggression and were unsympathetic to well-founded French anxieties.

British attitudes to France

Only a minority in Britain held to the view, which remained the French one, that because Germany had both caused the war and lost it, she deserved everything which the Allies imposed on her by the terms of the Versailles Treaty. Moreover, if the Germans attempted to ignore the Treaty, then they should be made to obey it by force. British politicians and public opinion became increasingly irritated by France's continuing hostility to Germany. They regretted the French occupation of the Ruhr in 1923 when Germany fell behind on the reparation payments. Nor did they support her attempts to create an anti-German defensive alliance with the new nations of Europe (Czechoslovakia and Poland in 1925, Yugoslavia in 1927). In fact in the 1920s, Britain's service chiefs regarded France with her large airforce as a greater threat than Germany.

Britain's attitude to Russia

Up to 1914, Russia had been a crucial element in Great Power alliances to prevent a single power from dominating Europe. After 1918, however, the Soviet Union was isolated, a mysterious and probably dangerous force working out the consequences of its extraordinary revolution of 1917. In the 1920s Britain was hostile to the Soviet Union. In 1919 the coalition government sent military aid to the anti-Communist White forces during the Russian Civil War – something which the successful Communists never forgot. Lenin, their leader, declared that his government would accept no liability for the millions of pounds which the Tsar's government had borrowed from Britain to pay for the war against Germany. The Conservatives feared the spread of communist revolution across Europe and, for most of the period, regarded the Soviet Union as more dangerous than Germany. Labour were marginally more friendly. MacDonald set up diplomatic links in 1924, which the Conservatives broke off in 1927 and re-established them in 1929. This failure to establish an anti-Nazi alliance with the Soviet Union played into Hitler's hands in 1938–1939.

Britain's gains

However flawed the Versailles settlement might be, Britain did well out of it. She had, beneath the waves of Scapa Flow the German navy scuttled by its own sailors. She gained most of the German colonies – German East Africa, South-West Africa and New Guinea. She also gained Palestine, Transjordan, and Iraq from the break-up of the Turkish Empire. Since Persia was already to a large extent British, most of the Middle East oilfields were now at Britain's disposal, just as the world was moving from steam to oil power.

As a world power, Britain was now substantially stronger than in 1914. Germany was crushed. Russia, formerly her greatest imperial rival, was convulsed by an internal struggle which was to place her on the defensive for the next 20 years. While the USA was indisputably the world's richest and most

> **Key term**
>
> **Mandates**
> The theory of 'mandates' was that the former German and Turkish colonies were mandated by the League of Nations to the care of Allied governments. They were responsible for the care of the native populations and should prepare them for eventual independence.

▲ The division of the Middle East after the First World War.

■ **Think about**

After the Second World War America played a major part politically in the reorganization of Europe and in the United Nations. She also invested millions of dollars through the Marshall Plan to help the economic recovery of Europe.

▶ How might the history of Europe and the world have been different if Congress had ratified the Versailles Treaty and allowed America to play a leading part in the League of Nations?

powerful nation, she had decided to keep clear of international commitments for the next 20 years unless they affected her immediate interests.

The other nation to do well out of the war was Japan who entered it as Britain's ally and used it to gain a firmer foothold in Manchuria and more commercial privileges on the Chinese mainland. However, though Japan was clearly an expanding power in Asia, Britain in the 1920s was the nation with by far the greatest international influence. She was therefore in a stronger position than any other nation to change the situation in Europe for the better.

British caution

However, for a number of reasons, Britain was unready to take a lead. Her politicians, diplomats and military advisers were unsure how strong Britain really was. As a Foreign Office memorandum put it in 1926, 'we have got what we want – perhaps more…[but] the fact is that war and rumours of war, quarrels and friction, in any corner of the world spell loss and harm to British commercial and financial interests.'

The Empire may have grown larger, but that made it harder to defend. India was restless with the charismatic Gandhi leading demands for greater self-government. The Foreign Office feared that the Russian Communists would stir up revolution in India and send revolutionary commandos through Afghanistan in support. In the Far East, the modern Japanese fleet posed a greater challenge than had the Russians before 1914. Though an Anglo-American-Japanese Naval Treaty had agreed a ratio of Britain and the USA 525,000 tons each to Japan's 315,000, the Admiralty did not think that it could simultaneously defend Far Eastern and home waters.

Another worry was the weakness of the British economy. The 1920–1921 slump was worse in Britain than anywhere else in Europe and recovery was comparatively slow. An active foreign policy implied extra spending when balanced budgets were the order of the day.

Perhaps the main reason, though, for inaction was that few politicians felt the urge to take a lead, particularly when public opinion seemed to favour peace and quiet. The nation was secure for the time being. Lloyd George had told his service chiefs in 1919 that they need not worry about a war for the next ten years. Bonar Law's insistence that 'we cannot alone act as the policeman of the world' summed up the prevailing mood in 1922.

Collective security to 1932

During the 1920s, Britain's foreign policy can best be described as one that favoured 'collective security'. When this failed in the 1930s, the National government of Baldwin and Chamberlain turned to 'appeasement'.

'Collective security' was the idea that peace would be maintained by the nations of the world, especially of Europe, working together 'collectively', frequently through the League of Nations. Solutions would be found through discussion and compromise. In theory, if agreement could not be reached by the nations in dispute, then they should be ready to accept the final judgement of the League.

If parts of the Versailles settlement did not work, 'collective security' should allow them to be revised peacefully. As Lloyd George put it to the House of Commons in 1919, 'if the Treaty is not perfect, I look to the League of Nations to remedy, repair and redress it.'

Collective security in action 1924–1933

Up to 1929 British governments had some real achievements.

- In 1924 at the London Conference, which was chaired by Ramsay MacDonald, France and Germany agreed to the Dawes Plan for the management of the repayment of reparations, and to the French evacuation of the Ruhr industrial area.
- In 1925, Austen Chamberlain, Foreign Secretary of Baldwin's Conservative government, played a leading part in the conference that ended with the Locarno Treaty. This treaty seemed very encouraging for the nations of Western Europe. France and Germany, represented by its new Chancellor Stresemann, agreed to respect each other's frontiers as laid down in the Versailles Treaty. Britain and Italy agreed to guarantee that this agreement was kept. Encouraging as the agreement was, even more encouraging was the mood of reconciliation. The obvious weakness of the Locarno Treaty, however, was its silence on Germany's eastern frontiers. All that Stresemann would agree to was to seek to change them peacefully. Germany would not accept them as permanent.
- In 1926, Germany joined the League of Nations.
- In 1927 Britain and France withdrew the Inter-Allied Military Control from Germany. At the time, this seemed an appropriate goodwill move but it meant that Britain and France no longer had the means to judge the level of German armaments.
- In 1928 Kellogg, the American Secretary of State, and Briand, the French Foreign Secretary, persuaded representatives of 65 nations to sign the Pact of Paris or the Kellogg Pact by which they promised never again to use war 'as an instrument of policy'. (Britain and France, however, retained the right to use military force within their Empires!)
- In 1929, at the Hague Conference, reparations were further reduced by the Young Plan. Britain and France also agreed to withdraw all troops from Germany by June 1930.

The successes of 'collective security' were possible because the comparative political stability of the late twenties and economic prosperity created an international climate of greater confidence and trust. That positive international climate was destroyed by the Wall Street Crash (see p. 199). Nonetheless the many statesmen committed to collective security persevered, though they had less and less success.

Source 5

THE GOOSE-STEP.
"GOOSEY GOOSEY GANDER,
WHITHER DOST THOU WANDER?"
"ONLY THROUGH THE RHINELAND—
PRAY EXCUSE MY BLUNDER!"

◀ The end of collective security. A *Punch* cartoon from 1936.

The World Disarmament Conference, held in Geneva in 1932–1933 proved a great disappointment. It failed to achieve anything very much. The reasons for its failure were indicative of the growing lack of trust. The Germans proposed that they should be able to rearm to the same level as France. The French refused, since they believed that once the Germans had equality of arms, another war was much more likely. The French then made a counter-proposal that they would agree to equality of armaments with Germany if Britain would guarantee French security against German aggression. Britain would not make this commitment.

By 1933, Hitler had become Chancellor of Germany. He withdrew Germany from the League and began rearming in earnest. The Japanese, meanwhile, had invaded Manchuria and resigned from the League at the end of 1932. The period of effective collective security had ended.

British foreign policy in the thirties

The situation which the National Governments faced between 1931 and 1939 was extraordinarily difficult.

The international situation in 1933

The British governments of MacDonald, Baldwin and Chamberlain had to operate in a world quite different to that of the twenties and far more dangerous. The world-wide slump caused considerable and damaging changes to national governments and to their attitudes to their neighbours.

Some nations became more aggressive. In the Far East, the militarist government of Japan invaded Manchuria and then China. The Italian dictator, Mussolini, noted the success of Japan and adopted a more aggressive foreign policy in North Africa. In Germany appeared an unpredictable and extreme nationalist dictator in the shape of Hitler, who was noisily committed to the destruction of the Versailles settlement.

The combination of Japanese generals in the Far East, Mussolini in the Mediterranean and Hitler in Central Europe was a particularly tough one for Britain. The defence of the British Empire was the first priority of the British government. Japan could be a dangerous threat to the Asian colonies and Italy to the vital routes to the Middle East and India.

Unaffected by the slump, the Soviet Union, under Stalin's exceptionally ruthless and bloodstained dictatorship, was modernizing fast. By its five-year plans, first initiated in 1928, it would create, by 1939, a powerful economy based on heavy industry which enabled it to create a massive army with modern guns and tanks.

Other nations, particularly the democratic ones, turned in on themselves. The USA, whose economy was the hardest hit of all, became even more isolationist. France, who also suffered economically and only made a slow recovery through the 1930s, experienced intense internal political and social conflict. In Britain, though the effects of the 1929–1931 slump were less severe and economic recovery comparatively strong, the government's instincts were to avoid trouble abroad wherever possible.

■ Think about

▶ Why should economic suffering in Germany, Italy and Japan have made their governments more aggressive while in democracies like the USA, Britain and France, governments became less eager to become involved in international conflict?

Bear in mind that Germany, Italy and, to some extent, Japan saw themselves as the 'have-not' nations of the world compared with the 'haves' – USA, Britain and France.

British public opinion towards peace and war

It is hard to judge just what public opinion really was at any particular moment about the complex issue of how best to keep the peace. There was certainly a widespread determination in Britain that the First World War would really be the war to end wars. Many Britons also had high hopes of the League and 'collective security'. They expected their leaders to go out of their way to avoid conflict. Some politicians believed that the anti-war mood was so strong that the electorate would not have supported rearming and standing up to the dictators much before 1939.

A number of episodes between 1933 and 1935, were interpreted at the time as evidence of strong anti-war sentiments among the British public. They may, however, have indicated nothing of the kind.

In 1933, a month after Hitler came to power, the Oxford Union, (the university's debating society), passed a motion that in no circumstances would it 'fight for King and Country'. The vote was widely publicized and was interpreted to mean that British youth had lost their patriotism and were now feeble pacifists. It could equally well have meant that they were prepared to fight for a better-defined cause, such as democracy, or simply that in student debate, one side argued their case better than the other.

In 1934, at a by-election in Fulham, the Labour candidate who had well-known pacifist views, won the seat from the Conservative supporter of the National Government. Historians now think that his victory had little to do with foreign affairs. However, members of the National Government, Baldwin in particular, interpreted it to mean that public opinion would be hostile to any spending on rearmament.

In June 1935, the League of Nations Union organized a 'Peace Ballot' of 11.5 million Britons. Of these, 10.5 million wished Britain to remain a member of the League, 10 million said that they would support economic and non-military measures against an aggressor nation, and 6 million would also support military action. The ballot also found that 2 million were opposed to military action in any circumstances. A large majority was in favour of disarmament. Again this ballot could be and was interpreted in different ways. Certainly most Britons appeared to favour collective security and disarmament. If faced with an aggressor, a majority favoured action, including war, but there was also a large minority strongly opposed to war.

Labour policy

Within the Labour Party, there were the same cross-currents. In 1931 the Party was committed to collective security and disarmament. However, its leader from 1931 to 1935 was the pacifist George Lansbury. By 1935, leading trade unionists like Ernest Bevin had decided that Mussolini's aggression in Abyssinia made nonsense of Lansbury's pacifism and that it was damaging to the Party's popularity. Bevin strongly criticized Lansbury at the 1935 Party Conference, forcing his resignation. The new leader of the Party was Clement Attlee. Labour's foreign policy became marginally less pacific. In 1938 Attlee strongly criticized the government for betraying the Czechs at Munich.

Fears of air attack

Throughout all sections of society there was a conviction that the experiences of the First World War had been so dreadful that another war must be avoided at almost all costs. Linked to this was the belief that the advance of air power

▲ George Lansbury, Labour leader 1931-35, off on a peace-keeping expedition to Poland and Czechoslovakia in 1937.

▲ The bomber threat. An Italian artist shows German bombers in action over London in 1940. In fact, though bombers did get through and did much damage, they could not do enough to break a national economy and could be shot down.

would make a future war particularly devastating for the civilian population. The writings of the Italian General Douhet were very influential. He argued that the next war would be won by air forces against which there would be no effective defences. Bombers would be used to break the population's will to resist. As Stanley Baldwin put it: 'the bomber will always get through.' The success of German bombers at Guernica during the Spanish Civil War seemed to prove, incorrectly as it turned out, that Douhet was right.

The choices facing British governments in the 1930s

Anyone who paused for a moment's thought about foreign policy issues in the early thirties realized that, sooner or later, there would be a major crisis over Germany's eastern frontiers; and that this was the major problem facing Europe. How the German frontier question was resolved would determine whether Germany could live in peace with her neighbours or would become again the threatening Great Power she had been before 1914 – or worse. This problem existed independently of Hitler. Most Germans believed that Poland in particular had gained far too much in 1919. At Locarno in 1925, Stresemann would only confirm Germany's western frontiers, not the eastern ones.

What should British governments do to solve the problem of Germany's borders and the linked problem of how to prevent a revived Germany from dominating Europe once again? Possible policies included the following options:

1 **A defensive alliance:** To insist that the borders as laid down in the Versailles Treaty were non-negotiable and form an alliance with France, Poland, Czechoslovakia and, if possible, Russia, to defend these borders. This was essentially the French policy. If it were to succeed, it needed strong nerves, continuous rearmament and Britain and France having mutual confidence in one another.

2 **A tough stand, taken through the League of Nations:** To sustain and strengthen collective security through a more active and powerful League of Nations. This was essentially the policy of the Labour Party. If it were to succeed, it needed a strong and sustained commitment from the Great Powers, notably Britain with France, to take action on the League's behalf if a member ignored its decisions.

3 **Appeasement:** To deal directly with Germany; accept that many of her demands were reasonable; and persuade the rest of Europe to accept them. Give way where appropriate to keep the peace. This was essentially National Government policy from 1935 to 1939. It was the easiest and least expensive policy to pursue. There was no need for alliances or to work with the League of Nations. It could only succeed, however, if Hitler would be satisfied with a limited revision of Germany's eastern frontiers.

4 **Do nothing:** To decide that what happens in Eastern Europe is of no significance to Britain. Let Germany do what she wants. If eventually that were to lead to a fatal conflict between Hitler and Stalin, so much the better. It would have been the easiest policy for Britain to follow and it was occasionally considered by some members of the government. However, it would have left one hostile power, probably Germany, in control of more than half the continent and a huge threat first to France and Belgium, then to Britain. It would have wasted all the sacrifices of the First World War.

Whether or not the German problem of the thirties could have been solved without war will never be known, but the chances would have been better if British governments had decided what their policy was. If they believed in firmness, like Option 1 above, then they would have needed a stronger alliance with France and to have re-armed earlier. If collective security, Option 2, was their choice, that needed energetic diplomacy, consistency and rearmament. If appeasement, Option 3, was the best way forward, they needed to be consistent, and to have an alternative in place, just in case Hitler did not turn out to be reasonable after all.

Until Chamberlain became Prime Minister, British foreign policy was inconsistent. MacDonald and Baldwin kept hoping that collective security might still work. Baldwin was also a slow-moving appeaser. Only in 1938 was the appeasement policy pursued with vigour and determination by Neville Chamberlain. Britain did rearm but at least a year too late.

Appeasement (and collective security) 1933–1938

The National Governments moved towards a more distinct policy of appeasing Germany for these reasons:

- Europe must avoid another war.
- The German case for revising their frontiers was essentially reasonable, and certainly not worth fighting another war for.
- German governments, including Hitler, were also, behind the threats and bluster, reasonable.
- British public opinion was strongly against an active foreign policy, which might risk war, and against rearmament.
- Britain was not as strong militarily as she seemed and would not be able to defend the British Empire against an alliance of Germany, Italy and Japan.
- The government's priority was the economic crisis at home and unemployment. It did not want to spend more on defence.

Japan and Manchuria 1931–1932

Japan made the first serious challenge to the League of Nations and collective security by invading Manchuria. Her reasons for doing so were not entirely aggressive. Manchuria was a lawless place and Japanese business had suffered. Only four years before, Britain had landed troops in Shanghai to protect British business interests there.

China appealed to the League of Nations. The only nation that could have taken decisive action on the part of the League was Britain. Britain, however, was not going to risk a single ship or sailor on behalf of China. Instead, the League ordered an inquiry, which reported back in 1932. It accepted that the Japanese had reason to intervene in Manchuria but criticized the methods. Japan considered herself insulted, left the League and stayed in Manchuria. The only way in which Japan could have been stopped in 1931–1932 would have been if the USA and Britain, who alone had military forces in the Far East, had been prepared to act on behalf of the League; which they were not. Britain wrung her hands collectively with the League but otherwise did nothing.

Italy and Abyssinia 1935–1936

Within Europe, Germany, with Hitler as Chancellor, was the major problem. The British government was keen therefore, to have Mussolini as an ally rather than an enemy. In April 1935, MacDonald for Britain, Laval for France and Mussolini for Italy met at the Italian resort of Stresa. They were worried by Hitler's rearmament programme and formed a common 'front', the Stresa Front, to maintain the Versailles settlement.

Appeasement

'[Appeasement] is best conceived as an underlying attitude of mind, deriving variously, in particular instances, from fear, guilt, superiority, insecurity or hope of economic advantage. It can be summarized as disposition to anticipate and avoid conflict by judicious concession and negotiation'.

Robbins, *Appeasement*, 1997

Robbins adds that agreement is impossible on what counts as a judicious concession; e.g. was Chamberlain's appeasement of Hitler at Munich in 1938 'judicious'. Chamberlain thought so; Churchill did not.

Japanese Empire 1928
Japanese conquests 1931–2
Further conquests 1933–39

▲ Japanese aggression, 1931–1939.

■ **Think about**

Economic sanctions

Banning trade with a nation which is behaving aggressively has often seemed a sensible move since it should end the aggression without a major war. However it did not work against Italy in 1936; nor against White Rhodesians in the 1960s when they refused to grant majority rule; nor against Saddam Hussein of Iraq in the 1990s.

▶ Why should it be so difficult to make economic sanctions effective?

Two months later, the British government came to a separate naval agreement with Hitler's Germany which allowed the German fleet to reach 35 per cent of the size of the Royal Navy. This agreement meant Britain could deploy the Royal Navy more flexibly but was in complete breach of the Versailles Treaty. Italy and France were not impressed.

In October 1935, Mussolini ordered the invasion of Abyssinia. Abyssinia appealed to the League. This was a simple act of aggression, and the League must act. It did, imposing economic sanctions on Italy.

The British government found itself in an embarrassing position. It needed Italy as part of the Stresa Front against Germany. The Admiralty was worried about the Mediterranean sea-routes if Britain went to war with Italy. Britain therefore refused to agree to oil sanctions (the only one that might have worked) against Italy. Instead the Foreign Secretaries of Britain and France, Hoare and Laval, devised a plan to partition Abyssinia, giving the most fertile parts to Italy. The British Cabinet approved the plan but before it could be discussed in Parliament, the details were leaked to the Press. There was uproar. Such weakness in the face of aggression was not what British public opinion understood by 'collective security'. Hoare had to resign. Nothing, however, was done to stop the Italian invasion. The Italians conquered Abyssinia in 1936.

Britain now tried to hold Italy in the Stresa Front by appeasement. That failed too. Mussolini left the League in 1937 and moved steadily closer to Germany. In 1938 he signed the Anti-Comintern Pact against Russia with Germany and Japan.

It is difficult to regard British policy towards the Italian invasion of Abyssinia as anything other than shabby and short-sighted. Britain and France could have prevented the invasion, which was brutal in the extreme. It allowed the League to be undermined fatally. Even in the most selfish terms, Britain gained nothing. Hitler concluded that if aggression paid for Mussolini, it would pay for him too.

Documentary exercise: Italy and Abyssinia

Source A

The Historian P.F. Clarke, writing in 1996

Mussolini's Italy remained a puzzle. It was harder to know if it should be conciliated, as a realistic strategy for isolating Germany, or opposed as another fascist dictatorship, which was the more ideological response of the left. Both Churchill and the government wobbled between the two courses.

Clarke, *Hope and Glory*, 1996

Source B

Anthony Eden, Minister for League of Nations' Affairs, addresses the League Assembly 10 October 1935

The League has two main tasks. First to avert war by the just and peaceful settlement of all disputes. Secondly, if we fail in our first objective, to stop war...it is by the League's effectiveness in realizing this (second) aim that the League will be judged. We cannot neglect our duties and our responsibilities. Action must be taken now...On behalf of His Majesty's Government in the United Kingdom, I declare our willingness to take our full part in such action.

League of Nations Official Journal, Special Supplement No.136

Source C

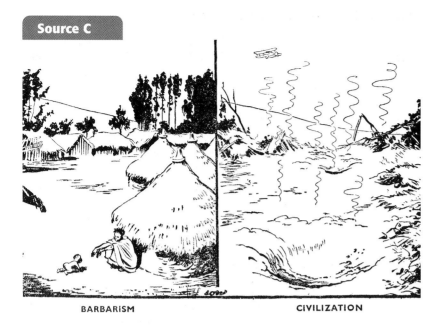

BARBARISM   CIVILIZATION

▲ This Low cartoon from the *Evening Standard* reflects in 1935 on the Italian conquest of Abyssinia.

Source D

0 — 500 km

ANGLO-EGYPTIAN SUDAN

Red Sea

FRENCH SOMALILAND

ITALIAN ERITREA

Aden

ABYSSINIA (Ethiopia)

BRITISH SOMALILAND

Addis Ababa

ITALIAN SOMALILAND

Indian Ocean

KENYA

☐ Land to be given to Italy
☐ Land to be controlled economically by Italy

▲ The ill-fated Hoare-Laval proposals of 1935.

Source E

Prime Minister Neville Chamberlain speaking to the House of Commons 2 May 1938

[An Anglo-Italian Agreement had just been signed to improve relations]

The Agreement is a step towards general appeasement...Today there is a new Italy, an Italy which, under the stimulus of the personality of Signor Mussolini, is showing new vigour, in which there is apparent new vision and new efficiency...I believe we may look forward to a friendship with Italy as firmly based, as that by which we were bound to the old.

Hansard

Quotation

During the Czech crisis when Bene, the Czech Prime Minister, was being threatened by Hitler, Haile Selassie the Abyssinian Emperor, whom the Italians had driven into exile, wrote to him saying:

'I hear that you are receiving the support of the British government. You have my profoundest sympathy.'

■ Examination-style questions

1 Comprehension in context
Using Source D and your own knowledge, explain what the Hoare-Laval plan was, and why it was drawn up.

2 Comparing the sources
To what extent do Sources B, and E support the claim that the British government 'wobbled between two courses' (Source A) in their response to Italy?

3 Assessing the sources
How useful is Source C as a reflection of public opinion of the government's response to the Italian invasion of Abyssinia?

4 Making judgements
Using these sources and your own knowledge, discuss the view that the British government should have pursued a more determined policy of appeasement towards Italy between 1935 and 1938.

The Spanish Civil War 1936–1939

In 1936 civil war broke out in Spain. The conflict was mainly between right-wing supporters of the Catholic Church led by General Franco and left-wing, anti-clerical supporters of the Republican government. European fascists supported Franco and European communists the Republicans. Nazi Germany and Fascist Italy sent troops to help Franco, Communist Russia money and supplies to aid the Republicans. For political idealists across Europe, the war in Spain was seen as part of the world struggle against fascism. The British government, however, was determined to stay out of it. In particular it did not wish to be seen as sympathetic to the Republicans as it still hoped to pull Italy away from her growing friendship with Germany. With France it tried to persuade the other Powers of Europe not to intervene. Germany and Italy pretended to agree but kept up their military backing to Franco, who eventually won. The British and French stance looked foolish.

Appeasing Germany 1933–1939

Hitler had no quarrel with Britain. The most constant elements in his political thinking were hatred of the Jews and Germany's eastward expansion. He expected Britain to turn away from Europe and concentrate on the British Empire. He could be persuasive and charming and convinced many British visitors, including experienced politicians, notably Lloyd George, that he was committed to peace.

However, he never hid his extreme nationalist views; expressed himself in violent language and denounced the Versailles Treaty with passion. The violence of the Nazis towards their political opponents in Germany was also common knowledge after 1934.

German defiance of the Versailles Treaty 1933–1938

All the steps described in the Timeline were breaches of the Versailles Treaty and substantially increased Germany's power in Europe. However, in each case the British government did nothing or positively encouraged Hitler in his defiance of Versailles.

The encouragement came in 1935 in the form of the Anglo-German Naval Treaty which as we have seen on page 237, seriously weakened the Stresa Front. In the same year, Hitler also began to rearm openly.

The reoccupation of the Rhineland was done by a small force which had instructions to retreat if it met any French or British troops. Hitler was gambling that Britain and France, who had allowed Mussolini to take Abyssinia, would let him have the Rhineland. He was right. The occupation was in breach of the Locarno Pact of 1925 as well as the Versailles Treaty. France was not confident to act without Britain's backing. Baldwin's government, however, and British public opinion, could see no harm in the German move. Why should German troops not have the right to move throughout Germany? The reoccupation was an understandable action. To Britain it was barely worth a protest.

The Council of the League met in London. Hitler had broken the terms of the treaties of both Locarno and Versailles, but only the Soviet Union suggested that action should be taken. German troops stayed in the Rhineland. Hitler said that he had no further territorial claims in Europe.

Timeline

Steps to War 1933–1938

1933 Hitler becomes Chancellor of Germany.
Germany leaves the League of Nations; secretly rearms.

1935 Germany openly rearms.
Anglo-German Naval Treaty.

1936 German troops reoccupy the Rhineland.

1938 Austria united with Germany by the *Anschluss* (Union).

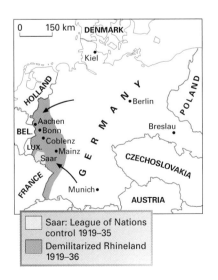

Saar: League of Nations control 1919–35

Demilitarized Rhineland 1919–36

Nothing happened, either, when German troops marched into Austria in March 1938 even though this gave Germany a much stronger position in Central Europe. Most Austrians seemed to want the *Anschluss*. It could be seen as an example of self-determination. The Prime Minister merely told the Commons that he particularly regretted the use of force by which it was achieved.

The Czechoslovakian crisis 1938

Chamberlain became Prime Minister in 1937 and immediately made foreign affairs his personal concern. His Foreign Secretary was Anthony Eden, who disliked Chamberlain's interference. They argued over Italy and then about how to respond to a suggestion from President Roosevelt of the USA for an international conference. Eden was in favour, Chamberlain considered that it would be waste of time. Eden resigned in January 1938.

Lord Halifax replaced Eden but now Chamberlain was entirely in charge of British foreign policy. He gave to the policy of appeasement new clarity and drive. He would work with Hitler to identify the legitimate grievances that Germany still had about the Versailles settlement. Solutions would be found to end these grievances and the peace of Europe would be secure. His method was personal diplomacy, with only the most limited consultations with allies like the French.

When the Czech crisis blew up, Chamberlain knew what the solution should be. In his view, the demands of the Sudeten German minority were reasonable according to the principle of self-determination. Either the Sudeten Germans should have self-government within Czechoslovakia or should be transferred to Germany. Even if the Sudeten case had been a poor one, it should be granted since he was told by his military advisers that Britain and France were not strong enough to save Czechoslovakia from a German attack. Chamberlain's task was to persuade the Czechs and the French that appeasement along these lines was the only sensible policy.

Ceded to Germany at Munich, 30 September 1938
Ceded to Hungary by Germany and Italy, October 1938
Seized by Poland, September 1938
Occupied by Hungary, March 1939
Boundary created by the Treaty of Versailles, 1919
Occupied by Germany, March 1939

◄ The destruction of Czechoslovakia, 1938–1939.

He decided that the best way to deal with the crisis was a dramatic exercise in personal diplomacy. Though he had never flown before, he would win Hitler's confidence by going to Germany.

He first met Hitler on 15 September, when they agreed that the Sudetenland should be transferred to Germany. Between his first and second visit, he persuaded an uneasy French and an angry Czech government to agree to this policy. He flew a second time to meet Hitler, expecting to sort out the final details of an agreement, only to find Hitler demanding an immediate occupation of the Sudetenland and the transfer of some Czech lands to Poland and to Hungary. Faced by such blatant bullying by Hitler, opinion in Britain and France hardened in support of the Czechs. Everyone prepared for war. At the last moment, nudged by the British Foreign Office, Mussolini suggested a conference of Germany, Italy, Britain and France at Munich. There Chamberlain was happy to give to Hitler everything that he had previously demanded on 22 September, except he insisted on a slower occupation of the Sudetenland.

Chamberlain returned to Britain triumphant. He received a hero's welcome from a nation hugely relieved that there was not going to be a war after all. He was particularly pleased with himself because at the end of the conference he had got Hitler to sign a declaration that the Munich Agreement and the Anglo-German Naval Treaty were 'symbols of the desire of our two peoples never to go to war with one another again.' This was for Chamberlain his 'peace with honour'. For Hitler it was a piece of paper of no significance.

From Munich 1938 to war 1939

The lesson Hitler drew from Munich was that Britain and France would let him have his way in Eastern Europe. When an easy opportunity occurred in March 1939, he occupied the Czech part of Czechoslovakia.

Within Britain, however, public opinion was turning rapidly in favour of resisting Hitler. The immediate feelings of relief after Munich were replaced for many people by the realization that the Czechs had been badly betrayed. As the rearmament programme gained momentum, the military chiefs, who by now regarded war with Germany as inevitable, became more optimistic about victory.

For most of Parliament, the occupation of the Czech lands was the final proof that Hitler could only be stopped by war. Chamberlain still stuck to his belief that his appeasement policy could still work; but he was prepared to agree with France to support Poland and to see if the Soviet Union could be drawn into an anti-Nazi alliance. The talks proceeded very slowly and ran into problems over the Baltic republics. The Polish government was also very uneasy about Soviet intentions.

In comparison, Hitler moved more swiftly and the Nazi-Soviet Pact opened the way to the German invasion of Poland.

To the last moment, Chamberlain obstinately searched for a way of avoiding war. On 2 September, when the invading German troops were deep into Poland, Chamberlain talked to a mutinous House of Commons not about the declaration of war but of the possibility of a conference. When Arthur Greenwood, the Deputy Leader of the Party, started his speech, 'Speaking for the Labour Party', a cry came from the Conservative benches, 'Speak for England, Arthur'. The Cabinet agreed to send an ultimatum to Hitler the following day.

Timeline

Dec. 1938 to Sept. 1939

1938 December German persecution of the Jews becomes more public through violence towards both people and property.

1939 March Slovaks split off from the Czechs, Germans occupy the Czech part of Czechoslovakia. Hitler now demands the Polish Corridor.

31 March Britain commits herself to support Poland against a German attack.

April/May hesitant British attempt to negotiate an alliance with the Soviet Union.

23 August Nazi-Soviet Pact announced. The Soviet Union declared that it would remain neutral should Germany go to war with Poland and her allies.

1 September German troops invade Poland. Chamberlain still hopes that a Munich type conference might restore peace.

4 September Britain finally declares war on Germany.

■ Activity   KEY SKILLS

Write an essay which a) describes the increasing aggression of Hitler and Mussolini and b) how the policy of appeasement evolved in relation to this aggression. You should include at least one diagram in your essay.

Neville Chamberlain. The guiltiest of the guilty men?

■ Biography

Neville Chamberlain
(1869–1940)

1890–1918 Runs a sisal plantation in the West Indies.

1897–1918 Birmingham businessman and local politician.

1911 Marries Annie Cole.

1915 Lord Mayor of Birmingham.

1916 Director of National Service. Not a success.

1918 Elected as Liberal Unionist MP for Birmingham, Ladywood.

1923 Minister of Health.

1924–29 Again Minister of Health, leads Local Government Reform programme.

1931 Helps to create National Government.

1931–37 Chancellor of the Exchequer.

1937 Prime Minister.

1938 Munich Agreement.

1939 Polish Crisis and Declaration of War.

1940 Setbacks in Norway. Resigns as Prime Minister but joins Churchill's War Cabinet, dies of cancer.

Neville Chamberlain was the younger son of the famous Joseph and half-brother to Austen. His father decided that Austen should go to university and into politics and Neville straight into business. He was a successful local politician but only when he was nearly 50 did he become an MP. His rise was then swift. A reforming Minister of Health and a firm and effective Chancellor of the Exchequer, he had no rivals when he succeeded Baldwin in 1937. All his efforts as PM were devoted to the German problem. When he was finally forced to resign as PM in 1940, unlike Asquith he joined the War Cabinet of Churchill who replaced him. This generous gesture helped the Conservatives to avoid the divisions which so harmed the Liberals.

If he had retired in 1937, he would be remembered not as a 'Guilty Man' but as a tough, clear-headed, hard-working and constructive minister, the best Conservative minister of the inter-war years and one who proved to the electorate that the Conservatives were committed to social reform.

If just one sentence were to be allocated to Chamberlain in a history book, he would be described as the British Prime Minister whom Hitler fooled. The one photo would be of him at Heston aerodrome on his return from Munich in 1938 waving a piece of paper and proclaiming that he had achieved 'peace in our time'. When he announced that Britain was at war with Germany in September 1939, he acknowledged that 'everything I have believed in during my public life has crashed in ruins.' His three years as Prime Minister seemed a futile misdirection of energy which ended in humiliation. His controversial appeasement policy is assessed later in this chapter. These pages contain evidence about the kind of man he was.

Source 6

A GREAT MEDIATOR

John Bull. "I've known many Prime Ministers in my time, Sir, but never one who worked so hard for security in the face of such terrible odds."

▲ A Partridge cartoon from Punch in 1938.

Source 7

INSPECTION OF THE CORRESPONDENCE COLUMN

▲ A Low cartoon from the *Evening Standard*. Dawson, the Editor of *The Times* (the Scoutmaster immediately behind Chamberlain), was an enthusiastic appeaser. *The Times* was then the most influential broadsheet newspaper in Britain.

Source 8

On his colleagues in 1932:

'It amuses me to find a new policy for each of my colleagues in turn and though I can't imagine that all my ideas are the best, most of them seem to be adopted faute de mieux (for want of better).'

On the impression he made on Hitler in 1938:

'H.W. (Horace Wilson, Chamberlain's personal adviser) heard from various people who were with Hitler after my interview he said that he had been very favourably impressed. I have had a conversation with a real man, he said, and one with whom I can do business and he liked the rapidity with which I had grasped the essentials. In short I had established a certain confidence, which was my aim, and despite the hardness and ruthlessness which I thought I saw in his face, I got the impression that here was a man who could be relied on when he had given his word.'

Chamberlain on Chamberlain

■ Questions

1 What are the messages of the two cartoons, 6 and 7? In what ways do their portraits of Chamberlain differ?

2 Study Source 8. What impression do you get of Chamberlain from himself?

3 What are the weaknesses of Sources 8 and 9 as evidence about Chamberlain as a personality?

4 In what ways does Source 9 differ from the other sources? How does it add to our knowledge and understanding of Chamberlain in 1938?

5 Using all the sources and your own knowledge, describe the character of Neville Chamberlain and indicate how it would have helped and hindered him as Prime Minister between 1937 and 1940.

Source 9

In conversation: during the war; Churchill described Chamberlain as

'The narrowest, most ignorant, most ungenerous of men'

In his book, *The Gathering Storm* which describes the years leading up to the outbreak of war in 1939, he judged that Chamberlain was:

'An upright, competent, well-meaning man (but showing) a lack of all sense of proportion and even of self-preservation.' He possessed a 'narrow, sharp-edged efficiency but had 'a limited outlook and inexperience of the European scene.'

Churchill on Chamberlain. Churchill was a back-bencher for most of the thirties, highly critical of the policies of the National Government towards India and Hitler. He led the critics of Chamberlain in 1938 and 1939

Source 10

I will always remember little Neville today, with his too long hair, greying at the sides, his smile, his amazing spirits and seeming lack of fatigue, as he stood there alone, fighting the dogs of war single-handed and triumphant – he seemed like the reincarnation of St George – so simple and so unspoilt – now in a few hours for the third time he takes a plane to a far country in the service of England. May God speed him and reward him for his efforts. I don't know what the country has done to deserve him.

Sir Henry (Chips) Channon Conservative MP for Southend. He is describing the end of a tense debate in the Commons during the Munich crisis of 1938

Was Britain ready to fight? Rearmament 1931–1939

Underlying the policy of appeasement was the belief that the British and French armies were not strong enough to defeat the German and Italian armies in Europe. Nor could the Royal Navy defend the Channel, Mediterranean and Pacific simultaneously against the German, Italian and Japanese navies. In addition, Britain's defences against the German airforce were believed to be inadequate.

In the 1920s, defence spending had been cut right back. It did not appear to be needed; the economy was fragile; through the League of Nations disarmament not rearmament was the priority. In the 1930s the National Government delayed rearming, despite the knowledge that Germany, Italy and Japan were all doing so. This was partly because the government had other economic priorities, such as unemployment benefit and housing, and partly because Baldwin believed that rearmament would be electorally unpopular.

Serious rearmament began in 1935 and was accelerated by Chamberlain in 1937. The most significant improvements were made in relation to air warfare. Watson Watt invented radar in 1935 and by 1939 most of the southern and eastern coasts were protected by a radar early-warning network. Simultaneously, a modern airforce was being built and the building programme was accelerating. In 1938, 240 aircraft were produced on average per month, in 1939 the number was 660. The army, including its tank regiments, was neglected until 1939 when the realization that the commitment to Poland was likely to mean another continental war led to the decisions firstly to re-equip the regular army, secondly to double the size of the territorial volunteers and thirdly to reintroduce conscription. Defence policy lagged behind foreign policy.

Historical debate: Was appeasement the right policy for Britain in the 1930s?

Interpretation 1: Appeasement was foolish, lazy, ill-informed, disastrous

This first interpretation was the work of men who were actually coping with the immense crisis of 1939–1940. For them, the disasters which overtook Europe as a result of Nazi aggression were evidence enough for the validity of their interpretation.

As early as 1940, they condemned appeasement as foolish, lazy and ill-informed. By failing to make a stand against the dictators, particularly against Hitler when he threatened Czechoslovakia in 1938, and by delaying rearmament, the MacDonald, Baldwin, and Chamberlain governments persuaded Hitler that aggression would pay and that he could pursue his dream of gaining living space for Germans in Eastern Europe without having to worry about Britain. Hitler could have been stopped either without a war or by a European war fought on terms much less favourable to Germany than the one which broke out in 1939.

The appeasers, therefore, had much to answer for. They made four bad mistakes.

1 They took Hitler at his word until much too late when there was abundant evidence that he was entirely untrustworthy and set on war.
2 They failed to make alliances which were the only sure defence against Hitler's aggression.

3 They took Hitler's boasting at its face value and let him trick them into believing that he was far stronger than was in fact the case. This was a particularly serious mistake during the Czechoslovak crisis of 1938.

4 They failed to inform public opinion of the dangers which were developing and consequently delayed rearmament too long.

This case was powerfully argued by three young journalists, Michael Foot, Peter Howard and Frank Owen who wrote their pamphlet *Guilty Men* in 1940 under the pseudonym Cato as the defeated British army was evacuated from Dunkirk.

The most influential critic of the appeasers was Churchill. In his view, he had warned them of their folly as a backbencher in the 1930s. As Prime Minister from 1940–1945 he had to save the nation from the consequences of their folly. He was able to gain a wide audience for his interpretation because he wrote a magnificent account of the causes and events of the Second World War (see Note on page 244)

Source 11

When Mr Chamberlain stepped out of his airplane on the return from Munich, he said, 'This means Peace in our Time'…Nobody can accuse Mr Chamberlain of being a wilful liar. He said those things because he believed them. He was absolutely satisfied that when Hitler signed that little piece of paper, the heart of the man who had built up his regime of treachery, lies and deception had changed.

At a dinner party shortly after Munich, the British Prime Minister found himself sitting next to a politician who had opposed the settlement [at Munich]. A discussion arose between the two men and was conducted in the most friendly terms…The Premier's opponent asked how any trust could reasonably be placed in Hitler's word. He pointed out that Hitler [had lied about having no territorial demands in 1934, again 1935 and again in 1936] and in March 1938 gave assurances that Germany had no hostile intention against Czechoslovakia.

Having recited all these broken pledges, this fellow guest turned towards Mr Chamberlain at the dinner table and asked. 'Prime Minister, in the face of all this, remembering all these things, do you not feel a twinge of doubt about Hitler's promises?'

Mr Chamberlain replied with complete gravity, 'Ah, but this time he promised me'.

Cato, *Guilty Men,* 1940

Source 12

On rearmament 28 November 1934
To urge preparation of defence is not to assert the imminence of war. On the contrary, if war were imminent, preparation for defence would be too late…What is the great new fact that has broken upon us during the last eighteen months? Germany is rearming. That mighty power is now equipping itself once more, 70,000,000 people, with the technical apparatus of modern war…Let the government give the lead, and the nation will not fail in the hour of need.

On public opinion 22 May 1935
I have been told that the reason why the Government has not acted before was that public opinion was not ripe for rearmament. I hope that we shall never accept such a reason as that. The Government has been in control of overwhelming majorities in both Houses of Parliament. There is no vote they could not have proposed for the national defence which would not have been accepted with overwhelming strength.

On the Munich Agreement 5 October 1938
All is over. Silent, mournful, abandoned, broken, Czechoslovakia recedes into the darkness…

I find unendurable the sense of our country falling into the power, into the orbit and influence of Nazi Germany, and of our existence becoming dependent upon their good will or pleasure. It is to prevent this that I have tried my best to urge the maintenance of every bulwark of defence – first the timely creation of an air force superior to anything within striking distance of our shores; secondly the gathering together of the collective strengths of many nations; and thirdly the making of alliances…It has all been in vain. Every position has been successively undermined on specious and plausible excuses.

Extracts from Churchill's speeches from Hansard

Interpretation 2: The revisionist view. Appeasement was a popular and realistic policy

The Churchillian interpretation was not seriously challenged for a generation. This is hardly surprising when one remembers that for the immediate post-war generation, Churchill's reputation was unquestioned and his account of the causes and events of the war was very widely held.

A generation had to pass until historians who had few personal memories of the 1930s and 1940s re-examined the evidence. This younger generation pointed out that in the thirties Churchill was in a small minority. Most politicians and the general public agreed with appeasement. Chamberlain was a national hero in 1938. They also pointed out that many people were deceived by Hitler and that the costs of rearmament were too great to bear until it was absolutely clear that Hitler was set on war. The appeasers helped to keep Europe at peace until Britain could rearm enough to survive in 1940.

Source 13

That is not to suggest that Chamberlain's psychological understanding and tactical methods were flawless. He did not grasp the dynamics of Hitler's regime and did not display a deep understanding of the aims, beliefs and practices of National Socialism...Even so it is difficult to assess what difference Chamberlain's shortcomings in this respect actually made to the conduct of policy. Lloyd George was blessed with much more imagination but his analysis of Hitler's mind and intentions was no better than Chamberlain's. Another set of men in power would no doubt have made some, but probably not a vast, difference to the policies that were followed.

Robbins *Appeasement*, 1988

Source 14

Unlike Churchill, Chamberlain had knowledge of what passed for the French war-plan and of the latest report of the British Chiefs of Staff...the French plan was to wait behind the Maginot line until the British had expanded their army and the economic blockade began to bite; this was not a strategy that promised speedy relief to the Czechs (as the Poles were to discover a year later)...The Chiefs were adamant that there was nothing that either Power could do to prevent Germany from inflicting a decisive defeat on Czechoslovakia. Britain was still a year away from the time when her rearmament programme would be substantially complete; the omens for war were not good.

Charmley, *Chamberlain and the Lost Peace*, 1989

■ Think about

▶ How do Robbins and Charmley defend the appeasers against their critics?

▶ From your own knowledge, comment on the strength of their arguments.

Interpretation 3: The counter-revisionist view

Source 15

There has been much propaganda on behalf of Chamberlain that he gained a precious year, that Britain was much stronger in September 1939 than in September 1938, I have little doubt that we lost a precious year...First we lost the Czechs who had a million and a half men behind the strongest fortress line in Europe, equipped by a highly organized and powerful industrial machine. They had a formidable air force. An attack on Czechoslovakia would have absorbed a large part of the German army and air force, in addition, considerable German forces would have been needed on the French and Polish frontiers...At that time the Germans were not well equipped with tanks and other armour. All that came later, much of it taken from the Czech army and some produced in Czech arsenals.

The Labour Politician Hugh Dalton considers whether Czechoslovakia could have been defended in 1938. Dalton, The Fateful Years, 1957

Source 16

This book argues that Chamberlain and his colleagues made choices among alternative policies. Those historians who have revised the earlier interpretation of Chamberlain, in which he was written off as an ignorant coward, imply that his foreign policy was dictated by a realistic assessment of economic and military weakness and by British opinion. This book suggests that Chamberlain led the government in 1938 and 1939, particularly in the months after Munich, into rejecting the option of a close Franco-British alliance, which might have dealt firmly with Mussolini's pretensions, and might have acted as a nucleus around which those states with reason to fear the Third Reich could assemble to resist it. We still do not know whether or not it was possible to induce the Soviet Union to hinder rather than help Hitler's attempt in 1939 and 1940 to forcibly prevent the Western Powers from interfering in Eastern Europe. Chamberlain refused to try; he thought collaboration with the Soviet Union undesirable and unnecessary. Yet Chamberlain had no intention of agreeing to a free hand for Germany in Eastern Europe. This book suggests that he could have tried to build a barrier to Hitler's expansion. After March 1939 British attempts to do so were either half-hearted or too late. Academically, therefore, this study proposes that the balance of evidence points to counter-revisionist interpretations. Led by Chamberlain, the government rejected effective deterrence. Chamberlain's powerful, obstinate personality and his skill in debate probably stifled serious chances of preventing the Second World War.

R.A.C. Parker in 1993 summarizes his criticisms of Chamberlain. Parker, Chamberlain and Appeasement, 1993

■ Think about

▶ Hugh Dalton, Source 15, was one of the best informed Labour politicians about defence issues. If he had still been alive, how might he have commented on John Charmley's defence of Chamberlain (Source 14).

▶ In what ways can R.A.C. Parker (Source 16) be described as counter-revisionist?

▶ Explain whether you consider Clarke (Source 17) to be more of a revisionist than a counter-revisionist.

▶ What is your own position?

Source 17

The name Munich has become synonymous with a pejorative sense of appeasement, and with some reason. The two jackbooted dictators received the two western Prime Ministers for four-power talks (excluding Czechoslovakia itself). The terms were no better than before; but Chamberlain, having undermined any French will to resist, now closed the deal and presented the bill to the Czechs. They now had no option but to cede the Sudetenland to Hitler. Chamberlain thus succeeded in his immediate aim of averting war. Thereby, as Sir John Simon chose to argue, he saved Czechoslovakia; and it is a melancholy fact, cited by later historians, that far more of the Poles for whom Britain ostensibly went to war in 1939 perished in the Second World War than the Czechs who were betrayed in 1938. This does not mean though that the Czechs were not betrayed. At Munich the fine arguments for appeasement as a process of mutual concession involved Chamberlain in making the necessary sacrifices, not on his own behalf, and not at his own expense, but that of the Czechs.

Peter Clarke, Hope and Glory, 1996

Interpretations exercise: The argument about appeasement

A historian analyses the international situation in the late 1930s

Britain's allies were no armour against the dictators. Chamberlain had serious doubts about the French. The United States offered no salvation. The extension of the Neutrality Act in 1936 confirmed American isolation and made it impossible for the United States to supply arms. The Soviet Union was a potential ally but Chamberlain was deeply suspicious of Stalin's motives.

Adamthwaite, *The Makings of the Second World War*, 1977

Source B

A historian analyses Chamberlain's motives for appeasing Hitler

Chamberlain felt sure that a British statesman could make all the difference between war and peace in Europe. It was essential to find out what the Nazis wanted, what they would accept as the price of peace and (if necessary) give it to them before they dragged the continent into war. This was Chamberlain's strategy for dealing with Hitler. The strategy was summed up in one word – 'appeasement'. For the most part, Chamberlain's desire to avoid war matched the anxiety of the British people about being brought into a conflict like that of 1914–18. Added was the new awareness that bombers could bring war to their cities.

On 30 September, Chamberlain returned triumphantly to London, bearing his piece of paper. He received a hero's welcome. That evening he declared from Downing Street, 'I believe that it is peace in our time.'

Howarth, *Twentieth Century History*, 1919

Source C

An historian analyses Great Britain's military position in the 1930s

Years of under-funding had left Britain and its Empire in a dreadfully weak position militarily – as the service chiefs were eager to explain after 1932, when the first attempts to assess the defence requirements of the Empire were made. A whole series of reports were laid before the worried Cabinet for the next six years, always with the same depressing message. The Royal Navy was incapable of sending a main fleet to Singapore and of maintaining a one-power standard in European waters (hence the Admiralty's concern to restrain German naval rearmament by the 1935 Treaty). There was not one adequately defended base throughout the entire Empire. A miniscule army could not possibly play a role in preserving the European equilibrium. Above all, perhaps, there was a weakness in the air; far from Britain being in a position to deter Germany by means of a long-range bomber force, it seemed much more vulnerable to aerial attack from the imposing *Luftwaffe*. Going to war against one of the dictator states would be difficult enough; fighting all three would be impossible.

Kennedy, *Appeasement*, 1986

Source D

A historian analyses the political difficulties facing the Conservative Party in the 1930s

Baldwin and Chamberlain had committed the Conservative Party in 1935 to a programme of social expenditure and house building which they were reluctant to abandon for a rearmament programme. Labour's attitude to even limited rearmament provoked Chamberlain to write that 'All the elements of danger are here…I can see that we might easily run into a series of crippling strikes and finally the defeat of the government.' In 1935 business leaders also warned Chamberlain that they would only co-operate with large-scale rearmament on their own terms. All of this put pressure on the government to tread warily with rearmament and to seek a settlement of outstanding national issues.

Overy, *The Origins of the Second World War*, 1987

Britain and Germany 1933–1939

1 (a) Account for the similarities and differences between Sources C and D in the reasons they give for appeasement.
(b) What do Sources A to D tell us about the extent to which the claim can be supported that Chamberlain was 'lulled into appeasement because he believed that Hitler was a reasonable politician.'

2 Consider the arguments for and against the suggestion that appeasement was the only solution to Britain's problems with regard to foreign policy in the 1930s.

3 How far can appeasement be seen as the most important reason for the outbreak of war in September 1939?

■ **Activity**

Look carefully at the different cartoons included in this chapter. Consider the techniques used to make it clear exactly what the cartoon is referring to, what view the cartoonist has of appeasement – and the way in which the cartoonist gets his opinion across.

Now design or plan your own cartoon that summarizes the counter-revisionist interpretation of appeasement.
What elements of this view, if any, make it different from the earlier criticisms of appeasement?

■ **Further reading**

*Alan Farmer, *Britain Foreign and Imperial Affairs 1919–39,* 1992
Winston Churchill, *The Gathering Storm,* 1948
Keith Robbins, *Appeasement,* 1988
D. Reynolds, *Britain Overruled British Policy and World Power in the Twentieth Century,* 1991
R.A.C. Parker, *Chamberlain and Appeasement* ,1993
P. Kennedy, *The Realities Behind Diplomacy,* 1981

Summary

- Britain did very well, in the short-term, out of the Versailles Treaty. She removed the German navy and added to her Empire. Apart from the USA, she had no rivals remotely as strong as she was, so her international position was apparently both impressive and secure. However, the weaknesses of the Versailles settlement and the international tensions which stemmed from those weaknesses undermined that position. Britain did not have the resources to defend the British Empire, act as the League's policeman and restrain aggressive dictators in Europe; hence the readiness of her government to pursue appeasement policies in the 1930s.

- Since Britain made major gains from the Versailles settlement, her aims to keep the peace and avoid change meant that British governments often took an unsystematic appeasing approach in the 1920s. However, during that decade, they made frequent use of 'collective security', most obviously at Locarno in 1925. The Labour Party committed itself firmly to collective security and disarmament into the late 1930s.

- The international situation deteriorated sharply after 1929. The aggression of Japan, Italy and Germany created an international climate where collective security had less and less chance of working. The League of Nations could only have been more effective if Britain and France had been ready to allow it more teeth in the settlement of international disputes and provided most of the teeth themselves from their military resources.

- The National governments of the early thirties pursued collective security and appeasement simultaneously. MacDonald played a leading role at the international disarmament conference in Geneva in 1932–1923, while appeasing Japan over Manchuria. Increasingly Britain moved more completely to appeasement. Chamberlain merely brought to the policy a sharper focus and greater vigour.

- Churchill and 'Cato' quickly condemned the appeasers as 'Guilty men'. Revisionist historians have defended the appeasers and in turn have provoked some counter-revisionism which argues that the first criticisms, though fierce, were essentially just.

Chapter 15

The Second World War
A good war?

Source 1

◀ St Paul's rising above buildings gutted by Nazi bombs in 1940.

Source 2

The Battle of France is over…I expect that the Battle of Britain is about to begin. Upon this battle depends the survival of Christian civilization. Upon it depends our own British life and the long continuity of our institutions and our Empire. The whole might and fury of the enemy must very soon be turned upon us. Hitler knows that he will have to break us in this island or lose the war. If we can stand up to him, all Europe may be free, and the life of the world may move forward into broad, sunlit uplands; but if we fail, then the whole world, including the United States, and all we have known and cared for, will sink into the abyss of a new dark age made more sinister, and perhaps more protracted, by the lights of a perverted science. Let us therefore brace ourselves to our duty and so bear ourselves that if the British Empire and its Commonwealth last for a thousand years men will still say 'This was their finest hour'.

Churchill in the House of Commons 18 June 1940 (and later that day on the radio to the British people and to the world)

Introduction

From a world perspective, if the First World War turned out to be quite unlike any other and much worse than anyone had predicted, the same was true only more so for the Second World War. The battles between Germany and Russia on the Eastern Front between 1941 and 1945 far surpassed those of the trenches in casualties and in savagery. The Nazi treatment of the Jews and of other peoples they considered inferior was so appalling that when the truth first began to emerge, the reaction of world opinion was disbelief.

For Britain, it was a strange war with contradictory characteristics. Britain started fighting alongside France, then fought alone and ended up playing third fiddle to the USA and USSR. Whereas Lloyd George came to power in 1916 and galvanized the country to *win* the first war, Churchill came to power in 1940 to galvanize the country *not to lose* the second one, and to hang on until 1941 when both the USSR and the USA became allies.

Britain's war effort was a triumph by which the nation contributed more to the freedom of the world than at any time in her history. In a genuine sense 1940 was, as Churchill had hoped, Britain's 'finest hour' (see Source 2) But it was also a disaster in terms of Britain's position as a Great Power. If Britain won the war, she also lost the peace. The economy was gravely weakened, and her standing as one of the world's leading nations with a huge and united empire was fatally undermined.

Simultaneously, the war caused a social revolution. The British people became more united and more equal. Most ended the war more prosperous and healthy. Again in marked contrast to the First World War, people looked forward to creating a better world once the war was over, not returning to the pre-war days.

This chapter describes how the six years of war marked major stages in two of the central themes of this book – in the decline of Britain as a Great Power, and in the progress of British society towards becoming wealthier, fairer and more caring than it was before.

The main phases of the war

Phase 1: 1939–1941 Germany triumphs in Europe

Though Britain and France went to war to defend Poland, they could not have chosen a more difficult European ally to defend. France had only prepared for a defensive war against Germany. Britain's army was still small and totally unprepared for continental warfare. The only way that Britain and France would defeat Nazi Germany would be slowly, by economic blockade and bombing, and by building up a massive joint army to attack should blockade and bombing not be enough.

Consequently, unfortunate Poland was rapidly crushed and divided by the Germans invading from the west and the Russians from the east. No one then knew what to do. Hitler had thought Britain and France were bluffing when they warned him that they would go to war over Poland, so he had no plans to fight them. For their part, Britain and France needed all the time they could get to strengthen their forces. The autumn and winter of 1939–40 was a war of curious inactivity. The British christened it the 'bore war' but the American phrase the 'phoney war' is the name that has stuck.

The phoney war came to a sudden end in April 1940 when the German army shocked Europe by some of the most brilliant victories in the history of

**The Second World War
1939–1941**
1939 September Germany invades Poland.
1939 Autumn–1940 Spring. Phoney war.
1940 April Germany conquers Denmark and Norway.
May Fall of France, Dunkirk evacuation.
August/September. Battle of Britain.
Autumn Blitz on London.
1941 June Germany attacks Russia.
December Japanese attack on Pearl Harbour. USA at war with Japan and Germany.

Key questions

- What part did Britain play in the defeat of Nazism?
- How effective a wartime leader was Churchill?
- What impact did the war have on British society?
- How did it alter Britain's place in the world?

warfare. By co-ordinating their air, armoured and infantry forces in a new and devastatingly effective way, and by attacking with speed, flair and confidence ,they conquered Western Europe in two months, April/May 1940. First to fall was Norway which Germany had to secure to safeguard her supplies of iron. Then the combined British and French armies, which were as large and well-armed as their German opponents, were taken apart by a surprise armoured attack through the Ardennes. While the main French armies tried and failed to prevent the Germans advancing deep into France, the British retreated hastily to Dunkirk. From there 300,000 British troops, plus another 100,000 French, were evacuated from the beaches by whatever ships small and large could get across the Channel from England. France surrendered.

In May Churchill had replaced Chamberlain as Prime Minister. What was the point of Britain fighting on alone? She had no chance of defeating Germany by herself. Where were her allies? The USA showed no sign of wishing to get involved in a war against Hitler.

Hitler and the rest of the world expected Britain to approach Germany for peace terms. Extraordinarily, the question never seems to have been formally discussed once by the British War Cabinet. Chamberlain and Halifax were in favour of at least exploring what Hitler had to offer. Churchill, however, made it clear that as long as he was Prime Minister he had no goal but total victory and that was that. The British people seem to have shared their Premier's bloody-minded obstinacy. They did not know how they would win, but win they would.

Churchill as a war leader

Churchill was 65 when he became Prime Minister. During the 1930s he was considered a vivid personality whose best political days were long since past, because, on the big issues, he had too often showed faulty judgement and took too many risks. As a young man, he had deserted the Conservatives to join the Liberals. No one denied that he had been a brilliant reforming minister in Asquith's government but few forgot his part in the Dardanelles fiasco. Though Baldwin had saved his career in 1924 by making this recent Liberal his Chancellor of the Exchequer, Churchill quarrelled with Baldwin in 1931 and took up so extreme a position against the government reforms in India that he lost any chance of leading the Conservatives in peacetime.

By temperament, Churchill was a warrior. When he became Prime Minister, he felt that 'he was walking with destiny'. Driven by his passionate love of the British Empire and his equally passionate hatred of Hitler, he threw himself into running the war with an amazing energy for a man of his years. His was a war dictatorship, with him much more of a dictator than Lloyd George had ever been. He was the grand strategist with his military chiefs clearly his subordinates.

His strengths far outweighed his weaknesses. His main contribution to victory, Attlee once said, was to talk about it. His eloquence in the House of Commons and over the radio after the 9 o'clock news sustained a united nation through the war and particularly through the dark days of 1940–1942. His other great achievement was to win the trust of President Roosevelt of the USA and, well before the USA formally went to war with Germany, to secure crucial aid in money and arms. As a strategist he made mistakes, sometimes major ones. The Singapore disaster of 1942 (see Spotlight) was as much his fault as anyone's and his pig-headed support for the continuation of the mass bombing of Germany in 1944 and 1945 is hard to defend.

Note

Hitler and Dunkirk

The British and French armies were at the mercy of the Germans for 3 days near Dunkirk but Hitler would not give the order for the final attack. This delay made the Dunkirk evacuation possible.

No one knows why Hitler made such a blunder. He was in a very excited state, hardly believing that his armies could have been so successful. He remembered the Dunkirk area from the First World War as treacherous ground and may have feared losing some of his tanks. Goering, the head of the *Luftwaffe* (German air force) was sure that the enemy troops could be destroyed from the air. On political grounds, Hitler may have decided to avoid imposing a humiliating defeat so that he could soon negotiate a peace with Britain, which would leave Europe to him.

Whatever the reasons, 460,000 Allied troops escaped from Dunkirk – troops which the Germans could have surrounded and taken prisoner without great difficulty.

■ **Think about**

▶ Re-read Source 2. What makes it so effective as an inspirational speech?

The fall of Singapore

Singapore was the most important British naval base in Asia. It had been reinforced in the 1930s with massive guns to deter the Japanese or anyone else from attacking from the sea. In 1941 it was defended by an apparently strong garrison of 88,000 troops, British, Australian, Indian and Malaysian.

As the main Japanese fleet attacked the Americans at Pearl Harbor in December 1941, General Yamashita, with a force of about 70,000, invaded Malaya. Expecting a possible Japanese offensive, Churchill had sent two of Britain's most modern warships, the battleship *Prince of Wales* and the battle cruiser *Repulse* to deter the Japanese from invading. Without adequate air cover, both ships were sunk on 9 December 1941.

Aided by their air supremacy, the Japanese quickly conquered Malaya and attacked Singapore from the north, where the defences were at their weakest, and forced a demoralized British army to surrender on 15 February 1942.

Source 3

[The fall of Singapore]. The greatest disaster to British arms which our history records.

Churchill

Source 4

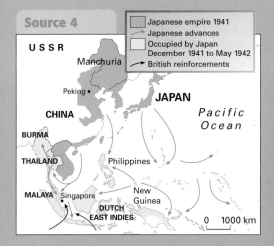

- Japanese empire 1941
- Japanese advances
- Occupied by Japan December 1941 to May 1942
- British reinforcements

USSR
Manchuria
Peking •
JAPAN
CHINA
Pacific Ocean
BURMA
THAILAND
Philippines
MALAYA Singapore
New Guinea
DUTCH EAST INDIES
0   1000 km

▼ British prisoners after the fall of Singapore.

Source 5

Before the war the heads of the Admiralty had scorned the idea that battleships could be sunk by air attack and Churchill had tended to support this view...

[President Roosevelt warned Churchill that he was putting too many resources into North Africa at the expense of the Far East]

None of these arguments altered Churchill's view. 'I would not tolerate the abandoning the struggle for Egypt', and was resigned to pay whatever forfeits were exacted in Malaya...It was clear that the responsibility for the failure to reinforce Malaya's inadequate defences rests principally with Churchill himself – and was due to his insistence on launching a premature offensive in North Africa.

Liddell Hart, *The Second World War*, 1970

Source 6

[The fall of Singapore] was the blow which did the most damage to Britain's imperial position in the whole war. Her power depended on prestige, on the idea that one Englishman could defeat ten Asians and could rule a province single-handed.

Lloyd, *Empire to Welfare State. English History 1906–1967*, 1970

■ Questions

Study Sources 4 and 5.

1 What was the main weakness of the defences of Singapore?

2 What were the main mistakes made by Churchill as far as preventing the fall of Singapore was concerned?

Study Sources 3 and 6.

3 Why do you think Churchill regarded the fall of Singapore as such a disaster?

4 Why did the fall of Singapore turn out to be such a blow to the British Empire?

The Battle of Britain

Britain came close to defeat in August/September 1940 in the air battle, which Churchill called the Battle of Britain. Hitler prepared an invasion force. It had no chance of success unless the *Luftwaffe*, the German air force, gained control of the skies above the Channel and southern England. If that air supremacy was won, the invasion had a very good chance of success since the British army had abandoned most of its weapons in France. The *Luftwaffe* mounted wave after wave of attacks on the RAF. For a few days in August, when it concentrated on destroying the radar defences and airfields and the RAF was running out of pilots, defeat seemed imminent. However, at a crucial moment the *Luftwaffe* switched to bombing London. The RAF regained the upper hand and caused Hitler to call off his invasion plans.

The Battle of Britain was a much greater setback for Hitler than it seemed at the time. Britain was clearly going to go on fighting and would not be easy to defeat. As long as she continued fighting she proved to be the rallying point of anti-Nazi resistance throughout Europe. When the USA eventually came into the war, the British Isles acted as a vast aircraft carrier from which the military might of the USA, with British support, launched itself decisively across the Channel against Nazism.

Phase 2: 1941–1942 world war: Japan USA and USSR

The nature of the war changed decisively in 1941. In the summer, Hitler turned his armies on the USSR. Then, in December, with characteristic recklessness, he declared war on the USA in support of his Japanese allies who had attacked the American fleet at Pearl Harbor. If the unlikely alliance of the USSR, the USA, and the British Empire could avoid military defeat in 1941–1942 and then hold together long enough, their combined resources were so much greater than those of Germany and Japan, they must win. Such was the common hatred of German Nazism and Japanese militarism that the Grand Alliance held together, despite considerable tensions, until victory was won in 1945.

1941 and 1942 were very bad years for the Allies. The German armies reached the suburbs of Moscow and then drove deeply south and east towards the oilfields of the Caucasus. In the Far East, the Japanese control of both sea and sky brought them another series of striking victories, the most notable of which was the capture of Singapore, Britain's most important naval base in Asia. Simultaneously in North Africa, where Britain's war effort was concentrated, the German *Afrika Korps* commanded by Rommel drove the armies of the British Empire back to the Egyptian border. And the U-boats seemed to be winning the Battle of the Atlantic

Phase 3: 1942–1943 the turning of the tide

By the summer of 1943, the war was effectively won. The most decisive battle was on the Eastern Front, where Russian armies outfought the Germans at Stalingrad. After Stalingrad, the Germans began the long retreat back to Germany. In the Pacific, the Battle of Midway ended the advance of the previously all-conquering fleet of Japanese aircraft carriers. After Midway, the Japanese were retreating too, bitterly contesting every island. In North Africa British Empire troops played their part. Skilfully generalled by Montgomery and now superior to Rommel's army both in numbers and weaponry, they first won the battle of El Alamein and then met up with the Americans to drive the Germans and Italians out of Africa. In Atlantic waters, better methods of detection helped the Allies get the upper hand over the U-boats.

Quotation

Churchill on Hitler
Churchill realized, earlier than most, Hitler's capacity for evil and his hatred of the Nazi dictator was one of the driving forces of his leadership during the war:
'This wicked man, this repository and embodiment of many forms of soul-destroying hatreds, this monstrous product of former wrongs and shame'
is how he described him in his weekly broadcast to the nation on 11 September 1940 as German bombers blitzed London.

Timeline

World War II 1942–1945
1942 February. Fall of Singapore.
June. USA fleet defeats Japanese at Midway.
October–November. British victorious in North Africa (El Alamein).
1942–3 Winter. Russians defeat the Germans at Stalingrad.
1943 Summer. Battle of Atlantic against the German U-boats turns in the Allies favour.
1944 Summer. D-Day invasions on the northern coast of France.
1945 May. Germany surrenders.
August Japan surrenders

▲ Churchill being Churchillian.

▲ Halifax, a loyal supporter of Chamberlain and convinced appeaser, whom the King and many Conservatives would have preferred to Churchill.

Note

Lend-Lease

In March 1941, before the USA had formally joined the war against Germany, Roosevelt persuaded Congress to pass the Lend-Lease Act which enabled Britain to borrow from the USA to keep her war-effort going. This economic support was vital if Britain was to keep fighting but it meant she built up a huge debt by the end of the war which she found very difficult to repay when Lend-Lease suddenly ended in 1945 (see p. 263).

Phase 4: 1944–1945 allied victory

The USA gave priority to victory in Europe. By the D-Day invasion of France in June 1944, American and British armies at last opened up the second front. However, remorseless bombing by both the British and American air forces failed to disrupt seriously the German economy. Nor did it break civilian morale. The Germans kept fighting until the American and British troops had crossed the Rhine and the Russians were shelling Berlin. Then Hitler committed suicide and the German resistance ceased.

American scientists with the aid of British and European colleagues had developed a new bomb of unprecedented destructiveness. Two of these atomic bombs were dropped on the Japanese, ending their fanatical resistance and beginning a new nuclear age where the human species had, for the first time, the technological means of obliterating itself.

As the war progressed, it became clear that the post-war world would be dominated by the USA and by Russia. At the Big Three conferences of Teheran (1943) and Yalta (1945), Churchill's aim was to gain the best deal for Britain. This meant sustaining his special relationship with the USA and as friendly a one as possible with Russia, while restricting Russia's gains in Eastern Europe as far as he could (see p. 278).

Political and social change
Political change

In 1939 Chamberlain's hold on the Conservative Party was such that, despite the failure of his appeasement policy, he remained unchallenged as Prime Minister for the first few months of the war. However, after Norway fell to a swift German attack in April 1940, opposition grew among his own Conservative backbenchers. Chamberlain made an ill-considered appeal to his friends to support him. Normally the government could count on a majority of about 250 in the House of Commons. On the Norwegian vote, it fell to 80 and Chamberlain resigned. He and King George VI wanted Lord Halifax to succeed him but across the country there was massive support for Churchill, who had rejoined the government as First Lord of the Admiralty. Churchill indicated that he would not be prepared to work under Halifax and Halifax indicated that he preferred not to be Prime Minister. So Churchill became Premier on 19 May 1940.

In Churchill's coalition Cabinet, Chamberlain and Halifax represented the Conservatives, Clement Attlee and Arthur Greenwood Labour. Attlee who was an effective chairman of committees and a doer rather than a talker later became Deputy Prime Minister. Ernest Bevin, the trade unionist leader, became Minister of Labour. Labour politicians thus gained valuable experience of high office and won the confidence of the public.

The costs of the war

About 360,000 Britons lost their lives, about half of the number killed in the First World War, though the Second World War lasted two years longer. A higher proportion were civilians, mainly as a result of bombing. Two out of every seven houses suffered some form of bomb damage and some cities, like London, Southampton, and Coventry were hit particularly hard. Bombing also led to the mass evacuation of children from the threatened cities into the safer countryside. There is some controversy among historians about the social effects of evacuation. However many middle-class Britons seem to have been genuinely shocked by the effects of deprivation on working-class children which they observed for the first time, and they became more supportive of social reform.

The economic costs were very high. In order to keep fighting, Britain sold off most of her overseas investments, mainly to the USA, and ended the war heavily in debt and with an economy ill-suited to peacetime trade.

Social change

The shared experience of the 'blood, toil, tears, and sweat' of the war made Britain a more equal and socially aware society. Food rationing was an obvious sign of equality. Rising taxation hit the rich harder than the poor and the latter were helped by food subsidies. Central government took on a more active role in social improvement, providing milk for babies and orange juice and cod-liver oil for children.

Unemployment dropped from 1 million in 1940 to 100,000 by 1945. Wages increased substantially above the cost of living. As in the First World War, the trade unions flourished. Membership rose by 50 per cent to over 9 million in 1947. As Minister of Labour, Bevin used his union experience to keep skilled men in the vital war industries and to bring in women to fill the vacancies of the men who had left for the front.

Women worked in a range of roles, not least in technical support roles for the army and air force. There is plenty of evidence that this wartime experience helped towards greater equality for women. Though after the war, women were still paid less than men for the same job, the custom that women lost their jobs when they got married fell into disuse and women working full-time or part-time became more usual.

Keynes was now the government's chief economic adviser. His influence encouraged the government to increase its expenditure – to finance the war effort, and reduce unemployment and provide additional welfare benefits. This successful experience of wartime Keynesianism meant that his ideas remained influential after his death in 1946.

A powerful mood developed that Britain after this 'people's war' should be a better and fairer place; in particular that the lives of those who were unemployed should be less desperate. As the British troops fought their way to victory at El Alamein, William Beveridge published his famous report – *Social Insurance and Allied Services* – which explained how poverty could be abolished by a national system of social insurance. The Beveridge Report eventually sold 600,000 copies and strongly influenced the welfare planning of the Labour government which came to power in 1945 (see Chapter 16).

▲ A woman working on the nose of a Lancaster bomber in 1943.

Source 7

So far as Britain's contribution is concerned, this war will have been won by its people, not by any one man or set of men…The people made tremendous efforts to win the last war also. But when they won it they lacked the lively interest in the social and economic problems of peace, and accepted the election promises of the leaders of the anti-Labour forces at their face value…The people lost that peace. And when we say 'peace' we mean not only the Treaty, but the social and economic policies which followed the fighting.

The Labour Party makes no baseless promises. The future will not be easy. But this time the peace must be won. The Labour Party offers the nation a plan which will win the Peace for the People.

'Let us face the future' Labour's election manifesto, 1945

■ Think about

▶ What do the authors of Source 7 mean by the claim that the people 'lost the peace'?

▶ In what ways did Labour intend the peace after the Second World War to be different from that of the inter-war years?

Source 8

I think that the war has made a lot of difference to housewives. I don't think that they will be prepared to go back to the old narrow life...They enjoy earning a little money for themselves, even though it all goes on the children. I have a feeling I won't go back into the home. I wouldn't like to keep any man out of a job, but I do hope there'll be more part-time jobs going after the war.

A 40 year old mother of two working part-time in 1944

A sign of the determination of Churchill's coalition government to create a better post-war future was the 1944 Education Act, which at last made secondary education for all a reality. However it retained class divisions in education by preserving the mainly middle-class grammar schools and creating mainly working-class secondary moderns.

A good war?

Few doubted – at the time or since – that the Second World War was a good war for Britain. A people unusually united played a major part in defeating a monstrous tyranny and moved decisively towards a better society.

Summary

- Britain played a major part in the defeat of Nazism. With France, she tried to deter Hitler from attacking Poland. After the devastating defeat of her armies in April and May 1940, she refused to consider making peace. She then won the Battle of Britain and kept the anti-Nazi struggle going until Russia and America joined the war against Germany in 1941. Thereafter she played a more minor role.

- Churchill was an inspirational war leader whose major achievement was to keep Britain fighting against the odds through 1940 and 1941. He united the British people in an unprecedented manner and ensured that Britain's resources were effectively concentrated to win the war. He also established a valuable personal relationship with President Roosevelt. As a military strategist he made some mistakes, the worst of which led to the fall of Singapore in 1942.

- The war made a substantial impact on British society. The massive demands it made on civilian society lessened inequality. The rich became less rich, the poor less poor. It also created a powerful mood for the creation of a fairer and more caring society once the war was over.

- The war proved immensely expensive for Britain and made her very dependent economically on the USA. It also weakened Britain's ability and will to maintain the British Empire. Consequently, after the immediate years of victory, Britain had a much reduced position in the world to which she took many years to adjust.

■ **Further reading**

Alan Farmer, *Britain:Foreign and Imperial Affairs 1939–64*, 1994
A.J.P. Taylor, *The Second World War, an Illustrated History*, 1975
P. Overy, *Why the Allies Won*, 1995
Sir Basil Liddell Hart, *History of World War II*, 1973
M. Gilbert, *Churchill A Life*, 2000

Chapter 16

Labour in power 1945–1951
Building the 'New Jerusalem'

Source 1

AND NOW–
WIN THE PEACE

V

VOTE LABOUR

◀ A Labour poster from 1945.

Source 2

The question is asked – can we afford it?...I cannot believe that our national productivity is so slow, that our willingness to work is so feeble or that we can submit to the world that the masses of our people must be condemned to penury [extreme poverty].

Clement Attlee to the House of Commons in 1946 introducing the National Insurance bill on which the 'Welfare State' was to be built

Introduction

> ### Source 4
>
> We shall not cease from mental strife,
> Nor shall our sword sleep in our hand,
> Till we have built Jerusalem
> In England's green and pleasant land.
>
> Extract from the poem *Milton* by William Blake

William Blake's great poem *Jerusalem*, written in 1804, tells how Albion (Britain) awakes from long sleep and, with God's help, dedicates all his energies to creating a better world. For Labour ministers in 1945, 'Building a New Jerusalem' was the perfect metaphor to describe their hopes for their new government. The four lines above, from another of Blake's poems, *Milton*, had been set to stirring music by Sir Charles Parry in 1916 and had become part of Britain's popular culture.

The builders of the 'New Jerusalem' used the Beveridge Report of 1942 for its foundations. They would abolish poverty from Britain and create a state that would guarantee to its citizens the essential elements of a decent life. However, as they began building, they had to grapple with one of the most difficult economic situations ever faced by any British government in peacetime. Source 1 shows Labour's determination to 'win the peace', Source 2 shows the government's confidence that the country could afford it. This chapter describes the achievements of the Labour government between 1945 and 1951 and the problems it faced. How successful it was in the long run remains a matter for debate (see pp. 266–267).

Key questions

- Why did Labour win the 1945 election by such a wide margin, yet lose the 1951 election to the Conservatives?
- What were the main reforms of the Labour government? How significant were they?
- How profound were the economic problems Labour faced in these years? With what success did the government tackle them?
- How effective a Prime Minister was Clement Attlee?
- Does the Labour government deserve its reputation as one of the great reforming governments in modern British history?

The 1945 election

Churchill had wished to keep his coalition government going until the war with Japan was over. Labour, however, withdrew from the coalition as soon as Germany had been defeated, and the general election was held in June with soldiers voting all over the world in special polling stations. Though the world and to some extent Churchill himself were amazed that in the moment of victory, the British people could vote out such a leader, many British politicians were not. Since the publication of the Beveridge Report, opinion polls had been showing Labour well ahead of the Conservatives. The electorate was not so much against Churchill as the Tories, whom it held responsible for the unemployment of the 1930s and for appeasement. Labour's 'Let us go forward together' theme for the election campaign struck the right chords, while Churchill's negative attacks on socialism seemed out of place and out of date.

Source 3

▲ A Conservative poster from 1945.

Think about

▶ Why do you think that the Conservatives' use of Churchill as their main vote-winner failed?

Facts and figures

Party	1945 Election Turnout 83%	
	No. of seats	% of vote
Labour	393	48
Cons.	210	40
Liberal	12	9

The new Labour government

This was a government of able, opinionated, powerful and quarrelsome characters, held together by a small, apparently unimpressive Prime Minister of few words and no passions – Clement Attlee. 'A modest man with much to be modest about' is how Churchill is supposed to have described him. In fact, in his quiet way, Attlee was a most effective Prime Minister with the valuable skill of holding together difficult colleagues and getting the best out of them (see p. 265). The most influential ministers were Ernest Bevin, Foreign Secretary, Herbert Morrison, Lord President of the Council with considerable powers over home affairs, Hugh Dalton, Chancellor of the Exchequer, and Stafford Cripps, President of the Board of Trade.

Creating 'the Welfare State'

Between 1945 and 1951, they kept the promises they had made in the their 1945 election manifesto, the most important being the creation of the 'Welfare State'. The term was coined by an Oxford professor, Alfred Zimmern, in 1934, when he contrasted democratic states whose main concern was the welfare of their citizens with the fascist states whose main concern was power. Throughout the world in the first half of the twentieth century, democracies were increasing the powers of the State to improve people's lives, especially the lives of those living closest to poverty. Britain, therefore, was not unusual in her various inter-war 'welfare' measures – national insurance, pensions, unemployment benefit, housing subsidies and so on.

What Labour did between 1945 and 1948 was to use the proposals of the Beveridge Report to take these various limited 'welfare' measures and make them 'universal'. The 'Welfare State' which it created provided benefits 'from the cradle to the grave' for all its citizens. Beveridge identified five 'giant evils' – want, disease, ignorance, squalor and idleness – which could be overcome by State action.

The government, Beveridge proposed, should extend the established principle of national insurance contributions, with additional funds being provided by higher taxation. Then the resources to slay the 'giant evils' would exist in a fair and effective system. Future Britons should be safe from poverty (ending want), need no longer worry about the costs of ill health (ending disease), enjoy a proper education (ending ignorance) and be housed decently (ending squalor). A well-managed economy on Keynesian lines would end long-term unemployment (idleness).

The Welfare State was created by a number of Acts of Parliament between 1945 and 1948.

The National Insurance Act 1946

This Act took the principles of Lloyd George's 1911 Act and made them compulsory for all adults. All employees had to make contributions weekly as did employers and the government. In return, every citizen was entitled to sickness and unemployment benefits, old age pensions (women at 60, men at 65) widows' and orphans' pensions, maternity allowances and death grants. The National Assistance Act of 1948 provided a safety net for those who fell through the mesh provided by the National Insurance Act.

'We have abolished poverty', claimed the leader of the Durham miners delegation at the 1950 Labour Party conference. There was something in his boast. The following year, Seebohm Rowntree made his final survey of poverty

■ **Think about**

▶ How is poverty defined?

▶ How much exists in today's Britain compared with 1951?

in York. Using the same measures as he had used in the 1930s, he found only 3 per cent living in poverty compared to 30 per cent 20 years earlier. Later sociologists regarded Rowntree's measures of poverty crude and his findings optimistic. Nonetheless the improvement was real.

Churchill's government had introduced family allowances in 1945 that allowed families to draw regular payments for their second and subsequent children.

The National Health Service 1948

One of Attlee's surprise appointments was Aneurin Bevan as Minister of Health. Bevan was the son of a coal miner and had himself worked briefly in the mines of south Wales before becoming MP for Ebbw Vale in 1929. A passionate left-winger, an eloquent speaker, with a sharp and witty tongue, he proved a brilliant choice.

He quickly decided that the way forward for Britain's muddle of different types of hospital was by nationalization, the creation of a National Health Service (NHS), managed by regional hospital boards, which answered to the Ministry of Health. The NHS would employ both hospital consultants and GPs.

Like Lloyd George in 1911, Bevan met with great hostility from the medical profession. They particularly disliked what seemed to them the loss of their independence and possible reductions in their earnings. Bevan eventually won them round by a mixture of tireless negotiation and more money. He agreed that consultants should keep the right to private practice and that GPs should be paid not by an annual salary but according to the number of patients on their lists. By the 'appointed day' in July 1948 when the NHS began, 90 per cent of Britain's doctors were ready to participate.

Quotation

[By 1959] the National Health Service had become accepted as an altogether natural feature of the British landscape, almost a part of the Constitution.

Professor Harry Eckstein, an American political scientist

Source 5

▶ Bevan versus the doctors, as seen by Vicky in the *News Chronicle* on the news of Bevan's appointment as Minister of Health in June 1945.

■ **Think about**

▶ Why should the doctors have been so hostile in 1945 both to Bevan personally and to the idea of a National Health Service?

▶ How did he overcome their opposition?

HERE HE COMES, BOYS !
7th August, 1945. Mr. Aneurin Bevan's appointment as Minister of Health is not welcome in certain circles.

The NHS was the most striking and best-loved part of the new Welfare State. It channelled far more resources into the country's medical services, particularly into the more deprived districts where the need was greatest. Previously the benefits of health insurance had been restricted to working men. Now women, children and the elderly were covered too. The extent to which it reduced pain and anxiety is incalculable. Such was the need to be met that expenditure in the first two years was 40 per cent higher than estimated.

Housing

Housing was also one of Bevan's responsibilities and another which he carried out with considerable success. The bomb damage from the war had affected millions of properties. Understandably, on all the questionnaires sent out by public opinion pollsters during the war asking the public to list their peacetime priorities, better housing was at the top of the list, well above health or education or unemployment benefit. After a slow start in 1946, 55,000 houses were built. The pace accelerated in 1947 with 140,000, rising to a record of 284,000 in 1948. At the end of the war, the estimated need was for 750,000 new homes. By the time Labour left office in 1951, it had built well beyond that estimate, mainly council housing for families on lower incomes. However, the 1945 estimate proved too low as more people married and had children than expected. Consequently, in 1951 there was still a housing shortage.

Another reform relating to housing was the New Towns Act of 1946 which created 14 new towns like Harlow and Crawley, healthy and pleasant places to live which people could move to from the crowded slums of the Victorian cities allowing these slums to be demolished. A Town and County Planning Act (1947) gave local government greater responsibilities and powers to ensure that land was developed in the best interests of the community. The government also gave more protection to tenants in rented property from excessive rent rises.

Education from 1944

The main task of Ellen Wilkinson as Minister of Education (see pages 218–219) was to make as effective as possible in years of economic difficulty as much of Butler's Education Act of 1944 (see p. 257) as possible. She held the Cabinet to the agreed date of 1 April 1947 for the Raising of the School Leaving Age (ROSLA) to 15 by threat of resignation. She also had 35,000 teachers trained in a year by the Emergency Training Scheme. As well as meeting immediate school building needs by a massive programme of prefabricated classrooms, 928 new primary schools were built between 1945 and 1950. The number of university places increased by more than 50 per cent between 1938 and 1948, from 50,000 to 77,000.

Nationalization

By Clause 4 of the Labour Party constitution (see p. 195), Labour had been committed since 1918 to the public ownership of the 'commanding heights' of the economy. What that meant in practice had not, however, been made clear either before the war or in the 1945 election manifesto. The minister with the greatest experience of making public ownership work was Morrison, who as leader of the London County Council had created the publicly owned London Transport, so it was to Morrison that Attlee entrusted the nationalization programme.

An early case was the Bank of England (1945). Then followed the British Overseas Airways Corporation (BOAC), the coal mines and cable and wireless in 1947, transport including the railways and electricity in 1948, the gas industry in 1949.

Massive though this change was, it was not that controversial. The Conservatives did not denationalize any of these industries when they came to power in 1951. The case for nationalizing the coal mines had been seriously considered by Lloyd George's coalition government more than 20 years earlier.

Note

Ellen Wilkinson and comprehensive education

Labour left-wingers criticized Ellen Wilkinson for not pressing local authorities harder to introduce comprehensive schools immediately after the war.

Only Anglesey among LEAs went fully comprehensive, though there were also some comprehensive schools in London by 1951. The 1960s and 1970s saw the big switch from grammar/secondary modern schools to comprehensive ones.

Nationalization and privatization

Margaret Thatcher's Conservative government was convinced that the poor performance of the nationalized industries and the over-mighty unions which ran them were a major cause of the economic problems which Britain faced in the 1960s and 1970s. She rejected the principle of nationalization and 'privatized' all the industries that Labour nationalized between 1945 and 1951. They either flourished like British Airways or withered away, like the coal industry.

▶ What is the attitude of the present political parties to private and public ownership?

▲ One of Attlee's first major broadcasts as Prime Minister. From the Cabinet Room at 10 Downing Street, he tells the nation that Japan has surrendered.

The gas industry was closely tied to coal. Already the government controlled the Central Electricity Board and the national grid. The private railway companies were struggling against the competition from motor vehicles. The only nationalization measure which the Conservatives wholeheartedly opposed was that of iron and steel (1951), since the industry was profitable. Churchill's Conservative government denationalized the industry in 1953. Nationalization then ceased to be a major issue in British politics for 30 years.

Economic problems

In reality, in order to keep fighting, Britain had become economically dependent on the USA as early as 1941. Neither side fully realized the extent of this dependency and the Americans were on their guard against being tricked by the cunning British into subsidizing the continuation of the British Empire.

When the war with Germany ended, Britain had run up debts of £3 billion and her industries were more concentrated on war production than any other nation in the world. To win the war she had kept her staple industries of coal, steel, shipbuilding and textiles running at full capacity in factories which had been obsolete in the 1930s. Once peace came they were even more out of date than they had been and the government needed a breathing space if it were to have a chance of operating a budget where imports were balanced by exports.

That breathing space was not forthcoming. By the Lend-Lease agreement, Britain was liable to pay her debts to the USA when the Japanese were defeated. Attlee's government hoped that in the interval between its election in July and the defeat of Japan, which most people did not expect until 1946, it could put the economy on a stronger footing. These hopes were dashed when Japan surrendered, and despite all the persuasiveness of Keynes, President Truman immediately ended the Lend-Lease arrangements.

As Peter Clarke puts it, Britain faced the desperate alternatives – 'beg, borrow or starve'. Keynes' begging failed. Starving was hardly an option for a government just elected to 'win the peace'. So borrowing it had to be. Keynes returned from the USA with a $3,750 million loan backed by another from Canada for $1,250 million. The snag about these loans was that in 1947 sterling would have to become convertible with the dollar. This meant that, within two years, there needed to be enough international confidence in the strength of the pound to prevent investors seeking to exchange their pounds for dollars. If they did there would be a run on the pound and another serious economic crisis.

Consequently, despite victory, the British people found themselves living in more austere conditions than during the war. Rationing continued and was extended, bread being rationed for the first time in 1946. Income tax stayed at wartime levels and tobacco duties doubled.

Fate then dealt the government a harsh blow in the shape of the weather. The winter of 1946–1947 was the worst for a century. First snow and ice, then floods from the thaw badly disrupted coal production and energy supplies. The crisis was made worse by Emanuel Shinwell's incompetence as the Minister of Fuel and Power.

When as agreed with the American government, sterling became convertible, there was a massive run on the pound. It was the worst moment in Attlee's premiership (see p. 265). Morrison, Cripps and Dalton plotted his overthrow but, with Bevin's support, he survived. Dalton resigned because of an indiscretion about the budget and Attlee made Cripps Chancellor. Almost simultaneously, the Americans decided, through the programme known the Marshall Plan, to launch a massive programme of financial aid to Europe to help economic recovery and thereby halt the advance of communism. Britain benefited greatly from Marshall Aid.

Source 6

◀ The big freeze of 1947. This was the worst winter of the century. Coal shortages led to power cuts. Big Ben froze to a halt.

■ Think about

The impact of the terrible weather and electricity cuts affected the government's reputation. Shinwell was the Minister of Power in 1947. The Conservatives coined the slogan 'Shiver with Shinwell'.

Cripps, a high-minded vegetarian who regarded waste as sinful, was the ideal Chancellor for this crisis. 'There but for the grace of God goes God' was Churchill's summing up of Cripps. In three years he kept a strict control of imports and encouraged exports. He imposed a freeze on wage increases and also restricted price rises. As his health failed in 1949, he agreed to the advice of three rising stars of the Party, Hugh Gaitskell, Harold Wilson and Douglas Jay to recommend that the pound was devalued. The Cabinet agreed to this recommendation and in 1949, the pound was devalued from $4.03 to the pound to $2.80.

By these measures, the 'dollar gap' was closed. Marshall Aid ceased in 1950. The British economy was much healthier. Comparing 1950 with 1937, exports had risen by 50 per cent and Britain's share of world trade had risen from 21 per cent to 25 per cent.

The 1950 and 1951 general elections

Despite all the economic problems it faced, Labour managed to hold its popularity with the electorate reasonably well. In 1950 its share of the vote fell by only 2 per cent. The Conservatives increased by about 4 per cent and this swing was enough to reduce the labour working majority from more than 140 to single figures. While the working-class vote seems to have held solid for Labour some middle-class votes were lost because of business criticism of too much government regulation and because of high income tax which hit the better off proportionately harder.

With so small a majority, Attlee had to call another election in 1951. Labour, now had a very public split between Bevan and Gaitskell, who had succeeded Cripps as Chancellor of the Exchequer. In order to pay for the costs of the Korean War (see p. 278), Gaitskell had introduced prescription charges to reduce the costs of the NHS. This led to Bevan's resignation from the government, followed soon by Wilson.

Nonetheless Labour did well, rallying the electorate to support them to safeguard the Welfare State. Though they polled fewer votes than Labour, the Conservatives won partly because their votes were better distributed and partly because many Liberals switched to them. Churchill returned as Prime Minister with a working majority of 17.

Facts and figures

General election results 1950/51

Party	1950 Election Turnout 84%	
	No. of seats	% of vote
Labour	315	46
Cons.	298	43.5
Liberal	9	9
	1951 Election Turnout 83%	
	No. of seats	% of vote
Labour	295	49
Cons.	321	48
Liberal	6	3

Attlee as Prime Minister

■ Biography

Clement Atlee (1883–1967)

Attlee came from a conventional middle-class background and was educated at public school and Oxford.

Somehow he found himself helping out at a boys' club in Stepney, in the East End of London, which inspired him to become a social worker and, by 1912, a socialist. He fought at Gallipoli, was seriously wounded and ended up a major.

Active in local politics in Stepney, he became Labour MP there in 1922 and was promoted to the post of Postmaster General in MacDonald's 1929–1931 ministry.

In the struggle to become Labour leader in place of Lansbury in 1935, both Herbert Morrison and Arthur Greenwood looked stronger candidates, but they both had enemies, while Attlee had none.

He was not particularly impressive as an opposition leader and there was plenty of talk about replacing him up to 1940. However, once in Churchill's coalition government, he proved himself a very effective Deputy Prime Minister and his position as leader of the Labour Party became secure.

■ Questions

Study Source 7.

1 Identify the man standing and the 4 seated ones.

2 Explain the reference to 'just a good committee man'.

3 What is the message of the cartoon?

Study Sources 8 and 9.

4 Using the sources and your own knowledge, describe the strengths which made Attlee an effective leader of the Labour Party for the best part of 20 years.

Source 7

◀ 'Tough lamb', a Low cartoon in the Evening Standard, October 1947.

Source 8

More complicated characters than Attlee, including Herbert Morrison and Nye [Aneurin] Bevan have found it incomprehensible that such a man could have attained the position he did and held it for 20 years. The truth, my experience would incline me to judge, was simpler. Attlee was a straightforward Victorian gentleman who believed one should do one's job and one's duty, whether as an army officer or Member of Parliament or Prime Minister…Secondly Attlee combined in rare measure the three qualities of honesty, common sense and intelligence: the first two to an outstanding degree and the third to a much higher level than many recognized.

Jay, *Change and Fortune, a Political Record*, 1980. Douglas Jay was a junior minister in Attlee's government.

Source 9

He was a strong, self-sustained man, with an indomitable will and iron courage…His reputation for modesty was entirely false. In old age, he wrote a little limerick, to mark his being enrolled as a Knight of the Garter:

'Few thought he was even a starter
There were many that thought themselves smarter
But he ended PM
CH and OM
An earl and a Knight of the Garter.'
[CH is Companion of Honour, and OM is member of the Order of Merit]

His qualities enabled him to hold together an extraordinary team of powerful personalities, to weld them, his party and his movement into a mood of united purpose unique in their history, to transform his beloved democracy into a welfare democracy, and the old Empire into a multiracial democracy.'

Morgan, *Labour People*, 1987

Historical debate

For the most part, the Attlee government has won an excellent reputation among historians, as Source A demonstrates. However, in the 1980s, it was savagely attacked by Correlli Barnett (Source B). Barnett has been particularly concerned to understand Britain's economic decline since the Second World War. In his judgement there were a number of interwoven reasons. The first was the Welfare State as created between 1945 and 1951, which was both far beyond what the nation could afford and gave its citizens false expectations of what the State could and should do for them. A second was the delusion that Britain could continue her role as a world power with the limited resources available to her. The third was the dominance among the ruling elite of a gentlemanly, Christian and liberal culture which undervalued industrial and commercial enterprise and neglected technical education. Barnett's criticism of the founders of the Welfare State fitted in well with the prevailing political values of the 1980s, when Margaret Thatcher was highly critical both of the costs of the Welfare State and of its capacity to undermine individual enterprise.

▲ Thanks to the National Health Service, this cheerful child views the world in 1951 through free spectacles.

Documentary exercise: Real progress or illusion?

Source A

The historian Peter Hennessy sees real progress

I've called this volume *Never Again* as, for me, the phrase captures the motivating impulse of the first half-dozen years after the war – never again would there be war; never again would the British people be housed in slums, living off a meagre diet thanks to low wages or no wages at all; never again would mass unemployment blight the lives of millions; never again would natural abilities lie dormant in the absence of educational stimulus.

Of course there were setbacks. The economy was a near constant disappointment. The bundle of social and economic problems the Welfare State was designed to break open and solve, proved tough to crack. But real progress there was; progress on a scale and a duration never surpassed in the nation's history.

Hennessy, *Never Again, Britain 1945–51*, 1992

■ Think about

▶ What would the situation of a similar short-sighted child have been in 1851?

Source B

The historian Correlli Barnett

And so it was, by the time they took the bunting down from the streets after VE Day and turned from the war to the future, the British in their dreams and illusions and in their flinching from reality had already written the broad scenario for Britain's post-war decline to the place of fifth in the free world as an industrial power, with a manufacturing output only two-fifths of West Germany's and the place of fourteenth in the whole non-Communist world in terms of annual GNP…As that descent took its course, the illusions and dreams of 1945 would fade one by one – the Imperial and Commonwealth role, the world-power role, British industrial genius, and at last, the New Jerusalem itself, a dream turned to a dank reality of a segregated, sub-literate, unskilled, unhealthy and institutionalized proletariat hanging on the nipple of State maternalism.

Barnett, *The Audit of War*, 1986

■ Questions

1 Study Source A. Summarize the author's evaluation of the six years of Labour government, 1945–1951.

2 Why, in contrast, is Source B so critical of these same years.

3 Is the author of Source C more in agreement with Source A or Source B?
What does he consider to be the main causes of Britain's comparative economic decline in the 1950s and 1960s?

4 Using these sources and your own knowledge, assess the domestic achievements of the 1945–1951 Labour government.

Source C

The historian Rex Pope

The post-war climate of economic management and of increased commitment of resources to education and welfare was beneficial to economic growth, so too was the world-wide pent-up demand for capital and consumer goods...The 1950s and 1960s saw a sustained record of economic growth which surpassed even that of the 1850s...Other countries however did better...One important reason for this was the diversion of resources into an international military role which was beyond the country's means. Research and development funds were over-committed to a narrow range of defence-related activities. The subordination of an industrial strategy to immediate political needs in the nationalized industries was another contribution by government to relative under-performance.

Pope, *The British Economy since 1914*, 1998

■ Examination-style questions

Post-war Britain 1945–1964

The policies of the Labour government from 1945 to 1951 included:

● The introduction of the National Health Service
● Changes in national insurance
● Reforms in education
● The nationalization of major industries and forms of transport.

1 Explain how the Labour government attempted to carry out any two of these policies.

2 Compare the success of the Labour government in implementing at least three of these policies.

■ Further reading

*Paul Adelman, British Domestic Politics 1939–64, 1994
*Kevin Jefferys, *The Attlee Governments 1945–51*, 1992
Peter Hennessy, *Never Again, Britain 1945–51*, 1992
Correlli Barnett, *The Lost Victory*, 1995
Kenneth Harris, *Attlee*, 1982
Alec Cairncross, *Years of Recovery: British Economic Policy 1945–1951*, 1992

Summary

● Labour won the 1945 election because of the development of a powerful public mood from 1942 that, after the war, the government must create a society which took better care of its citizens. The electorate did not believe that the Conservatives could provide such a government. They were remembered as the party of unemployment and appeasement. In contrast, Labour made clear that they would implement the Beveridge Report and its leaders had shown their competence in the wartime coalition government. Labour's majority fell by 1950, mainly because of a middle-class swing which was due mainly to the tax burden and to the irritation of business with too much regulation.

● The main reforms of the Labour government were the creation of the Welfare State and nationalization. The first was very significant because it transformed permanently the relationship of the individual to the State. It massively increased both the benefits available to all citizens, e.g. the NHS, and government spending. Nationalization was a major change, although, apart from iron and steel, not particularly controversial at the time. It was to last about thirty years.

● The economic problems that the government faced were particularly difficult. They were mainly the consequence of Britain's war effort and the debts to the USA which she had built up during the war.

● There were two major crises, the first over Lend-Lease in 1945, the second over dollar convertibility in 1947. The government handled them reasonably well in the circumstances, and, with help from Marshall Aid, had largely overcome them by 1950. The Korean War, however, brought with it another economic crisis.

● Despite superficial appearances to the contrary, Attlee was one of the best peacetime Prime Ministers in modern British history.

● Though there are a few dissenting voices, the present consensus of historians is that the Labour government of 1945–1951 was a gifted administration, which achieved much.

Chapter 17

Britain 1951–1964 'Life is better with the Conservatives'?

Source 1

A Conservative poster for the general election of 1959, which the Conservatives won by more than a hundred seats.

Source 2

In all our plans for the future, we are redefining and we are restating our Socialism in terms of the scientific revolution...The Britain that is going to be forged in the white heat of this revolution will be no place for restrictive practices or for outdated methods on either side of industry.

Harold Wilson addresses the annual Labour Party Conference, 1963

Introduction

The Conservative election victory of 1951 ushered in a thirteen-year period of Conservative rule. They were years of growing prosperity which the Conservatives used to good effect at election time (see Source 1). On economic issues, there appeared to be little to choose between the policies of the two main parties. The major differences tended to be on foreign policy. They were also years when, though the nation was prospering, Britons became increasingly aware that their main industrial competitors were prospering faster and, too often, were proving more competitive. In 1963, at the end of the Harold Macmillan (Supermac) era, there was a sensational scandal (the Profumo Affair – see p. 273) and much discussion about the nation's future. As Source 2 shows, Harold Wilson, the Labour leader, played cleverly on the mood that new policies were needed and won the 1964 election by a narrow majority.

Key questions

● Why were the Conservatives able to win three successive elections between 1951 and 1964
● The term 'Butskellism' was coined in 1954 to indicate that there was not much to choose in policy terms between Conservative and Labour. How much of a political consensus was there, in fact?
● How well did the British economy perform in these years?
● Why did Labour win the 1964 election?
● Were the years 1951 to 1964 wasted?

The Conservative ministries 1951–1964

Churchill again

Churchill was nearly 77 when he became Prime Minister. He was an old man in poor health whose main asset to his party was his tremendous national and international reputation. Though he sounded off angrily from time to time about the failings of socialism, he had no intention of destroying the Welfare State, or of pursuing significantly different policies, apart from denationalizing iron and steel and road haulage. For the most part, he left the business of government to his ministers of whom the most important were Anthony Eden at the Foreign Office, R.A. (Rab) Butler, Chancellor of the Exchequer, Harold Macmillan, Minister of Housing, and Sir Walter Monckton, Minister of Labour. The Party was also fortunate in having in Lord Woolton an able Party Chairman.

Butler at the Exchequer

Butler inherited a difficult situation – or so it appeared. The Korean War was at its height and had pushed military costs up to 30 per cent of the government's annual spending. However, international trading conditions were improving fast while prices were falling. Though defence costs remained high even after the Korean War ended in 1953, Butler was able to cut income tax before the 1955 election. The improving economic situation also allowed the government to end rationing and price controls.

Butler had achieved these successes by managing the economy in much the same way as Hugh Gaitskell, his Labour predecessor, had managed it. Consequently, in 1954, *The Economist* magazine coined the phrase 'Butskellism' to describe the economic policies of the 1950s. While the basic analysis was correct, Butler did make one important change from Labour's pre-1951 methods. He used the bank rate as a means of encouraging or discouraging economic growth. In November 1951 he announced a rise in the bank rate, for the first time for nearly 20 years, from 2 per cent to 4 per cent to take effect the following year.

Macmillan and housing

Macmillan was the most obviously successful minister. The failure of Labour to meet the housing needs of the country had been one of the main themes of the Conservatives' election campaign. They joked that Aneurin (Nye) Bevan, the Labour Minister of Health with responsibility for housing, had been so busy with the NHS that he had kept only half an Nye on housing. In fact, Bevan had more than met the targets set for him in 1945 and was getting 200,000 houses built each year to a good quality.

Macmillan's target of 300,000 per year was achieved in 1953, to a fanfare of publicity, with the backing of Butler and was sustained for the next five years. The new council houses were built to a lower standard than those built in Bevan's time, and it was not obvious that the proportion of the annual budgets devoted to housing was really in the national interest. Well-targeted investment to modernize key industries might have been money better spent.

Eden succeeds Churchill

Churchill took a long time to retire. He did not have a high opinion of Eden, his obvious successor. He believed that his country still needed him and set his heart on a major international conference to lessen the tensions of the Cold War. When King George VI died in 1952, he decided to stay in power long enough for the young Elizabeth to find her queenly feet. A stroke in 1953 left him more fragile but he hung on until April 1955. Eden succeeded him and immediately called a general election

Labour divisions

Attlee was also near retirement. His last years as Labour leader were not happy ones. He too suffered from poor health and he seemed to have run out of mental as well as physical energy. He was unable to end the divisions within the Party. Bevan had resigned from the government over Gaitskell's insistence on prescription charges, but he had widened his opposition by roundly criticizing official Party positions on foreign policy and defence, which supported German rearmament and Britain having nuclear weapons. There were about 50 Bevanites, including some of the most talented Labour MPs like Richard Crossman and Michael Foot. The trade union leadership, however, were hostile to Bevan. They looked increasingly on Gaitskell as Attlee's successor, and it was in fact Gaitskell who was elected as Party leader when Attlee retired at the end of 1955.

The 1955 election results

The Conservatives won so handsomely because they were united, well organized, appeared to be managing the economy well and had recently cut income tax. In contrast, Labour were divided and less well-organized and suffered from being associated through the trade unions with unpopular strikes in 1955 – affecting newspapers and the docks.

> **Note**
> **ROBOT**
> Butler also planned to introduce a scheme called Operation ROBOT of letting the pound float against other currencies if a balance of payments crisis loomed. This was almost certainly a good idea but was too novel for the Cabinet.

> **Quotation**
> Bevan, the miners' son, disliked Gaitskell, the public school boy and university lecturer. He famously, if inaccurately, described Gaitskell as 'a desiccated [dried up] calculating machine.'

Facts and figures

1955 general election results

Party	1955 election Turnout 77%	
	No. of seats	% of vote
Cons.	345	49.7
Labour	277	46.4
Liberal	6	2.7

Eden as Prime Minister 1955–57

Eden had been number two to Churchill for too long and was himself in poor health when he became Prime Minister. Handsome and intelligent, he looked the part but he was indecisive and easily flustered. The Suez fiasco of 1956 (see pp. 280–282) was entirely his fault. Having lied to the Commons and to the world about it, he could not recover his position. It broke his health and he had to resign in January 1957.

Macmillan as Prime Minister 1957–1963

There were two rivals for the succession, Butler, much the most experienced, and Macmillan, who was better at self-publicity. The Conservatives did not then have a formal method of selecting a leader – a name emerged through the Party grandees. In the difficult days after Suez, Butler, who had been a leading appeaser before the war, seemed a worse bet than the more positive Macmillan. Lords Salisbury and Kilmuir sounded out each member of the Cabinet individually. Their votes went overwhelmingly to Macmillan.

Harold Macmillan was the son of a successful London publisher. Educated at Eton and Oxford, he was decorated for bravery in the First World War. Elected MP for Stockton on Tees, he would not accept, like most of his party, that nothing could be done about unemployment, and gained a reputation for being a 'bit of a Pinko' (left wing). A supporter of Churchill's anti-appeasement campaign, he undertook some important commissions for the wartime coalition government and got to know both General Eisenhower, the future US President and de Gaulle, the future President of France. Churchill made him a Cabinet minister in 1951.

He made a particularly good impression as an international statesman. At one moment he was in Washington restoring Anglo-American relations after the tensions of the Suez affair. Then he was in Moscow negotiating a ban on the testing of nuclear weapons.

Note

As a young man Macmillan was shy and lacking in confidence. His private life was marred by the long and indiscreet affair, which his wife conducted with a parliamentary colleague and friend. Though he was always more nervous and pessimistic than he seemed in public, both his confidence and his skills in dealing with the media grew remarkably as a result of his experience in office. For the first half of his premiership, he seemed to have a magic touch.

▶ 'Introducing Supermac' from the *Evening Standard* in 1958. 'Supermac' was one of the most successful creations of the cartoonist 'Vicky'. Note the spectacles!

■ Think about

▶ What do you think Vicky's political beliefs were?

▶ Do you think he admired Macmillan?

Source 3

INTRODUCING: SUPERMAC

HOW TO TRY TO CONTINUE TO STAY TOP WITHOUT ACTUALLY HAVING BEEN THERE

NOTE: MAC'S TORSO IS, OF COURSE, PADDED

At home, Macmillan's main concern was to ensure that the economy continued to grow. His first Chancellor of the Exchequer was Peter Thorneycroft, who resigned along with two other ministerial colleagues when Macmillan prevented him from taking unpopular measures to control inflation. The apparently unflappable Prime Minister merely commented on 'a little local difficulty' as he flew off on an imperial visit. His new Chancellor, Derrick Heathcoat Amory, aided by favourable international trading conditions, then presided over a period of sustained economic growth which allowed him to make generous tax cuts in time for the 1959 election.

The 1959 general election

The Conservative victory seems to have been due to general contentment with the economic situation and confidence in the competence of the government and with Macmillan's leadership. Labour fought a solid campaign and appeared more united than they were before but the polling pundits (experts on voters' intentions) believed that Gaitskell made a serious mistake when he claimed that the Labour promises could all be met without a tax increase.

Macmillan loses his touch

After 1960, however, little went right for Macmillan. The economy over-heated and inflation became a serious worry. His plans to control the pay of public sector workers caused an outcry. His attempt to take Britain into the Common Market came to a humiliating end with de Gaulle's veto in January 1963. Trouble followed on trouble. In the summer of 1963 came the scandal of the Profumo Affair.

Macmillan then had to have an urgent operation and resigned. He was not so ill, however, that he could not influence the choice of his successor. He advised against Butler and, after much intrigue, the little-known Sir Alec Douglas-Home emerged as his successor. Many Conservative MPs were shocked that the Party was ready in the second half of the twentieth century to turn to an undistinguished aristocrat, however honest. Two Cabinet ministers, Iain Macleod and Enoch Powell, refused to serve under him.

Labour had a strong lead in the opinion polls and had a fresh and impressive Party leader in Harold Wilson, who had been elected after the unexpected death of Gaitskell in 1963. However, Sir Alec gave Wilson a close run for his money. The electorate came to appreciate his honesty and directness. What probably swung the result finally in Labour's favour was balance of payments figures which showed a serious imbalance of imports over exports. Labour accused the Conservatives, of mismanaging the economy so that there was an artificial boom before the election, which could not last.

Economic growth

In the 13 years of Conservative rule, from 1951 to 1964, the British economy grew on average at nearly 3 per cent each year. This was a much better performance than the 1.8 per cent of the preceding 13 years, from 1937 to 1950, and better even than the Victorian boom years of 1856 to 1873. Unemployment never rose to more than 2 per cent of the workforce (compared to the 10–20 per cent during the inter-war years). Consumer spending rose by 45 per cent. Families ate better and had more luxury goods.

A weakness of the government's economic management was what came to be called its Stop-Go approach. When the economy grew too fast, because in many sectors British industry was not competitive, the country imported too much and exported too little. That meant a balance of payments crisis and/or inflation. The government would then 'stop' economic growth by higher interest rates or taxes until imports and exports were back in balance and inflation under control. 'Stop' policies, however, were unpopular and liable to lose elections so interest rates would be lowered, taxes cut and the economy allowed to boom again. The periods of 'Go' were 1954, 1958 and 1963. All were followed first by elections and then by deflationary ('Stop') policies. The roller-coaster of Stop-Go made life difficult for British business. It failed to get control of inflation which led to constant pressure from the trade unions for wage rises. It discouraged long-term planning and investment.

Facts and figures

1959 general election results

Party	1959 election Turnout 77%	
	No. of seats	% of vote
Cons.	365	49
Labour	258	44
Liberal	6	6

Facts and figures

Compared with other countries Britain's economic performance was poor. In 1951 only the USA, Switzerland, Canada and Australia had been richer than Britain in terms of gross domestic product (GDP) per head. During the 1960s, France, Denmark, Sweden and the Netherlands moved ahead and West Germany caught up rapidly. British productivity was the lowest in Western Europe. Britain's share of world manufactured exports fell from 25 per cent in 1950 to 16 per cent in 1961.

Spotlight on 1963

The Suicide of a Nation

This collection of essays, edited by Arthur Koestler and published in the autumn of 1963, was a good example of 'progressive' opinion of the time. 'Britain is in deep trouble' was its theme. Her economic decline was extremely worrying. The main problem was the amateurism of the government, with the ageing Macmillan as the leading amateur. The country was stifled by class antagonisms. The nation had immense scientific and technological talents which were not being properly harnessed because the ruling class, 'the country's grand committee of management do not have the knowledge and understanding to apply them.'

That Was The Week That Was

This satirical TV programme ran from November 1962 to April 1963. Produced by Ned Sherrin with David Frost as the anchorman, it poked malicious fun at a wide range of political and social targets. It was cheerfully anti-authority. Members of the Cabinet, particularly the Prime Minister himself and Selwyn Lloyd, Chancellor of the Exchequer were favourite targets. They were made out to be pompous, incompetent and hopelessly reactionary.

The Stagnant Society

Written by Michael Shanks and published in 1961, this was a book that sold well in 1962 and 1963. Shanks was much impressed by what then seemed the dynamism of the Soviet economy, which he expected soon to be more productive than the British. Shanks identified class as the main cause of Britain's stagnation. Britain needed a more planned economy and more modern industries, run by classless people of merit.

The Profumo affair

This affair was a matter of rather sordid triviality, which the Press blew up into such a sensational scandal that for a time it looked as if the government might have to resign.

The Press were feverish anyway since there had already been a minor scandal, involving homosexuality, and some embarrassing discoveries about the number of upper-class Englishmen spying for Russia.

John Profumo, the Minister for War, was discovered to be having an affair with Christine Keeler (see below), a so-called model, whom he had met through an osteopath called Stephen Ward. The Cliveden stately home provided the environment where Ward and his women associates could mingle discreetly with the rich and powerful. However, Christine Keeler was suspected of having another affair, with a Russian official, so when the rumour of her liaison with Profumo began to circulate, Labour was able to raise the matter as a possible security risk. Profumo at first lied to the House of Commons but the Press, which now had a sensational story of sex and spies quickly found him out. Profumo had to resign. Sir William Haley of *The Times* used the scandal to accuse the government of being rotten to the core. The Press also hounded Stephen Ward, who was eventually charged with 'living off immoral earnings' and committed suicide.

Macmillan found the whole affair deeply distasteful and failed to take control of it until far too late. To his Conservative colleagues, the affair was another sign that Supermac had lost his touch.

▶ Christine Keeler photographed in 1963.

■ Think about

▶ How did *The Suicide of a Nation, The Stagnant Society, That Was The Week That Was,* and the Profumo affair, in their different ways, undermine the reputation of Macmillan in 1963. How much do you think that they contributed to the Labour election victory the following year?

Social reforms 1951–1964

Housing was the main achievement, and 6000 new schools were also built. Eleven new universities were founded and the existing ones were encouraged to expand. Subsidies were provided to help modernize British farming. Within the NHS, the treatment of mental health was improved by the Mental Health Act of 1959.

Document exercise: The 1964 general election

Source A

A vote for change – the view of Nigel Fisher, Conservative MP

In the general election of 1964, Alec Douglas-Home fought a gallant campaign in an atmosphere of heckling and sometimes near-hooliganism which must have been distasteful to him. He was often denied a hearing but he always behaved with dignity and courage… There were some who blamed Home, unfairly, I thought, for the Tory defeat; others attributed it to the defection of Macleod and Powell. In so narrow a result there were no doubt a number of contributory factors. But the main reason for the Labour victory was that Conservative governments had been in power for thirteen years and the electorate wanted a change. This enabled Wilson to capture at least part of the middle ground. Iain Macleod went to the heart of the matter when he said: 'I look to the centre – the centre decides elections…For the first time in five elections our grip on the centre has weakened. We must offer something better because we believe in something better.

Nigel Fisher, *Iain Macleod*, 1973

Source B

A historian's view of the Tory defeat

But was it such a famous victory? Given the state of the Tory Party at the beginning of 1964, the unpromising economic situation, the comparative lack of popular appeal of Alec Douglas-Home, should not Labour have won by a larger majority? Fewer people had voted Labour in 1964 than in 1959, even though the electorate was a larger one. A revived Liberal Party had secured some two million extra votes, some from Labour, more from the Tories. The Liberals in a sense had won the election for Harold Wilson…

[Wilson] was as conscious of this as anyone. He knew how much he had done, but he was aware how much he had still to do. He had convinced the electorate that Labour was fit to govern. Now remained the far more difficult task, to convince them that Labour was the natural party of government.

Philip Ziegler, *Wilson* (The authorised biography), 1995

Facts and figures

1964 general election results

Party	1964 election Turnout 77%	
	No. of seats	% of vote
Labour	317	44.1
Cons.	304	43.4
Liberal	9	11.2

Source C

▲ A Labour poster for the 1964 election.

Source D

▲ A Conservative election poster for the 1964 election.

■ Think about

Consider Sources C and D and
the 1964 election.

▶ What did each party consider their
main appeal to the voters?

▶ What do you think was the
crucial factor in the Labour
victory?

■ Activity   KEY SKILLS

Conservative electoral success 1951–1964

Use the information and the sources
on pages 270–274.
Consider these factors
  i) Growing prosperity
  ii) Improvements to the Welfare
     State
  iii) The abilities of their leaders
  iv) The divisions within Labour

a) Take two out of these factors and
explain how each contributed to
the success of the Conservatives
between 1951 and 1964.

b) How much did Britain really
benefit from these thirteen years
of Conservative government?
Your essay should contain references
to at least 2 sources and 1
picture/cartoon.

■ Further reading

*Paul Adelman, British Domestic
  Politics 1939–64, 1994
*Andrew Boxer, The Conservative
  Governments 1951–64, 1996
Alistair Horne, *Harold Macmillan*,
  2 vols, 1991
R.R. James, *Anthony Eden*, 1986
Henry Pelling, *A Short History of the
  Labour Party*, 1993

■ Examination-style questions

1 Comprehension in context
Study Source A. Explain the reference to the 'defection of Macleod and Powell'.

2 Comparing the sources
To what extent does the author of Source B agree with Source A about the
reasons for the Labour win in 1964?

3 Assessing the sources
How useful is the evidence of the election posters (Sources C and D) in
explaining the outcome of the election?

4 Making judgements
From your study of the sources and your own knowledge, explain what you
consider to be the main reasons for the Labour victory in the general election
of 1964.

Summary

● The Conservatives were able to win three elections in a row for a number
of reasons. Their success in 1951 coincided with an upswing in the
economy which gave most Britons a steadily increasing standard of living.
The Conservatives were able to make themselves the party of prosperity
and good economic management. They had popular leaders in Churchill
and Macmillan and a strong, well-funded Party organization. In contrast,
Labour were frequently divided and without a distinctive message.

● Butskellism is a meaningful term when it related to attitudes to economic
management. If Labour had won the 1955 election, Gaitskell would not
have acted very differently from Butler. The parties were more divided on
foreign affairs with a powerful group within the Labour Party fiercely
opposed to the Conservative defence policy, especially on nuclear
weapons.

● The British economy performed well between 1951 and 1964 by previous
British standards, but poorly in comparison with other national economies.
The stop-go policies of the government hampered long-term economic
growth.

● Labour won the 1964 election because enough of the electorate wished for
a change to overcome the Conservatives' 5 per cent lead of 1959. Labour,
well led by Wilson, had a forward-looking programme. The Conservatives,
led by the upper-class landowner Sir Alec Douglas-Home, seemed only to
offer more of the same. In a very close contest, concern about a balance of
payments crisis may have been the final nail in the Conservative coffin.

● The main achievement of the Conservatives in domestic matters was to
manage the economy well enough for most Britons to prosper. However, it
was a government with few positive ideas on domestic matters whose lack
of drive and low expectations of British industry and business meant that by
1963 there was amongst politicians and the media a sense of failure and
uneasiness about the future.

Chapter 18

British Imperial and Foreign Policy 1945–1964
An end to the Empire and no entry to the Common Market

▲ Midnight, December 11/12 1963. The Union Jack is lowered in Nairobi and the former colony of Kenya in East Africa gains its independence.

Source 2

We are a great nation, but if we continue to behave like a Great Power, we shall soon cease to be a great nation.

John Maynard Keynes in 1945

Introduction

One of the most striking changes in the history of the world after 1945 was the disappearance of the empires by which the nations of Europe had dominated the globe since 1890. Since the British Empire was much the largest, its fall was an international change of great significance. For British governments, Labour as well as Conservative, what happened to the Empire and how to maintain Britain's position in the world was an issue of the utmost importance, more important it seems to the politicians than to the British public.

As Source 2 opposite indicates, great nations do not have to be Great Powers and most historians agree that the attempts of a succession of British governments to maintain Britain as a world power were not only unrealistic but damaging to Britain's future. In the 1950s, commitment to the Empire by the leaders of both parties also prevented them from judging accurately the potential of the Common Market. As this chapter shows, by 1964, Britain had lost an Empire and had been refused entry to the European Economic Community (EEC) – to which she had applied for membership without much conviction.

Key questions

● Why and with what success did Britain sustain herself as a Great Power between 1945 and 1964?

● How and for what reasons did the British Empire break up between 1945 and 1964?

● Why did Britain first reject the idea of joining the European Common Market and then seek to join it?

● How true was the comment of the American Dean Acheson in 1962 that Britain had 'lost an empire and not yet found a role'?

The inability of Britain to maintain her Empire and her Great Power status after 1945 is only clear with hindsight. When the war ended, what seemed obvious both to the British people and the rest of the world was that Britain was a Great Power. She had emerged from the war victorious. Her troops occupied part of Germany. Her armed forces were 5 million strong, her navy had more than a thousand ships, her airforce was second only to that of the USA. By the agreements of Yalta and Potsdam, she had regained her Empire and had military bases strung across the world. If she had economic problems she expected to be able to overcome them by using the 'sterling area' for the economic development of the British Empire and to sustain an international economic role of a similar importance to that which she had possessed in the pre-war era.

If this mismatch between her economic weakness and these Great Power aspirations was clear to Keynes in 1945, it was not to most other people. Its reality only slowly dawned on politicians in the late 1950s and they were reluctant to come to terms with it. Churchill was a master of word images and he defined Britain's place in the post-war world as situated where three circles of international relationships overlapped – the Empire, Europe, and the USA/UK partnership across the Atlantic. In his view, this unique position gave Britain the potential to exercise indefinitely a unique influence in the world. This was not just a grand Churchillian view. Its essentials were shared by Attlee and Bevin, Foreign Secretary of the Labour government from 1945 to 1951 and by Anthony Eden, Churchill's successor as Conservative leader.

Attlee and Bevin faced some very difficult international problems in the years immediately after the war. The most serious were in Europe.

Ernest Bevin as Foreign Secretary

Bevin was a big man in every sense and Attlee gave him plenty of freedom on foreign policy issues. He hated Germans, Communists and intellectuals and had no doubt that Britain was a Great Power and should remain one. A typical comment, from 1946, was that Britain must have its own atomic bomb with a Union Jack flying over it! His major achievement was the cementing of the UK/American alliance with regard to Europe and committing Labour to a clear anti-Communist position.

Churchill's intersecting circles

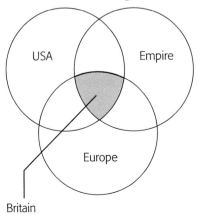

Britain and the Cold War

At Potsdam in 1945, the Allies failed to agree about the settlement of Europe. By 1947, relations between the 'Western' allies (the USA, Britain and France) and the Soviet Union had deteriorated into a 'Cold' War, where there was such fear and suspicion that both sides might have been at war except they were not actually fighting. The Soviet Union took control of virtually all the countries of Europe which her armies had reached in 1945; set up pro-Moscow governments in them; and erected a barrier of barbed wire fences and minefields (which Churchill christened the 'iron curtain') to cut this 'Soviet bloc' off from the West.

One of Bevin's greatest achievements was to persuade the USA that Russian Communism was a danger to Europe and the world and that the Americans must stay involved in European affairs and not retreat into isolation as in 1919. The USA–Western Europe link was forged in three stages.

The first stage was linked to the situation in Greece. There, British forces had restored the Greek monarchy and then stayed to defend it in a civil war against Communist republicans. The economic problems which Britain faced in 1946–1947 (see p. 263) convinced the government that it could no longer shoulder the anti-Communist responsibility in Greece. However, it was able to persuade the US President, Truman, to take it over. Truman announced the Truman Doctrine, that the USA could be counted on to support anti-Communist forces throughout the world. Marshall Aid then followed which helped in the economic recovery of Western Europe.

The second stage was a crisis over Berlin. West Berlin was a non-Communist island surrounded by Communist-controlled East Germany. In 1948, the Russians tried to force West Berlin, by a blockade, to become part of the Soviet bloc. The American and British airforces airlifted vital supplies into the city for more than a year until Stalin ended the blockade.

The third stage was the creation, in 1949, of the North Atlantic Treaty Organization for the defence of Eastern Europe against the Soviet Union. The USA dominated NATO and, for the next 40 years, the USA had military bases all over Europe, many of which were in Britain.

Between 1950 and 1953, Britain fought alongside American troops in Korea to prevent South Korea falling under Communist control. The costs of this war were an untimely extra burden for the Attlee government.

Spending on defence

Between the wars Britain spent about 3 per cent of her GNP on defence. Between 1945 and 1957 it ran on average at 10 per cent or more, and, though it was cut back thereafter, it was still running at about 6 per cent in 1964. The money went on keeping all three services – army, navy and airforce – well armed and maintaining military bases all over the world. In addition, both Labour and Conservative governments agreed that Britain would not remain a Great Power unless she developed her own nuclear weapons. Attlee and Bevin gave the go-ahead to develop the atomic bomb; Churchill and Eden the hydrogen one. A new fleet of bombers, the so-called V-bombers, was developed to carry these bombs.

Timeline

Britain and the Cold War 1945–1964

1945–7 Civil war in Greece.
1947 Truman Doctrine, Britain pulls out of Greece.
Marshall Plan.
1948 Berlin Airlift
1949 NATO formed.
1950–3 British troops support USA in Korea.
1952 Britain develops its own A-bomb.
1956 Suez Crisis Russia crushes Hungarian rising.
1957 Britain develops its own H-bomb.
1961 Berlin Wall built.
1962 Britain purchases Polaris submarines from the USA.
1963 Test Ban Treaty

▲ The Berlin Airlift 1948–49.

Note

Opposition to nuclear weapons

The Bevanites opposed the official Labour policy on nuclear weapons in the 1950s and the Party contained a strong element in favour of unilateral nuclear disarmament through the 1960s and 1970s.

Started in the 1950s, and active also in the 1960s and 1970s, was the Campaign for Nuclear Disarmament.

Source 3

▶ Led by Bertrand Russell, campaigners against nuclear weapons 'sit down' in protest outside the Ministry of Defence in Whitehall in 1961.

However, the Cold War arms race between the USA and the Soviet Union led to the building of increasingly sophisticated and expensive inter-continental ballistic missiles which could be fired from submarines. Britain tried but failed to keep up in this arms race. In order to keep the overall costs of her defence budget under control, she concentrated more and more on nuclear weapons. Eventually in 1962, Britain had to purchase Polaris submarines from the USA so she could maintain a semblance of an independent nuclear deterrent.

Decolonization 1919–1947

We saw in Chapter 14 how the Versailles settlement extended the British Empire and how the emphasis given to imperial defence strengthened the appeasers' case in the 1930s. However, Britain did recognize the virtual independence of the mainly white dominions, such as Australia, Canada and South Africa, by the Statute of Westminster 1931. A change of name marked the new status of the dominions. The British Empire was referred to more frequently as the British Commonwealth. British governments had no doubt that the Commonwealth was a major asset to Britain in terms of power, prestige and finance. The Ottawa agreements of 1932 established the sterling area which gave preferential trading terms with Britain to countries in the British Empire, and to others like Denmark and Argentina which had particularly strong trading links with Britain. On the whole, the Ottawa agreements benefited the industries of Britain's partners more than those of Britain but they helped the City maintain its position as the leading financial centre of Europe.

As in 1914, so in 1939, the British Commonwealth rallied to the Allied cause and provided some of its best fighting men. At the end of the war, Churchill's instructions to Eden as to Britain's negotiating position with America and Russia about the future of the British Empire could not have been clearer. 'Hands off the British Empire is our maxim and it must not be weakened or smirched to please sob-stuff merchants at home or foreigners of any hue.'

Independence for India and Pakistan

However, India, the former jewel in the imperial crown around which the Empire had originally been built, could not be held much longer. The British government had tried to win over the Indian nationalists by granting limited self-government in 1919 (the Montagu-Chelmsford reforms) and more in 1937 (The Government of India Act). However these steps offered too little too late. The nationalist Congress Party, skilfully led by Gandhi and Nehru, demanded first dominion status and, when that was not granted quickly enough, full independence.

Timeline

The British Empire 1914–1945

1914 Massive support from the British Empire in men and materials.

1919 Versailles settlement enlarges the British Empire.

1926 Balfour Declaration accepts the essential independence of the white dominions.

1931 Statute of Westminster recognizes dominion independence.

1937 Government of India Act gives some self-government to Indians.

1939 World War II Massive support again from white dominions, but many Indians hostile.

1942–43 Japan conquers most of Britain's possessions in the Far East.

Attlee was well informed about Indian affairs and sympathetic to the Indian's case. In addition, the Indian economy had developed considerably during the twentieth century and was no longer such a vital market for British exports. Consequently, even Churchill who had strongly opposed more self-government for India in the 1930s, agreed that independence was due. The chief difficulty was the friction between Muslims and Hindus, which led to the partition of the subcontinent in 1947 between mainly Hindu India and Muslim Pakistan.

Palestine mandate

Palestine proved a problem too difficult even for as tough and skilful a negotiator as Bevin. The problem was to a considerable degree created by his predecessors. Previous British governments had not only promised the Jews that they could make Palestine their national home but also offered guarantees to the Arabs already living in Palestine that their rights would be safeguarded. The Nazi persecution of the Jews brought an increase of immigration to Palestine immediately before and after the Second World War. Violence between the Israeli (Jewish) and Arab communities escalated. British troops tried to keep order but antagonized both sides. In 1947, Bevin decided that Britain was in a no-win situation and handed the problem over to the United Nations. Almost immediately an Arab-Israeli war erupted, which led – after a decisive victory by the Israeli army – to the creation of the state of Israel in 1948.

The Suez Crisis 1956

Britain and Egypt had had an uneasy relationship since the 1880s (see pp. 86–87). Egypt, unusually, had managed to be one of Britain's most vital overseas possessions without ever, formally, being part of the British Empire. British governments considered that the geographical position of Egypt made her vital to the Empire. The Suez Canal ran through Egyptian territory and Britain had important interests in the eastern Mediterranean and the Middle East. British governments were able to influence the direction of Egyptian policy through the corrupt King Farouk and a large army base defending the Canal.

However, Egyptian army officers overthrew Farouk in 1952 and, from 1954, Nasser, a strong Arab nationalist, was the effective ruler of Egypt. In 1954, he got the British government to agree to withdraw the troops from the Canal Zone. He also established better relations with the Communist world. A particular ambition of his was to build a high dam at Aswan to make much more of Egypt fertile. When the American and British governments withdrew a promised loan for the dam in 1956, he nationalized the Suez Canal which had been owned by a private company with many British and French shareholders.

Anthony Eden convinced himself that Nasser was an Arab 'Hitler'; a threat to vital imperial interests. This time there would be no appeasement. Nasser would be taught a lesson he would never forget; the Canal would be secured and Britain's prestige in the Middle East restored. Eden could count on the support of the French, who were worried about Nasser's influence on the Arab nationalists in their North African colony of Algeria, and on Israel who saw him as a danger to their very existence.

In the late summer of 1956, therefore, these three nations hatched a plot. Israel would attack Egypt. Britain and France acting as if in the interests of the world, would move in to separate the fighters. As they secured the peace, they would also reoccupy the Canal Zone and not leave it until it was restored as an international waterway.

Timeline

The British Empire 1945–1963
1945 Britain regains all her imperial possessions.
1946 Violence in India and Palestine.
Churchill's 'iron curtain' speech.
1947 Independence granted to India and Pakistan.
1948 Britain quits Palestine.
1956 Suez Crisis.
1957 Ghana independent.
Mau Mau violence in Kenya.
1960 Nigeria and Cyprus independent.
1963 Kenya independent.

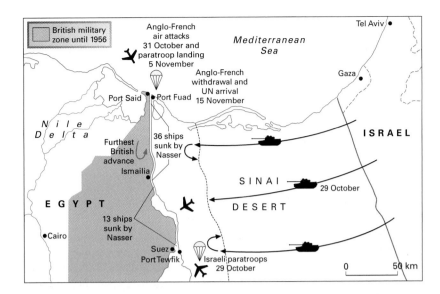

▶ The Suez Crisis, 1956.

That is not what, in fact, happened. Israel attacked Egypt and quickly gained the upper hand. British and French troops invaded and began to secure the Canal Zone. There was then international uproar as no one believed that Britain and France were acting for any purpose other than to strengthen their old empires. The Soviet Union made dire threats. The USA was outraged, withdrew financial support and there was a run on the pound. The Egyptians sank ships to block the Canal. Britain and France had to make a humiliating withdrawal. The Suez Crisis made clear both to Britain and to the world the days of successful imperial aggression were long since past.

Document exercise: The Suez Crisis 1956

Source A
Minutes of the Cabinet meeting of 27 July 1956

The fundamental question before the Cabinet, however, was whether they were prepared in the last resort to pursue their objective by the threat or even the use of force, and whether they were ready, in default of assistance from the USA or France, to take military action alone.
The Cabinet agreed that our essential interests in this area must, if necessary, be safeguarded by military action and that the necessary preparations to this end must be made. Failure to hold the Suez Canal would inevitably lead to the loss one by one of all our interests and assets in the Middle East.

Source B
US President Eisenhower to Eden 2 September 1956

...I am afraid, Anthony, that from this point our views on this [the Suez Canal] situation diverge...I must tell you frankly that American public opinion flatly rejects the idea of using force.

Source C
Secret agreement between Britain, France, and Israel, 24 October 1956 (the Sèvres Protocol)

It was agreed that:
The Israelis launch in the evening of 29 October 1956 a large-scale attack on the Egyptian forces...
In the event of the Egyptian government failing to agree in the stipulated time...Anglo-French forces will launch military operations against Egyptian forces...
These arrangements...must remain strictly secret.

Source D

Eden in the House of Commons 20 December 1956

We have been accused...of being in collusion with the Israelis. My right hon. and learned friend the Foreign Secretary (Selwyn Lloyd) emphatically denied that charge on 31 October. Since then it seems that the charge has been altered and Her Majesty's Government has been asked to prove that there was no foreknowledge of the Israeli attack...

I want to say this on the question of foreknowledge, and to say it quite bluntly to the House, that there was no foreknowledge that Israel would attack Egypt – there was not.

Source E

the historian Robert Blake writing in 1997

[The British invasion of the Canal Zone in 1956] was a military success but a political disaster. Eden underestimated American opposition, although the published evidence makes it clear that Washington was strongly averse to the use of force. The intervention was based on an obviously bogus pretext, the need to 'separate the combatants' in an Israeli-Egyptian war and safeguard the Canal.

Blake, *The Conservative Party from Peel to Thatcher*, 1985

■ Examination-style questions

1 Comprehension in context
Explain what circumstances in Egypt had prompted the British Cabinet to consider the use of force (Source A).

2 Comparing the sources
How far do Sources A and B contradict the claim in Source E that 'Eden underestimated American opposition' to armed intervention?

3 Assessing the sources
How useful is Source C to historians seeking to understand why British and French forces invaded Egypt?

4 Making judgements
Using the sources and your own knowledge, comment on the statement that the Suez affair was 'a military success but a political disaster' (Source E).

The European Economic Community (EEC)

As Eden was worrying about Nasser, six nations of Western Europe, France, West Germany, Italy, Belgium, the Netherlands and Luxembourg (the Six) were involved in discussions which were to lead to the formation of a European common market. They were building on the ideas of Jean Monnet and other European thinkers who believed that, after two wars of appalling destructiveness, the nations of Europe needed to come together in a European community that would give them shared goals and shared prosperity. Then the conflicts of the past would become unthinkable.

The first step towards the creation of that economic community was the European Coal and Steel Community (ECSC), established in 1951. Such was the

Timeline

Britain and Europe 1948–63

1948 OEEC (Organization for European Economic Cooperation) set up with Britain as a member.

1950 ECSC set up. Britain will not join.

1955 Messina Conference to plan the Common Market. Britain only observes and will not join.

1957 Treaty of Rome establishes the Common Market.

1960 Britain forms EFTA to balance the successful Common Market.

1961 Britain applies to join the Common Market.

1963 French veto Britain's application.

Facts and figures

British imports		
1953		1960
14%	Australia & New Zealand	8%
10%	EEC countries	15%
British exports		
12%	Australia & New Zealand	10%
11%	EEC countries	16%

▲ President de Gaulle of France, with an eloquent gesture of his hands, vetoes Britain's entry to the Common Market at a press conference in 1963.

success of the ECSC that ministers from the Six met at Messina in Italy in 1955 to decide how to build on what had been achieved. From the Messina Conference came the determination to create a more ambitious common market, surrounded by protective tariffs. The Treaty of Rome of 1957 created the Common Market, or European Economic Community (EEC).

Between 1945 and 1950, Churchill and Bevin had talked in general terms about the need for greater European co-operation and Britain's support for such an approach. However, when Britain was invited to join she took no interest in it. Ministers doubted that the ECSC would work and felt that Britain's world-wide economic interests were already well served by the sterling area.

The Six very much wanted Britain in the EEC and sent an invitation to Eden. The Cabinet decided not to send a minister to participate in the discussions, but only a representative whose function was to observe and report back. That official was Russell Bretherton from the Board of Trade. In fact, British policy had not really altered since 1951. The government still believed that Britain's future lay with the Commonwealth and that the EEC would fail. The official policy towards the Common Market negotiations was to offer 'a cold shoulder'.

1961–1963: Britain's first application to join

Britain's expectations about the Common Market proved spectacularly wrong. It was an immediate success, and the economic growth rates of its members were greater and more sustained than Britain's. Simultaneously, as the figures in the margin show, it became more significant as a trading partner to Britain than the Commonwealth.

Macmillan persuaded his Cabinet that the time had come to explore the possibilities of joining the EEC and sent Edward Heath, a committed European, to negotiate. Since the EEC had now been established for four years without Britain being involved, there were a number of EEC policies which Britain found distasteful, not least the Common Agricultural Policy which heavily subsidized European farmers and meant high food prices. However, after lengthy negotiating, Heath seemed to be on the point of success.

Then de Gaulle stepped in. He had been President of France since 1958 and was determined that France with Germany should continue to be the senior partners in the EEC. He disliked the extent of American influence in Europe and was suspicious of Britain's links with the USA. These suspicions were confirmed when Macmillan did a deal with President Kennedy for the supply of Polaris submarines in 1962. De Gaulle therefore announced a French veto against British entry. The British, he maintained, were not ready for Europe. For Macmillan, de Gaulle's veto was a major setback. As he noted in his diary, 'all our policies at home and abroad are in ruins'.

The reaction of British public opinion was mixed. The question of whether or not to join the EEC split the parties in the 1960s and continued to do so for the rest of the century. Only the Liberals were firmly pro-European. There was always a group within the Conservative Party which was strongly anti-European and wished Britain to strengthen its links either with the Commonwealth or with America. Labour was divided too. Both Gaitskell and Wilson were anti-European. Gaitskell argued that joining the EEC would end a thousand years of history and that by becoming a province of Europe the Commonwealth would be destroyed. Most trade union leaders were also against. At the same time, rising stars in the Labour Party, like Roy Jenkins and Shirley Williams, were strongly in favour.

The Messina Conference of 1955

Source 4

...if we had been able to say...that we accepted 'in principle' we could have got whatever kind of Common Market we wanted. I have no doubt about that at all.

Russell Bretherton, an official from the Board of Trade who represented Britain at Messina

Source 5

The French will never go into the 'common market' – the German industrialists equally dislike it, although Adenauer [the German Chancellor] is attracted to the idea of closer political unity on political grounds. This of course is very important, and I made it clear that we would welcome and assist the plan, although we could not join.

Macmillan, Foreign Secretary; diary 14 December 1955

Source 6

European Economic Community, 1957

European Free Trade Association, 1959

0   250 km

Source 7

Britain was warmly welcomed to participate in the negotiations [at Messina] but first hesitated, then prevaricated [played for time] and ultimately withdrew. The other six pressed ahead despite the empty chair...

The Foreign Office kept up the constant disparagement [criticism] of the European initiative...[by stressing how much more important economically the Commonwealth was] the Foreign Office succeeded in capturing the mood of the British public in watching with sceptical condescension while the six European countries set about pooling their inferior resources in a common market.

Peter Clarke, *Hope and Glory*, 1996

Source 8

We were still thinking of Britain and of standing between the USA and Western Europe and Russia and so on...as being an independent great power...I don't think that we really believed in the vision that Monnet had of forming a nucleus around which a new Europe could be built. After all, I don't know how many hundred years Britain had kept out of Europe. And suddenly to ask it to change, to give up its external, its world-wide role in order to join with a Europe which was down and out at the time, required a vision which I'm quite sure I hadn't got, and I doubt whether very many people in the UK had. Some may now think they had, but I don't think they did.

A civil servant, Edwin Plowden, looking back at the 1950s

■ Questions

1 What do Sources 5, 7, and 8 tell you about the attitude of government ministers to the Common Market at the time of the Messina Conference?

2 Study Sources 4 and 6. If we had played an active part at Messina and signed the Treaty of Rome in 1957, in what ways might the EEC have been different?

3 Britain's mixed feelings about the Common Market continued through the twentieth century, even though Britain joined in 1973 and her entry was confirmed by a referendum in 1975 by a 2 to 1 majority. In 1964 it could be said that Britain was only just coming to terms with the loss of the Empire. Why do you think British views remained so mixed?

4 What policies and opinions are held today?

Decolonization 1956–1964

The Suez fiasco undermined the British confidence in their imperial mission and increased the confidence of nationalist leaders in the colonies. A familiar pattern emerged of nationalist leaders being imprisoned by the British authorities as terrorists, then being freed to become, before long, the leaders of independent nations.

This happened with Nkrumah in Ghana which became independent in 1957, with Archbishop Makarios in Cyprus in 1960, and with Kenyatta in Kenya in 1963. Other African colonies to gain independence in these years were Sierra Leone, Uganda and Gambia. Backed by Macmillan, Ian Macleod, the Colonial Secretary, pushed forward the process of decolonization with vigour, to the anger of the Conservative right wing.

On the whole the policy worked smoothly with little violence, especially in comparison with the ending of the French and Belgian colonial empires. The Mau Mau rising in Kenya in the 1950s was one setback. Another was the failure of the Central African Federation in 1963, Macleod had hoped to mould Nyasaland, Northern Rhodesia and Southern Rhodesia into a single federation but this scheme foundered on the reluctance of the white settler population of Southern Rhodesia to risk their privileged position in a larger grouping with a huge African majority. The Conservative government allowed Nyasaland and Northern Rhodesia each to become independent as Malawi and Zambia respectively. It left the white setters of Southern Rhodesia as an unsolved problem to its Labour successor.

The main reasons for decolonization were the obvious decline in Britain's power, the strength of the nationalist movements in the colonies, the influence of world opinion and a lack of will within government. That will was sapped by the realization that the Empire was more of an economic burden to Britain than an asset.

Summary

- Britain aimed to sustain herself as a Great Power after 1945 since, to begin with, it never crossed the minds of either her governments or general public that she was not. When the mismatch between her economic resources and Great Power ambitions became apparent, the first reaction of governments was to look for ways of staying a Great Power more cheaply.
- The British Empire began to break up with the independence of India and Pakistan in 1947. The Suez Affair provided dramatic proof of Britain's declining international influence. African decolonization followed from 1957. The main reasons for the break-up of the Empire was Britain's declining power, a lack of will in British governments, the vigour of nationalism in the colonies and the fact that the Empire had become an economic burden.
- Until the late 1950s, British governments were cool about the movement to greater European unity because they believed the movement would fail and that Britain would do better by staying independent and by strengthening her links with the USA and the Commonwealth. In 1961 Macmillan's government changed this policy because the EEC was clearly working, and former colonies were trading less with Britain than was the EEC.
- In 1962 the Empire was, to all intents and purposes, lost and the first application to join the Common Market was failing. Britons might believe that they shared a special relationship with the USA. Americans did not. In 1964, it was far from clear what Britain's international role was or what it should be.

■ **Activity**

Churchill's 3 intersecting circles (see p. 277)

Comparing Britain's situation in 1964 with that of 1945, how had Britain's relationships with each of the following changed?

1 the Empire

2 Europe

3 the USA

What kind of international role would it have been sensible for Wilson's Labour government to have pursued from 1964?

What do you consider an appropriate role for Britain in today's world?

■ **Further reading**

*Alan Farmer, Britain Foreign and Imperial Affairs 1939–64 (1994) Access

*Alex May, Britain and Europe since 1945 (1999) Seminar

J. Darwin, *The End of the British Empire* (1991) Oxford

James Morris, *Farewell the Trumpets* (1973) Penguin

Michael Charlton, *The Price of Victory* (1983) BBC

John W. Young, *Britain and European Unity, 1945–92* (1993) Macmillan

Index

Main entries are indicated in **bold.**